Hiking Long Island

A Comprehensive Guide to Parks and Trails

Second Edition

Published By
New York-New Jersey Trail Conference
156 Ramapo Valley Road
Mahwah, NJ 07430-1199

Library of Congress Cataloging-in-Publication Data

McAllister, Lee, 1956-
    Hiking Long Island : a comprehensive guide to parks and trails / Lee
    McAllister.-- 2nd ed.
    p. cm.
    ISBN 1-880775-39-5 (alk. paper)
    1. Hiking--New York (State)--Long Island--Guidebooks.
2. Trails--New York (State)--Long Island--Guidebooks.
3. Parks--New York (State)--LongIsland--Guidebooks. 4. Long Island (N.Y.)--Guidebooks. I. Title.

GV199.42.N652L666 2004
917.47'210444--dc22   2004024061

Maps by Mike Siegel; Rutgers Geography Department
Photography by Lee McAllister
Cover Photo - Block Island Sound from Quadam's Hill in Theodore Roosevelt County Park
Cover design by Adrienne Coppola
Book design by Catfish Design

Although the authors and publisher have tried to make the information as accurate
as possible, they accept no responsibility for any loss, injury or inconvenience sus-
tained by any person using this book.

Hiking Long Island

A Comprehensive Guide to Parks and Trails

Second Edition

Lee McAllister

NEW YORK–NEW JERSEY TRAIL CONFERENCE
2005

This book is dedicated to my wife, Rosemary,
who gave me the support, inspiration
and encouragement that made it a reality.
Also, to my three daughters, Colleen, Katelyn, and Christie,
who helped me patiently with the computer.
May you always appreciate the beauty and wonder
of God's outdoor cathedral.

Table Of Contents

The Pine Barrens and Central-Eastern Suffolk County

The Twin Forks

Appendix

Abbreviations

The following abbreviations are used consistently in this book:

DEC	New York State Department of Environmental Conservation
DOT	New York State Department of Transportation
LIE	Long Island Expressway
LIGTC	Long Island Greenbelt Trail Conference
LIPA	Long Island Power Authority
TNC	The Nature Conservancy
USGS	United States Geological Survey

Acknowledgement

In the course of doing this labor of love, I have been helped by many people who have given me advice and information or have accompanied me on hikes. I would especially like to thank my editor, George Petty, who was the angel who brought the work together. The friends I have made in my wanderings these past few years have made it all worthwhile. Among them are Steve Biasetti, Kurt Billing, Mike Bottini, Tom Casey, Ray Corwin, Kim Darrow, Dai Dayton, William DeMilt, jr., George Fernandez, Louis Ferrara, jr., Louis Ferrara sr., Brian Gallagher, Wes Geahres, Bob Galli, Ritchie Lettis, Al Linberg, Bob Nellen, Larry Paul, Marty Shea, Don Sommerfield, jr., Ken Spadafora and Rick Whalen.

To all, I say thank you.

Paumanok

Sea-beauty! Stretch'd and basking!
One side thy inland ocean loving, broad, with copious
commerce, steamers, sails,
And one the Atlantic's wind caressing, fierce or gentle –
mighty hulls dark-gliding in the distance.
Isle of sweet brooks of drinking-water – healthy air and soil!
Isle of the salty shore and breeze and brine!

Walt Whitman

PART ONE

Introduction

Advice to Hikers

Hiking

Hiking is becoming a very popular sport. It is a fun, healthy way to get exercise and enjoy the outdoors; you can walk where you choose at whatever pace you like surrounded by natural beauty. It is a non-competitive sport; nobody keeps score. The distance, difficulty and vigor are up to you. Legions of folks begin by walking their neighborhoods for exercise. While that's not hiking, it's pretty close to the real thing. If you are in good shape from regular walking, you are only a few steps from being a hiker.

For some experienced woods walkers there are mental benefits as well. A hike may be the tonic required to help you sort out minor problems and find a solution to them. Each hike is a kind of adventure where you never know what you will see, or, if you're bushwhacking (walking off trail), where you may have to go before you finish. Completing a challenging hike can leave you with an important sense of accomplishment and a good tired and relaxed feeling both physically and mentally.

The following overview will provide beginners an idea of what to expect and how to hike safely and enjoyably. Veteran hikers may pick up a few tips or refresh their knowledge of hiking skills.

Preparation and Planning

One of the nicest things about hiking is that you can plan to suit your own capabilities or the experience of the group you're with. On Long Island there are no serious changes in elevation so the beginning hiker will not be surprised by unexpected steeps or rock scrambles. However, being in good shape will greatly add to the enjoyment you get out of the sport and will help avoid sore legs or fatigue. Regular stretching before and after a hike keeps the body limber and reduces strains and stiffness.

Planning for a hike entails choosing your route and learning a little about the area. Sometimes you may need two cars, one at each end of the trail. A local road atlas helps find trailheads and parking areas. Topographic maps are extremely useful and may show out-of-the-way features like ponds, kettle-holes, a hollow, a remote hill with a view, or a long-forgotten cemetery. Trail maps can be obtained from the Long Island Greenbelt Trail Conference. Detailed United States Geological Survey and New York State Department of Transportation topographic maps can be purchased from hiking and camping supply stores or ordered through the mail or via e-mail (see appendix). Maps are best kept folded in a clear lock-top bag where they'll stay dry and clean. If you want advice or experience with guided hikes you can turn to any of the hiking organizations listed in the appendix. They often offer group hikes.

As part of your planning, always let someone know the route of your hike and when you expect to return, and be sure to learn what the weather conditions are supposed to be. Always have a bailout plan in place and know the options available should weather or

A woods road in Eastern Long Island

injury force you to seek help or shelter. Of course being able to read a map and understand its features will help when such changes are necessary.

Clothing

The most important piece of equipment to a hiker is footwear. Since backpacking opportunities are rare on Long Island, day-hiking boots will do best for our sandy or uneven trails. A pair of lightweight nylon-and-leather boots with strong treaded soles will give your feet and ankles protection and support that sneakers cannot. It helps to have the boots waterproofed since dry feet are less likely to get blisters than moist ones. You don't need boots with the latest in Gore-Tex® or other waterproofing material; waterproofing with a commercial spray or other application will suffice. Regular maintenance of boots will help them last several years, and once they're broken in a good pair of boots will be your most reliable friend on the trail. Although they are not usually waterproofed, trail running shoes will suffice in terrain that is level, even and dry. Wool socks should be worn all year round. They help keep your feet dry and blister-free because wool retains its ability to hold body heat even when wet. Some people choose to wear a sock liner made of polypropylene or some other synthetic fiber, which wicks moisture away from the feet, keeping them dry.

You really don't need to buy special clothing for hiking, but there are a few simple cautions. *Hiking safely means staying dry and warm* in any season. It is a well-known fact that cotton readily absorbs moisture but once wet loses any ability to keep you warm. In cool or cold weather wet cotton draws body heat away from you, which can leave you uncomfortably cold, and in extreme cases may become very dangerous. For both inner and outer garments it's better to wear synthetic fibers which dry faster than 100 percent cotton garments. This is particularly true for t-shirts and tops. If you wear a cotton shirt, it's a good idea to bring a second shirt along to change into during a particularly sweaty hike. Pants should be loose-fitting with plenty of pocket room. Military-type fatigues, especially when constructed of rip-stop material, are the most durable, and the best are found in Army-Navy surplus stores. The large cargo pockets are great for hikers to store maps, cameras, energy bars, etc. They also dry quickly since real fatigues are never made of 100 percent cotton. Avoid wearing jeans if possible since denim is made from cotton and is therefore not a good choice for serious outdoor walks. In warm weather, shorts are a comfortable option. However, out in the Pine Barrens and on the East End there is always the threat of picking up ticks, so I wear light-colored fatigues that have tie downs on the ankles to prevent ticks from getting under the pants.

In colder weather you should dress in layers, which trap heat between them. Loose-fitting layers are best. Winter hiking can be exhilarating if you are in shape and properly dressed. If it is going to be cold (under 40 degrees) and you will be out for any length of time, you will want to wear long underwear, known as thermals, made from synthetic materials to keep you warm and dry. A good cold weather layer combination would be a wool shirt or sweater and a Polartec (or similar type pullover) over that. A tightly woven nylon shell, such as a windbreaker or parka, is the final touch in preventing convective heat loss from the wind. Sometimes this outer layer can double as raingear if it is waterproof. The key to comfort in winter is to put on layers early in the hike or during breaks and peel them off when you heat up on the trail. The idea is to maintain a level body temperature and avoid sweating, if possible.

Up to 40 percent of body heat is lost through the head, so a hat is important in cold weather. In warmer weather, a peaked baseball-type cap keeps the sun off the face and eyes. In winter, gloves and a scarf are also must-haves. A scarf around the neck keeps the blood-flow to the head warm and, hence, the head itself stays warm. Some people are more comfortable on cold days covering their ears with a wool headband that allows some heat to escape so they will not perspire too much. Protection of the skin in winter from sun and wind is often overlooked, but a cold day on the trail can leave your skin dry and red from windburn if you don't use skin creams. Sunscreen is important on bright days in any season. Lip balm prevents painful chapping. And don't forget sunglasses coated to filter ultraviolet light that can damage the eyes any time of the year. Lastly, pack a bandana: its many uses make it invaluable.

Equipment

Stores are full of high-tech equipment but you don't need to spend much money to enjoy hiking. A few essentials and some personal extras will suffice to keep your hike safe and enjoyable. When you're day-hiking keep equipment as light and compact as possible, but feel secure with all the essentials for the day on your back.

Day-packs (also known as rucksacks) and fanny packs can hold all that is necessary for even the longest of day-hikes. They come in various models and shapes. A top-loading pack is preferable since you can put outerwear under the flap and easily slide it out at a moment's notice. Better packs are made of tough nylon materials, like Cordura®; make sure you check the stitching, straps, and zippers when buying one. Popular brand names are usually of better quality and spending a few dollars more will reward you with years of durable use. A back pad and built-in padded shoulder straps make the pack more comfortable when carrying heavier loads. Small side compartments are either part of the pack or can be added. Some rucksacks are large enough (from 1,500 to 2,500 cubic inches) to use for short overnight camping trips, but for that purpose make sure there are loops on the pack where a sleeping bag and ground pad can be lashed.

As for what to take with you, the most important thing, though it's not an item of equipment, is knowledge; try to learn how to use your tools and your experience. Hikers in good shape with top-quality equipment can run into trouble, but with some knowledge and skills those situations can easily be remedied. For this reason you should read everything you can on the subject of hiking, no matter how much you think you already know. While the trails described in this book are well marked, it's always valuable to be able to read a map and use a compass. Knowledge of the wildlife you are likely to encounter on the trail will heighten your enjoyment and dispel your fears. You can plan your walks to provide experience of varied seasons and weather conditions even if you hike the same stretch of trail repeatedly.

A first aid kit is essential for any hiker. These kits can be purchased or they can be tailor made; the latter may be preferable. The kit need not be large but should contain a few essential items: *Band-Aids® and butterflies, antiseptic cream, aspirin or acetaminophen, gauze, bandages and adhesive tape* should be able to handle most cuts and scrapes. Decongestants and antihistamines alleviate sinus congestion but also reduce swelling from bee stings or insect bites. There are also small applicators that relieve the sting of insect bites. Other items that should be carried are an *ace bandage, extra toilet paper, nail clippers, safety pins, ammonia inhalants, a needle for splinters, tweezers, and moleskin* for painful blisters that can quickly crop up during a long hike. You will rarely use these items but having them when you need them makes the extra weight well worth your while. Anyone who's planning to do serious hiking should consider taking a first-aid course. Contact local Red Cross chapters for information on course availability.

The traditional list of essentials to be carried on each hike looks something like this:

• Map and compass
• Knife
• Water bottle (plus an extra one if possible)
• Waterproof matches/lighter and candles
• First aid kit and emergency foil blanket
• High energy trail bars and food
• Flashlight with extra bulb and batteries
• Extra wool or synthetic shirt
• Whistle/small mirror

Other optional items that can come in handy are:

• Sun block
• Sunglasses
• Hat
• Bandana
• Firestarter
• Insect repellent
• Change for phone call, or a cell phone
• Rope or nylon cord
• Toilet paper
• Ace bandage

- Raingear
- Extra socks

This list would include several other small items if you were a backpacker intending to camp overnight in more remote areas. These items will enable any person who knows how to use them to survive a night out in the woods if need be. You should know how to read a map and use a compass, and how to use a small folding knife in the woods. Three times anything – whistles, blasts, shouts, or flashing lights is the universal distress signal. Information on how to deal with emergencies can be found in one of the books about wilderness survival listed in the appendix.

Here is a list of personal items to help enjoy the walk to the fullest:

- Camera equipment and extra film
- Bird and wildflower field guides and a hiking book
- Binoculars
- Magnifying glass
- Notepad or drawing pad and pencil
- Foam pad for sitting
- Walking stick
- GPS (global positioning system) for the truly technical bushwhacker!
- All purpose tool

Some of these things may seem a bit extravagant, but if you don't mind a little extra weight, they can make for a more enjoyable outing.

Food

Your requirement for food depends on the temperature (you use more energy in winter), your metabolism, the hilliness of the terrain, your physical condition, the weight of the pack, the pace, and even meals eaten before setting out. How many calories you burn depends more on how far you go than on how fast you move; you consume energy at a fairly regular rate. The time to skimp or diet is not while you are hiking. Walk, burn energy, eat–it's a simple enough equation. For snacks it is best to eat carbohydrates that give the body a ready source of available energy. Whole-grain breads are fine; oranges, apples, or vegetables such as carrots can be munched on at breaks. But you don't have to be too health-conscious while hiking. A look at the ingredients in most "energy" bars tells you there are plenty of readily usable calories like sugars in them. Chocolate and GORP (Good Old Raisins and Peanuts) mix are also good choices. These snacks should be consumed regularly to keep your energy level up, especially on longer hikes. Fatigue from a precariously dropping energy level can lead to injury.

Lunch is a different matter. The rule here is if you're willing to carry it you're free to eat it. There are many good substitutes for the standard peanut butter and jelly sandwich. As long as they're kept out of the heat, cold cuts are a good choice. Pita bread holds up better in the pack than loaf bread since it doesn't crush much. Zip-lock bags are advised so you don't find those pretzels you packed scattered somewhere in the bottom of your pack; they also keep sandwiches fresh and clean. Pepperoni and cheeses are other choices for lunch, and they go well with crackers.

Each hiker should carry a minimum of one quart of water, more on hikes longer than half a day. Plastic water containers are available in all shapes and sizes. Even on cold days when you don't feel thirsty, your body loses water through evaporation and convection by wind. Don't wait until you feel thirsty; if you do, you're already dehydrated. High carbohydrate sports drinks are fine but not necessary unless you are hiking in very hot weather or burning calories at a steady pace on a long-distance hike. Small juice packets are a welcome change when stopping for lunch or a snack. There aren't many restrictions on trail food except not to eat heavy fatty foods that don't digest well. It also helps to bring foods that don't spoil or crush easily.

Safety Tips

Here are some tips to help you keep comfortable and safe while you enjoy hiking.

Ticks

There are two types of ticks found on Long Island: the American dog tick and the smaller black-legged tick, commonly known in these parts as the deer tick. The dog tick is found in both Nassau and Suffolk counties but seems more common farther west on Long Island. It prefers sunny locations like grassy fields and the edges of wooded areas. It has not been shown to transmit Lyme Disease, but can pass on a sometimes fatal but very rare disease called Rocky Mountain Spotted Fever.

The deer tick is the culprit that can pass on the bacterium that causes Lyme disease. There are many pamphlets available from local health departments explaining the symptoms of this illness. A red rash resembling a bull's eye may appear at the point of the bite, but not in all people. In any case, most people who are infected show other signs within a few weeks of being bitten. These include a flu-like fever, headache, malaise (tiredness), stiff neck, muscle and joint pain, and enlarged lymph glands. At this early stage, antibiotics can knock out the disease. In rare cases if the disease is left untreated, permanent damage to the joints, nerves or heart can occur. It should be stressed that these cases are not the norm.

Now that you understand a little bit about ticks, what can you do about them? First, remember that not all ticks (dog or deer) carry Lyme disease. Also, unlike mosquitoes, ticks don't usually bite as soon as they grab hold of their host. Instead, they prefer to crawl to a comfortable location before securely attaching themselves. It is at this stage when I have felt a tick crawling on a leg or arm. There is some time after the first contact to detect ticks before they even bite. Once attached, they anesthetize the area so the bite is not even felt; then they may start to draw blood from the victim. But deer ticks need about a day attached to their host before they begin transmitting Lyme disease, if they carry it.

Certain areas, like thickets near wetlands, seem to harbor many ticks, so avoid these areas if you can. Ticks cling to tall grasses and low shrubs and grab onto unsuspecting mammals that rub against them as they pass by. I have seen ticks at all times of the year, even in February if the weather is mild enough. Ticks are not active in below-freezing temperatures, so seeing them in winter is pretty rare. The concentration of deer ticks increases as one moves farther east on Long Island, especially on the South Fork and Shelter Island which are ground zero for these little pests.

Here is a list of precautions to take to reduce the hazards of your hike in tick territory:

1. Stay near the center of trails and avoid off-trail activity whenever possible. This is especially important for those hiking with small children. Most trailsides are trimmed back and it is possible to hike all day without having contact with vegetation. Some trails are predominantly on woods roads and wide enough to avoid any situation that could lead to picking up a tick.

2. Apply insect repellent to clothing, especially long sleeves and pants. The most effective repellents contain a chemical known as DEET, but that substance can produce rashes or illness in some people, particularly children. Caution should be taken when applying it to bare skin. A commercial substance known as Permanone® can be applied to clothing, but it must be done before hiking and is best used by hikers bushwhacking in heavily infested areas.

3. Wear light-colored clothing, which makes it easier to spot ticks if they do

attach themselves to your garments. Ticks are relatively easy to spot once you know what you are looking for.

4. Tuck pants into high socks or wear pants that have tie-down straps around the ankles, like army fatigue pants.

5. Do a regular tick check in the course of your walk. You can do it during breaks, or you can even check the person in front of you while you're walking. This is just a good habit, and there's no need to be obsessed with it.

6. Check your body when you get home and wash clothes as soon as you can. Take a shower after your hike. I've been in some heavily infested off-trail places and believe that a shower has gotten rid of many ticks, since I found none after I showered.

If you should find a tick crawling on you, don't be afraid to remove it by hand; ticks do not bite or sting like other insects. Killing it is another story; they have very hard-shelled bodies. Dropping it on the ground and stepping on it probably won't do, so place it between rocks to make sure it is crushed. If you are inside, the tick can be dropped into alcohol or flushed down the toilet. If a tick has attached itself to a person already, don't panic. A pair of small tweezers (the kind on some Swiss army knives works fine) will do the job. Grasp as close to the point of attachment as possible and pull steadily outwards without twisting or jerking. This is to prevent the mouth-parts that are imbedded in the skin from coming off and remaining in the person's skin. If the parts do break off, consult your physician for removal since infection is possible. In most cases, the mouth-parts will work themselves out over a few days. A magnifying glass will aid greatly in inspecting the site after removal. If a tick is hanging tough and doesn't seem to want to come out, smothering it with a drop of oil or a coating of petroleum jelly for a few minutes before trying again usually does the trick. Apply antiseptic to the site after removal. Be aware of possible symptoms, which usually show within 2 to 12 days after the initial bite. It should be noted that ticks become engorged with blood when they have been in their victim for a period of time. In almost every case in which I have removed a tick, it was not in this state, meaning it was not there for very long.

Dehydration

Common sense would tell you to keep drinking water regularly during the course of your hike, but some people are hesitant to urinate outdoors and hence don't drink enough. This can lead to headaches, muscle cramps, poor judgment and heat exhaustion. Each member of a hiking party should carry at least a quart of water or more on any hike. On longer hikes or in particularly hot and humid weather, much more water accompanied by rests is the rule. But no matter what, **do not drink any outside water source, no matter how clean it looks!** Microscopic organisms can cause sickness and disease. If you must drink from an outside source (and this happens extremely rarely on Long Island), you should use iodine water purification tablets.

Dehydration can occur on cold days as well as hot ones. The danger on cold days is that since you may not perspire as much you may not feel it necessary to drink. The body uses water much more efficiently if replenished before a shortage occurs. For this reason drink regularly during the course of the day and try not to wait until you feel thirsty.

To comply with low impact hiking principles, when you must relieve yourself outdoors, cover any toilet paper at least six inches deep under soil and leaves where it will degrade on its own.

Hypothermia

The condition where the body can't generate enough heat and body temperature starts to drop is called hypothermia. Commonly known as "exposure" in the media, hypothermia can occur in temperatures as high as the low 50s, and can set in with just a few degrees drop in body temperature. Wet clothing, especially cotton, worsens the hazard. Early warning signs are incoherent or slurring speech, uncontrolled shivering, stumbling, and lack of finger coordination. Probably the most dangerous symptom of hypothermia that sneaks up on the unsuspecting hiker is the loss of good judgment. This is very serious for hikers in remote mountainous areas where poor decisions can be life-threatening. On nearly level Long Island the danger is not so severe. Still, it is important while hiking in cold weather to keep fueling the body with simple sugars that can be readily metabolized. Hard candies are okay, as are fruits, chocolate, energy bars, or pretzels. Even high-carbohydrate sport drinks are good to keep energy levels up. Hypothermia is best treated by eating these, drinking hot liquids such as hot chocolate, and adding layers of wool or synthetic fabric clothing. Sometimes the simplest remedy is putting on a windproof shell to stop heat loss due to cold wind.

It is also a good idea to avoid smoking cigarettes or drinking alcohol while hiking in cold weather, since both constrict the peripheral blood vessels, increasing susceptibility to frostbite. Frostbite occurs when exposed skin freezes and becomes pale and cold to the touch. Should this happen do not rub the affected area, but try a gradual warm-up and get to a doctor as soon as possible. The extremities—hands, feet, ears, and nose—usually freeze first so take care to protect them. The extremely cold conditions that can cause frost-bite do not occur often in our area, and only experienced hikers are likely to venture out when they do. Still, it pays to take precautions in cold weather; take along a warm hat, gloves and extra clothing layers, and know how to deal with these situations if they come up.

Lightning

Should you be caught out in a thunderstorm, you should obviously seek shelter, but not under any tall trees. Hundreds of people are killed every year nationwide by being struck by lightning under an exposed tree, or hit by falling limbs broken by lightning. When a storm arrives, if you are not within a quick-paced jaunt to a car or other shelter, try squatting down amidst heavy shrubbery. Get out of exposed locations like hillsides or flat meadows where you are the tallest object. A person struck by lightning can be safely touched and should be given CPR if necessary.

Poison Ivy

This three-leafed plant can take the form of a low shrub or climbing vine. You should learn to identify it and avoid it whenever possible. Poison ivy contains an oil called urushiol that causes a severe reaction in most people. It can be contracted any time of the year, even when the plant is leafless. The oil can also be picked up off boots or clothing. The saying "leaves of three, let it be" is a good one to follow, but there are many three-leafed plants (wild strawberry is one) that are harmless. Learn to identify the different varieties of poison ivy; the leaves can either have "teeth" or be smooth.

The plant grows widely on Long Island but particularly in sunny locations such as the edges of woods and trails, overgrown fields, along wetlands and especially along the dunes and beach fronts. It is not usually found in deep woods but can be counted on to appear in disturbed second-growth areas. In winter the climbing vines can easily be identified by the fibrous hairlike rootlets that attach to tree bark. This "fuzzy rope" look is a telltale sign that the plant is in the area. Wearing long pants and learning to identify the plant are the best ways to avoid it. There are many over-the-counter remedies for the symptoms of poison ivy but I've found that the crushed leaves of jewelweed or touch-me-not, a wetland plant, will also alleviate the symptoms. Maybe you are one of the lucky 15-to-20 percent of the population that is immune to the plant's effects, but the rest of us have to take precautions to avoid it.

Rabies

This disease is transmitted from the saliva or bodily fluids of mammals and although a rarity, is still a very serious disease. It can be contracted by coming in contact with an animal that has the ailment, which can occur anywhere. Recently the public has been more concerned about rabies after the disease spread northward from Virginia a few years ago. Avoid any wild animal, such as a fox, a raccoon or a skunk, that acts strangely. The rabies carrier could be the classic "mad" animal with a foaming mouth or a docile animal that has no fear of people. Use common sense; when you come near a wild animal keep your distance, even if it looks harmless and in need.

Insect Bites

Although insects can be annoying, they're not really a big problem unless you have severe allergic reactions to bee stings or bug bites. If this is the case, you should carry antihistamine medication at all times. Insect bites are not a common problem encountered on the trail most of the year; rather they are situational. For instance, mosquitoes do most of their biting early or late in the day, and are usually active near sources of water or moisture. The West Nile Virus or Equine Encephalitis, also a mosquito borne disease, has recently entered the New York area. Though it can affect hikers like other people, it has not been reported to be a special problem. Deer flies can inflict nasty bites but are only active in hot weather in the immediate vicinity of a standing body of water, like a pond, lake, or slow moving river. Even ticks seem to be more numerous at particular times during the summer as their life cycle proceeds. I try to avoid being sweaty in hot weather when near water since sweat attracts insects. Most people can use a repellent and go on hiking as usual despite the nuisance that bugs bring.

Injuries

Although it is uncommon, someone in your party can fall and sprain an ankle or pull a muscle. The treatment for these injuries is best remembered by the memory word "RICE," standing for rest, ice, compression and elevation. On the trail aspirin can help reduce swelling, and an ace bandage will give support until you get home. A regular routine of home exercise and pre-hike stretching can lessen the chances of injury on the trail.

Small cuts and scrapes are fairly common to hikers. Treatment is to clean, cover, compress and elevate the injury to stop bleeding. The most common irritating injury to hikers is blisters. To safeguard against them keep your feet dry by wearing wool or synthetic socks all year round, and make sure your boots fit properly and are well broken in. Carry moleskin in your first-aid kit and apply it at the first sign that a blister is forming. Some people even put moleskin on before a hike to prevent blisters they know occur in particular spots. Cutting toenails short keeps them from jamming against the front of the boot, preventing a common soreness.

The Spire, a glacial erratic along the Paumanok Path

Natural Long Island: Geology, Flora & Fauna

The famous writer-naturalist-hiker John Burroughs said, ". . . the student and lover of nature has this advantage over people who gad up and down the world, seeking some novelty or excitement; he has only to stay at home and see the procession pass. The great globe swings around to him like a revolving showcase; the change of the seasons is like the passage of strange and new countries; the zones of the earth, with all their beauties and marvels, pass one's door, and linger long in the passing. What a voyage is this we make without leaving for a night our own fireside!"

Observe and enjoy.

Geology

Long Island was a part of the high continental shelf under water for most of pre-historic time before the era we know as the Pleistocene Epoch, or Ice Age. The last glacial age, known as the Wisconsin Glaciation, peaked about 20,000 years ago, and when the meltdown started it had reached as far south as present-day Long Island. It left a line of coarse debris that runs from Lake Success to Montauk Point. This is known as the **Ronkonkoma Moraine** and is referred to as a terminal moraine, since it marks the furthest advance of the glacier. After a brief retreat it once again advanced a little and stopped, leaving another line of debris known as a recessional moraine. This area of hills and bluffs runs the length of Long Island from present day Staten Island up to the north shore and out beyond Orient Point. It is called the **Harbor Hill Moraine**. The two moraines intersect in present day Lake Success. When the glacier melted the smoother and finer material ran off to the south. These areas are called outwash plains and tend to be lower and more level than the moraines. There are outwash plains south of each moraine. The long, smooth sandy beaches of the South Shore that are a result of the outwash plain contrast sharply with the rocky, steep beaches of the North Shore formed by the Harbor Hill Moraine. Hills that approach 300 feet in elevation in the Ronkonkoma Moraine afford surprisingly distant panoramas because of the flat **outwash plains** adjacent to them. Scattered on these morainal hills are large boulders called **glacial erratics** deposited by the retreating ice sheet. Although they are rare in interior Long Island there are many unusual erratics in the Manorville Hills.

Many undisturbed erratics in the Pine Barrens have rare lichens of various colors and shapes growing on them. Lichens are the combination of a fungus

A kettlehole along the Paumanok Path near Flanders

and an algae. The fungus provides moisture and the algae provides photo-synthesis for production of energy. The relationship benefits both organisms, a process called symbiosis. Lichens grow on rocks and trees and are an indicator of clean air, since they are sensitive to pollution. It is interesting to note that the number and diversity of lichen species drops off as one gets closer to New York City.

A **kettlehole**, also known as a glacial kettle, is a depression formed when a large block of ice fell or was deposited and outwash till filled in around it. They have a somewhat circular shape. Some are still full of water, like Wildwood Lake near Riverhead and Lake Success by the Nassau-Queens border. Lake Ronkonkoma is the largest of these kettle lakes on Long Island. Some are vernal, meaning they fill with water in spring and wet times but dry up in the warm dry weather of late summer. They are fairly common along the trail in the morainal sections. Some are completely dry and have trees growing in them. The kettles are interesting for their attractive topography and the types of vegetation found in those still wet. Animals not usually seen, including salamanders, frequent these kettles because of the moisture trapped in them.

Flora

Robert Cushman Murphy, in his book *Fish Shaped Paumanok*, describes nine distinct habitats found on Long Island: 1. Beach and Dune; 2. Salt Meadow and Bay; 3. White Cedar Swamps; 4. Pine Barrens; 5. Deciduous Woods; 6.

Prairie; 7. Grass and Shrub Downs; 8. Ponds and Freshwater Bogs; 9. Fjord-like harbors on Long Island Sound. All except the prairie (which were the Hempstead Plains) can still be seen.

The Long Island landscape looked much like modern day Canada up until a few thousand years ago. As the climate moderated more aggressive southern species began to dominate in places. **Sugar maples, yellow birches** and **American beech** as well as **hemlock** had their time in a forest succession that continues to this day. Out east, where the soils are very sandy, the **jack pine** dominated for a time, only to be succeeded by the now common **pitch pine** about five thousand years ago. Long Island had 68 native tree species not including several tall shrub-type plants. Some no longer grow here but today it has a surprising diversity of trees considering that it has little elevation or latitudinal change, no limestone soils, and no dramatic rock outcrops or deep gorges.

Long Island has a moderate climate influenced by the Atlantic Ocean, and a good deal of rainfall. It is in a temperate latitude between the steamy south and frigid north, producing favorable conditions for both northern and southern tree species. Soils also play a role in this diversity. The western portion, especially along the north shore west of Port Jefferson, has soil that is rich and moist, which promotes greater diversity and larger trees. Along the South Shore and East End where soils are drier and sandier various oaks are dominant.

Southern tree species, such as **sweet gum, tulip tree, persimmon, hackberry** and **sweet bay magnolia** from the Carolinian (Upper Austral) Zone that is extending its range northward, thrive in the western part of the island. There are northern species from the Alleghenian (transition forest) Zone like **sugar maple, white pine** and **hemlock** in a few places where microclimates or special conditions allow them to survive. Some of the "relic" species have hung on until relatively recently. Red spruce, a northern conifer, existed on Cid's Island near Orient until 1930 when fire destroyed them. Sometimes, certain species dominate an area and grow in pure stands, usually because of specific conditions that

Birdfoot violet

favor them. White cedar or red maple often do this in swamps; pitch pine, scarlet oak or red cedar in dry situations. In the "Sunken Forest" on Fire Island the **American holly** dominates an ancient forest growing in the shelter of the dunes on a thin barrier beach. Recognizing these differences can help the hiker find a wetland hidden off the trail or identify an area that was once cut or disturbed in some way. This is particularly important for bushwhackers, who can use these landmarks to locate themselves.

Starflower

A similar north-south mixture occurs with smaller plants and wildflowers. Since wildflowers are some of the most colorful and in some cases rare shows in nature, they are much sought after. Knowing not only where but when to look is the key here. A good field guide (see appendix for references) and a magnifying glass are helpful. The most showy flowers come from our native shrubs, the **mountain laurel, sheep laurel** and **swamp azalea**. These generally bloom in early summer. Mountain laurel grows best in the hilly moraine of the North Shore, being especially plentiful west of Huntington. It is also common along the north side of the south fork west of Sag Harbor. Sheep laurel is spread out in the pine barrens and the fragrant swamp azalea is found in wet areas. The moist woodlands near our rivers and watersheds have the beautiful starflower blooming along the ground in late May. Its six- or seven-petaled white star-shaped flowers are usually found with **Canada mayflower,** another more northerly plant. The trailing arbutus whose small pinkish to white flowers seem to hide amongst the leaves of early spring, has an exquisite fragrance which is often unnoticed because you must literally get down on your knees to smell it. **Trailing arbutus** is listed as rare or declining in its range in most field guides, yet is very common in the Pine Barrens.

Grass pink (calopogen)

Native orchids on Long Island mostly

grow in fragile bogs or swamps, except the **pink lady's slipper**, or moccasin flower, which is found from dunes to upland woods. Many lady's slippers have been dug out by collectors. This is unfortunate since this orchid, like most orchids, will die if transplanted because of its dependence on fungi in the soil.

Fauna

Long Island still has a wide variety of wildlife. Gone are the beaver, black bear, mountain lion, bobcat, timber wolf, elk, moose, timber rattlesnake, heath hen and many species of beautiful butterflies that once inhabited meadows and the Hempstead Plains, but I prefer to dwell on the surprises that, as Burroughs said, can still be found at our doorstep. Long Island is a place where much wildlife is transient, and unusual visitors can show up almost any time of the year and be gone just as quickly. I have memories of seeing harbor seals swimming in the Sound thirty yards offshore, and of a northern harrier flying low on the hunt in the dwarf pines. On morning runs I've surprised red foxes. I have seen a huge snapping turtle dragging its primitive-looking hulk along far from water, a great horned owl sitting atop a snag silhouetted against a rose-colored dusk, and a milk snake so long I couldn't see its tail and head at the same time as it crossed the trail! I have watched the ruby-throated hummingbird sharpen its long, thin beak while resting in a swamp full of flowering blueberry bushes, and on our island I spooked the first muskrat I ever saw (I don't know who jumped more!). Once I went to a place where I hoped to see the magnificently arrayed wood duck and wound up watching equally showy greenwinged and blue-winged teal as well. Another time I stood amazed watching a red bat fly around my backyard on a gray November day.

White-tail Deer

The thought that each time out you may see something that will surprise or enlighten is the thrill of the hike. It's what makes each outing an adventure.

The **white-tail deer** is the largest of our wild creatures and is probably more common than most people realize. The farthest west that deer can still be found is Heckscher State Park in East Islip on the South Shore. It should be noted that most of this herd is tame and used to being fed by people in the winter. Nearby Connetquot River State Park has a native population of deer

Fox den

that are thriving in a more natural environment. The mainstream population of deer inhabits the large public lands of the RCA tract in Rocky Point, the Carmans River watershed in Middle Island, Yaphank and Brookhaven, and all points east.

The largest mammal predators left on Long Island are the foxes. We have two species with distinctly different personalities. The most common is the flashy looking **red fox**, which inhabits mixed habitats of woodlands, brushy edges and open agricultural country. I have seen many dens throughout the Pine Barrens, usually on hillsides, and they are common in the Manorville Hills. The red fox also thrives in areas of Nassau County, especially the hilly, less developed North Shore. Dens have been spotted near the northern end of the Nassau-Suffolk Greenbelt. Although primarily nocturnal, red foxes may sometimes be seen in daytime, particularly early or late in the day, or on cloudy days. A true canine in every sense, the red fox differs from its cousin the **gray fox** in many ways. The gray fox looks similar to the red fox, but with more gray in its fur and a black-tipped tail instead of the white-tipped tail of the red fox. However, the gray fox is very catlike in its ways. It is much more secretive and skulky than its red cousin and never seems to travel far from the brushy, thick country it prefers to sneak around in. It is the only North American member of the canine family that climbs trees when pressed. It even walks in a feline-type way. Because of these shy habits the range of the gray fox is uncertain. It was seen in Alley Pond Park in Queens as late as 1957 but now appears only where undisturbed thick cover can support it. It is common at Montauk and probably survives in other places.

The **raccoon** is an intelligent mammal known for its curiosity and dexterity. A nocturnal animal with the familiar "mask" and ringed tail, it is a very formidable foe if cornered. It has very sharp teeth and claws as well as nimble fingers that can easily open door knobs or pry off garbage-can lids. It will feed on almost anything edible, from grubs, crickets and fruit to mice, birds' eggs, nestlings and scraps from our dinner tables. Raccoons are found from Queens eastward. They are most numerous near waterways. The raccoon is a rather handsome and smart animal in contrast to the **opossum** which has changed little through the ages. It is a primitive, somewhat dumb animal that continues to exist despite its shortcomings. It has a ghostly looking snout because of its short white facial hairs, and a naked ratlike tail that enables it to hang upside-down from trees. The opossum is more adaptable than the raccoon; it will eat things that raccoons won't. It has few requirements for den sites and is a real opportunist in this regard. It is often seen dead on roadways because it eats road kill and isn't smart in traffic.

Two other mammals found on Long Island are the **woodchuck** and **striped skunk**. The woodchuck is also well known as the groundhog of American folklore which gained fame by forecasting the length of winter better than the National Weather Service. I've seen "chucks" along the Northern State Parkway as far west as Hicksville. They are usually found near farms, old fields and pastures, and along hedgerows and woodland edges.

The striped skunk is rather timid and never seems to be in a rush to go anywhere as it forages for grubs, insects and small prey. This animal is not now and never was very common on Long Island. It is occasionally seen on the East End but is more likely to let you know of its presence by the smell of its repulsive discharge.

The beaver has long been extirpated from the Island, yet one of its close relatives, the **muskrat**, can still be found in wetlands throughout our area. The muskrat is a peaceful creature that inhabits ponds, rivers and even salt marshes. It looks like a smaller version

Leopard frog

of the beaver except that it has a long narrow tail instead of the beaver's paddle-shaped tail. Muskrats make a house from aquatic plants that looks very much like a beaver lodge. I have seen two houses next to each other in the old cranberry bog in Robert Cushman Murphy Park in Manorville. They were constructed of cattails and quite large. In some cases they can be eight feet long and five feet high. Some muskrats live in dens in banks on the side of a wetland. Muskrats like to burrow and this has resulted in damage to man-made dikes. To observe muskrats one must be very quiet and avoid detection since they are very skittish of people. When alarmed they dive underwater and can stay there for more than 15 minutes. When young are forced to look for new homes they can travel miles from water. Adaptable animals, muskrats can set up residence in fresh, brackish or salt water. For this reason they can be found in Nassau County, especially in the salt marshes where ample food and cover are available.

Farther east in some of the wilder marshes, with some luck one may encounter a **mink** or a **river otter.** These members of the weasel family are two of the rarest mammals on Long Island. Once quite common, they have both been extensively trapped for their valuable pelts. They both hunt along watercourses for their prey. The mink prefers to take muskrats and has been known to tear open their houses to get at the young within. Like their weasel cousins, they are fierce hunters with little fear of danger. On the other hand, the river otter has developed a reputation as a playful social creature that likes to slide down snowy slopes or body surf a rapid current. Otters prefer fresh water habitats and eat primarily fish, but they will take small mammals and crustaceans. Although trapping is no longer a hazard to the population, they are very scarce. The few remaining otters are likely to be found on the far East End. An undisturbed place like Mashomack Preserve on Shelter Island or the Long Pond Greenbelt offers the best hope of seeing them.

Long Island has two species of true weasels that inhabit varied terrain including forested and brushy areas, wetlands, farmlands, and open areas. As a result they are probably more widely distributed and common than one would expect. The larger and more common species is the **long tailed weasel**. It is known as a relentless hunter, its long slim body allowing it to chase prey into crevices and burrows most predators can't negotiate. They are surprisingly agile and quick as they chase down rabbits, chipmunks, shrews, birds, and just about anything else they can take down. They are prone to go on killing sprees when they smell blood. For this reason they have been a bane to poultry farmers, whose worst nightmare is a weasel in the chicken coop. In winter their coats turn white, helping them sneak up on prey in snowy conditions. The smaller version of the weasel is known as the **ermine,** also called the short-tailed weasel. Less common than its larger relative, it is no less a fearless hunter and displays similar traits. The black-tipped tails of the ermine have traditionally been used as the trim for the robes of royalty. Although they are fascinating to observe, you are not likely to see either of our native weasels; both are expert in their avoidance of people. If you learn to look for signs, you may be able to see one hunting along a hedgerow or field edge out east.

There are three species of tiny hunters called shrews found on Long Island. Shrews eat earthworms, snails, various invertebrate insects, some types of subterranean fungus and even other shrews and mice. The most common is the **short tailed shrew**, which is also the largest shrew in North America. It usually grows to between four and five inches long, and has a solid gray coat and the characteristic pointy snout and tiny eyes all shrews are known for. This shrew is particularly ferocious as it pounces on its victim, biting it in the throat and face, injecting its venomous saliva and rapidly paralyzing it. Two other smaller species, the **masked shrew** and **least shrew**, can also be found on Long Island. I have usually observed shrews in the springtime when they seem to be particularly active.

On any early morning or late day walk in the warmer seasons one is likely to see the **eastern cottontail** along brushy trails and woods' edges. The **New England cottontail** is also native to the island but is much less common. It can be distinguished from its cousin by its shorter ears and the black patch of fur between them. Another familiar animal in Long Island woodlands is the **eastern chipmunk**, usually seen rushing for cover as it lets out its familiar squeaky chirp. Its larger cousin, the **eastern gray squirrel**, is found all over the island. One mysterious animal that few people ever see or even know exists on Long Island is the **southern flying squirrel**. This shy, timid animal is a nocturnal creature that lives up in the treetops. They prefer tall trees so they can "fly" from one tree to the other. They do not really fly but glide on flat patches of fur growing between their legs on each side They are scarce in the settled west end of the island, but are fairly common in the wooded areas of the North Shore and in the Pine Barrens where trees have grown large along the Peconic River watershed. They den in small tree cavities, usually in an abandoned woodpecker hole.

Among the small critters that scurry around the unsuspecting hiker are field mice and the voles. The **white footed mouse** is found throughout Long Island. It is a beautiful tawny brown color with white feet and under-parts and has large eyes and a narrow snout. The young are gray in color. They scavenge for nuts, berries, and assorted insects. In winter they use abandoned birds nests for shelter by building a small covering to make a sort of roof. Like most small mammals, they are low on the food chain and are preyed upon by predators large and small. They are active all year round but will stay put during extremely cold spells, and usually habituate wooded areas and brushy clearings and hedgerows. Another mouse, the **meadow jumping mouse**, is not nearly so abundant as the white-footed. As its name implies, this creature requires open, moist meadows with tall grassland or vegetation. When startled it can leap three to four feet to escape detection and will remain motionless to elude predators. It too is brown in color but has a long tail used for balance while in the air.

Voles are very common mouse-like animals but not often seen because of their habit of spending much of their time in tunnels under leaf litter. They have rounder, chubbier bodies than mice, with short legs and tails. Two species of voles are most common on Long Island: the gray **meadow vole** found in clearings and open areas, and the **pine vole**, also known as the woodland vole. The latter is common in the Pine Barrens and North Shore woodlands. The last of the small ground mammals worth mentioning are the moles. The raised tunnels of the **eastern mole** can be seen in many places along the trails in eastern Long Island, especially in the Pine Barrens. They are truly awkward-looking animals, with a small head and large flipper-like legs designed for digging. Weirder-looking still is the **star-nosed mole**, which isn't common but has been found scattered about areas of Suffolk County, especially in Montauk. You are much more likely to see signs of moles than the animals themselves.

The **harbor seal** is our native seal, and it lives in island waters the year round. They can grow to five feet in length and weigh up to 300 pounds. Groups of seals "hauling out" onto rocks and beaches to sun themselves at low tide can be seen along Long Island Sound or in the bays of the eastern forks. In recent years the population of these seals has increased tenfold from 400 to about 4,000 so they are not as rare a sight as they once were. What's more, there are four species of arctic seals that now show up in our waters in winter. Sighting these seals even a few years ago would have been unheard of. While strolling our wonderful beaches you might also come upon a sea turtle washed ashore. These too have become increasingly common in recent years. Little is known about these creatures but scientists are starting to learn more about them and what role our local waters play in their lives.

Long Island has no native lizards but we do have a population of reptiles and amphibians around us, some familiar like the **fowler's toad** and **eastern box turtle**, and some rare such as the **tiger salamander** and **diamondback turtle**. All of these animals have become much less common near developed areas; hence the Pine Barrens are their last refuge. There are eleven species of snakes left on Long Island and their numbers are declining rapidly. Most people simply detest snakes, yet they are harmless creatures that would prefer to shun man at every opportunity. I have been fortunate to have seen seven of our native species. While moving debris on the Brookhaven Trail I came upon the beautiful **northern ringneck snake**, rarely seen because it spends much of its time under rocks and logs. I recall the time I found an **eastern hognosed snake** sunning itself in Manorville one summer afternoon. Although I did not disturb it, I have read of the theatrics of this animal. When threatened it will give a menacing hiss and strike at the air as if it means to do some harm, but it will not bite and is only bluffing to scare off its enemy. If this doesn't work it will feign death by going through a convulsion act leading to "death," where it rolls over onto its back and has its tongue hanging out. If picked up and placed down on its stomach again it will amusingly roll back over again. Its final act of survival is to attempt to flee. This is a perfect example of how knowing what animal you are dealing with prevents unnecessary fears. It should be noted that our only poisonous snake, the **eastern timber rattlesnake** has not been seen on Long Island since the last one was sighted along the Ronkonkoma Branch of the Long Island Railroad in 1914.

Long Island is a haven for many birds; in fact, 169 species have been identified as confirmed local breeders. Since we are on the Atlantic flyway, many migrating birds stop off here in spring and fall. Over 300 species have been spotted on or around Long Island. Some of the most interesting are overwintering arctic birds such as snowy owls and colorful grosbeaks and crossbills. Birdwatching, or birding as it is known, is a source of enjoyment to a growing number of people, and learning a little about birds can enhance any outing. You could see the flash of color from a **scarlet tanager** in the treetops, or hear the rush of a **ruffed grouse** from its haunt in the Pine Barrens, the mysterious and beautiful song of the **hermit thrush** at dusk in a pitch pine hideaway or a friendly group of **black-capped chickadees** checking you out on a cold winter day. **Wild turkeys** frequent the woods of the East End. **Great horned owls** prowl the night with no fear of other animals and hoot wildly on cold winter evenings. Bright yellow **prothonatary warblers** call from the wetlands of the Nissequogue watershed and **great** and **snowy egret**s wade through marshes looking for a fish dinner. Our state bird, the **eastern bluebird**, has returned to many open areas in the Pine Barrens and **rufous-sided towhees** seem to be everywhere in summer as they scratch the forest floor for food. The **ovenbird** trills its call of "teacher teacher" over and over again. **Northern orioles** add color and song as does the **rose-breasted grosbeak**, whose rich whistle soothes the ears. **Red-bellied woodpeckers** "chirr" from the trees while **gray catbirds** mimic other birds and scold from the briars. **Prairie warblers** sing repetitively from scrub-oak clearings while **red-tailed hawks** circle overhead. This is a small sampling of what you can expect to see and hear on the trail, and of course a pair of binoculars will help.

A Brief Long Island History

The first human beings to reach Long Island trekked across a frigid continent in the wake of receding glaciers some 12,000 years ago. These hunters of woolly mammoths and elk were nomads who lived in a moisture-laden climate that accelerated decomposition, so little trace of them remains. The first to leave any imprint were small groups of Algonquin-speaking peoples that settled here. It was once believed that there were thirteen original native tribes on Long Island. We now recognize them as extended-family groups, each inhabiting a different location. There were almost certainly more than thirteen groups, but since they were illiterate and some of their dwelling sites were taken over by the European settlers, we may never know how many there actually were. From contact with Europeans these tribes contracted diseases to which they had no resistance, decimating their already low numbers. They were weakened by the clash with a vastly different culture, and lost members to assimilation with the Europeans. Under these pressures a culture that had existed for at least 3,000 years disappeared with astonishing rapidity.

The English name of each group came from the Algonquin name for the area where they resided. Here is a list of the family groups as we know them and the approximate areas they inhabited: The **Canarsies** lived in Brooklyn and part of Queens. The **Rockaways** resided next to the Canarsie tribe in what is now Queens and the southern part of present Hempstead Township. On the North Shore were the **Matinecocks**, who occupied the land from Flushing to near present-day Smithtown. South of them resided the **Merikoke** tribe from Rockville Centre westward to Oyster Bay Township. The **Massapequa** territory included the South Shore of Oyster Bay Township to present-day Islip Township. The **Seacatoags** lived just to the east of them along the South Shore as far as Patchogue. To the north was the land inhabited by the **Nissequogue**, a tribe who dwelt in the watershed of the river that bears their name. Just east of the Nissequogues were the **Seataukets**, whose land was between present-day Stony Brook and Wading River. South of them were the **Patchoags** whose territory stretched from Patchogue to the Shinnecock Canal (then known as Canoe Place). The entire North Fork was inhabited by the **Corchaug** tribe. The South Fork had the **Shinnecocks** living from Canoe Place eastward to present-day East Hampton, where they gave way to the **Montaukett** tribe, who had the rest of the fork and Gardiner's Island. Lastly were the **Manhassets**, who lived on what we now call Shelter Island. These boundaries were loosely defined and probably overlapped in places.

Most archaeological sites have shown that the Algonquins located their villages near watercourses or sheltered areas along the coast where food was abundant. During the winter, the tribe would move inland away from the exposed windy coast. Some sites like Glen Cove, Stony Brook, Mount Sinai and Shelter Island offered protection and food sources making them habitable most of the year. Each group had a leader called a sachem who led them in decision-making. The most powerful sachems were Wyandanch of the Manhasset Indians on Shelter Island, and his western counterpart, Tackapusha, who lived among the Massapequa of the South Shore near what is now the Nassau-Suffolk border.

The Algonquins grew maize (corn), beans and squash. Fish and shellfish were abundant, as were whales, schools of which often moved along the coast. Oysters were a mainstay of most tribes' diet. Deer and turkey were plentiful in the woodlands. Long Island Algonquins were producers of wampum, fine purple and white beads meticulously made from whelk or quahog shells found along the beaches.

Even before the arrival of the first Europeans the Algonquins were preyed upon by their stronger neighbors to the north. The fierce cannibalistic Pequots of eastern Connecticut and the Narragansetts raided Long Island frequently. In one raid the daughter of the great sachem Wyandanch was kidnapped by the Narragansetts and held for a few years until a Scottish settler, Lion Gardiner, interceded and negotiated her release. The tribes farther west felt the wrath of the powerful Iroquois Confederacy of upstate, who exacted a tribute of crops and wampum each year as a sort of "protection" fee. When the Canarsies withheld their share one year, they were annihilated by their brutal foes as a warning to other tribes. Nevertheless, these peoples found Long Island a good place to live and established a network of trails connecting the tribal groups.

The exploration of the New World by Europeans reached the region on September 4, 1609, when Henry Hudson sailed into New York Harbor and made contact with the Canarsie Indians. Hudson's first mate Robert Juett wrote, "We found a land full of great tall oaks, with grass and flowers, as pleasant as ever has been seen." And this was in present-day Brooklyn! Later logs report sailors approaching Long Island could smell the fragrance of trees at sea before seeing the shore.

The first European settlers in the region where the Dutch, who established a small trading post on the southern tip of Manhattan Island in 1624. The commerce-minded Dutch were in this for profit and in no hurry to settle people in a wilderness that was 3,000 miles from their homeland. Small homesteads existed on the nearby shores of New Jersey and Brooklyn, but the colony stayed about the same size until the mid-1630s, when Dutch authorities became alarmed by English expansion in adjacent New England. Unable to muster much enthusiasm for the settlement in Holland, the Dutch started looking for other disaffected groups from neighboring countries, enlisting unhappy English and even French Calvinists who were suffering from religious intolerance in their native land. They acquired land from the local tribes and started to spread slowly eastward. Small settlements were set up in Gravesend, Flushing, Jamaica, Maspeth, and Hempstead. Most of these settlers were Englishmen paying tribute to the Dutch crown. The Dutch were intolerant of the native tribes and trouble erupted. Between 1643 and 1645 about 1,200 Indians and settlers died in hostilities in the area from Staten Island to western Long Island.

Meanwhile on the east end of Long Island the English were spreading their influence southward from New England. In 1639 Lion Gardiner obtained the island that still bears his family's name and that same year the wealthy New Haven merchant Stephen Goodyear purchased Shelter Island. There was an attempt to settle in Matinecock (Oyster Bay) in 1639, but the English were driven out by the already-established Dutch. In 1641 groups seeking more freedom settled present-day Southold on the North Fork and Southampton on the South Fork. The new settlement of East Hampton was founded in 1648. Farther settlement occurred in Setauket (1655), Old Field (1659) and Stony Brook (1660); smaller settlements sprang up in Babylon, Wading River, Lloyds Neck, and Northport. The English were careful to make deals to purchase land from the Algonquins, avoiding the problems the Dutch encountered to the west.

By 1660 the Dutch controlled a disparate group of settlers scattered as far east as the present-day western border of Oyster Bay Township. The English were in scattered wilderness settlements as far west as Huntington Township. The land along the present Nassau-Suffolk border was a no-man's land where it seemed a clash was inevitable. However, in 1664 the English took full control of the region without firing a shot as Governor Peter Stuyvesant surrendered to a superior English military force. New Netherlands became New York, named after the Duke of York, the brother of King Charles II. Dutch place names in western Long Island and especially Brooklyn remain from the Dutch occupation.

The number of small farms and large estates of wealthy landowners increased rapidly between the English occupation of New York and the Revolutionary War. Coastal areas were cleared first and then colonists spread inland. Fencing

Boundary tree in Stony Hill Woods

property was time consuming and expensive, so property boundaries were often marked by ditches or the bending of saplings to the ground. These old signs can still be seen by hikers today as strange crooked old "boundary" trees that seem to grow suddenly horizontal and then straight up again. Often they are in unlikely places in the middle of a forest. Boundary ditches are also discernible despite being overgrown and worn down with time.

By the time of the American Revolution, Long Island contained many small towns filled with artisans and craftsmen who traded extensively with neighboring colonies. Small family farms surrounded these quaint hamlets, and mills were constructed along local waterways. By 1770 there were about 30,000 people living on Long Island.

When the Revolution began Long Island was an important military location and food supplier, and the British coveted it. Early in the conflict, in late August, 1776, the British drove George Washington and his inexperienced army off Long Island and into Westchester. Long Island remained under British rule until the end of the war. Most of those sympathetic to the cause of the Revolution fled across the sound to Connecticut, some leaving families behind. Others stayed but didn't let their true feelings be known. It was from this group that a famous spy ring formed. A network was formed using invisible ink, secret codes and aliases. Robert Townsend of Oyster Bay, Abraham Woodhull of Setauket and Benjamin Talmadge of Brookhaven were three of the more notable figures in this espionage ring, which gathered critical information for George Washington himself. The penalty if caught was death.

Although no other major battles were fought on Long Island during the conflict, several raids were successful in forcing the British occupiers to keep important resources in place to maintain their hold. On several occasions the patriots came over from Connecticut in relatively small whaleboats under cover of darkness, crossing the dangerous "Devil's Belt," as the Long Island Sound was nicknamed. Hiding their boats along the steep rocky coast, they traveled inland and attacked British forts before returning, sometimes days later. Among the more notable places attacked were forts at Lloyd's Neck, Fort Salonga, Sag Harbor and the Manor of St. George in Mastic.

When the war ended in 1783, many exiled patriots returned to farm, raise livestock and take up their trades. During the occupation, the British cut down much of the hardwood forests for fuel. Still, the returning population flourished and once again Long Island became a bucolic place blessed with plenty of food from land and sea. George Washington even commented on what a tranquil place the island was during his historic 1790 visit. In his own words it had "a sense of stillness and sequestration from the world."

As the nineteenth century progressed, much of the remaining oak and chestnut forest was logged and shipped westward for fuel and raw material for industry. Even the pitch pine, a low-energy softwood, was used to make charcoal. This left the land cleared of large stands of mature forests and more susceptible to fire. One infamous Pine Barrens fire reportedly swept out of control from Setauket to Southampton during the Civil War. Wealthy sportsmen formed large preserves and game clubs to take advantage of the abundant fishing and hunting the area afforded. The western sections of Long Island had some of the wealthiest estates in the country, including those of well-known families like Vanderbilt and Doubleday.

With the completion of the Long Island Rail Road line from Brooklyn to Greenport in 1844 people could travel the length of the island with relative ease. Where the railroad crossed the unpopulated center of the Island, stagecoaches were set up to take passengers to towns on the north and south shores. Other rail lines were eventually built along both these shores. The effect of the railroad cannot be understated. Suddenly farmers could get their produce readily to the markets in New York City. Artists flocked to the Hamptons to paint in that special light that permeates the region. Tourism became a major attraction to the region as city folk fled the sweltering summers for the cool breezes and sandy beaches only a couple of hours train ride away. Sleepy little hamlets such as Quogue and Westhampton Beach went from stagecoach stops to bustling seasonal towns taking in boarders. Other railroad lines were built from Port Jefferson to Wading River, and from

Manorville to Eastport and Sag Harbor village.

All of these old railbeds are walkable now in one form or another in at least part of their former length. Parts of the Port Jefferson-Wading River line remnants can be walked as they follow a power line along the North Shore north of Route 25A. A bike trail has been proposed for this old section. It is hoped that an extension of the Brookhaven Trail will some day cross this old railbed on current LIPA land in Shoreham near Defense Hill. The

Isaac Conklin gravesite

Manorville-Eastport abandoned railroad grade is currently part of the Wampmissick Trail behind the Pine Barrens Trail Information Center in Manorville. Another section is walkable just south of the exit ramp for nearby exit 70 on the Long Island Expressway. The Sag Harbor railroad grade is now part of the Long Pond Greenbelt Trail System south of Sag Harbor.

Besides the tourism boom prompted by the railroad, local economies also benefited. East End farmers could now ship their produce farther and faster. Long Island became one of the leading producers of potatoes in the country. Duck farms also sprung up, and Long Island duckling became a specialty of city restaurants.

During this time of growth and awareness of Long Island's natural beauty the poet Walt Whitman (1819-1892) was born on Long Island, and though his family moved to Brooklyn when he was four he returned to the island many times throughout his life to work, ramble about and find inspiration in the landscape he loved. During that same time a school of artists led by native Long Islander William Sidney Mount, of Setauket, chose scenes of rural Long Island life as subjects.

At the beginning of the twentieth century, Long Island was still farm country, not just on the East End but west in Nassau County as well, and would remain so for another fifty years. Still, there were important non-farming activities taking place. The flat open Hempstead Plains became a natural site for airfields, and many test flights were made there by the military and civilians in the pioneering years of aviation. Charles Lindbergh took off on his famous first solo trans-Atlantic flight from Mitchell Field on May 20, 1927.

Possibly the most famous Long Islander of all was Theodore Roosevelt. He had a large family and during his presidency set up the summer White House at Sagamore Hill in Oyster Bay Cove. The site is now open to visitors. An avid hiker, he led his children on many an outing in the surrounding countryside. His belief that fresh air and exercise was essential for a healthy mind and body was a forerunner of today's hiker philosophy. He was an avid birder who challenged his friend, naturalist John Burroughs, to a weekend-long contest to see who could identify more species. He won by one species! Roosevelt was also ahead of his time as one who knew the value of setting aside land to protect it from development and preserve it for generations to come.

Hunting lodge in Connetquot State Park

There are several old points of interest whose traces the hiker can still see, including the old World War I Camp Upton, which is now Brookhaven National Laboratory. The northern section of the original camp is now Brookhaven State Park, which is traversed by the Brookhaven Trail. The early transmitting towers owned by the RCA Corporation are in the large hikeable preserves in Rocky Point and Riverhead (David A. Sarnoff Pine Barrens Preserve). Many of the larger state and county parks were once estates or game preserves, including Connetquot, Caumsett, Southaven and Terrell county parks.

The Great Depression of the 1930s slowed growth on Long Island, but that all changed after World War II. In 1947 on the Hempstead Plain developer William Levitt built tightly packed low-cost housing marketed toward veterans returning from the war. The landscape of Long Island changed dramatically as farms in Nassau County and then western Suffolk County were sold to developers to become neighborhoods with strip malls. More than 4 million people now reside in the two counties.

Amazingly, there are still fine hiking opportunities left in these developed areas, and that fact was part of the impetus for this book. At the beginning of the twenty-first century, the Pine Barrens Protection Act is the last chance for Long Island to preserve its precious groundwater and save large tracts of land for use by those who enjoy the outdoors as Teddy Roosevelt did a century ago. There are many unspoiled places waiting for walkers who choose to stay on Long Island and discover these little surprises right on their doorstep.

Preservation of Open Space and Hiking Trails

Public opinion has slowly changed recently as the people of Long Island have continually voted to pay a little extra to purchase land for recreational use and farming. Groups like the **Long Island Greenbelt Trail Conference (LIGTC), The Open Space Council, The Peconic Land Trust, The Pine Barrens Society** and **The Nature Conservancy (TNC)** have urged the protection of existing public lands and the creation of a plan for the preservation of remaining open space. Their efforts have led to the passage of the Pine Barrens Protection Act, which will preserve a central core of land in eastern Suffolk County from development. This will be the third largest forest preserve in New York State behind the Adirondack and Catskill preserves. Long Island hiking differs from many places I have walked because often township, county, state, and federal lands can all be crossed within the same hike. This makes one appreciate how much cooperative effort has gone into the preservation of Long Island open space.

The next challenge is the proper management of these areas as many different groups look to use the land. The immediate pressing problem is the explosion of ATVs and motorbikes that destroy trails and woods roads by tearing up the topsoil thinned by the last glaciers, making permanent scars on the land. This problem is especially accelerated when the ground is soft in the spring. Organizations representing hikers who use these public lands agree that there is no room for these illegal and destructive vehicles anywhere on walking trails. Mountain bikes and horseback riding are also causing erosion and drainage problems in some places. These issues must be addressed so that a compromise can be reached to allow different user groups to have designated areas where they can enjoy their pastimes without spoiling the experience for others. Each group is going to have to maintain its own trails and police its own members to prevent renegades from breaking the rules. This can be accomplished with public recognition that what we have is an exhaustible and limited resource; once destroyed it won't regenerate itself in our lifetimes. The land is not a pie to be divvied up among these competing groups but a whole ecosystem on which users should have as little impact as possible while still enjoying the open space.

Climate, Weather and A Trip Through the Seasons

The hiker's year begins in mid-March when it is usually cold and frozen in the morning and somewhat thawed by midday, making for muddy going in low-lying places. A sure sign of springtime is the deafening sound of spring peepers, tiny tree frogs that gather at ponds and bogs chirping and whistling around nightfall. For the walker, fickle weather means it's best to dress in layers. Wind is often something to deal with, especially in the open areas like beaches. As March moves into April, the first green plants can be seen poking their heads out of the wet ground of freshwater marshes. The first true wildflower of spring, the trailing arbutus, can be found hiding in the leaf litter. Listen for the first nesting birds; bluebirds choose nesting boxes and pine warblers sing while setting up territories in the Pine Barrens. By mid-April the trees in western Long Island will show flowers and new leaves. This will take place two to three weeks later in the East End, especially in the oak-dominated Pine Barrens.

Shadbush in bloom

Spring ephemerals, wildflowers that bloom on the forest floor and then disappear, can be found in moist woods from April into May. The weather usually starts to modify during this month but there's still a chance for a cold morning. Colorful songbirds, such as scarlet tanagers, rose-breasted grosbeaks, and northern orioles, help make this possibly the most musical month of the year. Just after sunset you may hear the repetitious whip-poor-will from the dark forest floor in the pines

Nature peaks in June as beautiful orchids light up in the cranberry bogs, irises send up brilliant flags above the shallow waters of lakes and ponds, and birds sing actively to defend their territories; all things wild are in full swing. This means great hiking during the longest days of the year. In July during the heat of the summer take plenty of extra water on walks; it is best to get out early or late in the day when the sun is low in the sky. The woods are generally quiet this time of year since most birds are busy feeding and raising their young and the last thing they would like is to call attention to themselves. One exception is the rufous-sided towhee, whose characteristic "towee" call is heard everywhere in the pine-oak woods out east.

In August a visit to freshwater marshes will reveal many wildflowers. The warm weather also offers a chance to see snakes and turtles that inhabit our area, but these animals seem to be declining and are not so easily found nowadays.

In September the woods and fields are filled with varieties of asters and goldenrods, and the fall migration of songbirds begins. The cooler weather is enough to get most hikers back in the woods again . In October the leaves in the wetlands are especially colorful early in the month, but the Pine Barrens foliage usually won't peak until month's end or later. In November and December as the days become shorter and temperatures colder, many people end their hiking for the year, but winter can be a great time to be on the trail. The cold clear days and long shadows cast by the low sun make for fine outdoor photography. The nights are filled with the deep hooting of the Great Horned Owl, which actually starts setting up breeding territories in December.

Most snowfalls on Long Island occur in January and February. Tracks of all sizes and shapes in the snow reveal the movements of the woodland creatures,

Snowy Peconic River

Morning mist on Peasys Pond

and learning to read them is fun. The woods are not as quiet as one would assume at this time of the year. Many of our year-round resident birds join together in late fall to form what are known as "mixed flocks" of chickadees, titmice, nuthatches, brown creepers, and small woodpeckers. Sometimes birds from the north country can be seen and heard at this time of the year. Large flocks of tiny kinglets will quietly pass by, and other larger birds like crossbills or finches seem to appear out of nowhere for a few days and leave just as suddenly. The mysterious snowy owl can be viewed along some of the dunes near the beaches as well.

Just when it seems winter is hanging on too long, there is a warm spell as March arrives. Listen for the soft warble of the bluebird as it returns ahead of most birds. The local ponds and rivers are filled with many species of ducks migrating north. The cycle of seasons comes around once again, and new experiences await the hiker.

Star haircap moss and mushrooms in early fall

PART TWO

The Trails

View from the bluffs where the Nissequogue empties into Long Island Sound.

Nassau County and Western Suffolk County

Nassau-Suffolk Greenbelt Trail
Stillwell Woods Preserve
Welwyn Preserve
Muttontown Preserve
Wantagh Nature Trail
Other Small Parks and Preserves in Nassau County
Walt Whitman Trail
Caumsett State Park
Target Rock National Wildlife Refuge
Gardiner County Park
Edgewood Oak Brush Plains Preserve
Long Island Greenbelt Trail
Stump Pond Loop Trail
Connetquot River State Park Preserve
Fire Island National Seashore

Nassau-Suffolk Greenbelt Trail

Length: 19.6 miles. Blaze: white

USGS topographic maps:
Amityville, Huntington

Tucked in along the border of Nassau and Suffolk counties is a green belt of land spared from the bulldozer. Amid a sprawling suburban population the Long Island Greenbelt Trail Conference has developed a trail free from the sights and sounds of busy everyday life. The Nassau-Suffolk Trail is located mostly within the eastern boundary of Nassau County but drops across the border into Suffolk at its far northern end. Many people are not aware that this 20-mile-long trail exists, connecting the flat coastal plain and freshwater courses of the South Shore in Massapequa with the hilly moraine and scenic waters of Cold Spring Harbor on the North Shore. The description provided here begins at the south end. The trail has surprising diversity with many opportunities to observe Long Island's wildlife and native flora up close. As with so many places I have hiked on the Island, I found delightful surprises where least expected. The trail is not without its problems though, as multi-use pressures, development threats, debris, and trail maintenance issues have all been encountered. Perhaps the most serious threat to face the trail was mountain bikes, which became popular in the 1980s. The dirt parking area on the north side of Jericho Turnpike (Route 25) became a popular place for bikers to meet and take to the trail. They descended on the trail in mass and overwhelmed the hikers. Within two or three years erosion and widening of the trail was so bad in places that some suggested closing it altogether. Meetings between the two groups achieved a solution: the trail was split into parallel paths where bikers and hikers would be separated, each on their own trail. In sections particularly susceptible to damage, the trail was designated for hikers only. From a hiker's perspective, the resulting parallel trails are a necessary evil, and although it is unsightly in places there is still a trail to walk. Problems still exist, but at least something was done to slow down the degradation of the land by the bikes.

At almost 20 miles (not counting side trails) this is the third longest continuous hiking trail on Long Island. Connecting side trails link the system to other options for the walker. The Long Island Greenbelt Trail Conference schedules at least one hike each year that does the entire trail in one day, but, of course,

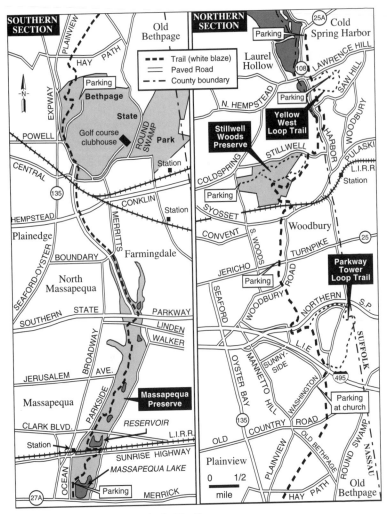

Nassau-Suffolk Greenbelt Trail

the trail can be walked in segments. As with most trails on the Island, you need a car at each end of your walk so you won't have to backtrack. At its southern end the trail begins on the north side of the corner of Merrick Road (Route 27A) and Ocean Avenue in Massapequa, 1.2 miles east of the south end of the Seaford-Oyster Bay Expressway (Route 135). Look for the white paint blazes on a tree on the west side of **Massapequa Lake**. This lake is the last fresh water lake in a drainage system that starts more than four miles north beyond Southern State Parkway. Just to the south of Merrick Road the water flows into a canal directly connected to the salty waters of South Oyster Bay about 1 mile south. This watershed is typical of the many southerly flowing streams that marked the South Shore prior to suburban development.

The **Massapequa Preserve** is owned by Nassau County and consists of 423 acres of freshwater wetlands (the largest wetlands in the county); it may not look like much on a map since it is strung out in a narrow band 4 miles long set between residential developments. Yet, the appearance to the hiker is amazingly natural since homes are out of sight most of the time. This is a prime birding spot for winter waterfowl and spring migrant songbirds. It was a wise move by the county to set aside this series of ponds linked by streams; they're like charms on a bracelet.

The trail initially stays close to the shore of the lake with a paved bicycle path on your left. This nearby path shares the route all the way to Bethpage State Park, nearly 8 miles away. Surprisingly many walkers choose the paved path, sharing it with bicyclists, rollerbladers and dog walkers, when a quiet and more scenic alternative is close at hand. At the north side of the lake (**0.34 mile**) the trail crosses a short boardwalk where a small stream flows vigorously (in spring) underfoot. The phragmites-lined stream is a pleasant sight and sound experience, especially if this is your first visit to the area. A few minutes farther north, I was surprised to find the trail in a pitch pine woods reminiscent of the Pine Barrens farther east. Wintergreen and various mosses could be found on the forest floor as well as signs of fire on the charred trunks of the pines. The trail straddles the wetlands on the right (east) and dry Pine Barrens flora on the left (west). On a winter walk I flushed a woodland hawk that darted away among the trees of the wetland. At **0.74 mile** the trail crosses over the bike path and traverses a fairly long narrow boardwalk through a wetland just south of Sunrise Highway.

At **0.94 mile** you will reach busy Sunrise Highway (State Route 27). This multi-lane road should be crossed only at the traffic light **0.1 mile** to the east. Follow the blazes to the light and cross to the north side. The trail turns left and heads north under the railroad tracks to the south shore of a reservoir at **1.25 miles**. The water spills over the dam here and it is a favorite area with fishermen. The trail heads west along the shore of the reservoir, picks up the bike path (**1.44 miles**) and heads north along the west side of the reservoir. A pair of binoculars will aid in identifying some of the many ducks and geese that spend the winter on Long Island. I saw an American coot for the first time near here. They are a purplish-gray bird that is sort of plump with a short neck, reminding one more of a chicken than a duck. Their bright white bill is also a distinguishing feature. Look for other ducks as well. Beyond the reservoir the trail crosses Clark Boulevard at **1.54 miles** and heads into wooded swamps on a narrow boardwalk at times. The entire wetland corridor is a great place to look for migrating warblers and other colorful songbirds in April and May. This short stretch north of Clark Boulevard can be especially rewarding, even in winter when chickadees, titmice and woodpeckers abound. Look out for wildflowers that bloom in spring in the wet woods. At **2.04 miles** the trail opens up at the shores of a **small pond** that is a great place to observe wintering ducks. Although many people use the bike path on the opposite side, colorful ducks such as green-winged teal, American wigeon, common pintail and gadwall all can be regularly observed here. The green-winged teal has a brilliant iridescent green head stripe that that seems to shine when the sun hits it just right. The teals continually whistle as they chase each other around in circles oblivious to the human activity so close by. When I researched a little more on these birds, I found that they breed in the far north and in the potholes of the Midwest prairies. They are certainly far from home when they choose to spend the winter on Long Island. The same goes for several other ducks you are likely to see here. So, despite all the talk of over-development, many birds still find Long Island a hospitable place to spend several months of the year.

The trail crosses a brook that feeds this pond on the north side and follows the north shore of the pond coming to a spillway where the water rushes over a dam. It then heads into a narrow path through woods where in spring you can observe much bird activity in the trees. The stream at the center of this watershed is out of sight on your left (east) but signs that wet ground is not far off can be seen in the form of small water-filled depressions in the woods. There are several sections where you will see many white-trunked gray birch trees, a sign that this is fairly recent second- growth woods. The silvery colored trunks of red maple can be seen in the wetter sections. At **2.54 miles** the trail comes out into a clearing at the south end of another fine pond for observing winter ducks. Cattails grow along the shore here providing food and cover for many animals. The water is clean and I observed a school of small fish along the shore. Pussy willows herald spring in March with their fuzzy heads readying to pop open. Tall tupelos rise above the western shore. You will be surprised by the wildlife activity and relative calm of the whole scene. The trail goes over a feeder brook on a narrow wooden bridge along the western side of the pond and heads northward into tall trees, crossing wetlands on a small bridge. Skunk cabbage can be seen poking up as early as the beginning of February. Ground pine covers the floor of the woods in places and inkberry as well as American holly can be spotted growing near each other. Both are members of the holly family but inkberry grows only in fresh-water areas. I found a little touch of Pine Barrens in the form of pitch pines and wintergreen growing close to large stands of red maples associated with the nearby watershed, a strange combination of plants indeed! This is Nassau County's last remnant of a Pine Barrens habitat that never was that common this far west anyway.

At about **3.35 miles** the trail meets a wide unpaved road and heads left (north). A short walk to the right will bring you to another **pond** in the series of ponds in the Massapequa Preserve. At **3.64 miles** the trail follows a wide dirt road along the back of residential property boundaries, finally coming to a crossing of Linden Street, dropping into a small wood lot and then over the Southern State Parkway at **3.84 miles**. Just over the parkway there lies another surprise. A **small pond** with people rollerblading and bicycling around it is filled with all sorts of colorful winter ducks. It is amazing how these wild ducks go about their business with so much human activity surrounding them.

Beyond this small pond, the trail follows the bike path a short distance while passing close to a residential neighborhood. The trail quickly leaves the bike path, crosses a short bridge over a creek that feeds into the pond and follows the wood lot between the bike path and nearby Bethpage Parkway. This section is almost totally hardwoods and the creek flows alongside the trail for a

Wintering Canada geese on Clark Pond in Massapequa Preserve

while. Just before reaching Boundary Avenue you may see a dark evergreen vine that is climbing all over just about everything it can cling to. This is English ivy, an escapee from a nearby backyard. At **4.94 miles** the trail rejoins the bike path, crosses the exit ramp at Boundary Avenue, goes under that road and leaves the bike path off to the left again. Watch for bicyclists here as the trail narrows under the overpass.

The area north of here is a necessary though forgettable section that links the trail through a heavily developed surrounding area. This is a disturbed narrow section; you'll see the trail is receiving heavy mountain bike use, making sections rutted, with squishy mudholes at times. One note of interest is the reappearance of pitch pines and Pine Barrens flora, and evidence of a past fire in the area adjacent to the trail. The trail again meets the bike trail and goes under Hempstead Turnpike (Route 24) at **5.84 miles**. After going under the overpass, the trail almost immediately leaves the bike path, again turning off to the left to follow the wooded corridor. Here notice the straight trunks and deeply furrowed bark of the black locust trees bordering this section of trail. A more southern tree planted for hedgerows, it has thrived on Long Island, especially on the North Shore, where it is fairly common. In late spring they have showy drooping clusters of fragrant creamy-white flowers. They grow long, dark hard-cased pods that fall off in autumn and open up in winter. The trail will now cross the bike path and run along undeveloped LIRR land. A short distance farther on you will see the railroad tracks and pass under them. A few minutes past this point, the trail crosses Central Avenue in Bethpage at **6.44 miles** and then goes up a short hill to the right leading into the woods. This slight elevation gain is the southerly fringe of the Ronkonkoma Moraine and is the first noticeable rise in the trail as you leave the flat coastal plain behind you. There is some sheep laurel growing among the oak-dominated woods here, which is the border of **Bethpage State Park**. The section of trail from Bethpage State Park to Cold Spring harbor State Park is now called **Trail View State Park**. At **6.64 miles** the trail drops down to the bike path, crosses a park road just east of a traffic circle and leaves the bike path to the right on the far side of the road. A few years ago the New York State Department of Transportation leveled a hazardous curve and hill that came down to the traffic circle here. The trail snakes through rolling terrain with a golf course to the east (right). Stay with the white painted blazes here as white triangular plastic blazes appear in sections. I believe these were put up by mountain bikers. At **7.24 miles** the trail crosses a park entrance off Powell Avenue. The Seaford-Oyster Bay Expressway (Route 135) is also nearby to the west. Bethpage State Park has five golf courses that take up a bulk of the park property, excellent places to cross country ski when snow conditions permit.

After following the bike path in Bethpage State Park for **0.3 mile**, the trail branches off to the right near power lines at **7.54 miles** and again enters the woods. This is a section I'm very familiar with, having grown up near here and run these trails many times. These woods contained many pink lady's slippers, a woodland orchid that added color to the area in late May and early June. I say "contained" because bike damage here is pretty serious and I'm not sure how many orchids still exist. Bike trails crisscross the greenbelt at several points, some marked and some unmarked. The poor management of this area should serve as an example of what can happen when trails are put in without a plan for maintenance or enforcement of rules. This section of woods is also cut up and segmented by horse trails which have been in existence for a long time. More recently mountain bikes have created new trails wherever old overgrown paths once existed, destroying the forest character that used to be here.

The greenbelt will meet a wide old bridle path and follow it northward to an overgrown clearing where small trees and shrubs are reclaiming what was once open field. Look for blazes on a railroad tie to guide you through this section. This corridor is the extension of Bethpage Parkway that was never completed. The few hundred feet wide strip is now overgrown with staghorn sumac, multiflora rose and the like and serves as a good example of plant succession. It is used by walkers, runners and bikers and is a vital link between the north and south sections of the trail. Haypath Road is reached at **8.74 miles** as the trail continues north through a sort of "open sky" section. This portion can be quite hot to walk in during daytime hours in summer since little shade is afforded. At **9.54 miles** the trail crosses Old Bethpage Road. Shortly thereafter it skirts some of the last remaining agricultural lands in Nassau County just before reaching Old Country Road at **10.24 miles**.

For the next **0.6 mile** the trail continues through overgrown fields past an industrial park on the right (east) reaching Washington Avenue at **10.84 miles**. The trail originally went straight across and under the Long Island Expressway (LIE) but construction of a service road has obliterated that route. The trail now turns right onto Washington Avenue, goes under the LIE (**11.1 miles**) and makes a left, where it heads into the woods again. Also note that the **blue on white blazes** of the **Parkway Tower Loop Trail** merge with the Nassau-Suffolk Greenbelt along this short stretch of road walking, then angle off to the right. The trail now climbs through the glacial moraine. A tall eastern hemlock or two is evident shortly before the trail turns away from the expressway, climbing among scattered thick stands of mountain laurel. There are also some small American chestnut saplings left over from a blight that nearly wiped this tree out early in the twentieth century. This tree was apparently quite common in this section of moraine and can be found growing for the next **3 miles** of trail. Unfortunately, the trail is suffering some erosion and widening due to mountain bike use.

At **12 miles**, the trail makes a junction with the other end of the Parkway Loop Trail. Beyond this it climbs uphill, where wooden steps or water bars have been installed to slow erosion, eventually crossing an exit ramp of the Northern State Parkway before reaching Sunnyside Boulevard where it crosses the parkway at **12.5 miles**. On clear days there is a view here of the Empire State Building and the New York City skyline on the horizon some 35 miles to the west (left). Unfortunately the overpass has been fenced in and the barrier raised, making it difficult to see the skyline unless you go right up against the fence and peer through it.

On the north side of the overpass the trail makes a right and dives back into the woods. Shortly thereafter, the mountain bikers are sent their own way, separated from the hiking trail to prevent erosion in the hilly areas beyond. Water bars and drainage ditches have been installed in some locations to stem the erosion damage that was caused by the bikes. Still, this is an enjoyable section of winding hilly moraine reaching above 300 feet in elevation at its highest point. Once again you will see American chestnuts along with some pretty stands of mountain laurel which bloom in June right along the trail. In late May you will see several wildflowers such as Canada mayflower, also known as false lily of the valley (it carpets the ground at points), Solomon's seal, stargrass, pink lady's slipper (also known as moccasin-flower), and a surprise find, shinleaf, a species of pyrola, a straight-stalked white flowering plant in the wintergreen family that is more associated with the cool woods of the Appalachians. Wood thrushes sing their flute-like song here. Red-bellied woodpeckers, a large colorful southern species, have been spotted in these woods as well. The trail will now descend the moraine and pass by some old fields. Just before reaching Woodbury Road you may notice the remains of an old stone wall, evidence of the former use of this land as pasture. Just beyond this, daffodils bloom in April surrounded by the small low lavender blooms of periwinkle. At **13.6 miles** Woodbury Road is reached and crossed. Walt Whitman taught in a school just up the road to the north (right).

On the west side of Woodbury Road the trail enters old fields in an advanced state of succession. The bike trail is separated from the hiking trail here. There is a section of wooden walkway to keep hikers' feet dry in wet weather. Russian olive, multiflora rose and poison ivy close in on the trail at points. I have seen some large garden-variety lupines growing alongside the trail in some of the more open areas just before reaching Route 25 (Jericho Turnpike.) at **13.9 miles**. Caution is urged in crossing here since this road is a major local route. A grocery store just to the west of the trail is a good place to get refreshment if you are on a long trek. An informational kiosk has been set up on the north side of the road and you are more likely to see mountain bikers than hikers here. You will also notice the hiking and biking trails are separated here once again (bikers to the left). The trail now passes through second-growth woods with occasional clearings. The first section is covered by wood chips, probably to cover prior damage by mountain bikes. It was in one of the second-growth clearings near here that I had to step over a brown mottled eastern milk snake during a late May hike. The snake was so long that when it crossed the trail its head disappeared before the tail could be seen on the three-foot-wide trail! No need to fear though; they're not aggressive snakes and are beneficial because they feed almost exclusively on mice, helping to keep that population in check. The trail rises up a short steep section where some huge old oaks provide shade. Once on higher ground, a view through the trees towards the northeast shows ridges of the Harbor Hill Moraine in the distance. The trail drops down to Syosset-Woodbury Road at **14.8 miles** and heads across the road and back into the woods just to the east (right). It will start a climb uphill, down and up again, sometimes coming very close to the parallel bike path. The trail reaches heights overlooking the railroad tracks of the Port Jefferson branch of the LIRR. Serious bike damage is evident here on the steep slopes. At **15.2 miles** the trail drops down to small, private Whitney Drive, makes a left and goes under the tracks, emerging on the other side to continue (left) back uphill north of the tracks. Look for spring wild-flowers such as solomon's seal and rattlesnake plantain, an orchid whose mot-tled leaves resemble a snake's skin, in the woods north of the tracks.

When the trail levels off it passes some side trails (including the mountain bike trail) before reaching the open fields of Stillwell Woods Preserve at **15.5 miles**. Here the trail follows a wide open unpaved road. The open grassy field on the left (west) is used for horse shows. On the right, the fields are more overgrown and in an advanced stage of succession. A shuttle car can be left in a parking area near the baseball fields to the west (left) beyond the field, with access from South Woods Road. The trail makes a right at **15.8 miles** and then a left into the woods at **16 miles**. Look for blazes on railroad ties set into the ground in these open areas.

The **Stillwell Woods Preserve** is a hilly wooded area that looks like Harriman State Park in places (minus the big rocks). Unfortunately, the area has been beset by mountain bike use, which has caused erosion problems on

Footbridge over a stream on the Nassau-Suffolk Greenbelt Trail.

the steeper sections. The trail winds through these hills along the eastern side of the property and occasional views through the trees (particularly in winter) give perspective to the hiker. Birds abound, especially during spring migration, when colorful warblers are moving through. Trailing arbutus thrives along the trail on well-drained slopes, and mountain laurel is common in the understory of this hilly terrain reaching above 200 feet in elevation. You will see the **yellow blazes** of the **Stillwell Woods Loop Trail** enter the trail and join it for a section. The yellow blazes continue to the left while the Greenbelt passes over a low wet area before reaching quiet and somewhat isolated Stillwell Lane at **16.75 miles**. Across the road the trail follows a course above part of Stillwell Lane that is level and seems like an old railroad grade, making a left to leave this roadbed at **17.2 miles**. It passes through a narrow ravine with a drop-off to wetlands on the right and a steep hillside on the left. The trees tower overhead while thick stands of mountain laurel close in on the trail at points. The trail seems remote here, and it is easy to imagine what travel was like on the back trails of Long Island a hundred years ago. In a few minutes you will come to the wetlands that eventually flow into Cold Spring Harbor. At **17.3 miles** the trail goes over a small stream and swampy section where there is a bench to sit on and muse about nature. Dragonflies buzz the wetlands in summer as they unceasingly defend their territories. Jewelweed and wild mints color the scene as well. In early springtime the subtle yellow of spicebush blooms line the stream borders. Just beyond the wetland the trail reaches Route 108, makes a left and follows alongside it a short distance before crossing at **17.4 miles** and entering Suffolk County in the process.

The trail now moves along the slopes of the hills of the Harbor Hill Moraine winding up and down through dense mountain laurel stands. Although Route 108 is down to your left, it is generally out of sight and cars are rarely heard. You may catch a glimpse of the blue waters of one of the ponds down to your left (west). This area also harbors a large population of the elusive red fox whose dens are located in the secluded sections of the hillside. At **18.0 miles** you will see the **yellow-blazed West Loop Trail** of The Nature Conservancy come in and join the trail for about **0.2 mile**, leaving it at **18.2 miles** going off to the right through a steep ravine. This side trail is part of a loop starting near the Uplands Farm Sanctuary that houses the Long Island Chapter Headquarters of The Nature Conservancy. The Nassau-Suffolk Greenbelt trail continues northward, passing around a horseshoe-shaped hollow filled with ferns and reaching Lawrence Hill Road at **18.6 miles**.

The trail goes steeply up wooden steps on the north side of Lawrence Hill Road, reaching the top of the ridge and following it with occasional views westward towards the waters of Cold Spring Harbor. Although interrupted by homes built in recent years, the views of the harbor are really impressive when the trees are leafless. If the day is clear, the blue waters contrast nicely with the surrounding browns and grays of winter. The trail drops and climbs a few more times, following switchbacks on the steeper grades. At one point it winds away from the edge of the ridge where, in late May, you may see some of the wooded glades brightly lit by the pinks, whites and violets of wild phlox. This land was added to the state holdings as **Cold Spring Harbor State Park** in 1999. The trail eventually reaches its terminus by descending steeply off the heights of the moraine and entering a parking lot with an information kiosk on Route 25A in Cold Spring Harbor at **19.6 miles** from its start in Massapequa. The waters of Cold Spring Harbor are directly across the street. The quaint shops of Cold Spring Harbor village are just to the east (right) on Route 25A and make a nice place to refresh yourself after your hike or to stroll and shop.

Access

Car

To reach the northern trailhead, leave the LIE at exit 44, turning north onto State Route 135, the Seaford-Oyster Bay Expressway, continuing until it ends. Turn east on State Route 25 for a little over a mile, then make a left onto Woodbury Road. In about a mile and a half make a left onto State Route 108.

Continue on to merge with State Route 25A and 0.7 mile later find the trail-head in an open parking lot on the right. The southern trailhead begins on Merrick Road (State Route 27A) in Massapequa at the junction of Ocean Ave. about 1.6 miles east of the Seaford-Oyster Bay Expressway (State Route 135). This 20 mile trail passing through some heavily populated areas can easily be hiked in short sections using two cars. The trail crosses no less than 17 roads, and all have nearby available parking except for State Route 108 and Stillwell Lane in the northern portion. For example, parking for several cars can be found in the Bethpage State Park parking lot and on State Route 25 in Woodbury where the trail crosses the road just west of Woodbury Road.

Train

The south end of the trail is accessible from the Long Island Railroad stations on Sunrise Highway (Route 27) at Massapequa to the west and Massapequa Park to the east of the trail. At the north end the Cold Spring Harbor Station is less than a mile from where the trail crosses Route 108. A Nassau and Suffolk County Hagstrom type of map should be sought to plan this type of trail access. In between, the trail may be accessed from the Bethpage train station: walk north up Broadway, turn right on Powell Avenue to cross the Seaford-Oyster Bay Expressway (Route 135) and find the entrance to Bethpage State Park on the left, where the trail crosses on the paved bike path just inside the entrance.

Buses

N78/79, N80, N81, N94

Stillwell Woods Preserve

Length: 3 miles. Blaze: yellow

USGS topographic map: Huntington

This preserve can be accessed from South Woods Road in Syosset. Owned by Nassau County, the park offers multi-uses including horseback riding, athletic fields, model-airplane flying, and mountain biking. The preserve has mixed woodlands and hills reaching well above 200 feet high. The primary interest to the hiker is the **yellow-blazed Loop Trail** that starts on the east side of the soccer fields and heads eastward into the woods. From the north end of the parking lot off South Woods Road opposite Syosset High School, head northeast through the soccer fields and between the two baseball fields onto an old dirt road that traverses overgrown fields. Cottontail rabbits are likely to be seen scurrying into the cover of the thickets, especially early or late in the day. You will soon pick up yellow paint blazes on trees and leave the second-growth fields of white pines shooting up above the usual shrubs, and enter hardwoods. From here the trail makes its way east and north with turn blazes relatively easy to follow. The area is beset by heavy mountain bike and illegal ATV use that is tearing up the steeper areas. White triangular markers for bikes and wide horse trails cross and merge for short distances as the trail finds higher ground.

The hills of Stillwell Preserve have impressive views north towards the tall ridges of the Harbor Hill Moraine in Cold Spring Harbor. Stillwell Road is the northern boundary of the preserve. Hikers can be rewarded with the views in winter if they explore a little off-trail on their own. The Nassau-Suffolk Greenbelt Trail merges with the loop trail on the west side of the property, and at this point the trail starts to turn southward and eventually westward back

The foamy flower head of False Solomon's Seal in Stillwell Woods in spring

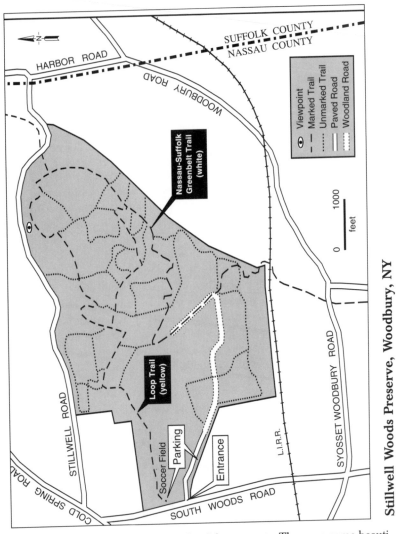

Stillwell Woods Preserve, Woodbury, NY

toward the old fields on the west side of the property. There are some beautiful specimens of trailing arbutus growing alongside the slopes of the old woods roads. They vary in color from white to deep pink and exude an exquisite earthy yet sweet fragrance when in bloom in mid- to late April. There are also fine stands of mountain laurel throughout these hills; it is the dominant plant in most of the area. To get an idea what this North Shore area was like before the heavy development took place, stand on one of the trailless hills and gaze north at the wooded ridges on a sunny late winter day. A few hours are all that is needed to hike this loop, which is **about 3 miles** long with a few side-trips for exploration. Contact Nassau County Parks Department to get a crude map of the preserve and trails.

Access

Car

Trails begin from the parking area on the east side of South Wood Road across from Syosset High School. To get there, leave the LIE at exit 44, turning north on Route 135, the Seaford-Oyster Bay Expressway. Continue to the end, then turn east and go about 0.75 mile on Route 25 (Jericho Turnpike) to East Woods Road. Make a left and the parking lot is on the right just past the high school.

Welwyn Preserve

Length: 1 1/2 hours. Blaze: unmarked

USGS topographic map: Mamaroneck

Located in Glen Cove on the famous "Gold Coast" of the North Shore, this lovely piece of land at one time was the Pratt estate. It is now owned and run by the Nassau County Department of Recreation and Parks and offers a fine example of the tall moist hardwood forests that covered the northwestern corner of Long Island when the first European settlers arrived in the 1600s.

A good place to start is a trail that heads back southward. From the parking lot follow the driveway back towards the entrance and look for the trail on the left just past the staff building. The impressive trees along the walk are protected and have been allowed to mature. Of particular interest are the tulip trees, also known as yellow poplars. More common in the southeast and Mid-Atlantic, they grow in moist, well-drained soils and can reach heights of 120 feet. The yellow poplar is one of the tallest and most beautiful trees in the eastern forests and the largest naturally occurring tree on Long Island. It is noted for its straight trunk and large yellowish flowers, which resemble tulips. Large tree trunks were hollowed out by local Indian tribes for use as dugout canoes, a skill picked up by the earliest settlers in colonial times. The giant trees are all but gone, but it is not hard to imagine what the primeval forests of Long Island must have looked like while walking amongst these stately survivors. Tulip trees have extended their range northward since the recession of the last ice age. In this western section of Long Island they mix with some more northerly species such as yellow birch and eastern hemlock, the former being especially rare on Long Island.

The balance of the walk goes through tall oak woodlands as the soil becomes better drained. Look for delicate spring wildflowers that grow along the trail in April and May. Eventually, the trail comes out to the beach with views across Long Island sound. The sand is smooth here because the former owners had the rocky beach scoured of rocks and replaced with fine sand some years ago. Note the osprey platform along this section. This is probably as far west as ospreys can nest on Long Island. As the trail winds around the tip of a point of land, it turns southerly and takes you back to the parking lot you started from. And hour and a half should be enough time to for you to enjoy the loop.

Access

Car

Take LIE exit 39 north (Glen Cove Road) a little over 6 miles to the end of the road in the village of Glen Cove. Make a right onto Brewster Street and in about 0.5 mile a left onto Dosoris Lane. Proceed about 0.7 mile and make a left onto New Woods Road. At the end of this road, make a right on to Crescent Beach Road and the preserve entrance is the first right.

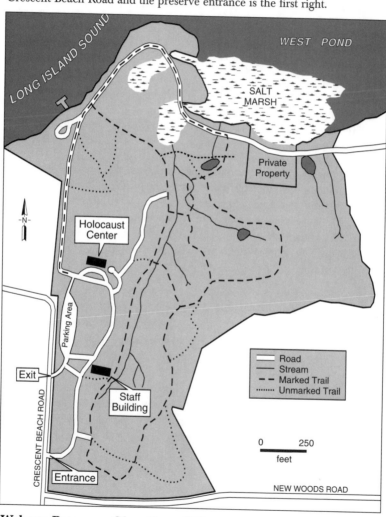

Welwyn Preserve, Glen Cove, NY

Muttontown Preserve

Length: self-guiding nature trail less than
2 miles

USGS topographic map: Hicksville

This Nassau County preserve comprises 500 acres of fields, woodlands and ponds. Ornamental non-native plant species remain from the days when this was an estate. The preserve is a compilation of three estates, the H.I. Hudson estate (known as the King Zog estate), the Landsdell-Christie estate and the Alexandra Moore McKay estate. The county took possession of the tract in 1968.

The terrain is relatively flat, with some rolling sections. Walkers can see the remains of the estate, a wall here, a vine-covered iron gate there; it all gives a sense of the wealth this area once knew. Kettle ponds dot the center of the property; there is activity here most of the year as birds, especially ducks and waders, seek refuge on their migrations.

Peepers announce the arrival of spring from these wet ponds every April. Indigo buntings, deep blue birds that nest in the brushy field edges and over-grown pastures, are known to breed here. They are uncommon on Long Island but regularly show up at Muttontown Preserve. A southern tree, the persimmon, known for its orange fruit, thrives in the preserve as well. The fruit is favored by people down South where it is treasured for its sweet flavor after the first frost. What the people don't eat is enjoyed by raccoons, possums and skunks.

The best way to enjoy this preserve is to pick up a map at the Muttontown Lane entrance and start from the north end near the nature center. There are several differently blazed trails starting either right or left which will take you south through woods and the fields that were farmed into the early 1960s. This variety of habitats brings a wealth of bird life to the area. The preserve is also used extensively by horseback riders who gain access from the Route 106 parking lot. The fall colors along the edges of the wide open fields are par-ticularly radiant in mid to late October and many migrating birds can also be seen at that time of year. The transitional second growth hardwoods are very colorful, and on sections of trail in the northwest portion of the preserve (along trail number 1) towering evergreens make the walk all the more diverse. The preserve is open year round but closes before dark; cross coun-try skiing is possible during winter. For more information or to acquire a map in advance, call the Nassau County Department of Recreation and Parks.

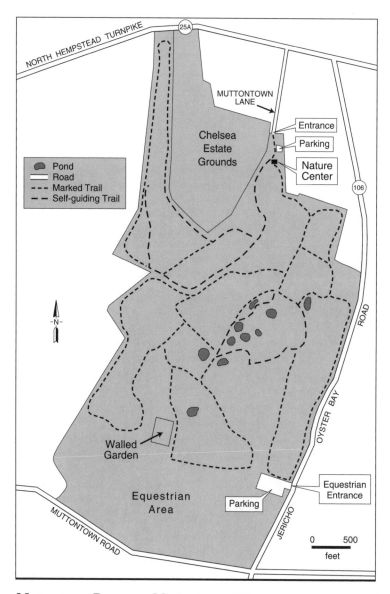

Muttontown Preserve, Muttontown, NY

Access

Car

To get to the main entrance and preserve building take LIE exit 41 north following the fork to the right to Route 106. Go north on Route 106 for about 3.75 miles and make a left onto Route 25A. Make another left in 0.1 mile onto Muttontown Lane. The entrance is straight ahead. Another parking area is located on the west side of Route 106 about 0.75 mile south of Route 25.

Pond along trail in Muttontown Preserve

The Wantagh Nature Trail

Length: 3.8 miles   Blaze: white

USGS topographic map: Freeport

On a topographic map Long Island's south shore is an outwash plain where all the fine glacial sediments ran off towards the ocean. Through this flatland many streams flowed southward off the hilly moraine. Indeed, Walt Whitman referred to Long Island as the isle of sweet brooks, and remnants of those brooks can still be found today. The Wantagh Nature Trail follows one of these watercourses along the west side of the corridor of the Wantagh State Parkway. The trail links the Nassau County Mill Pond Park with the Town of Hempstead's Twin Lakes Preserve making a loop that can be easily be completed in 1 1/2 hours. Along this trail walkers may stretch their legs in the shade of red maples and tupelos close to the ponds that are the center of these preserves. In this hike description distances are estimated since the trail has not yet been measured, and walking time at an easy pace is given for reference.

Members of the Long Island Greenbelt Trail Conference created this trail through a forgotten piece of open space tucked between suburban communities. Although never far from the sound of roadway traffic, the trail offers a chance to see the ponds and the changes of the seasons that bring new surprises throughout the year. The observant walker can discover beautiful native flowers along the shores of these wetlands and observe colorful songbirds, especially during spring and fall migrations.

Starting out from the gazebo on the south shore of **Mill Pond**, look for white blazes on a telephone pole with a sign designating the Wantagh Nature Trail. The path heads west with the pond on your right through Nassau County's **Mill Pond Park**. Mill pond is a common name in the northeast where dammed waterways powered mills for grinding grain into flour. Today on Mill Pond's south shore you can see a spillway through which water flowed to turn a mill wheel. The paved path turns north along the western shore of the pond where plants associated with wetlands dominate the scene. Sweet pepperbush and arrowwood are common along the path while aquatic plants such as pickerelweed grow out of the water.

My initial walk here was in late September when most wildflowers had peaked out, but I still noted the purple topped Joe-Pye weed and the orange jewelweed along the shore. A small bridge crosses over a clear, clean feeder

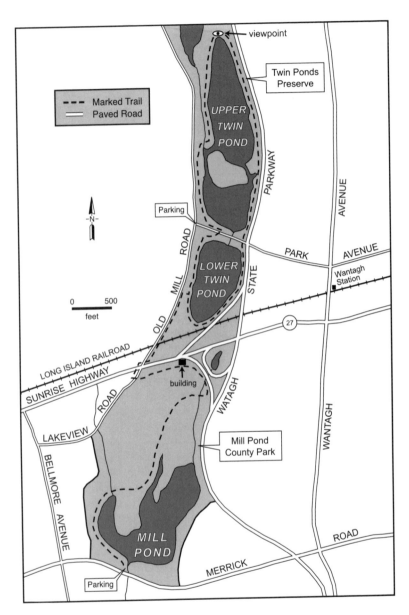

creek. This stretch will probably attract migrating warblers in the springtime. Known as the butterflies of the bird world because of their bold colors and patterns, warblers are always on the move as they flit from tree to tree. A small brook runs under the trail a little further on giving the walker a glimpse of what natural Long Island looked like before the development boom of the twentieth century.

After about 10 minutes walk (**0.3 mile**) on the path you will spot turn blazes signaling a left turn into the woods. This is shortly before it reaches the Wantagh Parkway, which can be heard and seen straight ahead. The damp woodland is dominated by tall red maples and various oak species. In a short distance a brick building spray painted with graffiti looms in front of you (**0.5 mile**). Bear left and follow the trail through a disturbed area to Lakeview Road. Crossing Lakeview, you will then have to cross State Route 27, known in these parts as Sunrise Highway. There is a button you can push to stop traffic on this busy six-lane road. I cannot stress enough how cautious one must be here, since cars travel very fast on this heavily used road. Crossing to the north side of the highway, you will then immediately turn east (right) across Old Mill Road (**0.6 mile**). Walk left (north) about a quarter of a mile up Old Mill Road to a small entrance opposite Lowell Lane through a fence on your right into the Town of Hempstead's **Twin Lakes Preserve** at about **0.85 mile**.

Once inside the preserve you will see **Lower Twin Lake** in front of you. Although it was September, looking closely I could see that wild irises in late spring and swamp rose-mallow in late summer would grace the shoreline with colorful blooms. The trail makes a left here and continues northward with the lake visible through the trees on your right. I noted some large old black cherry and sycamore trees along this stretch. White snakeroot was in bloom in the thickets here as well. In a few minutes the trail crosses Park Avenue (**1.2 miles**) and passes into the section of the preserve that contains the upper lake (about 30 minutes walking time). There were several fishermen's cars parked on this street, and I saw many small sunfish in the waters along the shore, attesting to the vitality of the lake. The trail continues north along a narrow corridor with Old Mill Road on your left and the water on your right. After reaching a small building at about 40 minutes time, the trail will make a right to cross over a bridge and then turn left to continue north again at about **1.75 miles**.

At about **2.0 miles** (45 minutes walking time) the trail reaches the northern shores of **Upper Twin Lake** with a nice view of the entire pond. This is the northern limit of the trail, and from here on you are heading back to the start. You will likely see fishermen along these shores in season since this pond is stocked with trout. At 17 feet deep the water can support a good population of fish, including largemouth bass and various species of sunfish. From here you will continue southward on the east shore of the lake with Wantagh State

Parkway on your left. Eventually the trail crosses Park Avenue again after an hour of walking (**2.5 miles**) and continues along the shores of the lower lake. One surprise that the observant hiker finds in early fall is the pink flowered gerardia, a member of the snapdragon family that resembles foxglove. This is a remnant of the once prolific native wildflowers that have fallen on hard times since more aggressive alien species have literally taken over roadsides and clearings. At about **2.75 miles** (1 hour 10 minutes) you reach the southern end of the lake and cross around a spillway to head west a short distance. A blaze on a huge old Sycamore directs you to head right (north) for a short distance to reach the place where you first came in through the fence, completing the loop around both lakes at about **2.9 miles**.

Leaving the preserve at a little over an hour's time you make a left and head back down Old Mill Road to Sunrise Highway. Retrace your steps along the same route you came up and you should reach the start point in about 1 hour 30 minutes walking time, about **3.8 miles** .

Access

Car:

The trailhead is located on the north side of Merrick Road about .3 mile west of the Wantagh State Parkway. Parking is available along Merrick Road. Start at the gazebo in the Mill Pond Preserve seen from the road.

Train:

The Wantagh train station is located about 0.25 mile west of the trail crossing on Sunrise Highway (Rte 27).

North Twin Lake on the Wantagh Nature Trail

Other Small Parks and Preserves in Nassau County

There are a number of smaller parks in Nassau County that make great places to get started walking, especially with young children. The **Tiffany Creek Preserve** is located in Oyster Bay Cove with access from Sandy Hill Road. Parts of three old estates make up this 197-acre parcel acquired by Nassau County in 1992 with the help of The Nature Conservancy. Only 45 acres on the west side of Sandy Hill Road has a marked trail. The larger parcel on the east side of the road will be blazed in the future. The marked trail takes you through a large stand of mountain laurel and mature oak dominated woodlands, which is common to this North Shore area. Other hiker friendly county-owned preserves include **Garvies Point** in Glen Cove, **Sands Point** in Sands Point and **Tackapusha Preserve** in Seaford. The latter contains the westernmost stand of eastern white cedar trees on Long Island. Another interesting preserve that allows walks is the **Shu Swamp Nature Sanctuary** located in Mill Neck on the heavily wooded North Shore. This preserve has a pristine brook running through it with towering tulip trees overhead. The Nature Conservancy's **Hope Goddard Iselin Preserve** in Upper Brookville has a mixture of fields and woods to walk through. These short walks can be enjoyed with small children and serve as good representatives of the various habitats remaining in the county. For information, contact the Nassau County Department of Parks or The Nature Conservancy located in the index on back of the book.

Walt Whitman Trail

Length: 3.7 miles. Blaze: blue, then white

USGS topographic map: Huntington

The Walt Whitman Trails are located in West
Hills County Park, just inside the border of Suffolk County amid suburban
sprawl. This hilly wooded section of the Ronkonkoma Moraine contains the
highest point on Long Island: Jaynes Hill, elevation 401 feet above sea level.
Traveling on the Northern State Parkway just west of Route 110 you pass
through the southern section of this publicly owned land. In winter when the
leaves are down its hills allow fine views and its small hollows are filled with
evergreen mountain laurel and eastern hemlock trees.

Hikers, horseback riders, birders and even mountain bikers all use the parklands. The resultant conflicts are not as bad as one might imagine and fine
hiking opportunities exist on the trail system put in and maintained by the
Long Island Greenbelt Trail Conference (LIGTC). The Walt Whitman Trail is
actually a system of trails running on the north and south sides of the
Northern State Parkway. There are loop trails in both sections that are connected to several access points by side trails. The approximately 8 miles of
trails within the park are connected to the Blue Dot Trail that roughly follows
the course of the parkway, linking them with the 20-mile Nassau-Suffolk Trail.
Through this connection you can walk from the south or north shores of Long
Island into the West Hills with hardly any road walking. While you're in the
area, you may want to visit the Walt Whitman birthplace located at the base
of West Hills Road on Old Walt Whitman Road. Although he only spent the
early years of his life in the house, he walked these hills on return trips later
in life. Some of those same paths are blazed for modern day walkers.

Since the West Hills are so associated with the poet, it is fitting that a hiking
trail starts at his birthplace and climbs West Hills Road to Reservoir Road
before joining the trail system in the park. Each year around the time of
Whitman's birthday on May 31, the LIGTC has a hike starting from the historic site after a reading of some of his poetry at the house.

All the main trails in the area have been blazed with a red dot, bar or cross
on a white background. To make things easier for trail maintainers and to prevent confusion to hikers, a new solid color trail blaze system is planned, and
is to be completed just about the time this book is published. If you have the
LIGTC maps note that the Red Dot Trail will be plain white-blazed, the Red

Cross Trail will be blue-blazed, and for the trails south of the parkway the former red cross trail will be blazed yellow and the former white trail will be blazed blue. In addition, there is serious talk of closing down the yellow-blazed White Birch Trail and the short white-blazed trail out to Mt. Misery Road. Check with the LIGTC before venturing out. All the walk descriptions herein assume the new blaze system has been completed.

The **white-blazed Main Trail** (formerly Red Dot Trail) that begins at the Walt Whitman birthplace is one place to start. However, this entails **0.8 mile**

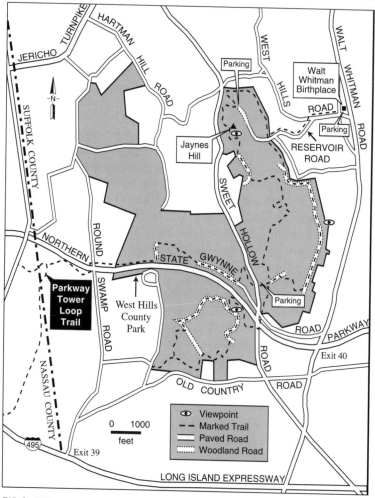

Walt Whitman Trail, West Hills, NY

of road walking through a quiet hilly neighborhood. For those who want to keep their walk on this trail in the woods, the end of Reservoir Road inside the park is the place to park, as it provides easy access to Jaynes Hill. At this point the two main walks in the area (which can be linked into one) start from more quiet surroundings.

The best place to start is from the parking area near the stables and picnic area off the east side of Sweet Hollow Road in West Hills Park. This is a short distance north of where Northern State Parkway goes over Sweet Hollow Road. From the parking area walk east across the clearing and you will see the **White Trail** (formerly Red Dot Trail) blazes on trees crossing north-south in front of you. Pass by these and pick up the **Blue Trail** (formerly Red Cross Trail) straight ahead and continue in a northeasterly direction. It will enter a wide bridle path and shortly break off to the right at **0.1 mile** to climb uphill through oak-dominated woods to meet another well-traveled woods road that is used by horses at **0.3 mile**. The sandier sections of trail can get chewed up in wet warm weather but are wide enough to allow you to walk easily under most circumstances. You are now on top of a ridge where the trail makes a left (north) and follows the woods road for a while. There are **views eastward** allowing you to look down at a large shopping center across busy Route 110. Beyond is another ridge of the moraine stretched out in a north-south alignment. This view is much better when the leaves are down. The trail continues north along the ridge with occasional short spurs to viewpoints to the east. When the trail comes to a rapid drop-off to the east, a fine stand of American beech trees is visible just below the ridge top. They are distinguishable in winter by their copper-colored leaves which stand out in contrast to the surrounding oaks. At about **1.0 mile** the trail goes by the back of a property that has a horse corral adjacent to the park. In a short while it makes a left onto an old woods road and then a right back into a wooded area, where you'll have to step over blowdowns left by trail maintainers to discourage mountain bike use. You may also notice the sweet birches that grow tall alongside the trail. At **1.5 miles** the trail crosses Reservoir Road and the blue blazes end. Immediately across the road the **white blazes** continue to show the way. From here the trail drops steeply down through open woods into a hollow at **1.6 miles**, then climbs steeply up. After cresting the other side it reaches a small wooded swampy area of the kind that used to be common in these hills. Due to development and changes in the land, many of these "wet spots" have been filled in or disturbed. They are important for animals as a source of water and breeding spots, especially the resident amphibian population of salamanders and frogs as well as snakes, which have become rare in recent years. This wet spot sits high up on the moraine where drainage is poor and water buildup occurs during wetter seasons.

The trail reaches a fence bordering the park at **2.0 miles** and reaches the picnic area at Reservoir Road in another **0.1 mile**. The trail turns right here and follows a wide path as it starts to turn in a westerly and then a southerly direction. There is a winter view west through the bare trees towards the ridges that comprise Manetto Hills. At **2.3 miles** the trail reaches a clearing with a glacial erratic and a bench facing a view to the south. This is **Jaynes Hill**, at 401 feet the highest point on Long Island. The Atlantic Ocean, more than 15 miles away, is plainly visible on clear days. In Walt Whitman's day the closer Long Island Sound could be seen to the north, but that was when much of the land was cleared. On my most recent visit there, the view was somewhat obscured due to the re-growth of vegetation. From this landmark location the trail drops off southward, winding back and forth down the hill. The trail reaches a horse trail at 2.5 miles and begins a series of sharp turns away from horse trails and into areas thickly covered with mountain laurel. At some places you will see overlapping post and rail fences that allow hikers through but bar horses and mountain bikes from entering sensitive areas where erosion would occur. The trail is well marked at these detours; just watch for turn blazes and you should have no trouble. Some newly cut sections wind under mountain laurel "tunnels" between horse trails. These sections are particularly showy when the mountain laurel bloom in early to mid-June.

At about **3.0 miles** the trail will descend past healthy stands of rhododendron and some small spruce trees. The spruce trees have probably escaped from cultivation and are not native. The rhododendron may also be escapees, but they do occur naturally in this climate. At **3.6 miles** the trail passes a large horse trail that was a mess on several of my visits (you will need boots here after a rain!). The trail reaches the picnic area again at **3.7 miles**.

Other hikes can be combined with the previous loop or done on their own. From the stables parking area the White Trail continues southward to cross Sweet Hollow Road, where it goes down Gwynne Road and immediately starts climbing through more hilly woods before reaching Round Swamp Road at Exit 39 of Northern State Parkway **1.37 miles** from Sweet Hollow Road. It then makes a left (south), passes under Northern State Parkway and goes down the road to Mary Court (**0.32 mile**) where it passes through a right-of-way along a fence line reaching the Parkway Tower Loop Trail at **0.43 mile**, totaling 1.8 miles from Sweet Hollow Road. This link is important as it leads to direct access by trail to the Nassau-Suffolk Trail, making longer hikes feasible.

The loop south of Northern State Parkway is shorter than the northern one but is a good leg-stretcher featuring an excellent view of Jaynes Hill. The total round-trip mileage from Sweet Hollow Road is 2.0 miles but any number of hikes can be put together using side trails. Starting from Sweet Hollow Road parking lot pick up the **White Trail** on a tree just across the small clearing to the east and head south (right) away from the clearing to reach Sweet Hollow Road at **0.23 mile**. Here you'll notice the White Trail continues down Gwynne Road southward to the parkway (**0.31 mile**) and turns right (west) going into a grove of eastern hemlocks, a tall evergreen more common upstate. There is a healthy patch of trailing arbutus growing on the almost bare forest floor straight ahead; in fact you'll find that this delicate and rare spring wildflower is quite common in West Hills alongside the trail in several places.

Once in the woods, make a right and you'll notice that the blazes of the **Yellow Trail** now take over and signal a turn to the left where the trail goes through a narrow path amidst mountain laurel. The Northern State Parkway will be on the right here. At **0.51 mile** you'll make a sharp left and head immediately uphill over a section that has had waterbars and steps installed to slow erosion. After a brief switchback and some huffing and puffing you will eventually reach a wide woods road at the top at **0.62 mile**. The **Yellow Trail** continues to the right (west). The blue-blazed trail comes in from the left; this is where you will end up later on to return to your car. Following the yellow blazes you'll notice, especially when the leaves are down, that you are pretty high up in these hills. This is Long Island's version of the high country as one can see another ridge across a valley below. At **1.04 miles** you will reach a junction of three woods roads. Straight ahead is an overgrown field displaying the spindly attractive white barked trees popularly called white birch but in field guides identified as gray birch, a fast-growing species that

can quickly colonize abandoned farms and clearings. It is a short-lived tree reaching 30 feet in height that is important because it stabilizes the soil and sets the stage for larger, longer-lived forest trees. It will be interesting to watch this transition from field to mature forest take place over the coming decades, providing

Stopping by a vernal pond perched high in West Hills County Park

there is no cutting or mowing to change the course of events.

Back at the junction, you will notice another triangle of blazes, this time yellow, marking the ending (note the upside-down triangle) of the **White Birch Trail** going off to the right. This trail is **0.81 mile** in length and gives access to the White Main Trail (forming a loop), and linking to the Nassau-Suffolk Trail to the west. The White Birch Trail passes into hardwoods and skims around the north side of the just-described field of birches and then descends steeply into a hollow at **0.2 mile**. Climbing out, it drops again before passing the base of a tall communications tower (**0.27 mile**). At **0.31 mile** the boundary of a day camp at the end of Mt. Misery Road is reached. The trail now gradually but steadily descends along the south side of Northern State Parkway where the many birch trees that give the trail its name are passed. Notice that some of the trees are already dying since other species are growing up around them. Someday this trail may have to be renamed! At **0.73 mile** the trail climbs an embankment and crosses over the parkway on a narrow right-of-way where it ends at **0.81 mile** on Round Swamp Road. As noted earlier, the White Trail can be picked up here and go either east back into West Hills Park on the other side of the parkway or proceed down Round Swamp Road to turn right and eventually meet the Parkway Tower Loop Trail in 0.43 mile. This allows access to the Nassau-Suffolk Trail, making longer hikes possible.

Back on the White Trail a sharp left is made at the junction with the White Birch Trail and the White Trail goes down the woods road. Keep an eye out for a right turn at **1.12 miles** where the trail goes down a narrow path among dense stands of mountain laurel. The trail then opens up in taller woods before reaching the end of the White Trail, which is designated by the inverted triangle of blazes. At this point the **blue-blazed trail** continues straight on the woods road. Don't get confused by the **white-blazed side trail** that climbs steadily uphill to the right to reach Mt. Misery Road in **0.22 mile**. This short trail may be closed at any time.

Continue on the blue-blazed trail as it passes along the northern edge of another old field in the process of being replaced by plant species such as sumac, catbriar, gray birch and red cedar. These trees will eventually give way to more permanent species as succession continues. Shortly thereafter, the trail makes a left (**1.55 miles**) near a short trail that goes off to the right to the Sweet Hollow Church. The trail climbs uphill from here and makes a right at **1.62 miles** where there are many young white pines growing on the hillside. It then drops down steeply to make a quick left onto a wide trail (**1.65 miles**) with taller pines overhead. In a short distance look for a turn to the right at

1.75 miles. where the trail winds uphill to reach the ridgeline at **1.96 miles**. A short distance to the right is a small clearing with a view out over the large industrial park in Melville. It is not hard to imagine the valley below as a patchwork of farm fields instead of the high-tech buildings that have sprung up in the past 30 years. From here, the trail goes left (north) along the fire road with views through the trees. The trail starts to turn west and at **2.11 miles** the last **fine viewpoint** is reached with a great vista of the tall ridgeline to the north where Jaynes Hill is the highest point visible. Shortly thereafter, at **2.16 miles** the loop is completed when the junction is reached with the yellow-blazed trail. Take a right and backtrack downhill and around to the right, eventually reaching Sweet Hollow Road and the parking area in West Hills Park in a 2.8 miles loop. Although not the quietest or longest of trails, the Walt Whitman Trail system is valuable for traversing some of Long Island's highest ground.

Access

Car

There are two places to access The Walt Whitman Trail system which is located in West Hills County Park. To find the trailhead recommended here, take LIE exit 49 north a mile or so and make a left onto Old Country Road, and then in about 0.1 mile turn right onto Sweet Hollow Road. Proceed north under the Northern State Parkway and the parking area will be on the right a short way farther on. Another popular access point is at the north end of the park. To get there, take LIE exit 49 north about 2.5 miles and follow signs for the Walt Whitman birthplace on the left. Turn left onto Old Walt Whitman Road past the Walt Whitman birthplace, left again on West Hills Road, and quickly left again onto Reservoir Road, which in 0.6 mile will take you to the park gate where there is space for a few cars.

Thick groves of mountain laurel in West Hills County Park

Buses

N95, S1

Caumsett State Park

Length: main path 3½ mile circuit

CAUMSETT S.P.

LONG ISLAND

0   20
miles

USGS topographic map: Lloyd Harbor

Located on the North Shore of western
Suffolk County in Huntington Township is
a large peninsula connected to the rest of Long Island by a thin strip of land.
This is a beautiful historic area of very exclusive homes with much woodlands

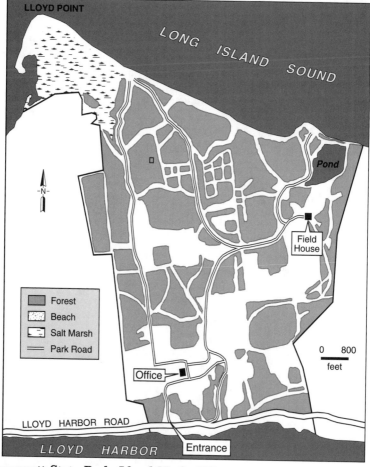

LLOYD POINT

LONG ISLAND SOUND

-N-

Pond

Field
House

Forest
Beach
Salt Marsh
Park Road

0   800
feet

Office

LLOYD HARBOR ROAD

LLOYD HARBOR

Entrance

Caumsett State Park, Lloyd Neck, NY

and beachfront. Once the Marshall Field estate, Caumsett State Park takes up a large portion of the peninsula and offers the walker respite from the malls and traffic a few miles away. Theodore Roosevelt used to lead his family on day hikes into the area when he was president and nearby Sagamore Hill was the summer White House. There is a huge old black oak tree at the corner of Lloyd Harbor Road and Forest Drive (east of the park entrance) that was a favorite spot for them to stop and rest. It is said to be the oldest and largest tree of its type in the country.

The tall trees and patches of woods adjacent to the Sound provide habitat for breeding and migratory birds. I have seen elusive species such as orchard oriole and indigo bunting here, but probably the most pleasant surprises come in winter when unusual migrants make their way to the area. On one New Year's Day walk my wife and I watched a seldom seen red-headed woodpecker working a tree with the Long Island Sound as a backdrop. The local papers reported a great gray owl one winter, a rare visitor from the far north.

These days Caumsett is an environmental education center and year-round place for the public to enjoy. The paths are excellent for cross country skiing when snow cover is adequate. One can spend the better part of a day strolling the wide lanes or exploring the lesser used side paths which are surprisingly tranquil and undisturbed by civilization. The park has fields, woodlands, and beaches with steep bluffs to explore. This is a good place for children to get acquainted with hiking. Maps can be picked up at the park entrance. This state park does charge a parking fee between Memorial Day and Columbus Day.

Access

Car

Take LIE exit 49 north several miles all the way into the village of Huntington. Make a right turn onto Main Street (Route 25A) and go a little over 0.1 mile. Make a right on to West Neck Road and continue about 5 miles onto the Lloyd Neck peninsula to the entrance on the left.

View over Fresh Pond to Long Island Sound from behind the Marshall Field Estate

Target Rock National Wildlife Refuge

Length: 1 mile. Blaze: nature trail

USGS topographic map: Lloyd Harbor

This 80-acre preserve is administered by the United States Fish and Wildlife Service. Located on the eastern side of the Lloyd Neck peninsula, it was the estate of wealthy Manhattan banker Ferdinand Eberstadt, who donated it to the Department of the Interior in 1967. The entrance to the refuge is located at the end of Lloyd Harbor Road, the main road into Lloyd Neck. Just continue past the entrance to Caumsett State Park and the entrance is on the right. The grounds have a variety of habitats: upland forest, salt marsh, second growth thicket, beachfront, and even formal gardens. Because of this diversity, 191 species of birds have been spotted at the refuge at various times of the year. In summer, gray catbirds mew from the thickets while warblers sing from the trees. In winter, diving ducks and mergansers can be viewed just offshore. The walk takes you down to a fine pebbly beach overlooking Huntington Bay. Eatons Neck with its lighthouse on the Sound lies directly across the bay. This spot off Eatons Neck has the unfortunate distinction of being the place where the most shipwrecks have occurred off Long Island.

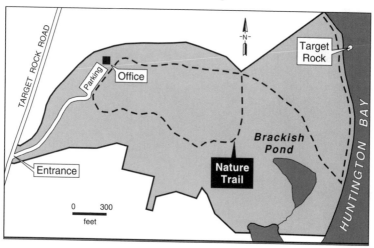

Target Rock N. W. R., Lloyd Harbor, NY

Target Rock gets its name from a huge glacial erratic boulder that can be seen just off shore near the northern border of the property. During the War for Independence the British used it for target practice. At that time the rock was imbedded in the bluffs, but the bluffs eroded around it from the constant action of wind and water on the shoreline. A guided pamphlet on the one-mile nature trail is available at the refuge office. Any walks here can be lengthened by extended exploration of the shoreline or the other trails on the interior grounds. An hour or two should be sufficient to tour the entire site. It should be noted that at this writing there is a small fee scheduled to go into effect. Call the main administrative office at Wertheim National Wildlife Refuge at (631) 286-0485 for further information.

Access

Car

Follow the same directions as for Caumsett State Park and continue on West Neck Road a little over two miles farther until the road curves left to become Sound Bay Drive. The refuge entrance will be on the right side

Gardiner County Park

Length: longest circuit under 1 mile

USGS topographic map: Bay Shore West

Gardiner County Park is a 231 acre preserve that gets its name from the Gardiner
family who owned it back in the seventeenth century. They were the first
European landholders on Long Island; having developed good relations with
the native inhabitants, they were able to bargain with them. Gardiners Island
is still owned by the family. The land became part of the grounds of the historic Sagtikos Manor built in 1697, which is on the north side of Montauk
Highway. George Washington is known to have stayed in the famous old
Manor house in 1790 while touring Long Island. The room he stayed in is still

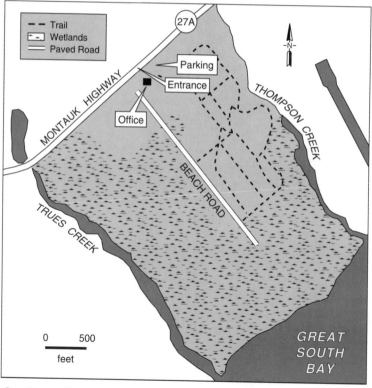

Gardiner County Park, West Bay Shore, NY

furnished much the same way it was when he stayed there. The park is bordered on the west and east by freshwater creeks.

Today, the park is a nice place to spend an hour or so wandering its wide wooded lanes down to the shore of Great South Bay. An exercise trail, bathroom facilities, and a pond are near the parking area. You will find old fields in the area immediately around the parking lot. The main path goes off to the south away from the restrooms. You may notice the remains of an old wooden post and wire fence that once was needed to mark off a boundary or keep animals in pasture. Now the land is becoming overgrown with hedgerows and second-growth woods. Red maples are dominant but some large tupelos grow around some of the marshes in the park. The main lane will take you through woods and marsh right down to the edge of Great South Bay. The Fire Island Lighthouse with its blinking light and 168 foot spire dominates the barrier beach across the water. Completed in 1858, the light was restored in 1986 and can be seen 20 miles out at sea. Off to the right (west) is the green bridge of the Robert Moses Causeway connecting Captree State Park to the mainland. There are other lanes and paths to wander on to the east of the main path once you return from the water. This is a good place to stroll with young children or to get acclimated to walking before tackling longer hikes elsewhere.

Access

Car

Robert Moses Causeway south to exit C2 onto Montauk Highway (Route 27A) going east about 0.75 mile to the entrance on the right.

Bus

SCT40

Edgewood Oak Brush Plains Preserve

Length: 3 miles. Blaze: blue

USGS topographic map: Greenlawn

When the first European settlers arrived they found Long Island varied dramatically in habitats and plant species from one end to the other. From the Queens border to the Nassau-Suffolk County border was a vast 60,000 acre flat grassy plain called the Hempstead Plain that is said to have been the largest natural prairie east of the Appalachians. In colonial times the plains were used for horseracing and polo playing. Later on the flat rock-less grassland was a natural airstrip for early civilian aviators and important to the military for its strategic defensive location. It became known as the "Cradle of Aviation" and had seven airfields built on it. Although many noteworthy pioneering aviation events happened here, the most famous undoubtedly was Charles Lindbergh taking off from Mitchell Field on his dramatic solo non-stop trans-Atlantic flight. After the postwar development boom there are only 86 acres of this unique natural grassland left, most of it disturbed by invasive species. Adjacent to Nassau Community College 19 acres of grassland are owned and managed by The Nature Conservancy, which is using managed burns to maintain the dominance of native species. Many of the current names of today's towns in the area reflect their relationship to the Hempstead Plain. East Meadow, Plainedge, Plainview (where the plains were visible from Manetto Hills) and

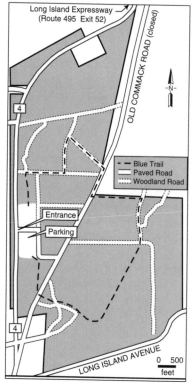

Edgewood Oak Brush Plains Preserve, Brentwood, NY

Island Trees all get their names from the plain. Island Trees suggests the small isolated groups of trees that sprang up towards the eastern end of the plain. As the Hempstead Plains gave way to more trees and scrub growth they became known as the Oak Brush Plains. This was a transition zone between the grasslands and the vast tracts of Pine Barrens to the east. Fire also played a key role in keeping this area as Oak Brush Plains (see on Pine Barrens, p. 111). There were nearly 60,000 acres of Oak Brush Plains in western Suffolk County until postwar suburbanization took over. It was here that the last heath hen on Long Island was seen in 1844. An Atlantic Coast subspecies of the greater prairie chicken, it roamed the Hempstead Plains and Oak Brush Plains, where it fed off the acorn mast of the scrub oaks. The Oak Brush Plains were its last stronghold on Long Island. The loud booming call of the males could be heard for up to a mile during early spring courtship. Over-hunting and loss of habitat proved too much for this wild bird. The last of its species died on Martha's Vineyard in 1932. It's a shame that this symbol of the wild eastern prairies couldn't have survived so its call could still echo through the scrub oaks for today's hikers to enjoy.

Today, about 2,000 acres of the original Oak Brush Plains exist. This is chiefly due to the protection given by Edgewood State Hospital and the adjacent Pilgrim State Mental Hospital that once stood here. Imagine the once vast tracts of land where scrub oak and various grasses dominated. One could see for long distances because the vegetation rarely grew higher than head height. Groups of pitch pine grew here and there amongst the thicket understory, small islands of pine trees in a desert of scrub. This land was transferred to the state as a preserve in the mid 1980s. It contains 711 acres but with future acquisitions will likely top 900. There is also adjacent undeveloped land and 50 acres of multi-use town land that makes the preserve seem even larger than this. This is a good piece of open space considering the density of western Suffolk County. Although the heath hen no longer thrives here, several rare plants and animals still inhabit this dry, sterile, and sometimes hostile environment. Many of the plants of the Pine Barrens can also be found here. Members of the heath family such as wintergreen, bearberry, blueberry, staggerbush and trailing arbutus thrive here. One big surprise that I have read grows here is fireweed, a tall, bright pink-flowered plant that blooms in midsummer. Common in the north country (as far north as the sub-arctic), where it invades clearings and burn areas, it is found in no other area on Long Island. A rare chocolate-brown phase of the eastern hognose snake, also known as the puff adder, is also found in the Oak Brush Plains Preserve.

Near the parking area on the east side there is a large clearing where the hospital once stood. The New York State Department of Environmental Conservation (DEC) manages this property, so a free permit is necessary to hike here. Call (631) 444-0273 to obtain one. A rough map is also available from them and is helpful in locating your place along the trail. Biking is permitted only on hard roads within the preserve. Model airplane flying is allowed in this clearing due east of the parking lot.

From the parking lot locate on a tree the blue plastic disc blaze of the trail going south (right) from here. The trail is well-marked but take care to look for blazes at intersections where the trail may make a turn. The state does not use the universal (two blazes leaning in the direction of a turn) system, so be alert for this. You will head away through the clear areas with signs of cottontail rabbit all around. You'll then enter a woods dominated by pitch pines and will cross an old woods trail or two before reaching Old Commack Road, the old route that is no longer used. As can be seen from the map, this paved road bisects the park in roughly a southwest-to-northeast direction. Continuing across the road through pines, look for signs of an old fire on the trunks of the trees. The charring tells which way the fire was blowing. Since the fire occurred years ago the ground cover has become thick and the litter layer is building up; the area is due for another fire to clear this ground cover out and keep the pine habitat healthy. The woods road eventually takes a sharp left and heads northeast through

On the trail in Edgewood Oak Brush Plains Preserve

scrub oaks with tall pines towering over them. Going straight for a while the trail will cross another woods road and come out to a clearing of disturbed ground that is being reclaimed by large clumps of some of our native grasses. Skirting the edge of the clearing you will notice some bigtooth aspen trees growing on the left. These trees are pioneer species that grow quickly and are short-lived, invading after burns and disturbances that clear the land. They have a gray green bark and generally grow in groves of several trees together. They are quite common in the preserve.

Continue straight past the clearing and watch for a narrower trail that crosses diagonally. Look left to spot the blue blazes as the trail makes a sharp left (west) here. This is classic oak brush plain flora with groves of pines and even aspen rising above thick scrub oak. Once again you'll reach paved Old Commack Road where you'll make a right and proceed up the road a hundred yards or so and then make a left (note two blazes on the tree). The trail now follows an old road; closer inspection of the roadside reveals it was once paved. Proceeding down this road you'll see large thorny bushes growing on the sides. This is multiflora rose, an introduced wild rose that blooms in late spring. Watch for another left turn, which was hard to see on my visit. The next section of trail was badly overgrown at this writing but I have been told that the DEC plans on trimming back the thorny multiflora rose that is now overrunning the trail.

The trail soon makes a left onto an olds woods road, a very pleasant trail shaded by pitch pines. It makes a right at an intersection and goes west for a few minutes. Watch for a place where the trail turns to the left and then left again. Commack Road is close at this point and in winter you may see traffic through the trees. The final section is through a pine grove with much bracken fern, growing three to four feet tall in places. Shortly thereafter you'll come out into the clearing with your car in front of you. The entire trail is a bit more than three miles of easy flat walking and can be covered in an hour and a half to two hours.

Access

Car
Take exit 52 on the LIE to Commack Road, going south 2.1 miles to the entrance in a large field on the left (east) side of the road.

Bus
SCT33

Long Island Greenbelt Trail

Length: 31.8 miles. Blaze: white

DOT topographic maps: Bay Shore East, Central Islip, Saint James, Northport

This is the second longest of the "superhighway" trails and the first long hiking trail on Long Island. The trail opened in 1978 after two years of hard work by the then-fledgling Long Island Greenbelt Trail Conference (LIGTC). It is a 32-mile-long sanctuary for the walker linking Great South Bay to Long Island Sound. At times it is a thin thread of "Greenbelt" among development but more often it is a quiet place that passes through some of Long Island's more scenic terrain. From the sandy beaches, creeks, and woods of the South Shore's relatively flat coastal plain, through the watersheds of two of the island's largest rivers, to the hilly and wooded glacial moraines and bluffs looking over Long Island Sound to Connecticut this trail offers striking diversity along the way. The LIGTC offers scheduled group hikes throughout the year (some even under moonlight) of varying lengths and group sizes. There is even a hike of the entire trail for those hardy enough to want to take on such an outing. The main Long Island paper, *Newsday*, lists these hikes every Friday in the "Events" section. Membership in the Long Island Greenbelt Trail Conference entitles you to maps and a quarterly newsletter detailing all group hikes among other pertinent news.

The trail is best explored using two cars since loops are not common along its length. This enables hikers to cover more ground without having to backtrack to the starting point. But backtracking is not always such a bad thing. I have found hiking a trail backwards gives an entirely different perspective; things that were missed on the way in are often seen on the return trip. Although the trail can be hiked from a number of points, I will describe it from south to north beginning from Heckscher Park on Great South Bay. Of course a detailed map will help you choose. Part of the fun of hiking is the planning of where to go and when.

At the southern trailhead in **Heckscher State Park** (there is a fee in season) park in parking field seven or eight. There is a difference of 0.4 mile more of walking along the beach from lot seven. This is a wonderful place to start a hike, especially in early morning when the beach is empty, or at dusk when

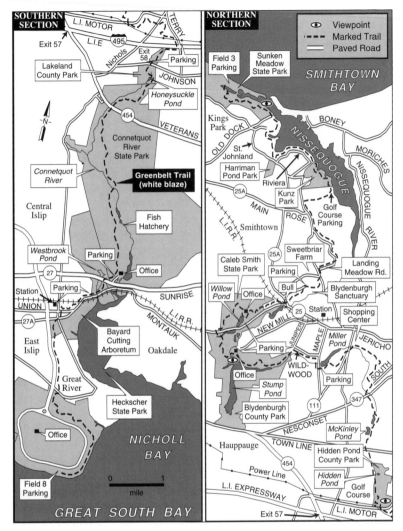

Long Island Greenbelt Trail

the moon is full. Across Great South Bay lies the barrier beach of Fire Island with the Fire Island Lighthouse's flashing light the most obvious landmark. The communities of Fire Island are to the east of the lighthouse. Farther east lies the wild undeveloped Fire Island National Seashore.

One memorable hike I took along this trail began shortly after sunrise. The sun was reflecting off the water, the salt breeze was blowing in my face and the cry of gulls awakened my senses to the walk ahead of me. The trail goes off to the east and in a little while turns away from the beach at about **1 mile** onto an undeveloped sandy road called the Clam Road. After a short distance, it turns right to resume a northerly course. The proximity of the salt marshes influences the growth of tall phragmites grasses lining the trail. The woods are dominated by black cherry and tupelo. Wildlife abounds here, and deer can be spotted any time of the year. A chipmunk is likely to dart across your path at any moment. Bird life seems particularly abundant here in the shelter of the trees, which give cover from predators and protection from the wind. In a short distance a bench overlooking a channel from the bay is reached, affording a good place to rest. Continuing on through wet ground containing many young red maples, the trail meets the blue-blazed **Timber Point Trail** at **1.4 miles**. This trail goes off to the east (right) and reaches the canal at West Marina at Timber Point in less than .3 mile. Even on a short trail such as this there is much for the observant hiker to see. I found an owl pellet on the trail, the undigested bones and fur regurgitated by the owl after it has devoured its prey. You will see many woodpeckers in the trees and brilliant red cardinals in the cover afforded by briar thickets. On a cold March morning a large mourning-cloak butterfly fluttered by me in near-freezing temperatures. It was an astonishing sight in those conditions.

From the junction with the Timber Point Trail, the Greenbelt continues on an old jeep road, making a sharp right parallel to the park road on a well-used dirt road, and then a left through a campground (**1.8 miles**) that is open in summer. Contact the park for information about campsites. The trail goes back into the woods and passes around a tall water tower at **1.9 miles**. The oak trees here signify the transition from the wetland species now behind you. Here on the outwash plain of southern Long Island the first signs of the pine-and-oak woods that dominate much of the island can be seen. American holly trees, an evergreen native, can also be found growing here. From here the trail follows the woods along the east side of Heckscher Parkway, and the trees are noticeably smaller. Damage to the trail from bike use is obvious in this section. As you approach Timber Road (**2.1 mile**) the first pitch pines become noticeable here and there, precursors to the great Pine Barrens stands out east.

The trail crosses Timber Road and is fairly straight through oak woodlands in a narrow corridor, with the parkway to the west (left) and the backyards of residential homes to the east (right). Although a rather uneventful section, it does drop down to cross a small brook that runs under the parkway. It is said that the water table has dropped about three feet since the heavy postwar development on Long Island. You can just imagine the effect this has had on many small waterways like this one. Some are now dry, especially on the South Shore. At **3.8 miles**. the trail reaches Montauk Highway. I observed four ospreys calling overhead just south of the road. What a great sight these large chocolate-brown and white birds were! Perhaps no other creature better symbolizes the beauty, grace, and freedom of nature on Long Island than these stately birds. The snags in this section of woods also offered glimpses of woodpeckers and migrating warblers. You should cross busy Montauk Highway (state route 27A) at the nearby corner. The area immediately north is overgrown with vines and large bushes of multiflora rose, a wild rose with sweet-smelling clusters of white or pink flowers in June. Note the red cedar trees indicate that this transitional section of flora was once an open field of some sort. This type of vegetation is preferred by many types of birds, including the cardinals and mockingbirds I observed flitting around the area.

After crossing Union Boulevard at **3.9 miles**, a definite change of plants is evident. First, you will notice that coniferous trees become more numerous. Some of the first ones visible are larches, trees that lose their needles in fall, a rarity amongst cone-bearing trees. Some really large oaks are interspersed as well. The pines become dominant and in no time you will be in a pure white pine grove now simply known as "the Pines," at **4.2 miles**. These neat, straight rows of trees were originally scheduled for plantings on local highways but now give shade to hikers glad to get out of the hot sun. A small clearing with some dead trees is from a fire in the 1980s. Watch out for blazes on the trees as the trail heads to the east and northeast at this point, coming out onto State Route 27A. Across the street is an entrance to the Bayard Cutting Arboretum; its beautifully landscaped paths make for an excellent side trip. Route 27A now heads up and over the Long Island Railroad Montauk branch.

The trail enters a brushy area that was once the Westbrook Farm (**4.6 miles**), where racing horses were kept. A large sign tells you the Town of Islip Westbrook Soccer Fields now occupy the land. In another 0.3 mile the Westbrook dam is reached (**4.9 miles**). The pond was dammed in the late 1800s for ice skating. The sound of rushing water flowing over the dam makes it a nice spot to rest and observe some of the waterfowl found here. This is especially true in winter when seasonal visitors are in residence. The water rushing beneath your feet is part of the West Brook, a tributary of the Connetquot River, into which it will merge a little farther on. The trail continues north along the east bank of **Westbrook Pond.** Islands containing tall pitch pines make this pond especially scenic and photographic. There is much bird activity on the pond all year round. Looking west, winter sunsets can be

The Great South Bay just after sunrise

quite a show over its clean waters. A bench about midway along the pond is a fine place to take in the scene.

At **5.2 miles** the trail goes under busy State Route 27 on a catwalk. Look for some small alder trees flourishing along the shore here. The small brown attractive cones are a giveaway. These trees are found in fresh water environments along rivers and ponds. A short distance north of Route 27 the trail comes to a small wooden platform with a pretty view of this portion of Westbrook Pond. There are a couple of eastern white cedars nearby. A rare coastal species, they are discussed in more detail on p. 147.

You are now within the confines of the **Connetquot River State Park Preserve**. Heading away from the water, the trail passes through dry oak dominated woods to reach the main parking area of the preserve. Don't be surprised to see deer innocently grazing within feet of the cars in the lot. Wild deer these are not, as one can pass within a few feet of them before they even flinch or appear to notice you. The lack of predators or hunting within the park allows the deer to multiply unchecked and over-browse their preferred vegetation. This makes the deer smaller and more susceptible to diseases in severe winters.

The parking area at **5.5 miles** from the beginning of the trail on Great South Bay is a good place to leave a car since it gives the hiker options to hike north or south, or to shuttle to other starting points. Entrance is off the south side of Route 27 (Sunrise Highway). Expect to pay a five dollar fee to leave your vehicle in the lot during the warmer seasons. A day permit is issued at this point if you are hiking the Greenbelt Trail. For use of other trails in the park as well as fly fishing etc., you must send a self-addressed, stamped envelope to NYS Parks, Box 505, Oakdale, NY 11769. The permit is good for one year, and the park is open in summer from 6 a.m. until sundown and 8 a.m. until 4:30 p.m. in winter. Call ahead at (631) 581-1005 for further information. Don't let this scenario of permits stop you from exploring Connetquot River State Park Preserve; it offers a glimpse into some of Long Island's natural beauty with a feeling of serenity unmatched in this part of Suffolk County.

Leaving the parking lot you will head north past the entrance booth and pass the large old building housing the park headquarters. This stately structure, parts of which date to 1820, was a former country inn and stagecoach stopping-point. The good fishing and hunting opportunities in the area transformed it into the Southside Sportsman Club (reminiscent of the situation along the Carmans River in what is now Southaven Park). The calm waters of the dammed-up **Connetquot River** flow by here; they provided power for the Nichols Mill, which was built in 1760 and still stands on the banks of the river. At about **5.7 miles** the trail turns behind the headquarters (left) and follows a course just to the west of a paved park road that heads to a fish hatchery. More docile deer are likely to be seen here as you pass through woods and small meadows. A walk here on a sunny morning can easily make you forget that you've just left busy Montauk Highway behind. The trail crosses the park access road at **6.4 miles** and reaches the fish hatchery at **6.6 miles**. The hatchery raises trout that are to be released at various locations on Long Island. It is fascinating to be able to see such beautiful fish up close. The pristine waters of the Connetquot keep these fish in good health; the size of some of them attests to that. One can follow the development of the trout in a few well-spent minutes, as the fish are kept apart by size in holding areas.

The hiker now has two options: until the harsh, icy winter of 1993-94 when the historic Bunces Bridge was washed away, the trail followed the west side of the river (the same side as the hatchery). After the bridge was gone, rerouting became necessary, so the trail was blazed to cross an artificial berm just north of the hatchery. You will see the blazes as they make a right (east) and cross a relatively wide dammed-up section of river. You may get a glimpse here of snowy and great egrets (distinguished by beak and foot color) or of a great blue heron wading the sides of the river. The trail turns north (left) and follows the east side of the river, which is out of sight at this point. It connects with a woods road and meets the original path at about **7.6 miles**. The second option is the original path, since the bridge was rebuilt in the fall of 1996. It follows the river closely. It is a joy to observe the vibrant colors that begin in September with the scarlet tupelos and climaxes with the intensity and varying hues of red maples in mid- October. Some of the old blazes are still in evidence but they are soon to be newly blazed so the trail on the west side can once again be followed. From Bunces Bridge, the serenity and natural beauty of the Connetquot shines. You may see a fly fisherman quietly tossing for the elusive trout or a small flycatcher swooping over the water to catch a fly; maybe the fragrance of swamp azalea will catch you as you take in warm sunshine on a June morning. The quietness and calm of the lazily flowing water is soothing to the soul.

Throughout Connetquot River State Park Preserve you'll notice markers of different colors designating hiking or cross-country ski trails, depending on the season and conditions. A network of trails, mainly on woods roads, offers hours of strolling in this large preserve. A brief description is given in the Connetquot River State Park Preserve section.

From Bunces Bridge the trail will shortly make a right onto a horse trail at **7.7 miles** and then a left onto another trail at **8.1 miles**. This stretch has some particularly good blueberry bushes that will make your hike all the more enjoyable in July and even August. The trail continues north through dry woods reminiscent of the extensive pine woods farther east, although the river is never far off to your left (west). Some of the tallest pitch pines on Long Island are located along this stretch of trail. Except for the occasional woodpecker flying from tree to tree or a noisy blue jay sounding an alarm, all seems calm here. Of course in May and June breeding birds will be singing from the trees, but no human noises are to be heard in this woods-insulated environment. But farther on, after crossing a few more wide fire roads, the sound of automobiles whipping by will invade your senses again as Veterans Highway (Route 454) is reached some **9.1 miles** from the start of the trail on Great South Bay. A gate in the fence is your way out. The Connetquot River is just down the road to your left where it passes under the roadway.

Use caution crossing Veterans Highway and enter on the opposite side into the north edge of Connetquot Park. The trail heads straight on an old firebreak or woods road. At **9.3 miles** the abandoned paved Old Wheeler Road is crossed. The Connetquot River headwaters can be viewed close-up if you take a short detour to the left. The river can be quite dry in some seasons but usually has water flowing southward under the road. Return to the trail where it goes into the woods and continues a generally northerly course away from the road. On the left (west), the land drops off slightly into the **Dismal Swamp**, a wooded swamp containing red maples, tupelos and other wetland species. The swamp is really the watershed of the upper Connetquot. It is seasonal since water levels vary due to rainfall and any snow meltoff, creating a floodplain effect. A small wooden boardwalk crossing a particularly wet area is reached at **9.7 miles**. The trail then opens up into a dry area that has some

The Long Island Greenbelt Trail in Connetquot State Park

very large oaks and pitch pines, survivors of an old fire (note the charring on some tree trunks), while younger trees sprout alongside the trail. Sheep laurel proliferates in some open areas. Some side trails crisscross the trail here, likely created by illegal bike use.

At **10.1 miles** the railroad underpass is reached. The end of a residential street is on the right. This is the border between Connetquot Park and **Lakeland County Park** on the north side of the tracks. Once on the other side you will see **Honeysuckle Pond** on your left (north). This small pond and the wetlands beyond it are the headwaters of the Connetquot River. The trail passes onto part of a network of boardwalks (**10.3 miles**) traversing the swampy land that feeds Honeysuckle Pond. They are handicapped-accessible and allow you to walk quietly through an area that only diehard naturalists would generally see first-hand. Leaving the boardwalk, the trail comes out along the parking area, turns right to the entrance of the park on Johnson Avenue at **10.6 miles**. This is a good spot to leave a car if you plan on using the car-ferry method to hike. The trail makes a right and crosses Johnson Avenue continuing into a wood lot between two houses. It reaches a chain link fence (**11.0 miles**) and follows it, eventually reaching the south service road of the Long Island Expressway (LIE) between exits 58 and 59 at **11.3 miles**. The woods beyond the chain link fence are notable because they contain wetland species of trees and signify the first visible above-ground source of the Connetquot River. The trail follows along the service road east (right) for 0.2 mile, reaching Terry Road where it turns left and proceeds under the LIE. White blazes can be seen on poles along this stretch.

North of the LIE the trail gives way to some road walking, leaving Terry Road at **11.6 miles** and heading west (left) along the open LIPA power lines right-of-way. It quickly turns away from the power lines into a large wood lot bordering an attractive horse farm on the left (west). A trail reroute was evident on my visit here; watch for blazes that leave the wider, more worn path. There has been some disturbance here due to a fire and the subsequent damage by brush trucks putting it out. Old Nichols Road is crossed at **12.0 miles** as the trail goes into woods within view of some greenhouses on the right; they're more easily seen when leaves are down. In a short distance a sign directs mountain bikers to detour left while the Greenbelt starts a short uphill on wooden steps (to prevent erosion) to the top of a wooded knoll. Although a modest climb by any standards, this begins the ascension of the south side of the **Ronkonkoma Moraine**, the central moraine that runs the length of Long Island and out along the South Fork. If the leaves are down, a view of how obviously the moraine rises above the flat outwash plain of the South Shore can be seen. American chestnut trees are common along the trail here. These small trees are remnants of once big and numerous chestnuts that favored the morainal soil, but were devastated by a blight early in the twentieth century. The trail winds among scrubby second-growth trees before reaching power lines, makes a right (north) and climbs uphill. Glancing back to the south you can see for several miles toward the South Shore. A red-tailed hawk screeched overhead while I was taking in this scene on a clear cold March afternoon, a reminder that wild things are still in evidence in suburbia if given a little space to claim their own.

At **12.9 miles** the trail reaches Motor Parkway, which it crosses, and quickly winds to a **superb viewpoint** north from this morainal vantage point 180 feet above sea level (**13.0 miles**). This area is the furthest south the great glaciers of the last ice age reached some 20,000 years ago. Two benches near each other give slightly different views towards the North Shore. Only the high bluffs along the Harbor Hill Moraine prevent you from seeing the Long Island Sound and Connecticut. The first view is north by northwest and sweeps over woods towards the northwest (left) where the building rising just above the horizon is the old Kings Point Psychiatric Hospital near the north end of the trail some 17 trail miles away! The second view is more northeast. The prominent building is the SUNY Medical Center at Stony Brook. This view is more encompassing and impressive when the leaves are down.

In a short distance the trail will start down the north side of the moraine. A reroute due to erosion problems takes the trail left to a third bench alongside a chain link fence bordering the golf course property of a large hotel that dominates the top of the moraine just to the west (left). Continuing to descend, the trail passes behind the buildings and pool of the Town of Islip's **Hidden Pond Park**. Sharp eyes will notice that the trail passes alongside an old over-

View from the top of the Ronkonkoma Moraine

grown boundary ditch in this area, a throwback to the days when that was an economical method of marking one's property. The trail makes a right **13.5 miles** into the confines of Hidden Pond Park along a path which reveals three kinds of evergreens in winter, white pines, pitch pines and red cedars. It turns left and passes a picnic area at **13.8 miles** before coming to **Hidden Pond** at **14.0 miles**. The small pond is dry much of the year, a sort of backwoods hidden wetland surrounded by large red maples that are ablaze with color in autumn. The trail turns right and then left to go around the pond. Make sure to watch for white blazes in this area as the trail makes a few turns away from junctions with other paths in the park. The stretch of woods north of Hidden Pond is interesting since there are several types of ground cover that dominate specific locations alongside the trail. For instance, wintergreen will be prevalent and seems to blanket the forest floor in one spot. Then ground pine, a low-growing evergreen member of the clubmoss family, which was once picked extensively for Christmas decorating, dominates another area. In spring, wildflowers like starflower and Canada mayflower can be found here. One rarity I found growing in a spot alongside the trail was pipsissewa, an evergreen relative of the common striped wintergreen. It blooms in early July on Long Island. In all of my wanderings on the Island I have only seen it growing in two sites in Middle Island. This plant is more often associated with the north woods than with the coastal plain of Long Island. In a short distance the trail will reach the fence bordering the golf course again and turn north (right) traveling between it and residential backyards. I found a few stray golf balls here, just another one of those unexpected surprises of hiking. The trail turns left alongside Town Line Road and crosses it at **14.5 miles**.

Immediately north of the road the trail parallels a ditch behind residential homes before reaching a seasonal freshwater wetland at **14.7 miles**. This wetland is the headwaters of the Nissequogue River, which the trail will more or less follow until it empties into Long Island Sound. Now within the watershed of the Nissequogue, the trail will come to **McKinley Pond** at **14.9 miles**. Sometimes referred to as **Bow Tie Marsh**, this pond is in one of the largest freshwater marsh systems left on Long Island and does have a rough bow-tie shape. If you approach it quietly you may see some waterfowl on the pond. Beyond this point the trail alternates between second-growth clearings on the right and wetlands on the left. Watch closely for blazes as the trail makes some quick turns here. One particularly sharp left turn enters the edge of the swamp and crosses several short boardwalks connecting root stumps of red maples. The water level here varies greatly depending on rainfall and seasonal changes.

The trail leaves the wetland temporarily and crosses an open grassy strip of land owned by the Town of Smithtown. On the far side is a small metal bridge that crosses the young Nissequogue (**15.3 miles**), where the trail makes a sharp right and heads north. Crossing a few wet places on short boardwalks, the trail comes out to the eastern border of what was open farm fields until the 1980s when the Hidden Ponds condos were built. The condos are on the left and the wetlands of the Nissequogue are on the right at this point. Soon, the noise of traffic can be heard as Nesconset Highway (Route 347) is reached at **15.8 miles**. Care should be taken crossing here as one of the biggest perils awaiting the hiker on the Greenbelt doesn't have four legs but four wheels (and sometimes eighteen!).

On the north side of Route 347 the midway point of the trail is unceremoniously reached (**15.9 miles**) just before the end of South Avenue. The trail makes a left onto West Avenue at **16.0 miles**. and heads into the woods at the dead end of this street. You can leave your car in this residential neighborhood if you're planning a day-hike in either direction. These wet woods are a typical freshwater wetland habitat along the Nissequogue watershed, which is off to the immediate west (left) at this point. Skimming the edge of the wet woods the trail cuts along the property boundaries of suburban backyards before reaching another of suburbia's trademarks, a shopping center. It's a good place to refuel if you are so inclined. Obviously, this is also another location to leave a car or arrange a pickup. Just beyond the shopping center, the trail crosses a bridge over the still-small northeast branch of the infant **Nissequogue** at **17.2 miles** before crossing Route 111 at **17.6 miles**.

After Route 111 the trail dives into dense woods circling around a development that is, for the most part, out of sight. A sharp right is made at **18.0 miles** and you will notice that wetlands make their appearance again as the land drops off to the right. In a little while a short side trail will lead down to a view of **Miller Pond**. On my first hike here, the trees obscured all but a narrow view across the water, leaving me with the impression that the pond was undisturbed and remote. The trail will soon prove otherwise as the head of the pond has a big parking lot off Maple Avenue at **18.4 miles**. It is not unusual to see mothers with their youngsters feeding ducks or kids fishing here in warmer weather. Miller Pond was dammed in the mid-1800s and was used as a source for ice; after being cut from the pond, the ice would be packed in hay in cool places to preserve it.

The trail goes up Maple Avenue and turns left onto Wildwood Lane at **18.5 miles**. It proceeds down Wildwood Lane past pleasant gardens in front of neatly kept homes. At **19.0 miles** the trail makes a left onto Juniper Avenue, reaching Brooksite Park at its terminus in a short 0.1 mile (**19.1 miles**). This bit of road-walking is necessary for linking public lands and, gratefully, makes up only a small percentage of the Greenbelt mileage.

Across Brooksite Drive the trail enters the confines of **Blydenburgh County Park**. The **blue blazes** that go off to the left are part of the **Stump Pond Trail** that goes around the entire pond for about six miles. It's worth a short detour in that direction as far as a small bridge over the northeast branch of the Nissequogue River. The river flows out from a culvert under the road and heads westward into wetlands that eventually open up into Stump Pond. Its banks are enclosed by alders and other wetland-loving shrubs. The Greenbelt Trail now follows wide woods roads used as bridle paths that are chopped up by horseback use. In a short while it skims the edge of an old field (**19.5 miles**) in a state of succession into scrub woodland. Russian olive trees and multiflora rose can be seen along with other pioneer species that will eventually give way to longer living trees if the area is left undisturbed. Shortly past here one may notice the beginnings of **Stump Pond** on the left (south) side of the trail if the leaves are down. In spring many wildflowers that prefer damp woods can be found growing alongside the trail. This section of trail becomes very wet after rains, with large puddles covering most of the width of the path. Waterproof boots may be necessary here in wet season. Another indicator of the moist soil nearby is the sweet pepperbush whose fragrant white spikes bloom here in summer. Ground pine is very common along here also. At a junction at **19.8 miles** the trail turns left back towards the pond. The trail will follow a path slightly above the shores of the pond (which is really quite a good-sized lake) in what is a very scenic section, particularly when the leaves are down. Many types of ducks and geese can be spotted here in winter. I saw canvasback, northern shoveler and common pintail among more common species. Visit this area in December for an opportunity to learn to identify waterfowl. The trail next makes a right turn through a small cleft in the hillside and then a quick left up some log steps put in for erosion prevention. A small outbuilding passed on the right is the first sign that you are nearing the **Blydenburgh-Weld House**, first built in 1821 (**20.5 miles**). The house will appear on the right in a clearing that affords a great view of the length of **Stump Pond**. The **Long Island Greenbelt Trail Conference** headquarters is located in this old house. There is parking near here which makes this a good spot to begin or end a hike (access is from New Mill Road). If the office is open (the door on the left), the first-floor store is worth a visit.

After enjoying the view from the front of the house, head back down the trail on a well-kept boardwalk-like staircase to the site of the **Millers House and New Mill**, which dates back to 1798. The mill is a good example of how water power was used to do work that would have been backbreaking if done by hand, in this case the grinding of grain into flour. Just past the mill, the trail goes over an outlet where you can hear the sound and feel the power of the rushing water. The trail makes a right turn here (west) away from the shore of Stump Pond. Just down this woods road the trail makes another right at a gate that enters **Blydenburgh State Park Nature Preserve**. There is a combination lock here designed to limit access to the preserve. The combination can be obtained from the Caleb Smith park headquarters off Route 25 in Smithtown. You can call ahead to (631) 265-1054 or even stop in the day of your hike and get a permit for access to the parks along with the lock combinations you'll need.

The trail now enters the upland woods of the **Harbor Hill Moraine** as the sound of rushing water fades away while you amble uphill. In winter, you may catch a glimpse of the blue waters of Stump Pond through the trees. Oak trees and plants associated with drier woods once again prevail. A woodpecker may attract your attention as it probes the trunk of a tree looking for insects under the bark, or in spring the song of a bird such as the common yellowthroat may drift up from the river ravine on your right. This is a relaxing, more private stretch of trail contrasted with the wide bridle paths you have just left. You will appreciate the combination locks that keep some people out. At **21.1 miles** the trail reaches an abandoned paved road that is the former route of Old Willets Path, which was originally a stagecoach route from Smithtown to Central Islip. Turn right and walk down this road a short ways before making a left that starts to drop down back into moist woodlands. At the bottom it reaches a small stream, which is part of the Nissequogue watershed. The trail winds around and through this wet section. Spring and fall are the best times to explore areas such as these when the contrast with the drier uplands is more pronounced. At **21.4 miles** the trail reaches the gate that exits the park at the corner of Old Willets Path and Route 25. Another combination-type lock is found here.

Cross the road at the light since traffic is heavy and moves fast. Head east (right) a hundred yards or so and enter **Caleb Smith State Park** (formerly **Nissequogue State Park**) north of Route 25 (**21.5 miles**). The trail ascends into dry oak-dominated woods passing some side trails that traverse back sections of the park. It then proceeds downhill, coming to another stream that is part of the Nissequogue watershed. Along the way you may notice colored blazes marking short trails within the park. The trail turns sharp right (**22.0 miles**), crosses the stream and turns right again, crossing a bit of higher ground with wet areas on either side. At **22.2 miles** it reaches a paved park where it turns right onto the road. Following this road it reaches pleasant **Willow Pond** in a short while. Look for waterfowl here anytime of the year. Just beyond the pond, the park headquarters (**22.4 miles**) is located in a building that used to belong to the Wyandanch Club, a wealthy sportsman's club that took advantage of the fine fishing and hunting afforded by the Nissequogue River and its tributaries. There is small natural history museum inside that is worth a look since it displays some of the wildlife found in the area. Parking is available just west of the headquarters.

Caleb Smith State Park has some trails good for those with young children or for those just learning about hiking, or who want to take a walk in the woods but have limited time to travel. An interpretive brochure and map can be obtained at the park office. You can spend anywhere from a half hour to an hour and a half on these well-marked nature trails, which coincide with the Greenbelt for part of its length through the park. Cross country skiing is also an option here. On one summer exploration of the trails near the wetland portion of the park (west of the office), I found the tall orange blooms of the turk's cap lily in the wet woods. The bright golden prothonotary warbler has also been known to breed here. A bird of the wooded swamps of the South with a loud repetitive song, it is very rare on Long Island since this is near the northern limits of its range. This is another of the north-meets-south natural history examples wildlife observers on Long Island have come to appreciate.

The trail continues behind the headquarters on a woods road, making a right turn at **22.6 miles** into a clearing containing several red cedar trees and an area set up with many bird feeders in winter. Crossing more park trails, it enters rolling hilly terrain and then drops down to **Peacepunk Creek** at **22.9**

miles. In late winter one can spot the mottled maroon colored hoods of skunk cabbage; this "harbinger of spring" is technically the first flower of the season despite its strange appearance. Later in spring the plant grows large, bright green leaves that exude a skunky smell when crushed. The only drawback to this area is the proximity to Route 25 and the sound of traffic. Continuing through areas in various stages of succession, the trail passes the somewhat historical-looking buildings of SCOPE (Suffolk County Office for the Promotion of Education) at **23.1 miles**. At **23.2 miles** the gate leaving Caleb Smith Park is reached.

Coming out on Meadow Road, make a right and proceed up to Route 25, turning left under the train trestle to the statue of the bull (**23.4 miles**) and left again to a crossing of Route 25A just beyond at **23.5 miles**. The bull memorializes the legend of how the town was founded. As the story goes, a Richard Smith made a deal with Chief Wyandanch to purchase all the land he could ride around on the back of his bull "Whisper" in a day, thus creating the township of Smithtown. Although many historians doubt this ride ever occurred, the noble bronze five-ton local landmark has stood here since 1941.

Once across busy Route 25A, the trail passes through a wooded swamp on a thin boardwalk. These wetlands are just north of the **Nissequogue River.** Spring wildflowers abound here in this section of county land fronting the river. The golden blooms of marsh marigolds fill the wetter sections of trail. The trail rises up to drier land with some large beech and oaks overhead. There are a few places where "widowmakers" are above one's head. These are old trees leaning precariously on other trees; although the immediate situation is not as dangerous as may appear, it does make one realize that they'll eventually come down. From the higher ground one can look down on the Nissequogue to the south (right). Although the river itself is hard to see, the high phragmites (reeds) growing along the river shore give it away. A few small feeder streams are passed over on bridges in this section. At **23.8 miles** a side trail down to the river is passed.

After a few more minutes walking, you will notice that the trail is nearing the backyard boundaries of local residences; in fact I once had a large dog charge a fence, all the while barking furiously at me. Experienced Long Islander that I am, I kept moving fast without even looking at it, despite the fact that a chain link fence stood between us. The trail passes through a narrow public-access corridor and comes out onto Sommerset Drive where it turns right and proceeds a short ways down to the end of that street. Here a gate leading past a chain link fence (**24.5 miles**) allows entrance onto the Sweetbriar Farm property.

The **Sweetbriar Farm** is actually a public environmental study and nature preserve center run by the Environmental Center of Setauket-Smithtown. The 27 acres of land surrounding the farm on the south and east are owned by The Nature Conservancy, while the middle 20 acres are Sweetbriar Farm proper. The conservancy calls this preserve the **Vail Blydenburgh Sanctuary**; it has 1000 feet of frontage on the Nissequogue River on its southern border. You may choose to explore the other paths in this lovely area. The Greenbelt Trail passes through the area on wood trails with many briars alongside them. It then passes open fields with a stable in the distance on the left. This short but pleasant walk is reminiscent of what much of Long Island probably looked like in the 1800s when much of the land was cleared for farming and grazing. In fact this was once a working farm with cows, cider-making, and the works until the 1940s. It was donated to The Nature Conservancy in 1966 by Mrs. Vail Blydenburgh in memory of her husband. Passing back into the woods, the trail crosses the park access road and descends toward a small field that abuts against Landing Avenue. The shiny gray-bronze bark of sweet birch is evident alongside the trail as it descends. This tree is common in the cool moist woods of the Appalachians, growing in elevations of up to 6,000 feet in the southern part of its range. It grows here in places along the North Shore woods. It has an aromatic bark and twigs that smell like wintergreen when crushed. Its sap was once used for flavorings in candies and the making of birch beer, though this process is now done synthetically with wood alcohol and salicylic acid.

At the north end of the field the trail reaches the corner of Eckerkamp Drive and Landing Avenue at **24.9 miles**. From here the trail has its largest stretch of road-walking. The LIGTC is working to reroute the trail alongside the shore of the Nissequogue behind the housing development. But for now this piece of walking on relatively quiet suburban roads will have to do. Follow the white blazes as the trail makes a left (north) and proceeds up Landing Avenue to Landing Meadow Road (**25.0 miles**). Turn right and follow this road as it curves northward to once again meet busier Landing Avenue at **26.1 miles**. Make a right (north) until the entrance to the Smithtown Landing Golf Club is reached at **26.7 miles**. Enter the club property and follow the blazes across a parking lot back into the woods again at **27.2 miles**.

The trail now follows the course of the **Nissequogue River** until it empties into Long Island Sound. The trail enters **Arthur Kunz County Park** along this beautiful section. Several excellent viewpoints are reached where one can rest and study the view. You are likely to hear the resounding rattlelike call of the belted kingfisher along one of the open sections along the river. These long-billed greenish-blue birds have large crests on their heads and move

Nissequogue River from the trail

about their territories plucking fish from the water with seeming ease. Sailboats are moored here and there. Late afternoon is a great time to explore this fine woodland section. The trail will occasionally leave the river, reaching some glacial erratic boulders and passing a brick foundation where an old homestead once stood alongside the river. The trail makes a sharp right turn (northeast) in a small wooded swamp at **27.9 miles**. This is a place to look for spring wildflowers or observe migrating birds (especially warblers). At **28.0 miles** a woods road, an extension of Landing Road, is crossed. The trail then climbs above the riverbank before reaching the south end of Riviera Drive at **28.1 miles**. Now the trail follows the river where it widens along this road, passing a deli where you can buy refreshments at **28.6 miles**. Continuing alongside the road, it reaches St. Johnland Road at **29.2 miles**, turns right and goes a short distance before making another right and once again entering the woods. You may want to cross the road and take a short rest at pleasant little Harriman Pond Park, owned by the town of Smithtown. Also just up the road on the same side as the trail is the Obadiah Smith House, which dates back to 1700. There is a state historic marker in front of the house.

Once the trail leaves St. Johnland Road and re-enters the woods, the Nissequogue again makes its presence known. At **29.4 miles** a bench with an **excellent view** is reached. Looking east, the scene is very peaceful over wetlands towards grassy marshes in the river. The Nissequogue River is tidal; the river seems to display a variety of moods as the water runs up and then is sucked out of the river corridor in a cyclical rhythm. The water is brackish in this entire section as the freshwater that began its journey way back in McKinley Pond in Hauppauge is running into the salt water of Long Island Sound. Many marine animals and fish find this somewhat protected environment essential in their early years which makes the upper Nissequogue a nursery of sorts.

Continuing on the trail passes through the northern boundary of the Kings Park State Hospital, which is mostly in disuse at this time. Many buildings (some very large), roads, and staircases mark an area long past its heyday. The trail actually comes out to a road within the grounds and makes a right (northeast) turn (**29.7 miles**) before reaching another bench with another fine view at **30.0 miles**. From here the trail winds along the side of the hillside overlooking the river before dropping down to its sandy shore at **30.1 miles**. The trail now makes a left and heads northwest with the water on your right. This section of shore walking is a sharp contrast to the woods you've been hiking in, and in winter you'd best wear a windproof shell as the north winds can bite hard. In summer, you'll need to protect yourself from the sun. At **30.5 miles** the parking lot of the Old Dock Inn restaurant is reached.

The trail follows this parking lot up to its second (higher) level before ascending the Harbor Hill Moraine beyond. Climbing a narrow path the trail angles right and follows a route where views back over the parking lot and the river are passed. You are now in **Sunken Meadow State Park**. In a short distance you'll reach a sort of corner where the trail turns left (west) and comes to a **magnificent viewpoint** overlooking the place where the Nissequogue empties into **Long Island Sound**, at **30.9 miles**. From this vantage point you can see how the sandbars below are formed by the constant action of water currents and wind. The shores of Connecticut are visible on any reasonably clear day. To the east you can see across the wooded area of Nissequogue towards Crane Neck Point in Old Field. From this vista the trail follows along the top of bluffs that are over 100 feet above the shore below.

Eventually the trail makes a left turn away from the water. Be careful to follow the white blazes of the Greenbelt along the bluff section as there is another well-marked trail with bright yellow blazes that continues along the bluffs and a red-blazed trail in another section of the bluffs. As far as I have been able to tell these trails do not have the sanction of any authorized agency. They may even be gone by the time you are reading this, although they've been there for more than a year now. In any case the Greenbelt Trail will leave the bluffs and drop down behind them into an area protected from wind and the sound of water. The trail works its way southward, merging into an unpaved interior park road. The woods here are filled with many briars and thick ground cover, the result of a 1984 fire. If you were to follow the road you would come to the top of "Cardiac Hill," a 170-foot hill that has presented a challenge to cross-country runners for decades. The Greenbelt Trail makes a right before reaching the hill at **31.3 miles** and starts winding its way back toward the bluffs where it passes around a chain link fence at **31.4 miles**, makes a left and heads downhill along an open lane near a hill that is also part of the cross-country course called Snake Hill. Watch for white paint blazes on the paved portion of the path and at the bottom as it makes a right (north) and crosses a pond bridge. This will take you out to parking field three and the northern terminus of the Long Island Greenbelt, **31.8 miles** from Heckscher Park. There is a concession stand open across the lot in season.

It should be noted that **Sunken Meadow State Park** has some very walkable woods roads, beaches and bluffs to explore. As you become more familiar with the area you may choose to hike here at different seasons and put together loops using these paths. Of course the shores of Long Island Sound invite the walker as well, but keep in mind that a parking fee will be charged in the park during summer. The park is located at the northern end of Sunken Meadow Parkway. Make a right and proceed down to the second (last) parking lot on the left to find field three and the trail's end—or beginning.

Access

Car

This 32 mile trail cuts across Long Island north to south through Suffolk County, crossing many roads which offer possibilities for shorter hikes using two cars. To get to the north end of the trail take exit 53 from Sunken Meadow State Parkway north to its end at Sunken Meadow State Park. The trail begins south of lot #3 which is to the right of the big parking areas at the end. There is a $5.00 fee between May and October. The Southern terminus is located at the end of Heckscher Parkway in lot #8 of Heckscher State Park. Heckscher Parkway continues from the eastern end of Southern State Parkway. Other good access points are Caleb Smith State Park, Blydenburgh County Park, Lakeland County Park and Connetquot River State Park Preserve.

Trains

From the Great River Train Station on the Montauk Branch: walk south on Connetquot Avenue about .25 mile to Union Avenue. The trail crosses Union Avenue southwest to northeast at this intersection.

From the Smithtown Train Station on the Port Jefferson Branch: walk west on Main Street (Route 25 & Route 25A) about .9 mile to where Route 25A branches off to the north from Route 25 across the street from the famous statue of the bull. The trail crosses Route 25A just north of this spot.

Buses

SCT3C, 3D, 40, 42, 54, 56, 58, 62

Stump Pond Loop Trail

Length: 5.4 miles. Blaze: white, then blue

USGS topographic map: Central Islip

Stump Pond is a large L-shaped lake located within the boundaries of Blydenburgh County Park. Many people are not aware of this beautiful body of water so close to suburban neighborhoods. The pond is a great place to observe all kinds of wintering ducks. The LIGTC had long desired to have a complete loop around Stump Pond; this became a reality in 1996 when a key link was completed. The best place to start is from the Long Island Greenbelt Office located in the historic Blydenburgh-Weld House. Park in the first lot on your left once inside the park and walk ahead to the large house beyond it. A beautiful but unheralded view is seen from in front of this house. Stump Pond lies southward with little evidence of the busy world that is just beyond it.

The Long Island Greenbelt passes through this grassy area and I prefer to do this hike going to the East (left) first. Follow the white-blazed Greenbelt Trail down past an outbuilding through a small ravine where it turns right to join the wide trail along the shores of the pond at **0.1 mile**. Make a left along this picturesque section above the lake shore. Large oaks hang over the water and in winter ducks can be observed. Among the more colorful are canvasbacks, a red-headed, large goose-size duck that visits the Island from the Midwest during the winter months. Other waterfowl seen here include ruddy ducks, Canada geese, gadwalls, and American wigeon. On one visit in February, I found a huge flock of American coots all over the lake. The path turns right at **0.5 mile** and continues past some sections that can be quite wet if it has rained recently. A small stream runs under the trail as it flows into Stump Pond on the right. Look for ground pine, a low-growing evergreen member of the fern family, growing alongside the trail in places. At **1.0 mile** the trail skirts the south border of an old field in the process of becoming overgrown with red cedar and other pioneer species. At **1.3 miles** the border of the park is reached and the white blazes of the Greenbelt Trail continue straight ahead to cross Brooksite Drive. Follow the wide path to the right and pass over the northeast branch of the Nissequogue River. Here, the calm waters of the Nissequogue flow placidly underfoot in a pretty setting lined with alders and red maple. You will notice that the trail is now **blue-blazed** and will remain so until you are almost back to the Greenbelt office.

The wide woods road will turn right along the fence that borders the park and head back to the west. Watch for turn blazes that, in a short distance, will take you off the wide trail onto a much narrower path closer to the wetlands on your right. The trail will come back to meet the wide bridal path a couple of more times, each time heading onto a narrower path. There are some young white pines growing alongside the trail and it should be interesting to watch them grow tall and eventually tower over many of the surrounding trees. The trail opens up here to some excellent views, possibly the best of Stump Pond from any point around it. I enjoy having the lake pop back into view every few minutes; there is something special about hiking on dry land with a large body of water nearby. At **2.3 miles** a small footbridge is crossed over a wetland and a sharp corner or "elbow" is reached at **2.5 miles**. From here you can see a wide expanse of Stump Pond with the historic buildings across the way. The Blydenburgh-Weld House where this walk started is the one on the upper right.

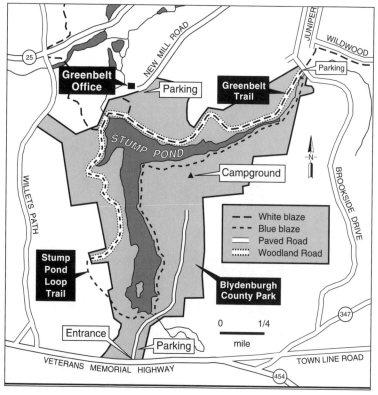

Stump Pond Loop Trail, Smithtown, NY

Cutting back to the south, the trail follows along the east shore of the lake again, reaching a boat-rental and launching area at **3.3 miles**. Farther on it makes a left, heads away from the lake to temporarily join the main wide road before heading back closer to the lake. Some large trees tower overhead here, particularly red maples and tulip trees, the latter of which are the tallest native species growing on Long Island. The furrowed bark and yellow-green tulip-like flowers are identifying marks. Pretty clusters of delicate white wood anemones grow here and there in the woods in this section in late April. At **3.5 miles** the paved park entrance road is reached. The trail follows the road where it goes over the wetland that flows into Stump Pond and leaves the road at **3.6 miles**. This is the main road into the park and can be accessed from Veterans Memorial Highway (Route 454). A campground is located in the park farther down this road.

After leaving the road follow the blue blazes behind a park building and you'll head into an area roped in with white poles to provides access to the handi-capped. Shortly beyond at **3.8 miles** you'll reach a perky running stream; it's the east branch of the Nissequogue. A wooden bridge built by the Telephone Pioneers of America Nesconset Club goes over the water. It is nice to hear rushing water underfoot in wetter seasons. Beyond this the trail passes a wet-land filled with tall reeds before going up into an old field.

Stump Pond seen from the loop trail

The trail passes behind some buildings of the county-court complex and mercifully makes a right turn onto relatively quiet Croft Lane at **4.0 miles**. At this writing the trail is scheduled to be moved off this road to a track through an Atlantic White Cedar grove. After walking the road for **0.3 mile** the trail makes a right back into the tangled woods onto a bridle path in Blydenburgh County Park. The small horse corral in a backyard on the left is a reminder that this area is popular with horse owners since they have the large park to ride in literally at their doorstep. At a junction the trail turns left (north) onto a main bridal path. It is interesting to note that there are more pitch pines mixed in on this west side of Stump Pond than in the woods dominated by hardwoods on the east side. The waters of Stump Pond can be seen through the trees on the right (east) if the leaves are down. An occasional side path is worth exploring for a closer look. The trail then goes down a slope and crosses the West Branch bridge (**4.9 miles**) over the shallow but flowing water of yet another branch of the Nissequogue feeding into Stump Pond.

The trail then meets a wide bridal path again and makes a right (north) again coming to the shores of Stump Pond with the Millers house complex visible. The blue blazes end at **5.2 miles** where the Greenbelt merges to take you up the wooden staircase to your car beyond the Blydenburgh-Weld House at **5.4 miles**. This is a good time to stop in at the LIGTC office to browse the gift shop. A last look at that great view is a fitting way to end this loop, which can be completed in two to three hours depending on how much time you stop or explore side trails.

Access

Car

The best place to start the trail is from the LIGTC office in Blydenburgh County Park. To reach the park entrance turn south off Main Street (Route 25) in Smithtown onto Edgewood Ave. Just after crossing the railroad tracks make your first right on to New Mill Road. Proceed straight into the park entrance.

Bus

SCT62

Connetquot River State Park Preserve

Length: 8.4 miles. Blazes: blue, green, red, yellow

USGS topographic map: Bay Shore East, Central Islip

This 3,473-acre park protects the slow moving Connetquot River as it makes its way southward towards Great South Bay. It has a historic past as power for a mill built by the Nichols family in 1780. That structure and a huge old house still stand along the banks of the dammed-up river. The house was originally the Snedecor Inn in the 1820s, and was a stop for stagecoaches on the South Shore route. Later in the century the land became the Southside Sportsmen's Club, a refuge for public figures and wealthy businessmen including names like Belmont, Vanderbilt, Whitney, and Tiffany. Politicians also enjoyed the natural beauty and outdoors activities here, including President Ulysses Grant, Daniel Webster, and Henry Clay.

Today the land is part of the state park system and a preserve for activities such as fly fishing, hiking, nature observation and horseback riding. A look at a street atlas of the area will show the preserve has housing developments to the west and east. It has a large herd of white-tail deer and a flock of wild turkeys. Other than a tame herd in nearby Heckscher State Park there are no deer or turkeys until you get several miles farther east. The main entrance is a parking lot off Route 27 (Sunrise Highway) in Oakdale about a mile and a half east of the Heckscher Parkway exit 45, which is actually the southern spur of Southern State Parkway. Another access point is a pull-off on Route 454 (Veterans Memorial Highway), which cuts across the property at its northern tip. There is a gate on the south side of the road just east of Connetquot Avenue where the road goes over a small stream that, at this point, is the Connetquot River.

The Long Island Greenbelt Trail with its white blazes cuts through the park north to south and is described in its own section. Four color-blazed trails also loop around sections of the park. They are fully described on a map available free at the park entrance off Route 27, where a parking fee of $5 is charged in the warm season. The trails are as follows, **Blue Trail (8.4 miles loop), Green Trail (3.9 miles one way), Red Trail (3.7 miles loop) and Yellow**

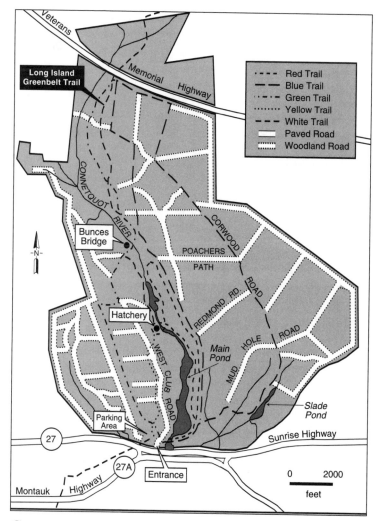

Connetquot River State Park Preserve, Oakdale, NY

Trail (1.0 mile one way). I found them to be inconsistently marked with colored arrows on trees at junctions. They were marked more in the clockwise direction than the other, and I had to pay close attention to the map at intersections. The preserve is crossed by several wide woods roads and fire lanes. Some of the trails are on these sandy fire roads, where use is shared with horseback riders. Although these lanes are wide and clear, they are quite soft from the horse use, and for some not easy to walk on. To be sure, there are some interesting things for hikers to see, especially those who are not too experienced. The deer in the interior sections are not as tame as the pets found by the main parking lot but are not nearly as jittery as wilder deer found out east, so you can observe them feeding in clearings if you keep your distance. There is always the chance of spotting a flock of wild turkeys running through the woods. Wild migratory ducks can be observed in winter. Check out the more secluded Slade Pond located in the southeastern portion of the property off the Blue Trail. The fish hatchery is a fascinating place to observe trout in various stages of development, but on the Green Trail off the north side of Bunces Bridge on a sunny afternoon in the off season you may spot some fat veteran trout swaying in the currents of the **Connetquot River** (the Long Island Greenbelt also crosses here). The preserve is also a great place to cross-country ski, with wide paths and flat terrain that can take you away from the busy entrance off Route 27 into more quiet woodlands.

The **Red Trail**, 3.7 miles long, offers the most interesting family hike. It avoids the wide sandy woods roads, and for most of its length horses are forbidden. You walk on comfortable wood chips and stay closer to the water where plants and birds are more abundant. In late April and early May there is a profusion of wood anemones, violets, and marsh marigolds. You may take an optional side loop through the fish hatchery. The **Blue Trail**, 8½ miles long, offers the most exercise. This long trail seems particularly intended for horses; it keeps to wide soft sandy roads, and the blazes are far apart and high on trees at eye level for a rider. It stays in the dryer parts of the park, where vegetation is less interesting and there are not so many birds. It heads northward along the east side of **Main Pond** on wide roads up to the northern edge of the park until turning right (east) near Route 454, where it will eventually head south, traversing the eastern side of the property. In the northeastern section there is an old burn reminiscent of the Oak Brush Plains that once covered western Suffolk County. It is particularly striking in its own way when seen late in the afternoon on a clear winter day. The trail then goes south on Cordwood Road, a wide fire road graced by tall pitch pines, passes **Slade Pond**, and crosses three brooks that feed the Connetquot before merging with the Red Trail and returning to the main parking lot. Since the Blue Trail is wide, unobstructed and flat, it is excellent for cross country skiing. The **Green Trail** is similar to the Blue Trail in length and appearance, except it traverses the park's west side, crosses the river at **Bunces Bridge**, and heads north, ending at a junction with the Blue Trail which returns you through the center of the preserve. The **Yellow Trail** is a simple one-way access trail to the hatchery. For more information call the park office at (631) 581-1005.

Access

Car

The entrance to the preserve is on the north side of Sunrise Highway (Route 27) about 1.4 miles east of Southern State Parkway exit 44. Note that you can only enter the preserve going westbound since Route 27 is a divided highway.

Buses

SCT40, 54

The Connetquot River as it runs through the middle of the preserve

Fire Island National Seashore

Length: 7 miles of unmarked beach

USGS topographic maps: Pattersquash Island, Howells Point

A group of barrier beaches not connected to the mainland runs most of the length of Long Island's South Shore. They are really large masses of shifting sand constantly shaped by storms and tides. They act as buffers for the mainland in storms and contain some of Long Island's world-famous sandy beaches. For the hiker they offer an opportunity to walk in relative solitude along the place where earth meets sea. The plants and animals that have adapted to this barrier beach existence are hardy indeed. Some are year round residents and some transients from afar. Most keep out of sight and are rarely seen. The barrier beaches offer a look at life between dune and swale, forest and thicket, ocean and bay, compacted into an area over a hundred miles long and averaging less than a half mile wide.

Within this ever-changing elongated land mass is New York's only designated Federal Wilderness area. One can hike over its 20 miles of beach bordering the thundering Atlantic, explore life in the dune-lands and see an ancient forest. There is even a primitive camping area for those willing to brave poison ivy and ticks. At night, the sky is so clear the milky way reaches down to the horizon. This can soothe and relax the mind and the body. The ocean calms the senses; the rhythms of the earth are more obvious here. Being aware of the native wildlife heightens interest and enjoyment. The seasons each offer something different to the walker. Spring brings the migration of birds northward and the blossoming of showy plants such as beach plum and shadbush. Wind is an almost constant presence along the barrier beaches. It is helpful in summer when the sweltering sands heat up to dehydrate hikers who walk long distances here. Of course, in summer you are most likely to run into others along the beach.

Make sure to protect yourself from the sun's rays reflecting off the water and sand. The constant wind magnifies the hazard to your skin all the more. A few year round precautions are in order. Sunblock, sunglasses, a hat, lip balm and possibly facial cream will make your hike safe and enjoyable. Boots or sneakers are recommended; walking in bare feet or even sandals can leave the sensitive skin on your feet exposed to severe burn. Water or liquids should be carried as well. Probably the best time of year to hike the beach is autumn, when it is still warm but the extreme summer sun is gone. The migration of birds that begins in August with the arrival of wading birds such as sandpipers, curlews, and godwits peaks this time of year; warblers and countless other songbirds move along the barrier beaches in their long journeys south. This is also a good time to backpack for those inclined to experience a true sense of solitude. In late autumn the infamous nor'easters rake the coast with

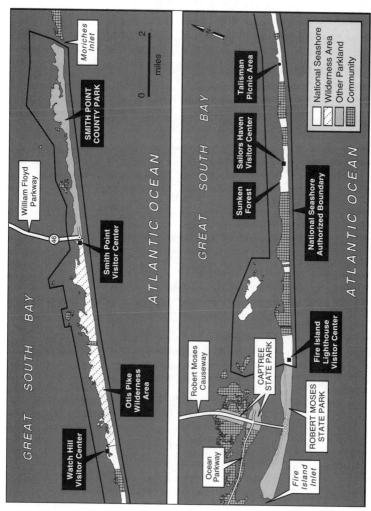

Fire Island National Seashore

high winds and rough surf. In winter northern birds such as the snowy owl, snow bunting, Lapland longspur, gyrfalcon, and crossbills visit the barrier islands. A pair of binoculars and appropriate layers of clothing, especially a windshell, are essential.

A good place to start a hike is from Smith Point Park at the southern base of the William Floyd Parkway. There is a small visitor center run by the National Park Service on the west side of the traffic circle. The parking area is on the east side. A fee for parking is required. From the visitor center pick up a map and check out what displays they have on at the time. You will undoubtedly see the boardwalk that goes off to the west. It is a fine way to get acclimated to the barrier beach environment. A brochure from the visitor center will guide you and explain life between the dunes. The real way to see the National Seashore in its splendor is to walk the beach heading west or continue on the boardwalk for a while and pick up the beach on the south side on a boardwalk path that leads to it. Either way, there will be nothing in front of you except sea, beach and dune for the next seven miles until you reach the Watch Hill Visitor Center. Beyond that the small communities of Fire Island begin. If you are interested in backpacking out and camping under the stars you must pick up a permit from the Smith Point Visitor Center (631-281-3010), where they will fill you in on the details of where to camp and what you need to pack in.

A good place to view the surrounding terrain is from a wooden boardwalk that goes northward to the bay. The first high dune this crosses is a fine place to stop and have lunch. From here you can see Great South Bay and pick out some distinguishing features on Long Island and beyond. The short radio tower to the north is located near Wertheim National Wildlife Refuge. This is where the Carmans River empties into the bay. Farther in the distance to the north is the tall communications tower with flashing white lights in Ridge located just north of Route 25 about 10 miles off. Looking to the west, Patchogue can be located by large docks along the water. A pair of binoculars will help in picking out the Vietnam Veterans Memorial high on Bald Hill in Farmingville. A glance to the east or west reveals the barrier beach stretching out in either direction. Here and there a high dune crops up. The great expanse of the Atlantic lies to the south. If you follow the wooden trail to the bay side, you can get a feel for what the interdunal terrain is like. Beware of the mosquitoes that proliferate here a good portion of the year. On one hike with my family in mid-October, there was no sign of the biting pests as we had lunch on a breezy day with temperatures in the low sixties. The night had been chilly enough to have a light frost, yet when we descended into the middle of the barrier beach we were beset by them. It is amazing how much shelter from the wind the primary dunes offer; this makes the temperature warmer and gives mosquitoes protection from the elements. Unless you are an experienced hiker who knows how to protect yourself from ticks, stay on the sandy trails or boardwalks in the interior of the island. Poison ivy is also prevalent here. One might get a glimpse of a white-tail deer if lucky.

There are many other points of interest for the walker to explore in this South Shore area. The Sunken Forest located at Sailors Haven to the west is a truly fascinating place. Here, within the shelter of the dunes lies an ancient forest of American holly trees with a few sassafras mixed in. The canopy of the trees grows only as high as the primary dunes since the winds and salty air keep them from growing any higher. The understory is surprisingly cool in the shade of the trees. To the west, the Fire Island Lighthouse alerts sailors to the hazards of sand bars and the beach. The lighthouse was originally built near the western end of the barrier island, but the shifting sands have extended the land four miles westward, evidence that the barrier islands are constantly being changed by the forces of nature.

It should also be noted that one can hike westward from the Smith Point parking lot about five miles through Smith Point County Park to the rough water of Moriches Inlet. Four-wheel-drive vehicles are likely to be encountered here. Across the bay to the north lies the William Floyd Estate. This little-known site was the homestead of William Floyd, Long Island's only signer of the Declaration of Independence. It is well worth the visit when open in the warm season. The grounds are vast and front Moriches Bay. Information can be found in a brochure on Fire Island put out by the National Park Service.

Access

Car

From the LIE take exit 68 to William Floyd Parkway (County Route 46) south to its end at Smith Point County Park. There is a fee ($3.00 at my last visit) in season to park in the lot.

Buses

SCT7E, 74 (summer only)

Hiking the open expanse of the ocean barrier beach

The Pine Barrens and Central-Eastern Suffolk County

The Pine Barrens
Pine Barrens Information Center and Wampmissick Trail
Paumanok Path: Pine Barrens Trail Section
Rocky Point Natural Resources Management Area
Cathedral Pines County Park and Prosser Pines Preserve
Warbler Woods
Randall Pond Preserve
Wertheim National Wildlife Refuge
Southaven County Park
William Floyd Estate
Brookhaven State Park and the Brookhaven Trail
Robert Cushman Murphy County Park and the Coastal Plain Ponds
Navy Co-op Pond Walk
Wildwood State Park
Terrell County Park
Otis Pike Preserve
Manorville Hills
The Summit and Hampton Hills
Dwarf Pines and Westhampton Burn Area
David A. Sarnoff Pine Barrens Preserve
Peconic River County Park
Cranberry Bog County Nature Preserve
Sears-Bellows County Park
Hubbard County Park
Red Creek Trails
Quogue Wildlife Refuge

The Pine Barrens

In central and eastern Suffolk County the region called the Pine Barrens is dominated by various species of oak trees and the tree scientifically named *Pinus rigida*, known to most of us as the **Pitch Pine**. This evergreen sometimes resembles a giant bonsai in its twisted and contorted form on exposed hilltops, but it can be straight and proud when growing out of the bottom of a sheltered hollow or kettlehole. Thought to have a limited value commercially, it was bulldozed in large numbers during the postwar housing boom, destroying about three quarters of what was once 250,000 acres of pine barrens. The Pine Barrens' sandy, nutrient-poor soil holds little moisture on the surface, making agriculture difficult. The acidic soil slows decomposition and allows pine needles and leaf litter to accumulate within a few years. Periodic fires that "clean" the barrens are a part of this ecosystem; they keep invading species out and lay the foundation for pine and oak to sprout like a phoenix from the ashes and begin a forest anew. It's no wonder that early settlers called them

"barrens," even though they have a haunting beauty that is not easy to catch in words or pictures. I am one of those who once thought of the Pine Barrens as monotonous or lacking the green variety of the mountains of the Northeast. I am now a believer. In the Pine Barrens the walker can still find deep solitude. It is not wilderness like the remote sections of our northeastern mountains; the spectacular and grandiose are not found here. Yet they have a subtle beauty that grows on you the more time you spend in these primeval woods.

For starters, they are anything but barren. The large tracts of the central Pine Barrens preserved from development by

The pitch pine, the fragrant tree that grows throughout the Pine Barrens

the Pine Barrens Protection Act still harbor many surprises for those willing to keep an eye out for them.

The most important but hidden resource of the Pine Barrens is the tremendous amount of pure clean water contained in the **aquifers** that lie beneath its surface. The porous soils scoured and overlaid by the last receding glaciers act as a giant natural filter removing impurities and sediment from the rainwater that percolates through it. Some water in the upper aquifers may take only a few years to reach there. This water is obviously most threatened by pollution. Water in the pure untapped lower aquifers takes thousands of years to reach its destination and is undoubtedly some of the purest water found anywhere in the country. It is estimated there are trillions of gallons stored beneath the Pine Barrens that can be preserved best by just leaving the forest alone. The need to protect this resource may prove to be the best reason to save Long Island's last large wild undeveloped area.

In the Pine Barrens I first became involved in the exploration and blazing of the Paumanok Path. I spent many days with other trail builders in the large tracts of undeveloped and somewhat unknown lands of the Manorville Hills. We developed a good-natured and humorous way of naming some of the region's more significant features; it became our "Pine Barrens nomencla-

Thin ice on Woodchoppers Pond in the Pine Barrens

ture." We gave many glacial erratics, hollows, hills and other features names that I will refer to.

Classified as the **Northern Pine-Oak Forest**, the Pine Barrens are a unique ecosystem. They run along the coastal plain from southern New Jersey through Long Island and up into coastal Massachusetts at Cape Cod. They are also found in smaller scattered locations away from the coast in several northeastern states, most notably in the Albany Pine Bush northwest of the state capitol, and on the Shawangunk escarpment on the west side of the Hudson Valley. They are found nowhere else on earth. The acidic porous soils lacking nutrients and swept by periodic fire create conditions to which plants (and animals, to a lesser extent) have been forced to adapt, creating rare species with specialized needs.

Fire is crucial to the continuance of this novel ecosystem; its plants have developed special characteristics not only to survive fire but to make use of it to aid their growth. Some plants, like sweet fern, bayberry, and pitch pine, even encourage the burning of fires with their combustible strong aromatic oils. It has been said that up to 90 percent of the energy in the dominant pine barrens plants is underground in the root systems. The plated bark on pitch pines is a form of protection from all but the hottest fires. Some species of pine cones actually need the heat of a fire to open them so they can germinate. Oaks, especially the scrub oak, are amazingly adept at springing back after a fire. Even the ashes left after the fire provide a layer of nutrients to be released back into the soil to promote quick growth.

To watch for these fires a system of fire towers was set up on Long Island (as well as the rest of the state). They were manned by forest rangers who with maps and compasses located the fire as soon as possible. As many as ten towers were built on Long Island but only six were state run at any one time. These were located at Brentwood, Kings Park (near present day Sunken Meadow Park), Telescope Hill (near Bald Hill in Farmingville), Upton (present-day Brookhaven Lab), Flanders (atop Flanders Hill) and Stony Hill (north of Amagansett). Other towers were located in Connetquot and West Hills. The towers are all gone now, their heyday in the 1940s and 1950s a forgotten but interesting part of our history.

The several different forest communities in the Pine Barrens are classified according to the ratio of pitch pines to oaks found within a specific area. Observant hikers will find the forest type does change markedly during a hike. You can be walking through a classic pitch pine forest under the shady canopy of fragrant evergreens only to pass into an open area dominated by impenetrable thickets of scrub oak, and then find yourself back in an open forest of taller oaks with few or no pines and either grasses or bracken fern growing in the understory.

The ground cover in the Pine Barrens is dominated by a family of plants known as **heaths**. These plants prefer the dry acidic soil of the barrens and can be evergreen or deciduous. They are sometimes fragrant and some even thrive in the moist conditions found in the wetlands scattered through the area. The most common are the blueberries (both short and highbush); their close cousins are the huckleberries. Be sure to sample them from mid-July through August as they are small but sweet and one of those treats that are still free! You'll see such familiar Pine Barrens plants as wintergreen (including striped), trailing arbutus, bayberry, staggerbush, maleberry, bearberry and sweetfern, along with the showier sheep laurel and swamp azalea. Other plants, such as goat's-rue, several species of violets (including the showy and rare birdfoot violet), hudsonia (known as heather), several species of orchids, cow-wheat, wild indigo, wild lupine, frostweed, blue curls; sickle-leafed, stiff and Maryland golden aster are also common. Throw in the interesting assorted species of sedges, lichens, and ferns and you start to get an idea of how un-barren these Pine Barrens really are!

A great variety of wildlife calls the Pine Barrens home. The most visible and noisy are the many species of birds that breed here. The New York State bird, the eastern bluebird, thrives in the burnt and open areas in the barrens. Once common, it has been pushed away from farmhouses and orchards by the introduced and aggressive house sparrow and starling. Those birds evict the bluebirds from the tree cavities they like to nest in. In more wooded areas of the barrens with large clearings, particularly burn areas, one can spot this most attractive of birds. You haven't seen deep blue until you have seen a male bluebird in sunlight in early spring. Nest boxes put up by wildlife and birding clubs have helped this bird stage its comeback. I have seen eastern bluebirds at all times of the year in the open burn areas just north of Whiskey Road, where the great fires of 1995 opened the woods up.

Other birds found within the pines are the scarlet tanager, northern oriole, great crested flycatcher, white-breasted nuthatch, eastern wood peewee, black-capped chickadee, tufted titmouse, brown creeper, several species of woodpecker, ruby-throated hummingbird, yellow-billed and black-billed cuckoo, brown thrasher, goldfinch, and several species of warbler including black and white, pine, prairie, blue-winged, ovenbird and American redstart. In summer, rufous-sided towhees seem everywhere, scratching the forest floor calling their familiar "towee-towee" when other birds have ceased singing.

Their trademark song of "drink-your-tea" is a familiar sound throughout the Pine Barrens in spring and early summer. There are also many species of hawks inhabiting the pines, but perhaps no other bird exemplifies the wildness of the Pine Barrens like the whip-poor-will that unceasingly sings at night. The deep hooting of the great horned owl also fills the night air. Lastly, the hermit thrush, with its haunting, mystical song, breeds in secluded places in the pines, which is unusual since the only place farther south where this bird breeds is in the higher elevations of the Appalachian Mountains.

Many other species of wildlife are found in the Pine Barrens. Colorful butterflies dart along the woods roads in spring and summer. You might see anything from the exquisitely colored spring azure on those early clear spring days to duskywings, skippers and swallowtails all summer, just to name a few. The white-tail deer and red fox are common. There are also eleven species of snakes in the barrens, though they're in decline in most other places on Long Island. Other rarely seen animals include the muskrat, pine vole, salamander, tree frogs, southern flying squirrel and several species of bats.

The Pine Barrens have a special effect on a walker seeking solitude and an opportunity to refresh the soul. Sure, surprises await, but they are rare and fleeting. The therapy of the pines is more intangible and subtle, different from the overwhelming sensation experienced above tree-line on an Adirondack peak. Both feelings are unique; both are to be treasured. Lawrence Paul, whose out-of-print work, "*The Pine Barrens of Ronkonkoma*" inspired me and countless others to explore this special area, wrote, " The hills, rising to 300 feet, afford magnificent panoramas extending to 20 or more miles. The prospect of gnarled and grotesque pines reaching in thousands to the four horizons is at once so wild and so melancholy as to approach the sublime."

Pine Barrens Information Center and Wampmissick Trail

Length: 0.62 mile. Wheelchair accessible. Blaze: white

USGS topographic maps: Wading River, Moriches

Located just 0.2 mile north of exit 70 of the LIE on the County Road 111 extension is the Pine Barrens Information Center. This is a good place to stop on your way east to get maps, information, or day permits for some of the public lands. The Center has a large wall map of the Paumanok Path and photographs of other public nature trails on Long Island. There is also a hands-on display for youngsters featuring many natural objects found in the Pine Barrens. Behind the information center is a short 0.62 mile loop known as the Wampmissick Trail. It gets its name from the Indian word for blueberry, the common shrub of the understory throughout the Pine Barrens. The LIGTC usually has a "blueberry hike" during the summer to pick ripe blueberries and huckleberries and bake the berries that make it back into pies for the hikers. The trail is a good introductory hike in the Pine Barrens and a way for adults

The Pine Barrens Trail Information Center

and kids alike to stretch their legs before continuing east. Behind the trail center you can pick up the white blazes that lead away from the building and turn right at **0.21 mile**. You are now on a track bed abandoned by the old railroad through Manorville to Eastport on the South Shore. Close inspection of the trail side may reveal leftover cinders, and hikers will notice the track embankment. Curious explorers can walk the railroad grade on the other side of the LIE just south of the service road where the exit 70 eastbound ramp is located. A Suffolk County parklands sign here designates the track bed as a public right of way. In a short distance (**0.27 mile**) the trail will make a left. Typical dry Pine Barrens plants like sweet fern, bracken fern and wintergreen grow along the trail as well as mushrooms in summer and fall. The trail loops and rejoins the railroad bed at **0.48 mile**. Make a right and then a left to return to the information center completing the loop in **0.62 mile**. A yellow-blazed connector trail leaves the Wampmissick Trail and heads through typical pine barrens woodlands to Mill Road in about 0.4 mile. The Paumanok Path can be picked up where it comes out to the road at that point.

Access

Car

Take LIE exit 70 north about 0.1 mile; the Center will be on the right side just past the church. Hours are 9:00 a.m. to 5 p.m. Friday through Monday from Memorial Day through Columbus Day. Call ahead to (631) 369-9768.

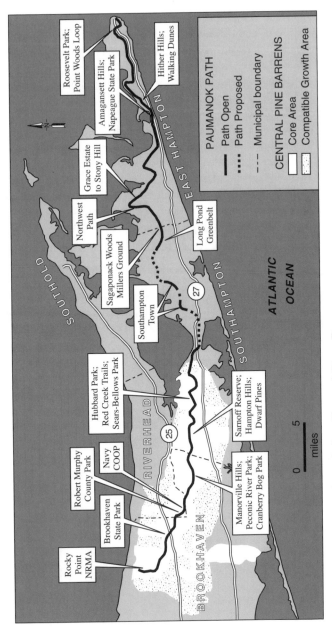

The Paumanouk Path and the Central Pine Barrens

Paumanok Path: Pine Barrens Trail Section

Length: 46.77 miles. Blaze: white

USGS topographic maps: Middle Island, Wading River, Moriches, Riverhead, Eastport, Mattituck, Quogue

The word Paumanok meant eastern Long Island in the tongue of the Algonquins, and was used by Walt Whitman in his poem on Long Island. Paumanok Path, the premier hiking trail on Long Island, begins on the North Shore, in Rocky Point, running southwest away from the Harbor Hill Moraine and through the coastal plain in the Rocky Point Natural Resources Management Area (also known as the Co-op). It then goes through the old Route 111 corridor in Ridge. Passing the Pine Trail Nature Preserve south of Route 25 it enters Robert Cushman Murphy Park and an area of coastal plain ponds. In Manorville it passes close to the Peconic River and some dry burn areas before entering the Manorville Hills south of the LIE in the heart of the Pine Barrens. From these morainal hills it passes into Hampton Hills and near Wildwood Lake before traveling through the dry hilly terrain of the state-owned David A. Sarnoff Pine Barrens Preserve. East of here, amid pine barrens, the trail passes Maple Swamp and then Owl Pond. Beyond this, beautiful Sears Pond is approached before reaching the edge of the vast salt marshes in Flanders' Hubbard County Park. The trail then goes through Red Creek Park and takes a road route to the Shinnecock Canal. In all, it covers almost 50 miles. There are still reroutes going on within this blazed section as new land is acquired. Although the Paumanok Path was originally conceived as the Pine Barrens Greenbelt by the LIGTC, new plans would extend it through Southampton and East Hampton townships on the South Fork to form a 145-mile trail all the way to Montauk Point.

The trail can be accessed from one of the many roads it passes and I leave it up to the individual to choose a hike that suits the desires of the particular group doing the walk. No primitive backpack camping is allowed along the trail but a few county parks do allow camping adjacent to the trail. A permit is required to hike on the Rocky Point and Otis Pike Preserve (former Navy Co-op lands) in Manorville. Call the DEC at (631) 444-0273 for an application or write them at NYS DEC Fish and Wildlife Division, Bldg. 40, SUNY Stony Brook 11790-2356. The permit is free and good for three years.

The northern end of the trail begins in a state-owned parking lot on the south side of State Route 25A in Rocky Point, across the street from a Burger King 0.4 of a mile west of Rocky Point Road. This is the north border of the large 6,150-acre parcel of state-owned land known as the **Rocky Point Natural Resources Management Area**. The tract lies within the borders of the towns of Rocky Point, Middle Island, and Ridge, and is commonly called the "Rocky Point Co-op" since it is used by hikers, hunters, mountain bikers, horseback riders, naturalists, joggers and even occasionally by fox hunters.

The area was owned by the Radio Corporation of America (RCA), which in the early 1920s built tall transmission towers and antenna fields for international wireless communication. When new technology made the towers obsolete, the land became idle, and was sold to the state in 1978 for $1. The Department of Environmental Conservation currently manages the area and there are regular patrols by state forest rangers.

The main buildings on the property were removed in the early 1990s and all that is left of them is grassy clearings. Armed with a compass, trail map, and a Middle Island topographic map you can spend many full days exploring the area. Those who are watchful will spot the large cement footings that once supported towers that dominated the horizon. They are usually in groups of four and one might even come across part of a tower, although most of them have long since been removed from the property. The occasional transmission pole or other remnant can be seen here and there. The land is predominantly dry as the few wetlands are small and located in little-used pockets. Rocky Point Road cuts through the area roughly north to south with most of the land, about 3460 acres, located on the eastern side of the road. Whiskey Road cuts across the southern portion of the property in an east-to-west direction. My favorite times to ramble around in this area are late spring, when wildflowers such as birdfoot violet and goats-rue abound along the sides of the woods roads, and September-October when asters and golden-rods fill the grasslands. In winter cross-country skiing is permitted.

Plants and wildlife in the area were transformed by the great fires of August, 1995 which made national news. Coming during a long dry spell, the fire began on Monday, August 21, 1995 somewhere on the east side of Rocky Point Road, about 2 miles north of Whiskey Road. The cause is still unknown, but driven by a strong dry northwesterly wind it quickly became unmanageable, spreading south of Whiskey Road and consuming almost 2,000 acres over several days. New sunlight after such wildfires promotes plant life suppressed by dense tree cover, providing increased food for animals and unusual flowers for visitors. Over the coming years the area will change as new plants and trees take over and continue the process of succession.

Today, the walker can explore any section of the land on about 75 miles of woods roads and 20 miles of firebreaks built to service and protect the RCA operations. Some of the firebreaks are more than a hundred feet wide, creating a diversity of habitats and edges for wildlife and plants.

From the parking area follow the **white blazes** out to the left (east side) and proceed south a few hundred feet on the old paved road that accessed the building once standing on this portion of the property. Following the white blazes on the pavement and the **blue-NY State disks** you will turn to the right at the first junction and go westward into the woods. If you were to proceed straight, southward, instead of turning right here, you would be on the red-blazed trail. Following the **white blazed** trail into the thickets you pass through an area where I have frequently startled white-tail deer bedded down during the day. This is a no hunting zone, being close to Route 25A, and the deer seem to know it since they frequent this area. The trail reaches **Sitting Rock**, a large glacial erratic, at **0.32 mile** and the woods open up into rolling terrain along the southern fringe of the Harbor Hill Moraine. At **0.62 mile** the junction with the yellow-blazed trail is reached. On my last visit here the sign post was down but the trail is nonetheless evident. Heading south (left) this side trail passes a lookout and links the blue trail with the red trail in about **1.2 miles**. It can be used as part of a 2.5 mile loop to return to the parking area on Route 25A via the red trail. I did this loop with my family in mid-July during a hot spell. We did it late in the day and picked blueberries and huckleberries all along the route. This loop is a good one for young children since it can be covered in a little more than an hour at an easy pace.

The trail continues slightly uphill from here before crossing a woods road. There is a quaint hollow down to the right (north) of here that belies its proximity to Route 25A. There is also a horse trail that goes through this area. At **0.81 mile** the trail returns to a short stretch of woods before crossing a firebreak that has become overgrown in the middle, leaving a wooded path on each side. Once back in the woods the trail angles downhill past some large anthills. Look for dirt mounds on the side of the trail. Yellow-shafted flickers, a large woodpecker, like to come to these anthills to feast by lapping the ants up with long, specialized tongues. Beyond this the trail traverses a dry upland stretch of oak-dominated woods. On clear winter days you have the impression of being in a forest far from civilization. At about **1.75 miles** you will drop into a dry **kettlehole**. Any water has long since dried up in this one since it now houses fairly large trees, most notably bigtooth aspens. This is one of eleven kettles in the vicinity that form what geologists call a **kettlehole**

valley. They are all located in the outwash plain that drained the Harbor Hill Moraine. This kettle is shallow compared to some of the others and it is also the southernmost of the group. If you want to investigate them closely, you must get off the trail. The best time to do this is when the leaves are down so local visibility is better. The USGS topographic map for Middle Island is helpful for finding them. They vary in size and depth, but all are dry. Probably the most dramatic is the **Crater** located just to the west and slightly north of this kettle. Lying on the western border of the state property, it is just west of a firebreak near a new development off Radio Avenue in Miller Place. Probably because of its steep slopes it was spared the bulldozer. It sinks 80 feet below the surrounding terrain, making it the third-deepest kettle on Long Island. Standing in it is like standing in a tree-filled crater.

Beyond the kettle, a jeep road with a horse trail is crossed as the trail now follows a fairly straight overgrown woods path before eventually coming out to some clearings alternating with wood lots. You may notice that many pitch pines are dead in some sections. This is due to an insect pest that attacked the trees in the early 1990s, killing them in large numbers. Like most natural problems it played itself out without any human intervention. A little farther on the trail passes one of several man-made clearings in the park. This one is on the right (south) side. Nesting boxes are put up to encourage birds to take up residence. Tree swallows are most common but house wrens and even eastern bluebirds can be found in these boxes. In June the swallows put on a show as they swoop and dive while moving fast on the wing after flying insects to feed themselves and their young. In these spots the DEC also plants crops, such as sorghum, that provide food for birds like the bobwhite quail and ring-necked pheasants; the crops also give cover for rabbits and deer. These feed-lots create a diversity of wildlife greater than if the property were all woods.

After several turns the trail reaches a woods road at **3.33 miles**. Here another short **yellow-blazed side trail** leads to the right (southeast) in about 0.1 mile to an access point with parking on Rocky Point Road. This access point is located just north of the main parking area used by mountain bikers. Hikers can also use the lot for easy access to the Paumanok Path by walking north and picking up the yellow access trail to the main trail. The blue-blazed trail continues straight across this access road reaching Rocky Point Road **3.51 miles** from the start on Route 25A.

Use caution when crossing Rocky Point Road; cars move at highway speeds here. Once on the east side you will shortly enter a section burned by the great fires of 1995. For the first two years after the fires, blue toadflax flourished. The blue-tinged stalks of this flower are usually not too obvious but they grew in such profusion in the re-opened forest floor that they formed attractive stands that caught the eye. Now that they have declined, scrub oak and staggerbush have taken over the area. The staggerbush are full of white bell-shaped flowers in mid-June; they resemble those of blueberries, but are much more numerous. These plants turn crimson red at the end of October. As the forest grows back these shrubs will yield to the taller trees taking most of the sunshine from the plants in the understory. At about **3.7 miles** the trail makes a right to head in a more southerly direction into an area of woods that didn't burn as hot as the section you just left. Many of the taller trees have leaves despite their charred trunks. After crossing a jeep road at about **4.0 miles**, the trail passes into the woods once more, reaching another dirt road at about **4.4 miles**. In late spring or early summer you are likely to hear the rich whistle of the colorful northern oriole from the treetops or catch a glimpse of tawny brown flash into a thicket as a brown thrasher seeks cover. The noisy great crested flycatcher is often heard in these wooded sections as well as the raucous blue jays in their gregarious flocks.

In a little while you will start to see signs of the fire again and then many trees downed by the brush trucks that battled the blaze. Shortly thereafter at **5.0 miles** the sign designating the junction of the **red-blazed trail** is reached. The state blue-blazed trail terminates here and the white blazes of the Paumanok Path will now follow the red trail southward (right). I usually hear the plaintive song of the hermit thrush in this area in June and July. The trail now goes through burn areas into a hollow before coming out to the parking lot on Whiskey Road at **5.4 miles**. This dirt lot is a good location to plan a loop hike in the area or to leave a second car for an end-to-end hike.

South of Whiskey Road the Paumanok Path follows a **yellow-blazed trail** through the woods and past an access road created after the fire jumped the road to continue burning southward. Just beyond this you cross another fire-break which allows good access for exploration of the southern portion of the state property. Soon an area cleared by an earlier fire in the 1980s is reached. Keep an eye out for birds of prey, particularly red-tailed hawks, surveying the open terrain for rodents and other small mammals. They will likely take off at first sight of you. You may also see the bright yellow goldfinch in this burn area. On the far side of the burn a woods road with a power line running along it is reached (**5.8 miles**). This marks the boundary of the state land and the end of the yellow disks.

The trail now enters a county-owned corridor that was scheduled to become an extension of County Route 111 but is now part of the Pine Trail Preserve. It's a green belt of land that passes through the hamlet of Ridge for several miles. After going through a narrow stretch of woods you'll reach the wide, sandy extension of Wading River Hollow Road at **5.87 miles**. This was likely once the road that connected Wading River with Middle Island, and this unpaved section acts as a firebreak or access road. Beyond here the trail passes through the woods and past a small kettle on the left (north). It then enters a clearing that has subtle signs that a homestead once stood here. You may notice a thorny non-native shrub called barberry that was often planted by settlers for its fruit. In a short distance farther on the trail will cross an unmarked path. This path can be taken to the south (right) into the most recent addition to the state landholdings, part of the old Baier Lustgarten Nursery property. This area is described in more detail in the section on the Rocky Point Natural Resources Management Area. A loop trail may begin here in the future. A little farther on the trail reaches Wood Lot Road at **6.16 miles**. There is room to park one or two cars along the road at this point. On the east side of the road the trail passes through an area that had a minor fire a few years back. Alert hikers will see blackened tree trunks and fresher vegetation growing on the ground. One common pine barrens plant that thrives after light fires is sweet fern. Its name comes from the leaves, which resemble fern fronds, but it is not a fern at all; it is a heath closely related to bayberry. Crush a leaf and you will smell a strong fragrance; the aromatic resins given off by the plant "sweeten" the air on hot stifling summer days. Many pine barrens plants exude similar fragrances, containing volatile oils that actually promote fires! A fine tea can be made from the leaves of sweet fern. A comparison can be made to the bracken fern, by far the most common true fern growing in the Pine Barrens. It branches into three large leaves and can grow up to three feet tall. This fern often starts to turn brown as early as late July if we get a cold night or two.

At **6.27 miles** the trail passes through a cut in an old boundary trench line, dug long ago to mark property, before reaching Raynor Road at **6.39 miles**. Cars could be parked a short ways up the block if necessary.

On the east side of Raynor Road the trail passes through the private land of a plant nursery, so please stay on the trail and respect landowner rights. You are likely to hear a nearby dog barking, but in all of my many trips here I have never seen it. On the east side of the nursery border you'll cross an old wide dirt road lined with very large hickory trees. A pause here during early morning or late day from late April through June will usually reveal a lot of bird activity in the trees. The birds are here because the area is a transitional zone between the open nursery land and the second-growth thickets bordering it on the east. Prairie warblers and goldfinches are found on the open nursery side, with blue-winged warblers, tufted titmouses and woodpeckers in the second-growth woods. After passing through low-growing Russian olive trees and overgrown eastern red cedars you'll reach Ridge Road **6.74 miles** from the start. Parking is not available since the road is narrow along here.

The trail enters a narrow section for a short distance on the

Charred tree trunks contrast with the foliage of the woods

other side of the road. Watch for horseback riders along here; in fact, the entire stretch of trail from Whiskey Road to William Floyd Parkway is used by horses since it is the only corridor connecting them. Continuing eastward you'll notice the border of the Ridge School on the south side (right) through the trees. The Randall Pond Preserve is directly south of the school property, but a connecting trail has a locked gate permitting access only to classes at the present time. Someday a link between these trails may open up. The trail passes through a thin wood lot with development on either side before opening up on a woods road. Trail erosion from bike and horse usage is evident on a small slope just before reaching William Floyd Parkway at **7.7 miles**. Exercise caution crossing this wide roadway since cars travel at high speeds here. Fortunately the traffic is not usually heavy and there is a wide grassy median. On the other side the trail continues on a straight pathway through dry Pine Barrens terrain dominated by scrub oak in the understory with lots of pitch pines above. The first wide overgrown path you cross is a good connector to Brookhaven State Park to the north (left). After passing a few unmarked trails and making some winding turns you'll reach Route 25 at **8.56 miles**. Extreme caution is advised in crossing this busy road.

The large **Pine Trail Nature Preserve** parking area is located on the south side of Route 25. A kiosk has been set up to inform hikers of trail news, and it's a good place to consult a map. The parking lot is located about a half mile east of William Floyd Parkway and makes a good place to gain access to the trail, going in either direction. South of here the trail crosses several dirt roads and skirts the boundary of a housing development. Despite the nearby houses there's still ample opportunity to see wildlife. White-tail deer can be spotted, especially very early or late in the day. A chipmunk may scamper in front of you, or you may see a garter snake. Noisy birds such as the bright orange northern oriole and red northern cardinal are also common.

As the trail starts to turn more easterly you may notice that the houses are no longer near the trail. The land to the south is the property of Brookhaven National Laboratory and is strictly off limits to hikers, or, for that matter, any trespassers. After joining a dirt road the trail reaches a wide fire break (9.9 miles) where power lines pass overhead. This essentially ends the Pine Trail Preserve section of the trail and, despite the dry surroundings, you will now be entering a magnificent coastal plain pond system and the Peconic River watershed within **Robert Cushman Murphy County Park.** Details on this area are found in the chapter on that park.

Turn left (north) and follow the power lines about 250 feet to where the white blazes of the trail can be spotted on the right entering into a section of low-growing woods still recovering from a 1994 fire. At **10.13 miles** you will reach a junction with the **yellow blazes** of the **Brookhaven Trail** on the left. This fine trail will take you northward to Route 25 in about 1.25 miles and go all the way to the parking lot of Shoreham-Wading River High School on Route 25A, some 5.25 miles to the north. An end-to-end hike can be fashioned using the Brookhaven Trail and finishing up either to the east or west on the Paumanok Path. The truly adventurous can hike a nice loop trail by bushwhacking northward off the Paumanok Path from the section of trail between William Floyd Parkway and Route 25 and passing through Brookhaven Town land into the west side of Brookhaven State Park. Unmarked trails and woods roads can be used to make your way back to the trail's north end.

Shortly beyond the junction you'll cross a woods road (**10.2 miles**) and enter land dominated by scrub oak and re-growth of other oak species such as scarlet oak. It's all low-lying so there's little protection from the sun in hot weather along this stretch. The puff adder (also known as the hognose snake) has been spotted sunning itself in this section of trail, but sighting one would be a real rarity. While hiking this section with my family in October, I ran into men cutting brilliant red scarlet oak saplings and tying them into bundles. They had come from New Jersey and South Carolina to cut the colorful foliage to sell to big-city florists in the Northeast. I was told that when kept below 50 degrees they will keep the vibrant colors for a long time and are therefore of some value to the industry. One of the men also explained to me that they had been doing this since they came here as children with their fathers. I don't know if this was legal but I later found out that a year or so later they were caught by park police and told to stop.

Another woods road is crossed and shortly thereafter the trail skims the edge of a wetland between **Woodchoppers Pond** to the north and Sandy Pond. Take a walk here in the early evening in April or May and you'll hear the deafening chorus of thousands of spring peepers calling in the night. The observant will notice that the vegetation changes here as wet ground allows plants such as inkberry, a native holly, to flourish. The shore of the pond is lined with tupelo trees. This species is not unusual in this setting. Tupelos are the first tree to turn a brilliant scarlet in early fall, sometimes as early as mid September. If you are lucky you may spot the beautiful white fringed orchid blooming alongside the trail in July. This tall orchid is a noble-looking flower with a showy white spike of flowers atop a green stem. Like all orchids, it is a rarity to see one in nature; orchids have a strict set of growing requirements and take several years to flower.

At **10.62 miles** a **wooden bridge** is reached which fords the outlet between Sandy and Grassy Ponds. It was built by Eagle Scout Forest Lewandowski in 1993 and is a much more attractive and stable crossing than the crude logs that were here before. In some dry seasons the water may dry up beneath it since coastal plains ponds are dependent on rainfall to maintain water levels. Beyond the bridge the trail enters a corridor of wet woods under a canopy of trees filled with birds, especially warblers and vireos during migration. Shortly, at **10.71 miles**, the trail comes out onto a grassy clearing where you will see **Sandy Pond** to your left (east). The trail joins a woods road that goes to the right past **Grassy Pond** beyond a clearing on the right. There are some very colorful trees in fall across the pond as red maples turn red, orange and yellow. A little farther on the trail passes one of the "feedlots" planted with sorghum and the like to provide winter food for pheasant and quail. This is a reminder that small-game hunting occurs near here from October through February; hiking is safe except during what is usually a three week big-game season in January. The trail now joins another woods road, turns right and passes another feed lot at **11.25 miles**, after which it turns left and then right as it heads back into the woods on a well-defined path skirting the nearby hidden Twin Ponds. This path angles southeast and traverses a section called "Pepperbush Alley" because of the tall fragrant shrubs that line the path here and bloom in early to mid August. At **11.72 miles** a view of **Jones Pond** is evident on the right. There is a small path on the right that takes you to a viewpoint of this large pond. In late winter look for migrant ducks, including the ringed-neck duck, which is common in the acidic waters of the Pine Barrens ponds. The male is an attractive duck with a dark-blue head and a distinctive ring around its bill. The faint ring around the neck is a difficult feature to see unless the duck is inspected up close. The common name was given by hunters who obviously have handled the ducks, but ringed-bill duck would be more suitable.

At **11.90 miles** the trail reaches Schultz Road in Manorville. There is parking available along the road for a few cars. If you were to take Schultz Road southward (right) you would come to exit 69 on the LIE in less than 2 miles. The next section of trail heads through shaded woods of pine and oak with an occasional American chestnut along the way. In about **0.2 mile** the trail opens up into an area that had a minor fire; there are some tall trees spread out among the regrowth. The land north of here is explorable and interesting. A nearby swamp is a short bushwhack but can reward the adventurous with surprises such as the large owl that flushed out of a tree when I approached it. On a gray February day, I spotted an albino deer in this area. One can explore the public land beyond Wading River Road as far north as Grumman Boulevard, where several interesting ponds are located. See "Navy Co-op Pond Walk."

Taking a break on The Block, one of the several glacial erratics along the trail

Continuing eastward on the Paumanok Path watch for a turn where the trail makes a right off a wide trail onto a narrower path. Here the wetlands of the Peconic River come into view on the right (south). In April the red tinge of the swamp (or red) maples gives this location away. The Peconic is a flood-plain type of river that doesn't see much elevation drop during its course so it meanders slowly and swells or recedes with the rainfall. Thus it is surrounded by a wide buffer of swampy low ground. During the severe drought of summer 1995, it shrank up to a narrow trickle or series of small stagnant pools and hikers were able to walk right up to the meager sliver of river. The trail moves down closer to the river where there are wetland species on the right and dry pine barrens plants on the left. It is an opportunity to see just what a slight gain in elevation can do to affect the surrounding vegetation. You will shortly pass some fine highbush blueberries that can produce large plump berries in July if the season has had sufficient rainfall. You will enter a wetland and cross swampy ground on a wooden bridge before following a berm out to the edge of a small junkyard. Public land extends out twenty feet here but stay close to the small pond on the right since the landowner has not taken well to hikers. Just beyond is Wading River-Manor Road at the **13.31 miles** mark.

Once on the road make a right and go over the Peconic River on a low bridge. Take a moment to pause here (be careful of any climbing poison ivy) and get a close look at the meandering, lazy river which is still quite small at this point. You may catch a glimpse of a snapping turtle submerging at your approach or see a flycatcher diving at the many insects flitting above the water surface. Cross the road to the east side and view the river on its easterly course toward Peconic Bay, which is a few miles to the east. There is room to park on the east side of this rural road. The trail heads into the woods on the right with the wetlands and river now on your left (north). In a little while it will turn right and continue along the south side of the river. There is a red maple swamp through the woods on your right. After crossing over a wet spot on a board the wetlands become more obvious on your left, particularly when the leaves are down. Continue on for a few minutes with the river corridor and wetlands off to your left. Many birds can be seen in this pleasant section of trail through most of the year. At **13.95 miles** the trail makes a sharp right away from the river. Keep your eyes peeled for some old boundary mounds past here; they are telltale reminders of the land-use history, some dating back to the 17th century. All that is left now is just an overgrown ditch in the woods. The trail will reach the Greenport branch of the Long Island Rail Road (**14.16 miles**) in a secluded setting. Although only two or three trains pass by each day, the railroad will not let hikers cross the tracks for liability reasons. A re-route around the tracks was put in a few years back. The trail takes a right (west) just before the tracks and follows the south side of them, at one point reaching a rise of land 30 feet above the tracks. Mill Road is reached at **14.46 miles** and you will note a power line crossing the road just to the south. This power line has an open sandy path underneath that can be taken about 0.5 mile west (right) to a bar-restaurant called the Maples (you're in Manorville hamlet here) or to the Pine Barrens Trail Information Center, which is just around the corner from it. The Maples is a popular meeting spot for hikers on some group hikes.

Back at Mill Road you'll dive back into the woods south of the tracks and follow them until you reach the point where the trail turns right and away from the tracks at **14.73 miles**. Should that rare train pass, you will hear a sound hikers have heard for the last 150 years. Once you turn away from the tracks you reach a clearing under the power lines and head into the woods, passing a wetland on your left. The swamp is a tributary of the Peconic River and is the last you will see of that watershed on this trail. Reaching Mill Road again at **15.12 miles**, you make a left and walk a short distance past the wetland, and another left to head away from the road. Take note that a yellow-blazed side trail across Mill Road starts on an old woods road and heads through the open forest to link up with the blue-blazed Wampmissick Trail before reaching the Pine Barrens Trails Information Center in about 0.4 mile.

The trail now winds through shaded woods, passes a woods road and enters a recent second-growth area that was burnt sometime in the past few years. It comes out to Mill Road again at **15.54 miles**, crossing the road and continuing through an area burnt over in the late 1990s. The scrub oak is interspersed with an occasional shady area of pitch pines. In May listen for the song of the prairie warbler in these low woods. In winter you may see mixed flocks of chickadees, nuthatches, kinglets and brown creepers noisily foraging as they pass through. At **16.26 miles** the trail comes out to Halsey Manor Road, makes a right and crosses over the LIE. The trail will make a left (east) on the south side of the expressway at **16.54 miles**.

The next 10 miles of trail traverse the **Manorville Hills**, the most rugged and hilly part of the entire trail. This is the Ronkonkoma Moraine that runs through the central part of the Island and becomes the South Fork farther east. This area is discussed in more detail in the Manorville Hills section. The trail also unceremoniously enters the state owned Otis Pike Preserve which was passed from the federal government to the state in 1997. Once in the woods south of the LIE, the trail makes a quick left and remains close to the Expressway for over a mile and a half. New acquisitions to the south will permit a re-routing of the trail to some of the more interesting features in the area, such as Sunset Hill. The potential improvements to this trail are mind-boggling for those of us that have explored this beautiful area. For the time being we'll just have to use the existing section that has been put in place. There is already a debate as to how much new trail should be opened up, since this section is seeing serious abuse from the motorbikes besieging the entire Manorville Hills. Until there is some serious crackdown on these illegal motorized uses (and that requires funding), the problem will continue.

Continuing eastward, the trail makes a sharp left (north) at **16.93 miles** onto an old boundary road where it quickly turns right to continue its eastward trek alongside the LIE. Shortly thereafter the terrain starts to rise a little, the first sign of any hills at all. Eventually the trail rises on the northern side of a 160-foot hill called the **Northern Spur** since it has a ridge that seems to extend off to the northeast. Exploration up this gradual slope will reward the hiker with the discovery of **Grouse Rock**, a glacial erratic that is a ruffed grouse drumming site in springtime. Another worthwhile goal is a fine view back westward towards the Brookhaven National Lab and beyond. There is a fairly steep hollow between the Northern Spur and nearby 190-foot **Sunset Hill** just to the south. This is a little over a mile from Halsey Manor Road and is worth the off-trail scramble to see this fine view to the west and northwest. On clear days one can spot the SUNY Medical Center in Stony Brook some 25 miles in the distance.

The trail now heads eastward to meet a wide jeep road alongside the fence that borders the LIE. There is a woods road going southward into the hills at this point that gives access to the interior of Manorville Hills. The trail continues straight along the LIE here; the only note of interest is a glacial erratic on the north side of the trail nicknamed **The Nose**. It is not a particularly large rock, standing only about three feet tall, but it does look somewhat like a nose (use your imagination). Eventually the trail makes a left and leaves the wide road. It then comes out to another dirt road, turns left (**17.65 miles**) and passes three large erratics on a hillside on the right. Named **Tres Huevos** ("three eggs" in Spanish), they are an excellent place to rest. There are actually four erratics on the hill but the last is smaller and inconspicuous. The land behind these erratics rises up steadily and is yet another place to go exploring off-trail. Follow the trail as it rolls eastward to join a major woods road at **18.12 miles**.

At this point the trail finally leaves the expressway and heads southward on a wide jeep road. At **18.30 miles** it takes a left onto a more obscure grassy woods road for a short distance before turning right at **18.42 miles** and heading into tall trees and past a kettle with a relatively open understory. It goes uphill past a glade of ferns; they're not the common bracken or hay-scented varieties but something more tropical-looking. You are now on a loop known in hiking circles as the **Thumb Loop**. Once it reaches its high point, it starts back downhill, reaching the bottom of the kettle once again at **18.87 miles**. You'll then turn right (east) and pass through some beautiful rolling terrain with a deep drop-off to the right at one point. This section of trail is particularly pretty in winter with some snow on the ground as you can see several layers of the rippling land off to the southeast. At **19.09 miles** the trail makes a sharp right onto a wide dirt road and heads downhill. It is hoped that eventually the trail can continue straight and avoid this section of unsightly dirt road walking. As the trail heads uphill again severe erosion is evident as motorized vehicles have created a ditch more than six feet high on the sides! This is an extreme example of the fragility of the thin layer of topsoil and how susceptible it is to permanent damage. The trail curves to the left at **19.25 miles** where a small erratic is passed on the left that makes for a good place to take a break.

The trail makes a right (**19.28 miles**) and heads onto a narrow path in a cozy hollow between hills. I have spooked more than one bedded-down deer here, so be alert. This is also a great spot for huckleberries in July: They line the trail all along here. Another woods road is crossed at **19.52 miles** as the trail continues southward before turning left at **19.66 miles**. This section of trail was cut to give access to the woods roads off to the east. It goes uphill to a small 240-foot hill called **Little Knob** at **19.74 miles**. There is a partial view through the trees to the west, just enough to show you are fairly high and deep within these hills; only the surrounding pine-clad ridges are visible through the trees from here. The trail descends to reach a major North-South boundary road at **19.86 miles**. It turns right and heads south along this well-used, eroded dirt road. This is another section of trail that hopefully will be re-routed directly across this road in the future.

Following the boundary road for some time the trail rises and falls until it takes another road to the left at a fork at **20.23 miles**. The road you were just on goes steeply up to the top of a 270-foot unnamed hill with views through the trees of the surrounding land. As the trail proceeds here, looking to your left, you'll see the land drops off sharply to the bottom of **Deep Kettle** which bottoms out at 140 feet in elevation, making a 130-foot difference from the bottom of the kettle to the top of the hill. It may not sound like much to seasoned mountain hikers but that is roughly equivalent to a thirteen-story building. The fact that it takes place on "flat" Long Island makes it all the more surprising. Deep Kettle is worth a short bushwhack to the bottom, where the dry bottom is a thicket with huge pines towering over an understory of scrub oak, bracken fern, and blueberry and huckleberry bushes. The trail shortly leaves the sandy road to turn left at **20.32 miles** and head into the woods, traveling almost completely around Deep Kettle before reaching a large unnamed erratic at **20.53 miles**. Along this section, when the leaves are down, the hulking mass of the hill towers impressively over the hollow in the background. Following the contours of the land, the trail makes a sharp right turn onto a more worn path at **20.81 miles** where it once again is heading easterly.

The trail now winds through and past a few balds. These are open grassy areas usually located on hillsides under tall pines. Balds are great places to rest and stretch the legs in a shady location. They are named after the large open areas in the high elevations of the Great Smokies of the southern Appalachian Mountains. This section of trail passes some small ones at first before coming into a rather large bald with a small glacial erratic right along the trail there. There is a view eastward through the trees with nothing but pine-clad ridges to be seen. Except for the sound of an occasional distant plane, the wind rustling through the trees is all you can hear.

The trail then winds back up to the right and climbs a fairly steep pitch of a hill before heading down to the left. Here it takes the left fork of a trail junction (**21.40 miles**). A few minutes farther on keep an eye out for a hill just up to your right. This is the southern "summit" of a 250-foot hill called **Doubletop** since it has two tops at the same height that are distinctive when viewed on the USGS topographic map for Eastport (the upper left corner). The view from this southern hill is a fine one (albeit through the trees), for you are looking out over the flat outwash plain and can clearly see Moriches Bay some six miles distant as well as the barrier beach and vast Atlantic Ocean beyond. The trail will climb up to the northern summit of Doubletop; it has a few trails running over it that have been eroded by illegal motor-bike use. Here at **21.63 miles** the trail takes a sharp left and heads steadily downhill. As you reach the bottom you will see the wide sandy Toppings Path through the trees. At **21.76 miles** the trail makes a left onto a path that parallels Toppings Path for a short distance before making a right turn and crossing it at **21.80 miles**.

Toppings Path is a landmark of sorts as it bisects the Manorville Hills by running north-to-south between them, separating them into western and eastern sections. Being unpaved and very wide it is not especially attractive, but it serves as a fire road and allows access to four-wheel drive vehicles. It is apparently quite old and runs more than four miles from just south of the LIE at Exit 71 to County Route 111 on the south. It bears the name of Captain Thomas Topping who acquired this land from the Shinnecock Indians in 1662.

The trail enters the eastern Manorville Hills across Toppings Path and almost immediately makes a left (**21.83 miles**) onto a smaller trail. Look for a white blaze so you don't bypass it. You will then wind gradually uphill and past an old wooden ladder on the left, remnants of a long-forgotten hunter's tree stand. Deer hunting still takes place in sections of these hills, though the number of hunters is regulated for safety purposes. There are some big white-tail deer here and hunting helps keep the population in check, since there are no natural predators.

Old tree stands are scattered throughout the area but are easily overlooked since they weather and tend to become rather inconspicuous with the passage of time. If the leaves are down, you may catch a glimpse of the blue Atlantic Ocean through the trees to the south (right).

The trail will make a right turn just below the crest of the hill at **22.0 miles** near a white-and-green DEC sign marking the cooperative hunting area. Before making the turn you may want to continue up the unmarked trail to just beyond the top of the hill. There you will see a large, wild-looking glacial erratic just beyond the crest of the hill on the left. This is **Split Rock**, so named because it was split in two by the forces of nature ages ago. It may have occurred when the rock came crashing down from the melting glacier or maybe a small crack filled with a bit of water that froze and thawed, eventually splitting the solid mass after thousands of years of this action. The boulder is covered with rock tripe, a scaly-looking lichen that actually receives it nutrients from the rock itself! At the base of the northwest side of the rock you will see an abandoned fox den that was active in the spring of 1994. Split Rock is one of several erratics strewn on this hillside in a boulder field left by receding ice between 15,000 and 20,000 years ago. Close examination of some of these boulders show pieces of white quartz and pink granite, probably scoured from the Green Mountains of Vermont or the Berkshires of Massachusetts. Although this 250-foot hill is unnamed, I think **Split Rock Hill** would be appropriate.

Back on the Paumanok Path you'll see some erratics on either side of the trail. Shortly, you'll make a left onto an overgrown woods road and head in a northerly direction. A short distance south (right) on this road just past some large erratics you may glimpse some large boulders off to the left (east) through the trees. This is much easier when the leaves are down. Closer inspection will reveal a slope with the largest concentration of inland erratics to be found on Long Island. There are dozens strewn around the west and south sides of the hillside; hence, I call this **The Boulder Field.** Back on the trail, as you head northward on the woods road away from the junction, about

The view from Bald Hill

40 yards through the trees on the left at the base of Split Rock Hill you may catch a glimpse of a tall pointy erratic named **The Spire** (photo p. 16). Shortly, the trail takes a right (**22.17 miles**) onto a narrower path where it proceeds to meander around, over, and between hills, never staying flat for long. In late summer you may see many kinds of mushrooms alongside the trail under the shady canopy of the woods. Mushrooms come in many different shapes and sizes. Whites, yellows, reds, oranges, and even the violet-colored purple cort can be seen popping up out of the soil almost anywhere along the trail in these hills. While you are looking down for mushrooms you'll likely notice other modest ground growth, such as the fragrant wintergreen, the trailing arbutus and probably even the pale, ghostly finger-like Indian pipe rising in bunches through the brown leaf litter. The entire area begs for off-trail exploration as many unheralded views can be found on some of the isolated hilltops in the southern section of these wild hills.

As the trail continues its winding trek up and down watch for a sharp right at **22.73 miles**, where it skims the top of **Deep Hollow** down in the drop-off to your left. Were you to continue on the path without making this turn you would shortly head straight down into this elongated hollow. It is named for the pitched slopes that make it such an interesting feature for the hiker wishing to explore it. The trail will eventually drop down into the eastern end of the hollow and wind around to the right, then angle up-slope away from a glacial erratic called **The Block**. This lichen-encrusted boulder is about the size of the top half of a Volkswagen beetle. You will see it off to the left about 30 to 35 yards away. The trail was originally supposed to go right past it but DEC wildlife officials have identified it as a drumming site for ruffed grouse and asked to have the trail moved away so as not to disturb them during this late April and May ritual. Most birds sing in springtime to attract a mate and establish a territory, but the ruffed grouse sits on a large stump (rare in the Pine Barrens) or a rock and beats its wings so rapidly that a drumming sound results. Being a classic northern hardwoods forest game bird, this grouse is quite rare on Long Island. Environmentalists try to help the birds' mating rituals to maintain populations. You are not likely to see one but may be startled

A short access trail runs the length of Birch Creek to link with The Puamanok Path

by the astonishing speed (over 40 mph) with which they burst from the forest floor when approached. The Block can be inspected most of the rest of the year without disturbing these wild birds.

At **22.97 miles** the trail goes to the right over a slight slope and arrives at the side of a vernal wetland, a wetland filled with water in spring but dry in summer. This depression does not look like a kettle and probably exists because the soil underneath has a high percentage of clay or some other nonporous soil that does not allow drainage. In late spring when the ferns are opening on its banks it resembles a mini bayou-type swamp; large red maples grow out of

the water like bald cypresses do down south. In the late summer it is not nearly so attractive but there are some fine highbush blueberry bushes along the
shore, a real treat in August. At **23.12 miles** the trail reaches a woods road,
makes a right turn (south) and heads uphill. The eroded sides have some
healthy-looking specimens of trailing arbutus growing out of them. This road
was obviously cut as a north-south boundary road since it is arrow-straight
going uphill and then down to unpaved Hot Water Street. The trail stays on
it for only 0.1 mile, making a sharp left (east) and cresting **High Hill** at **23.29
miles**. At 300 feet above sea level, this is not only the highest point in
Manorville Hills, but I believe the highest point east of the familiar Bald Hill
(north of exit 63 on the LIE) in Farmingville. Unfortunately, this hill has not
been preserved in its natural state as the trail follows a somewhat disturbed
road apparently cut by bulldozers to access a fire. The downed trees and
mounds along the road attest to this; still, in winter there is a good view
towards the east from off to the left (north) side of the trail just before it begins
to descend. The County Center can be seen as well as glimpses of Peconic
Bay. The trail will then descend and rise up again to a shoulder of the main
hill where at **23.37 miles** there is a view through the trees northeast (left)
towards the Northville area. From here the trail drops abruptly down, bears
right at a fork and leaves the woods road with a left turn onto a narrow path
at **23.50 miles**. It meets a wider path in a short while (**23.57 miles**) and follows it to the right. From here, the trail loops around to the right (north-north-
east) and enters an area you can tell is second-growth because the trees are
short and close together. There is a hillside on your left; it's easier to see when
the leaves are down. This is **Burnt Hill** and well worth the short bushwhack
just to the west of north on your compass. You will notice some scattered tall
pitch pine survivors rising above scrub oak, bracken fern, and huckleberries
as you make your way up the incline of the slope. Burnt Hill was given its
name because a fire swept this hill and cleared views in every direction. At
250 feet in height it is not the highest hill in the area but the effects of the fire
and its excellent placement make it a real find for the hiker. The clear April
day we first found this prize is one of my most memorable in these hills. The
Paumanok Path was originally slated to go right over it but fear of ensuing
damage from motor bikes caused us to move the trail to an existing path just
to the south. Views abound in every direction from various points around the
summit. Near the top you will be able to look back southeastward towards a
stout water tank and tall tower, a sort of Mutt and Jeff pair that helps hikers
orient themselves in these hills. Beyond them is the mass of Bald Hill and the
white radar dome on the top of The Summit in Hampton Hills. Move around
to the east a little and a beautiful view of the blue waters of Peconic Bay
becomes visible. Around to the northeast side you can see the hills of the

Harbor Hill Moraine and if it is clear enough, the coastal Connecticut land-mass. A pair of binoculars will verify this. Perhaps my favorite spot on Burnt Hill is a nice open bald (called George's Bald) on the slopes of the west side where there's a great panorama of the surrounding hills (including High Hill, which you just came off a little while earlier). The area is perfect for stretching out and taking off your boots for a little while.

Returning down to the trail, continue your eastward progression until you reach a woods road at **23.95 miles** onto which you'll turn right and then left at a junction of woods roads. If you continue straight here you will come to **Hunter's Garden** in a few minutes. See the Manorville Hills section for more info about that. After a short distance make a right onto another woods road at **24.07 miles**. This is another straight north-south old boundary road probably created when developers had a vision of putting subdivisions into this entire area.

The trail leaves this boundary road at **24.16 miles** where it turns left at some junked cars and reaches the fence enclosure of the aforementioned stout water tank and tall tower at **24.26 miles**. The tank and tower are good landmarks seen from various locations within Manorville Hills (and outside the hills as well). Beyond this point the trail drops into a secluded steep-sided hollow and the tank and tower drop out of view. Here, surrounded by the dark brooding pines, it meanders back uphill to a fine ridge with a couple of good views to the north (**24.73 miles**) at the country beyond Riverhead. Looking in the opposite direction you can see the shaggy pine-clad hilltop of 295-foot Bald Hill. This familiar shape can be seen from as far away as Sound Avenue way up in the northern portion of Riverhead Town because it rises prominently above the nearby hills. The trail drops quickly off the ridge to meet a wide dirt road at **24.84 miles**. The trail hangs a right here for a short distance and leaves the road at **24.97 miles** where it takes another right onto a fainter path. In a short distance you come to a junction with the light-blue-blazed Bald Hill loop trail. This loop is blazed counter-clockwise as it traverses Bald Hill. The blue blazes double up with the white blazes heading right and passing through open woods, then make a left to start a steady ascent of **Bald Hill** (not to be confused with Bald Hill in Farmingville, which is to the west) at about **25.5 0 miles**. Though it was once an open hilltop with a fire tower on top, it has become overgrown through the years. Serious trail erosion from illegal motor bike and mountain bike use almost caused the LIGTC to bypass Bald Hill completely. However, volunteer work in recent years has put an end to this; log erosion blocks make vehicle access difficult and have also stemmed erosion. A **spectacular view** from the top overlooking the Riverhead County

Complex and Peconic Bay has been cleared. See if you can pick out Robins Island on the horizon in the middle of the bay. Looking right (south) you get an excellent view of Moriches Bay, the barrier beach and the Atlantic Ocean beyond. Binoculars will bring in detail of surviving houses on stilts at the ocean's edge. It is possibly the best view to be had in this area. Bald Hill is also a short walk from County Route 51. The road runs just to the south of the hill, but is obscured from view and out of earshot, making Bald Hill seem more remote and secluded than it actually is. The light-blue blazed trail can be found from County Route 51 on the north side of the road about 0.5 mile west of Speonk Riverhead Road. A metal gate across the woods road here along with county parkland signs mark the spot.

Coming down off Bald Hill, The Paumanok Path follows a woods road to the right and then makes a left across the wide access road that comes in from County Route 51. At **25.86 miles** the trail makes a left as it rolls up and down while snaking through typical oak-dominated woods. A right turn is made at **25.93 miles** before the trail crosses an unmarked trail, descends and then rises to meet County Route 51 at **26.19 miles** where it finally leaves the Manorville Hills behind.

Cars move fast on wide County Route 51 so be careful crossing it. Once on the far side the trail drops down almost immediately into a large dry kettlehole. Here the trail runs adjacent to the Suffolk Community College, Riverhead Campus, a good place to leave your car. Look for a y**ellow-blazed interpretive trail** (**26.22 miles**) on the far (south) slope of the kettle. It goes off to the right to another trail which you should take to the left. You'll go under a road within the college grounds and eventually come to a large clearing with a parking lot on the left in 0.35 mile. A kiosk is located at the corner of the lot with a map of the trail. This is an excellent location from which to launch a hike either to the east or west. The lot can be accessed from Speonk-Riverhead Road just south of County Route 51. Make a right from Speonk-Riverhead Road then a first left and quick right to bring you to the parking lot.

From the kettle the white-blazed trail turns left and reaches Speonk-Riverhead Road at **26.42 miles**. The trail now enters the **Hampton Hills**, another hilly morainal section of over 2,000 acres of county-owned land acquired through The Nature Conservancy in 1990. The trail is narrow as it winds back and forth among these tightly packed hills. In the fall you can't help but notice the bright lemon-yellow sassafras trees in the understory; in an autumn woods dominated by reds they stand out in sharp contrast. In April you'll likely hear the trilling song of the pine warbler, a little yellow bird that nests and lives exclusively in pine trees, so it naturally likes the Pine Barrens. At **27.10 miles** the trail crosses a woods road. Farther on, it passes a junction with a **yellow-blazed access trail** on the left that winds its way northward to reach County Route 51 in about a half a mile. The parking area for this trail is just southwest of the power lines on the south side of the road. This trail is little-used and a bit brushy at points so keep an eye out for blazes and wear long pants. The options for day hikes are obvious, as one can hike either south or north of County Route 51. A loop trail is planned to go north from here into the far eastern Manorville Hills, where small ponds are located.

Back on the Paumanok Path, the trail hardly ever seems to be level as it is either climbing, descending or traversing a hillside. A power line is reached at **27.47 miles** and a **view** towards the northeast can be had where the ground is kept clear under the lines. More bumpy terrain is traversed before a hill allows a view northward at **27.72 miles**. A little farther on you will cross another woods road before reaching the paved Hampton Hills Road at **28.17 miles**. This road gives access to the Hampton Hills Country Club and golf course tucked in the pines. Beyond this, the trail drops down into the woods and crosses another woods road at **28.24 miles** and shortly after that reaches a view of **Wildwood Lake** at **28.26 miles**. The trail is about 60 feet above this glacial kettle lake and the view is most impressive in spring when things are just opening or in fall when foliage is in full color, say about mid-October. The trail makes a right (south) and leaves the wider path it was on and moves away from the lake. If you continue a little farther on the wider path, a clearing down to the left makes a good place to stop and soak up the scene. For a close look from the lakeshore, continue farther down this woods trail and you can get down to the shore on your left.

Beyond the lake the trail will cross a few more woods roads and then enter (unceremoniously) **The David A. Sarnoff Pine Barrens Preserve** after crossing a woods road at **28.52 miles**. The state trails in the Sarnoff Preserve are described in detail in its own section. The Sarnoff section of trail is impressive as one gets deeper and deeper into the preserve; the only sound to be heard is the wind through the trees or an occasional bird. It is lightly used and a good hike for those seeking some form of solitude. The trail goes through some fine stands of pines and open clearings filled with uplands heather (hudsonia) and reindeer lichen. Other small yet intriguing lichens you may spot are the brilliant scarlet British soldiers and the fairy-like pixie cup. The finer contours of the land seem to be followed at times as the trail coils up on itself at one point and wriggles back and forth. Woods roads are crossed at **29.20 miles** and again at **30.35 miles** before the trail starts to climb up to higher ground where **views** through the trees towards the north reveal the Northville

Maple Swamp, the largest of its type found in the Pine Barrens

oil drums just south of the bluffs overlooking Long Island Sound. This marks the beginning of the wine country of Long Island's North Fork. At **30.48 miles** another **view** from this wooded 180-foot hill allows a glimpse of the blue waters of Peconic Bay to the east. These views are superb in late afternoon on a clear winter's day. At about **30.80 miles** you'll pass a faint path off to the left which is the **yellow-blazed trail**, a shortcut toward the parking area on Route 104. At this writing it was poorly maintained and somewhat overgrown. As the trail continues its eastward march it begins a slow ascent up a nameless hill that had all its tall trees cleared by a severe fire sometime in the past. The result is a **great open panorama** northward (**31.30 miles**) over the scrub oak vegetation towards the hills of the Harbor Hill Moraine. This vantage has a somewhat airy feel despite not being much above 180 feet high.

You now descend the hill where the trail eventually makes a right turn around a **large kettlehole** by heading north on the opposite side. There is a place to pause and rest at **31.80 miles** under the trees on the east side overlooking the crater-like depression. Notice this dry kettle no longer holds moisture and contains dryland species. This is one of those places where a micro-climate is formed by cool air settling into the kettle at night, causing the trees at the bottom to leaf out much later (sometimes weeks) than the surrounding woods and change color earlier than the oaks around it.

From here, the trail heads straight northward reaching the DEC parking area on Route 104 at the **32.35 mile** mark. The **yellow-blazed** connector trail that was passed about 1.5 miles back goes off to the west (left) from here. A restaurant once stood in the clearing just west of the parking lot and traces of asphalt and glass attest to this. The Paumanok Path now follows the yellow-blazed trail as it heads north away from the lot into the woods where it turns east (right) and crosses Route 104 at **32.64 miles**. It heads on a straight path and continues ahead when the yellow trail goes off to the left (north) to join a **blue-blazed loop trail** described elsewhere. There is an interesting vernal kettlehole a little beyond where the trail turns right onto a dirt road. Look for it down to the left; it is surrounded by some big old pitch pines and usually has water in it in spring or after wet periods of weather. It has a wild remote look to it. At **33.11 miles** the trail makes a sharp right and heads southward back to Route 104 at **34.03 miles**. There is some fine terrain just east of here; the trail may be rerouted to encompass it in the near future. However, rerouting the trail may require acquisition of some of the land, so it is unclear when this will occur. When it does, 1.83 miles of easterly road walking will be eliminated. The trail takes a left onto Pleasure Drive road and goes back into the woods (**34.93 miles**) at a point where the road turns left. There is room here for a few cars to park.

The trail now moves through the woods within earshot of Route 27 (Sunrise Highway, Exit 64), crossing under a power line at **35.29 miles** while it goes through somewhat rolling terrain. This power line can be followed eastward up the long ridge of **Flanders Hill**, which is more than 230 feet high. Here a fire tower once stood with a commanding view of the surrounding countryside. Today adventurous hikers should include Flanders Hill in their exploratory hikes or bushwhacks of the area to the south and east toward Sears Pond. Flanders Bay can be seen on the way from a few places.

A main woods road is crossed at **35.84 miles** where shortly thereafter you'll see wet swampy ground down to the left of the trail. Red maples are evidence here that there is more moisture in the ground than in the surrounding barrens-type soil. At **36.18 miles** the trail makes a left onto a woods road that takes you to **Maple Swamp** on the left at **36.39 miles**. This is the largest of the maple swamps found in the Pine Barrens. They are like oases amid the dry sandy landscape of the barrens. Maple swamps represent an area where the water table is close to the surface, and thus they will never really dry up no matter how dry the weather may get. This swamp is a haven for all sorts of birds throughout the year and a very pretty spot to rest or have lunch beneath the shade of overhanging red maple trees. To get a different perspective on the wetland, go back a short distance and make a right. You'll find a dead end path with a fine view over the open water of this unusual place. In April 1996, Governor George Pataki joined County Executive Robert Gaffney and a group of Greenbelters to hike this section of the trail to Maple Swamp. It was an occasion for the governor to view this jewel of the Pine Barrens and see why it is essential to preserve the Pine Barrens for future generations. The county executive hiked more than 15 miles that day to see the Pine Barrens firsthand, and he seemed impressed with what he saw.

The land beyond Maple Swamp is some of the finest available to the walker. The trail rises away from the water through beautiful rolling terrain, a pleasure to hike in any season. Try October, when the woods are in full color and the yellows of occasional maples or sassafras contrast with the burgundy of the blueberry ground cover. Or try a clear winter's day, when views of the undulating land towards Flanders Hill give a perspective not experienced many other places in the Pine Barrens. This section of the trail crosses abandoned woods roads at **36.72 miles, 37.04 miles** and **37.12 miles** respectively. All the while you will be alternating between stands of pines and open oak woods while occasional kettles and depressions heighten the features of the land. At **37.60 miles** the trail has a partial view eastward from a ridge over the low ground below. It gradually drops down from here and perceptive hikers will see evergreen trees (when the leaves are down) displaying a shade of green different from the pitch pines. These are Atlantic white cedars that grow adjacent to Owl Pond.

A junction with the **yellow-blazed Birch Creek Trail** is reached at **37.85 miles**. This side trail runs along the west side of pretty **Birch Creek Pond** to County Route 24 where it makes a right, reaching Spinney Road about 0.4 mile from the junction. Ample parking at the head of Spinney Road makes it another good place to set up a loop or end-to-end hike. There is another yellow-blazed trail that leaves Spinney Road to follow the east side of the pond, joining the Paumanok Path at Owl Pond in about the same 0.4 mile distance. In late May and early June there are some dry openings filled with the yellow flowers of hudsonia (also known as beach heather).

From the Birch Creek junction the white-blazed trail heads southward, with the wetlands of Birch Creek on your left. At **38.02 miles** the trail goes over a small berm or earthen dam where water trickles underfoot. As it approaches Owl Pond you'll see (and smell) Atlantic white cedar trees alongside the trail. Also known as swamp cedar, this tree grows only in freshwater in a narrow belt along the coastal plain from central Maine to the Gulf Coast in Mississippi. Its pleasant fragrance has long been known to repel insects but it

Pretty Owl Pond is one of the highlights of the eastern section of the trail

is the rot-resistant wood of this tree that spelled its downfall. Early colonists prized this durable wood for fence posts, log cabins (especially floors) and shingles, among other uses. During the Revolutionary War it was used to produce charcoal for gunpowder. Needless to say, the once-great stands of this tree are long gone and it is now quite rare in our area. But the tree is making a comeback of sorts in a few groves on eastern Long Island. The best are located in the Riverhead area of Sweezy Pond and Cedar Swamp off County Route 51. Owl Pond has a small but growing grove on its west and south sides. The trees can be seen in lesser numbers around many of the local wetlands, such as the ponds within Sears-Bellows County Park and Penny Pond. There are many rare plants and butterflies not found elsewhere that are associated with these trees.

At **38.18 miles** the trail comes to the shores of attractive little **Owl Pond**. The cedar grove can be seen directly across. The aforementioned second **yellow access trail** goes off to the left towards the Spinney Road-Route 24 parking area in about 0.4 mile. This location is a nice peaceful place to rest and take in the scene before moving on to cross a crude log bridge over a drainage of the pond at **38.21 miles**. As you proceed you may see young Atlantic white cedars on your right growing in the wet acidic soil. A little farther on the trail crosses a sandy backroad at **38.39 miles** before reaching wide Spinney Road at **38.73 miles**. Spinney Road is closed to public auto use and paved for only a short distance from Route 24. It gives walkers easy access to the interior of public land as far south as Flanders Hill and even south of Route 27. It was near here on an October morning that I first saw a buck moth in flight. I had read much about this bright orange, black, and white moth that is on the endangered species list in New York State (and has caused developments to be halted) but I had never seen one. These large moths flutter around during the day for a two-week period and I was impressed with how vivid the Halloween colors of the male moth appeared. I now consider myself a true "piney" for having seen one.

Once it's on the east side of Spinney Road the trail climbs gently and then descends quickly to a **wet kettle** at **39.35 miles**. Spring peepers give this wetland away with their loud chorus in early springtime. At **39.51 miles** the trail reaches a little-used woods road and follows it to the right, leaving the road at **39.66 miles** with a left turn. You may notice wetland species like Atlantic white cedar and tupelo on the left as you approach Sears Pond, visible through the trees on that same side of the trail. At **39.80 miles** you will reach an open view of **Sears Pond** as the trail traverses its southern shore. Sears Pond is alluring any time of the year and I consider it probably the most attractive body of freshwater on Long Island. There is something about it that reminds me more of an Adirondack lake than a Pine Barrens pond. In *Walden*, Henry David Thoreau wrote, "A lake is the landscape's most beautiful and expressive feature. It is earth's eye; looking into which the beholder measures the depth of his own nature." This seems especially appropriate for Sears Pond. It wouldn't be too unusual to see an osprey circling over it or a flock of wild ducks come in for a splash-landing on its surface. At **39.87 miles** the trail takes a sharp right and heads for higher ground away from the pond before coming back near the shore at **40.17 miles** where it turns right again onto a wider path. The trail makes another right onto a sandy access road and it then almost immediately leaves it. Heading onto a newly cut path, you will traverse some upland sections of the park with a more secluded feeling than was provided by the old road trail. Some kettleholes can be seen below the low ridge the trail follows. This section passes a few narrow horse trails, and you will notice **royal blue blazes** marking a side trail back to the parking area near the entrance of Sears-Bellows County Park; they join right along with the white Paumanok Path blazes. At about **40.65 miles** the blue-blazed trail continues straight ahead on an old woods road junction where the Paumanok Path turns left. The blue trail will eventually circle around Bellows Pond with some fine views before going through the campsite and parking area near the park entrance in a little under a mile. This is a great camping spot in the off-season, and it's a good place to access trails for longer hikes in the region.

From this junction the Paumanok Path goes along the shore of **Division Pond** before reaching a wide unpaved park road where it turns right. At **40.85 miles** the trail will make a left away from this sandy road to head towards County Route 24. The park road takes you to the right past House Pond to Bellows Pond and the public campground in a little less than a mile.

The trail crosses Route 24 at **41.22 miles** and passes through a short section before reaching Red Creek Road at **41.31 miles**. There is room to park a car along the road here but be sure not to block off the unpaved gravel road the trail follows northward. This road takes you to the Black Duck Lodge and the shores of Flanders Bay described in the Hubbard County Park section.

The trail follows this road and you may notice some large specimens of mountain laurel in the woods off to either side. This is the first of this showy shrub to be seen along the trail since the Peconic watershed back in Manorville. Surprisingly, it is nonexistent in the morainal sections of Manorville Hills, Hampton Hills, and the Sarnoff Preserve. At **41.56 miles** the trail makes a sharp right off the road and heads into an oak-hickory woods adjacent to salt-water wetlands that appear through the trees on your left (north). In a short distance you'll cross a wet area and go alongside a boundary mound, passing close to **Hubbard Creek**. The creek can be seen up close by taking a short path off to the left at **41.70 miles**. Here, you can get a nice overview of a tidal wetland that usually has flocks of ducks on it from October through April. This is an especially nice place late in the day when the sun is behind you and the long shadows creep toward the creek.

Heading away from the water, the trail again reaches Red Creek Road (**41.91 miles**) where it makes a left and follows it over Hubbard Creek. Here, the creek is still a narrow river-like waterway draining toward the bay. The tea-colored water is characteristic of Pine Barrens streams, which contain tannins from the surrounding vegetation (Atlantic white cedar and oaks).

Just beyond this, the trail turns right (east) and continues on what appears to be an old overgrown woods road at **42.06 miles**. The trail will soon link up in Red Creek Park with the Red Creek trails system with **yellow and white diamond-shaped blazes.** At about **42.3 miles**, look for an unmarked side-trail on the left that heads down to **Penny Pond**. This will take you to an old duck-hunting blind on the southwest shore of this lovely pond. I've seen ospreys nesting in trees on the northeast side of the pond and fish jumping to the surface of the water to catch insects. You may also see a belted kingfisher zigzagging over the pond surface. This green bird is bigger than a blue jay, has a crested head, and makes a noisy rattling call. It feeds almost exclusively on the fish it catches. The southern flying squirrel is common around this region. Rarely seen, it is one of the more mysterious mammals found on Long Island.

It is strange to see such a quiet freshwater pond tucked away in the woods so close to the salty waters of Great Peconic Bay. Return to the trail and continue eastward (left) and in a short distance you'll see another path leading to the left (north) that will take you to the east side of Penny Pond (down to the left). You will see a dense stand of Atlantic white cedars that grows right down to the shoreline. Past the pond, this path will eventually lead to Lower Red Creek Road.

At **42.69 miles** the trail leaves the woods road (left) and heads into the woods of **Red Creek Park**, run by the town of Southampton. The trails of this park are described in detail in the section devoted to it. In a little while you'll cross another woods road (**42.86 miles**) by making a left and quick right. At **43.08 miles** you'll reach a junction with the **yellow trail**, which you will now follow straight ahead instead of the yellow-white trail you've been on for some time. If in doubt, look for the white paint blazes of the Paumanok Path. There's a bench to rest on here as well, courtesy of the Southampton Trails Preservation Society, an organization that maintains the Red Creek trails. As the trail proceeds along, it passes a white trail on the right; though it's part of the Red Creek Trail system you should instead make a left (**43.36 miles**) and continue to follow the yellow trail. A short distance later, you'll make a right at **43.43 miles** and shortly thereafter another right onto an old road at **43.57 miles**. The trail makes a left turn onto another road at **43.74 miles** and another left near a bench at **43.95 miles**. It passes around a **kettlehole** and makes a right at **44.22 miles** and another right onto partially paved Old Squires Road at **44.33 miles**. There are a few quiet residences on this section of road. At **44.77 miles** you will reach paved Red Creek Road.

From here, the trail is all road walking to its terminus at the Shinnecock Canal some two miles distant. It is hoped that some crossing of private land can be secured in the future but more needs to be done to accomplish this. Nonetheless, the road walking is pleasant and on roads that don't have much traffic. After making a left onto Red Creek Road the trail makes a right onto Newtown Road at **44.89 miles**, passing **Squire Pond** on the left and passing through the Shinnecock Indian Reservation land in a wooded area (sand dunes block a view of nearby Great Peconic Bay here). One option is to head off the road northeast (left) just past the last road on the right (Washington Heights Avenue) and make your way to the beach. Here, you can walk along a great stretch of beachfront on the bay to the Shinnecock Canal. The trail currently ends at the Montauk Highway underpass (there is parking here) at the **46.77 mile** mark but changes in the trail with further acquisitions will undoubtedly lengthen it. Beyond this point, the trail will head east onto the South Fork, but there is much private land in Southampton Town to deal with and furthermore, the land just beyond the canal is quite narrow. Hopefully, this all-important link in the Paumanok Path will be completed soon. Then, the trail will go all the way to the Montauk Point Lighthouse at Long Island's easternmost point.

Access

Car

This 46.77 mile trail crosses at least 18 paved roads offering opportunity to plan shorter hikes using two cars. Access to the trail can also be gained by using side trails such as the Red Trail or Yellow Trail in Rocky Point Natural Resources Management Area, the Brookhaven Trail, the Yellow Access Trail in Hampton Hills, the Main Loop in the David A. Sarnoff Pine Barrens Preserve, the Birch Creek Trail, the Blue Trail in Sears-Bellows Park or the main (yellow) trail in Red Creek Park. Access to the western trailhead in Rocky Point is located in an unpaved parking area on the south side of Route 25A .4 mile west of Rocky Point Road. There is a Burger King directly across the street from the lot. The eastern end of the trail is located at the Shinnecock Canal where one can park along the western side of the canal on Canal Road West. This trailhead can be reached by taking Sunrise Highway (Route 27) to exit 65 south to Montauk Highway (county Route 80). Proceed east on Montauk Highway a little over 2 miles and make a left onto Newtown Road and the first right onto Canal Road West after crossing over the railroad tracks.

Buses

SCT5A, 8A, 62

Access for Short Interior Hikes

There are also popular starting places for interior hikes which allow parking for several cars. Here are some of them: the parking area on the north side of Whiskey Road in Middle Island located about 1.1 miles west of Rocky Point Road; The Pine Trail Nature Preserve parking area on the south side of Route 25 (Middle Country Rd.) in Ridge, about 0.4 mile east of William Floyd Parkway; and Halsey Manor Road in Manorville just south of the LIE, which can be reached by taking LIE exit 70 south about 1.2 miles and making a left onto Halsey Manor Road where cars can be parked in the grassy area just south of the LIE overpass about 0.8 mile after the turn. Another good place to begin hikes is the northern parking area of Suffolk Community College Riverhead campus located off Speonk-Riverhead Rd just south of County Rd 51. The campus can be reached by taking LIE exit 70 south to the exit for Route 51, then making a left and proceeding east to Speonk-Riverhead Rd. Make a right onto that road and the first right will take you in to the college. When you enter, bear to the left and make your first right into the parking lot. Park as far back in the northwest portion of the lot as possible and pick up the yellow trail that takes you into the college kettlehole and junction with the white blazes of the Paumanok Path. Farther East, the state parking lot on the west side of County Route 104 is located about 0.75 north of the junction County Route 31. County Route 31 is exit 63 on Route 27 (Sunrise Highway).

Rocky Point Natural Resources Management Area

Length: 5.3 miles. Blaze: red

USGS topographic map: Middle Island

This 6,150 acre area is often referred to as the Rocky Point Co-op because of the cooperative use of the land by hikers, naturalists, horseback riders, hunters, and mountain bikers. For more information on the history of this large piece of Pine Barrens terrain see the Paumanok Path section, p. 119. This is predominantly dry land, laced with many woods roads, firebreaks, and side trails with much evidence of prior use by the RCA Corporation. Marconi Boulevard, formerly called Rocky Point Road, is named for the Italian radio pioneer whose research led to the first international radio communications. Evidence of RCA's presence can be seen in the concrete footings that once supported 440-foot towers, cables, and transmission networks. The nearby Rocky Point Post Office has a large mural that commemorates the "First Trans-Atlantic Shortwave Message from Rocky Point to Europe," which was sent on November 5, 1921.

In the Pine Barrens evidence of fire is widespread, but the fires of August 1995 were the largest in memory. Amid the burned trees re-growth is occurring, particularly by blueberries that take advantage of increased sunlight. Native Algonquins and colonial berry-pickers would set blazes to improve their harvest. A permit is required to hike here; applying will help the DEC justify the funding for more enforcement and management. You can obtain a permit at the DEC Regional Headquarters on the SUNY Stony Brook campus, or call them at (631) 444-0273, or request one by writing to NYSDEC, Division of Lands and Forests, Building 40, SUNY-Stony Brook, Stony Brook, NY 11790-2356.

This parcel is bordered by Route 25 on the south, Route 25A on the north, unpaved Wading River Hollow Road and Woodlot Road on the east, and Radio Avenue on the west. Marconi Boulevard (Rocky Point Road) cuts through it north-to-south, and Whiskey Road east-to-west. Most of the land lies north of Whiskey Road, and the larger parcel is on the east side of that road. The USGS or DOT topographic map for Middle Island and the LIGTC Pine Barrens Trail Map (western section) will help you follow trails and identify landmarks. The DEC also gives out a crude map; it locates intersecting horse and bike trails. Access roads and fire lanes created by RCA make for fine off-trail ramblings, but without a detailed map you may wind up far from your car. A map and compass should be carried with you on any such forays. Most of the area is in the coastal plain between the Harbor Hill and Ronkonkoma moraines; the northern section just touches the Harbor Hill Moraine. The land is flat with some rolling terrain, hills and kettleholes in the

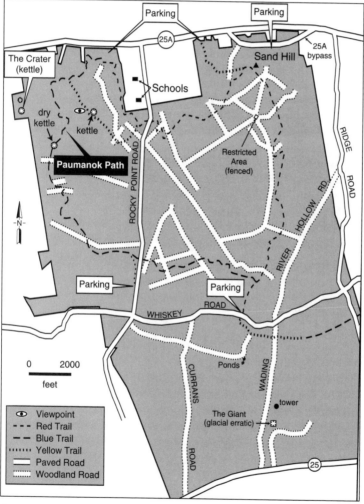

Rocky Point N. R. M. A., Rocky Point, NY

northern section. There are a few small seasonal wetlands in the southern sections. On a small coastal pond in early December I saw a tundra swan (also called whistling swan) resting during its migration from west of Hudson Bay. You may also see the rare buck moth in this habitat.

In spring birdfoot and woolly blue violets, common cinquefoil and trailing arbutus line the sides of the woods roads, and later blue toadflax grows in small clearings. Bluebirds can be found in burnt open areas. In June, tree swallows fly about in the wider grassy fire breaks, where nesting boxes have been set up for them. In autumn the showy aster, goldenrods and thoroughworts bloom among scarlet oaks and staggerbush. In late fall small active flocks of cedar waxwings pass through. During the winter cross-country skiing is permitted on the woods roads.

The Giant

There are two main hiking trails within the area, a **blue and a red trail**, both of which are about five miles long. An excellent 10-mile hike using both trails can be launched from several different access areas. **Four shorter yellow trails** connect to the main trails. The DEC cuts and maintains the trails, and blazes with their plastic round disks. The trails mostly follow abandoned woods roads or herd paths created by deer, but some new cutting was necessary to complete them. Since the Paumanok Path follows the length of the blue trail, you should consult that section of the book begining on page 123 for a description. The other trails will be discussed here.

The preserve's newest acquisition is on its southern border running to Route 25 (Middle Country Road). The land was acquired from the Baier Lustgarten Nursery, which was once the largest plant nursery in New York State. Today, the hiker can wander among tall hedgerows of evergreen spruces and see exotic plants slowly being overtaken by the surrounding native vegetation. There is an old barn put together without the use of nails near Route 25 but this structure will probably be leveled as it is a hazard to anyone exploring it and funds are not available for restoration. A house Mr. Lustgarten lived in still stands on Middle Country Road (Route 25). A large glacial erratic named **The Giant** is located about 0.7 mile north of Route 25, just north of the bend in the only paved road to pierce the property (it is closed off now). The recent DOT map shows the road turning eastward right near the boulder. A tall communications tower about 0.2 mile north of the rock can also be used as a reference point. The fires of 1995 reached The Giant as evidenced by the burnt trees on the north side, but firefighters must have stopped it at this point.

The Rocky Point Red Trail

The **5.3 mile red trail** runs north from the Whiskey Road parking lot to the parking area on Route 25A where the Paumanok Path begins. This trail makes a great 10-mile loop when hiked in conjunction with the blue-blazed trail. It can also be hiked in smaller sections with younger children, say from Whiskey Road to another car at the Rocky Point Road parking lot, by using the blue-blazed trail as well. This hike, which is just over a mile, traverses some of the burn areas from the 1995 fires.

The Whiskey Road parking lot is on the north side of Whiskey Road in Ridge a little more than a mile east of Rocky Point Road. A large sign put up by the DEC shows the red disks the DEC uses for this trail and the white rectangular paint blazes of the Paumanok Path. There is room for several cars in this gravel lot. Whiskey Road got its name in a colorful way. In the 1700s workers were hired to cut a road through the forest from the Randall Homestead in what is now Ridge to Coram some 7 miles away. They were paid partly in whiskey, which they drank while the crude road was being hewn out of the heavily wooded terrain. The result was this winding road, and believe it or not, the road actually had to be straightened into to its present curvy route!

From the parking lot you head north into an area that had some of the hottest fires in 1995. I was in this area just three days after the fires burnt out this section on the night of August 22, 1995. It resembled the moon; there was no color at all, just black and gray with no sign of life of any kind. The smell of burnt wood permeated the air and ash rose up with every step. This section had a hot crown fire, which means that the tops of trees burnt as windswept flames jumped from tree to tree. It has been interesting to watch as this section has "sprouted up;" the once shaded woods have now become clearings filled with thickening clumps of quick-growing scarlet oak. They are now six to seven feet tall. I have seen the New York State bird, the eastern bluebird, in this area every year since the fires have opened the woods up. At **0.4 mile** a junction is reached where the white-blazed Paumanok Path goes off to the left with the blue trail. As you head north away from this junction you will notice an area where brush trucks battling the 1995 blaze mowed down many small trees. Just beyond this, you'll cross the first main woods road at about **0.45 mile**. Along this road in either direction (especially west) trailing arbutus blooms in late April and early May and, since the fires, a healthy growth of birdfoot violet has sprung up to the southwest (left). Look for them in early May lining the roadside, especially where it turns northwest.

The trail enters a section of oak-dominated open woods before reaching another woods road about **1.0 mile** from the parking lot. After crossing this old access road you will pass some open clearings on the right (east). The DEC maintains these clearings by mowing them and planting grasses that offer food and cover to game birds such as bobwhite quail and ringed-necked pheasants. The trail used to pass through a dense stand of small pitch pines here but they were obliterated in the fires. Beyond here the trail curves to the west and passes a mature sugar maple off to the left of the trail. This tree is a real freak in these parts and is the only isolated specimen growing here that managed to survive the fire. It was damaged in the fires but fortunately the crown survived. Sugar maples are rare on Long Island and non-existent in the Pine Barrens. It is this species, associated with the cool moist woods of the mountainous northeast, that is tapped for its sweet sap, which is boiled to make maple syrup. What this tree is doing out in the middle of these woods here is anyone's guess. The trail then turns north and goes down a long relatively straight section that may have been a woods road at one time but is now overgrown. On a late March afternoon I once paused along here and suddenly found the ground at my feet to be full of activity. Dozens of little animals were in motion back and forth going under and over the leaf litter on the forest floor. Closer inspection revealed them to be shrews, most likely a species called least shrews. These little animals are very small and resemble field mice a first glance; closer inspection reveals pointy snouts and tiny eyes that are quite different from those of mice. They have a very high body metabolism requiring them to constantly seek food. Pound for pound shrews are among the most ferocious predators in nature.

As the trail continues northward you will cross a firebreak created by the fire departments to contain the 1995 fires. Growth will be slow to come here since a bulldozer was needed to cut a swath in the woods to gain access to the area, thus stripping the thin layer of topsoil, and a bike trail now uses it. You will notice that the sandy soil is exposed in this 20-foot-wide opening. Beyond this there are no more signs of recent fire damage.

The trail eventually turns left, crosses a bike path (note the yellow markers), and skirts a clearing on the left that is maintained by the DEC for wildlife habitat and food sources. Nesting boxes are placed here for bluebirds, house wrens, and tree swallows. Soon at a junction of woods roads the trail turns right onto a wide, overgrown path that may have been an RCA access road. In this stretch of oak-pine forest the terrain slopes down to the right into **Telegraph Hollow,** named for an old telephone pole still standing at the bottom. Telegraph Hollow was known for years by hunters and hikers, but in recent years a series of looping mountain bike trails have been made in it.

The Red Trail crosses a faint path and continues northward until it crosses a horse trail on a busier woods road. A little farther on it crosses a wide sandy

road that was once a main access road to one of the RCA control buildings. Down to the left (south by southwest) is a clearing guarded by two brick pillars marking the location where the building once stood. The DEC removed them in the early 1990s to eliminate a potential hazard to hikers. To the right the wide road will take you to parking area 26 on the Route 25A bypass in Rocky Point in about half a mile.

The trail continues through a woods before crossing another road and feedlot. You will then go straight uphill. Keep an eye out here for the tiny purple wood violets that bloom on this slope in April. You will reach the top of **Sand Hill** at **2.8 miles**, and when the leaves are

A winter moon over the burn area around sunset

down you can see through the trees over the coastal plain towards the South Shore. At 210 feet Sand Hill is the highest point on the Rocky Point property, marking the fringe of the Harbor Hill Moraine, which runs the length of the North Shore. An old sand-mining operation created the open steep slope on the east side of the hill. Long Island Sound lies 1.4 miles north of where you are standing. The trail heads to the west (left) from the top. Recent growth has

obscured a view of the SUNY Medical Center some miles off. In a saddle between this and a nearby 180 foot hill, the trail takes a left and heads into the woods. The path straight ahead is a **yellow-blazed access trail** which takes you to parking sites 26, 27, and 28 on the Route

A morning of solitude cross country skiing after a snow

25A bypass. Besides the typical pine-oak forest in these hills there are also American chestnut, pignut hickory, sassafras and even some flowering dogwoods more reminiscent of western Long Island.

The Red Trail heads away from this hilly section, crosses the same fire break as before and passes into thick scrubby woodlands. In a short distance it crosses another less used woods road and continues through open barren areas before following an overgrown path through a small recent burn area. The tall pitch pines have charred trunks but have survived. The open understory has patches of aromatic bayberry alongside the trail. Keep an eye out off to the right of the trail for the sets of concrete footing that are all that remain of the antenna field that once stood here. One afternoon I almost stepped on an eastern box turtle right in the middle of the trail. I could tell it was a male from the bright red eyes that stared out at me from underneath its shell. The trail crosses a bike path and after some twists and turns reaches Rocky Point Road at **4.3 miles**. Just before crossing the road you pass a large area of hay-scented ferns. They grow on hummocks created originally to support RCA's tall communication towers. Hay-scented ferns are a bright green with a nice scent about them. They are smaller yet more attractive than the more common bracken fern.

On the west side of Rocky Point Road you proceed through the woods reaching a junction with another **yellow-blazed trail** at **4.45 miles.** This trail goes through uneven terrain close to some of the dry kettleholes that dot the region. It links up to the blue-blazed trail (and the Paumanok Path) in 1.2 miles; the red-yellow-blue trail combination makes an easy 2.5 mile loop from the Route 25A parking lot. Just beyond this junction you reach a wide fire-break that is mowed over every few years to prevent tree growth. Tall natural grasses such as broomsedge and little bluestem flourish here as well as such sun-loving flowers as blue curls, Maryland golden aster and slender golden-rod. In winter, the grasses give off a bright copperish hue in the low shining sun. Beyond here the trail passes through the woods behind the Rocky Point schools, eventually reaching an old paved access road to this northern portion the RCA property. A right turn takes you past thick viney bittersweet growth to the parking area on Route 25A some **5.3 miles** from Whiskey Road.

Access
Car

The trailhead for both the Red and Blue Trails (as well as the Paumanok Path) is located in the unpaved parking lot on the north side of Route 25A 0.4 mile west of Rocky Point Road directly across from Burger King. Hiker access can also be found in the parking lot on the west side of Rocky Point Road a little over 2 miles south of Route 25A. This lot, used primarily by mountain bik-ers, is only about 0.25 mile north of Whiskey Road. Hikers should head through the clearing along the road (north) away from the lot to pick up one of the yellow blazed connector trails. Go left on the Yellow Trail a hundred yards or so to the junction with the BlueTrail (which is also the Paumanok Path at this point). Another access point is the previously mentioned parking lot about 1.1 miles west of Rocky Point Road located on Whiskey Road. There are two good access points from parking areas on the south side of Route 25A bypass in Rocky Point. Both lots are located east of Rocky Point Road. about 0.5 mile apart, the first being a little over 0.5 mile east of this junction. Be aware that during 3 weeks in January these lots will be used by deer hunters Monday through Friday. Permits are required; see page 150 for more information.

Buses
SCT5A, 62

Cathedral Pines County Park and Prosser Pines Preserve

Length: 2 to 3 hours. Blaze: none

USGS topographic maps: Middle Island, Bellport

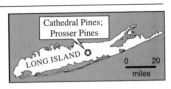

There are two fine parks located in Middle Island, one on each side of County Route 21 (also known as Middle Island-Yaphank Road). Driving south from Route 25 in a little more than a mile you come to the smaller of the two, **Prosser Pines Nature Preserve**, on the east side of the road. A little farther on opposite the junction with Longwood Road is the entrance to **Cathedral Pines County Park** about 1.5 miles south of Route 25. In Prosser Pines park mammoth white pines tower over the visitor in what I think of as Long Island's mini-version of the sequoia forests of Northern California. This unusual forest has an equally unusual history. Jonathan Edwards, who served as an officer for the British in the French and Indian War, was awarded 300 acres of land in Middle Island north of this site in 1759. He reportedly brought some white pine seedlings from Quebec to plant on his property. White pines were rare on Long Island and certainly didn't exist in the Pine Barrens. Yet, they thrived and in 1812 "Uncle Billy" Dayton obtained some seedlings and planted them on his farm on this site. In time, they were named cathedral pines as they reminded folks of a cathedral towering overhead. The site was named for the Prosser family, who bought the site in the early 1900s and preserved it for future generations. When we first came to eastern Suffolk County, my wife and I pulled our daughters on sleds through its snowy trails, cross-country skiing under the shelter of the pines during a snowstorm. I once came upon a wedding being prepared in this outdoor cathedral, and during an early morning run I observed a barred owl mysteriously staring me down from one of the pines.

The cool canopy of the pines has created a sort of micro-habitat of vegetation not expected amidst the dry surrounding Pine Barrens. Sweet birch with its wintergreen-smelling bark, American beech and American chestnut are all found in the understory and grove edges. These trees cannot be found for miles around. You'll notice that not much grows in the shade of the pines since so little sun reaches the forest floor. Still, you can see lovely pink lady's slippers blooming in late spring and witch hazel trees blooming in late autumn. Notice the occasional old mound of raised earth and boundary ditches that show the land has been owned and used for a long time. Since the parks are not very big they are suitable for walks with children (though you can find loop hikes and spend a couple of hours here). The preserve is bordered by nurseries on the east and has some old deteriorating buildings in the grassy areas on the north side. The nursery land has been purchased by Suffolk County as part of a land-preservation initiative. The meadow-like area on the north is very colorful in late summer as brilliant orange butterflyweed and bright yellow Maryland golden asters predominate in places. You may see the

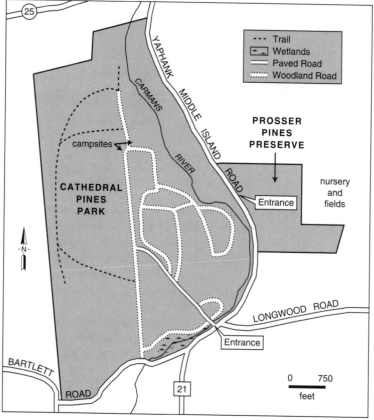

Cathedral Pines Park, Prosser Pines Preserve, Middle Island, NY

A walker dwarfed by the cathedral of white pines in Prossers Pines Preserve

stumps of trees that were downed by Hurricane Gloria in 1985. The death of the older trees has allowed younger ones to receive sunlight to grow and preserve this special grove.

Just down the road to the south is the entrance to **Cathedral Pines County Park**. A much larger area than Prosser Pines, the park is used for group camping, shows, and the like. A mountain bike trail has been put in the park, which has compromised off-trail exploring and caused damage to fragile soil in remote sections. Yet it remains a good place to get acquainted with hiking. When you first enter you can see the upper Carmans River as a small, slow-moving creek. Not far from its source, the Carmans borders the park on the east as it meanders close to County Route 21. In autumn the brilliant colors of tupelos and red maples that thrive in the moist soil of the river make this stretch of road memorable. A walk along to the left (south) from the small booth just inside the park entrance takes you to the wetlands of the upper Carmans (on your left). Here skunk cabbages, the first flowers of spring, push their odd maroon hoods through the ice in February. In May the starflower, Canada mayflower and pink lady's slipper bloom in this area along the dirt road. From the entrance booth uphill through the pine woods you come to a fenced-off clearing on the right where in April and early May the increasingly rare birdsfoot violet grows along the edges. A few years back the flowers carpeted half this clearing, but constant mowing from park employees and subsequent use of this area for recreation has confined the flower to the trail edges. The marked bike path starts here as well.

Returning to the large clearing on the north side of the park, find the dirt road that passes the numbered campsites and head into the woods in the northwest corner, following the dirt road northward. Look for the uncommon wild-flower pipsissewa blooming rather inconspicuously on the forest floor in July. A close relative of the more common spotted wintergreen, it is associated with the mountains and north country, yet it is found here and in a patch of woods in nearby Middle Island and is quite rare on Long Island. A long loop can be made as this road ends and a trail can be picked up heading west and back to the south again. This trail traverses the little-traveled backwoods (west side) of the park among oaks, hickories, an occasional chestnut and mountain laurels that flower in June. A wide path will take you back to the east to make a complete circuit ending at the campsites and the large clearing where all the park activities take place. Quiet walkers may see white-tail deer or red fox with a little luck. Two to three hours should be time enough to walk this park.

Access

Car

To get to the entrance of Cathedral Pines County Park take LIE exit 66 (County Route 21) north a little over 3 miles to the park entrance on the left (west). The entrance to Prossers Pines Preserve is on the same road about 0.3 mile farther north on the opposite (east) side of the road. A green key to Suffolk County parks is required to avoid a parking fee in season.

Warbler Woods

Length: 2 miles one way. Blaze: none

USGS topographic map: Bellport

A mile north of Yaphank on either side of County Road 21, Warbler Woods is a favorite place for birders to observe spring and fall migrations of these small, active and colorful "butterflies of the bird world." Parking is very limited; only two or three cars can fit on the west side of the road in a small pull-off area. You can see warblers best flitting among the bare branches of late spring. Keep in mind that bow hunting is allowed here between November 1 and December 30, so stay on the trails and wear bright colors if you hike here at that time of year.

The topography of the area ranges from hilly glacial moraine to the bottom-lands of the Carmans River and its floodplain, offering a diversity of habitats. The west side of the road is flatter and a smaller area to explore. Unfortunately, ATV damage is occurring at an alarming rate in this beautiful area. A dirt road goes off into the woods here to the right, circumventing a red maple swamp. Notice all the dead snags of older trees that woodpeckers and some other small animals use for nesting holes. This area is very colorful in autumn. Continuing west away from this swamp you pass through an open oak dominated forest; take a left here and the straight path leads you through wet woods with large trees. The understory of this part of the path has a lot of sweet pepperbush, a shrub also known as soapbush because the flowers can be worked into a lather when rubbed with water. You will soon come to a dead end with a fine view of the **Carmans River** looking northward. Ducks are usually flushed out of hiding here. The banks are dominated by spicebush, a plant whose leaves are fragrant when crushed. Look for winterberry with bright reddish-orange berries along its branches in fall and winter. During peak foliage time red maples and towering tupelos adorn the banks of the upper Carmans River here. On one October exploration along the river I came face to face with a coopers hawk sitting in a tree waiting for some unsuspecting songbird to come by. Bushwhacking along the banks of the river is hazardous as it is thick with prickly stands of briers and heavily infested with deer ticks. You must return the way you came.

The east side of the road offers longer hikes since there is more land adjacent to undeveloped woods. A path leads away from the road on the east side just

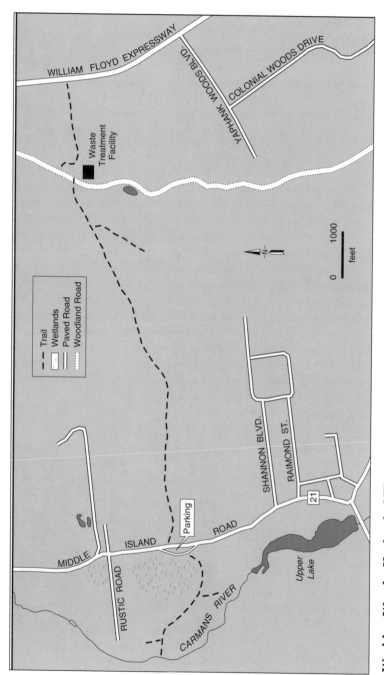

Warbler Woods, Yaphank, NY

south of the pull-off area. The trail heads slightly uphill as it climbs the Ronkonkoma Moraine. Off to the right (south) the moraine reaches over 190 feet in elevation. As the trail starts down the other side you may notice that the plants are more typical of the North Shore than the Pine Barrens. Hickories grow among the tall oaks and flowering dogwood thrives in the understory. You will also come upon some small wetland ponds on the left (north) side; I have spotted wood ducks here on occasion. This area is dotted with small vernal ponds that surely harbor salamanders in springtime. There are also side trails to the south useful for longer outings once you have become more familiar with the area.

The trail passes through a transition woods where vines and shrubs close in on the trail at points. Eventually you enter a full pine barrens environment and come to an area opened up by a fire in the early 1990s. Shortly thereafter a side trail goes off to the right (south) into a heavily wooded area offering several hours of exploring all the way to the Yaphank Hills of the moraine again, with views through the trees in winter across the coastal plain. If you continue on the main trail from this junction, you will come upon an old sandy woods road associated with the Longwood Estate to which it leads heading north (left).Turning north on this road in a short distance you can pick up a path off to the right (east); take this to the William Floyd Parkway more than 2 miles from County Route 21. If you continue north you will find other trails just east of the Longwood Estate. One note of caution, though: a mall may be built near the Par Meadows Race Track to the south, which could adversely affect walking in the southern part of this area.

Access

Car

Take LIE exit 66, continuing north on County Route 21 about 1.8 miles. Look for a small area to pull over 2 or 3 cars on the west (left) side of the road. The trailhead for the longer hike described in the book is on the opposite side of the road just south of the parking area.

Bus

SCT7E

A perched wetland on the Rokonkoma Moraine in Warbler Woods

Randall Pond Preserve

Length: 3 miles. Blaze: red, then blue

USGS topographic map: Middle Island

The Ridge Environmental Conservation Area has long been known to sportsmen as a center of hunting activities on Long Island. The hunters' check-station is located there, as well as holding pens for ringed-neck pheasants which are stocked at various sites throughout the area. The 184 acre parcel was purchased by the state in 1914 and used to raise bobwhite quail and pheasants, but that operation is now upstate. The land has a surprising diversity: open grasslands, transition shrublands, forest, wetlands, and ponds. It is mainly flat but has some gently rolling terrain in a few spots. This is a great walk for families with children or folks looking to get acclimated to hiking, and is also a fine example of how the land changes through time if left alone. These

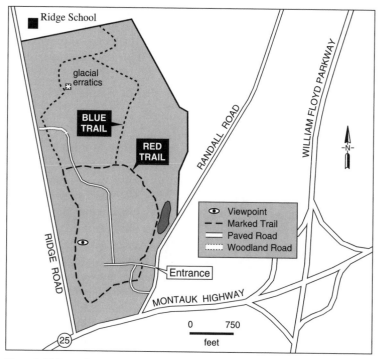

Randall Pond Preserve, Ridge, NY

changes, called succession, show how plant species replace (or succeed) each other as field eventually becomes forest. Because of its diverse habitats, you see a great variety of wildlife, especially birds, in this preserve.

The Randall Pond Preserve is bordered by Randall Road on the east, Route 25 on the south, Ridge Road on the west and the Ridge Elementary School on the north. The school is linked to the preserve by a small side trail through a locked gate open only to the school. If the gate were open to hikers, it could link to the Paumanok Path just north of the school, offering new walking options.

At the park entrance there are picnic tables and restrooms as well as the hunters' check station. You can pick up a brochure at one of the nearby informative kiosks that describes the **Randall Pond Nature Trail**. There are two loop trails in the conservation area. The southerly loop is blazed with the red disks used by the state and the northerly one is blue. Together, they form a large figure eight. Look for the beginning of the **red-blazed trail** on the east side of the kiosks near a large rock with a plaque. The trail goes north along the shores of Randall Pond. Wetland species such as pussy willows and sedges grow in the shallows. The pond is bordered by large red maples hanging over the water. Rainbow trout are stocked for anglers. The trail goes over a small bridge where a gully drains into the pond in excessively wet weather. While leading a hike here for one of my daughter's classes, I observed two shrews, probably short-tailed shrews, fiercely fighting amongst the leaves at our feet. They were so intent on each other they did not even know we were watching.

The trail eventually turns away from the pond and heads into the dry uplands of Pine Barrens terrain. The woods here are second-growth mature forest. Observant hikers will undoubtedly see some surprises. I have seen nesting

red-tailed hawks in the tall pitch pines here. On another hike I caught a glimpse of a snake, a northern black racer darting across the trail in front of me. The wooded section of the northerly trail is blue-blazed and also holds delights. On a walk with one of my daughter's classes we spotted a yellow-

An eastern box turtle seen along the trail

shafted flicker, a rather large woodpecker. It was nesting in a hole in a dead tree alongside the trail. It was amusing to watch it stick its head out of the hole when I tapped on the tree. On another hike we saw a little brown bat sleeping upside-down while hanging to a branch in thick shrubbery along the southern portion of the red trail. Some of the clearings on the west side of the **blue-blazed trail** are covered with colorful wildflowers. In spring, wintercress brightens the scene with its carpets of brilliant yellow. Later on, in early summer, the pink-purple crown vetch seems to be in every opening. Nearby, the small white flowers of wild strawberries dot the path in spring, and the fruit is ripe in June.

As you walk south on the west side of the red trail the area becomes very shrubby and full of thickets. This is prime habitat for the eastern cottontail rabbit. A walk in early morning or late afternoon will undoubtedly start a few scurrying in front of you. The nesting boxes here are put up for tree swallows. Bobwhite quail can also be heard near here. As you continue south the terrain opens up to grasslands that are mowed to prevent the invasion of shrubs and woody vegetation. This grassy valley was farmed up until the 1970s. On a late spring walk I heard an energetic almost frantic song from a bobolink, a yellow and black grassland bird that is quite uncommon on Long Island. On another hike I saw a black-billed cuckoo, the only time I've ever seen this somewhat secretive bird. There are two benches located nearby which make excellent places to rest. From the more southerly one atop the slope you can look back and see all three different habitats featured in the preserve. The nearby grasslands give way to the shrub and small tree habitat. In the distance you can see the mature forest-stage of plant growth. A brochure describing the trails with explanations for each numbered station throughout can be obtained in a wooden box attached to one of the kiosks near the beginning of the trail. During the small-game hunting season beginning in October, you can get a close look at the beautiful ring-necked pheasants that are held in wire enclosures across from the picnic tables. These birds are released onto public lands during the season. The males have the colorful heads while the females are a mottled brown color.

Access

Car

Take LIE exit 68 to William Floyd Parkway (County Route 46) north about 4 miles to State Route 25, turn left (west) and make the first right (north) onto Randall Road where the preserve parking lot will be a short distance up on the left.

Wertheim
National Wildlife Refuge

Length: 3 miles. Blaze: posted signs

USGS topographic map: Bellport

For trail map see next section, page 177

Southaven Park;
Wertheim N.W.R.

LONG ISLAND

0   20
miles

The US Fish and Wildlife Service oversees eight National Wildlife refuges on Long Island, three of which are open for regular public use. Wertheim National Wildlife Refuge is the largest of this group, comprising 2,400 acres of woodlands, fields, freshwater tributaries, salt marshes, and ponds, as well as brackish, salt, and freshwater wetlands. The refuge is bisected by the Carmans River where it empties into Bellport Bay. Long Island Rail Road tracks also cross the refuge in its northern section. The Carmans estuary is one of the largest undeveloped estuaries left on Long Island. It can be best explored by canoe from Montauk Highway where you can paddle out into Great South Bay. Whichever way you choose to explore Wertheim, the USGS topographic map of the Bellport quadrangle will be useful.

The refuge is named after Cecile and Maurice Wertheim, who donated most of the land to the government in 1975. The land was originally inhabited by the Unkechaug tribe of Native Americans, who lived on the area's rich harvest of fish and shellfish. This unspoiled tract of property still has some of the Island's best habitat for rare mink and weasel as well as some of the least-seen breeding waterfowl, reptiles and amphibians, animals that seem to be on the decline across much of Long Island. There are also healthy populations of wild turkeys, hawks, and owls.

The word refuge takes on a special meaning at Wertheim; there's no hunting here, and the property is maintained throughout the year by mowing and controlled burns for the benefit of wildlife. Follow the entrance road over the river to the headquarters. The **White Oak Nature Trail**, a loop on the west side of the river, is about 3 miles long with the option to short cut it at 1.5 miles. This long easy trail is a good one for families or beginners wishing for a quiet walk with a chance to view wildlife of many kinds. It is also a good winter walk since it is somewhat sheltered from the blustery northwest winds on clear winter days. A very good descriptive brochure can be obtained from the refuge office; it has an interpretive map that follows several numbered stations along the trail. A kiosk with a map and some interesting information about wildlife in the refuge is located by the parking area. Although the map is excellent, I'll describe the trail so you can decide whether it is the type of walk you would like to do. It is important to note that the refuge keeps the trails open only from 8 a.m. to 4 p.m. The office remains open until 4:30 p.m.

Snags like this provide nesting or roosting habitat for birds and other animals

Starting out from the information center, you will cross the road through young second-growth hardwoods on a wide trail that has wood chips spread out to make walking dry and easy. You may notice that the most common tree here is black cherry, and that the trees are heavily covered with lichens; so much so that at times the dark-colored trunks appear a crusty gray-green. Keep an eye out for wildflowers in spring, particularly the lovely starflower in mid-May. Although not blazed the trail is marked by signs at each intersection and is easy to follow. The walk is almost completely on wide woods roads. The preserve puts up nesting boxes for birds and has forest openings and clearings offering a variety of habitats and ecotones (edges between two habitats) for wildlife. There are many deer in the refuge and it is possible that you may see some scamper out of sight as you stroll quietly along these wide paths.

A few minutes into the walk, look for signs for a side trail off to the right that takes you to station #2 where a **wooden blind** with cloth coverings over viewing slots allows you to sit quietly and observe wildlife in a natural, undisturbed state. Approach this blind quietly and you will probably be rewarded by having the chance to watch white-tail deer browse. Early morning or late afternoon are the best times for such viewing. You may also see wild turkeys or catch a glimpse of a red fox if you are lucky. Farther on down the trail you will reach a junction where the shortcut back to the parking area goes off to the left (east) to complete the 1 mile short loop. This loop is a good walk for young children. The long trail continues southward past a grassy forest glade (station #7) and through some tall pitch pines. Eventually you will catch a glimpse of the bay and barrier beach of Fire Island National Seashore to the south. You will also see the wetlands of **Yapahank Creek** emerge on your right (west). This tributary of the **Carmans River** is best explored by canoe. Once near the wetlands you won't see much over the tall phragmites along its margins. Turning right you will come to station #8, which overlooks the Carmans River estuary across the straw-colored reeds to the pine woods of the opposite bank of the river (which itself is hidden). In late summer look for the showy large pink flowers of swamp rose-mallow rising above the grasses on the shoreline. The opposite side is also part of Wertheim National Wildlife Refuge but only reachable by canoe.

The trail now heads back northward with the river corridor on your right. There are tall pitch pines that leave the path covered with needles in late fall and winter, making for a pleasant walk. You will pass an active osprey platform as you continue north to another **blind** at station #10 down a side trail on the right (east). This blind will enable you to view a backwater where you may see muskrats or wild ducks.

Continuing on the trail you will pass a vernal pond (station #12) and its associated red maple forest which is very colorful in early autumn. Resident tupelo trees also turn scarlet in September as nights turn cooler and the days shorter. Farther on is **Owl Pond**, a freshwater pond with a lot of wildlife around it. Look for flycatchers darting after a meal or for turtles to quickly drop out of sight as you approach. Eventually the trail comes out to a grassy picnic area near the refuge office on the shore of the Carmans River. The river is still fresh water here although it is only 3 miles downstream to Bellport Bay. It becomes brackish in about 1.5 miles.

At one time there was direct access to the refuge on the east side of the river from Smith Road but problems with vandalism caused that to close. It's a shame because there is fine walking through woodlands and past **Woods Hole Pond** in a mile-long loop as well as side trails to explore. The beautiful wood duck has been spotted breeding in this pond. This loop trail, known as the **Indian Landing Trail**, is only accessible if you canoe to **Indian Landing** from the river. It is hoped that this trail will become useable again from the car parking lot on the east side of the refuge. If you choose to canoe through Wertheim, you may canoe all the way down past Fireplace Neck into the open waters of Bellport Bay. Fireplace Neck was so named for the large fires that used to be kept burning on the shoreline here to help alert whalers returning from sea. If you canoe into the bay be careful not to get stuck trying to return against the outgoing tide, or your going will be tough.

For information on trail availability call the headquarters at (631) 286-0485.

Access

Car

Take LIE exit 68 to William Floyd Parkway (County Route 46) south about 3 miles to Montauk Highway (County Route 80). Go west (right) about 0.7 mile and make a left (south) onto Old River Road (which shortly becomes Smith Road). Go a short distance to preserve signs for entrance on the right.

Train

From the Mastic-Shirley Train Station on the Montauk Branch cross William Floyd Parkway and proceed west on Northern Boulevard about 0.9 mile to its end on Smith Road. Turn right and the entrance to the preserve is a short distance down on the left (west) side. The walk to the refuge headquarters and White Oak Nature Trail is another 0.5 mile in nice surroundings as you pass the Carmans River and its wetlands.

Southaven County Park

Length: 5.2 miles. Blaze: unmarked

US topographic map: Bellport

The beautiful Carmans River is the center-piece of Southaven County Park. One of Long Island's four main rivers, it is over 12-miles long with a drainage basin of seventy-one square miles. The Carmans begins as a small brook in Middle Island near Route 25. It is best explored by canoe since car access points are limited. Very little of this river's banks are developed since public parks, preserves, and wildlife refuges protect much of it. The balance is made up of undeveloped private or agricultural land. Several miles of the Carmans with its wildlife and rare plants are explorable within the 1,366 acres of Southaven Park. The value of the land that comprises this park did not escape notice in the past. In the 1800s it was known as the Suffolk Club and was probably the most exclusive sportsmen's club in the New York area. Daniel Webster caught his famous 14-pound brook trout in the Carmans just south of present-day Montauk Highway. In the early 1900s it was purchased by Anson W. Hard and used as a private hunting and fishing lodge. It later became known as the Suffolk Lodge Game Preserve, and its reputation warranted an article in Look magazine in 1955. It became the first park opened by Suffolk County and today is used for group gatherings in the southern part of the park near the entrance on Victory Avenue (north service road of Sunrise Highway).

As you wander north on the typically sandy woods roads of the pine barrens, the noise of the crowds soon fades and nature prevails. Several trails going off to the east will lead down to the river. Waterfowl abound at any time of the year. On one spring outing I was startled to see a Canadian goose sitting on her nest on a small island in the river. As I watched silently the gander swam boldly towards me and looked ready to defend his turf. In the breeding season birds not often seen on Long Island such as the American redstart, the veery, and several flycatchers can be found here. North of the Long Island Rail Road tracks spring wildflowers rise out of the water in the many little inlets along the river. In spring look for clumps of bright yellow marsh marigold and deep-purple swamp violets. The rich soil along the banks also fosters starflower, Canada mayflower and the inconspicuous and rare Indian cucumber-root. In fall tupelos, red maple and highbush blueberry all turn crimson in a riot of color along the river. The park extends north of the Long Island Expressway and you can cross under it alongside the river between exits 67 and 68. The small pond just north of the Expressway at this point is

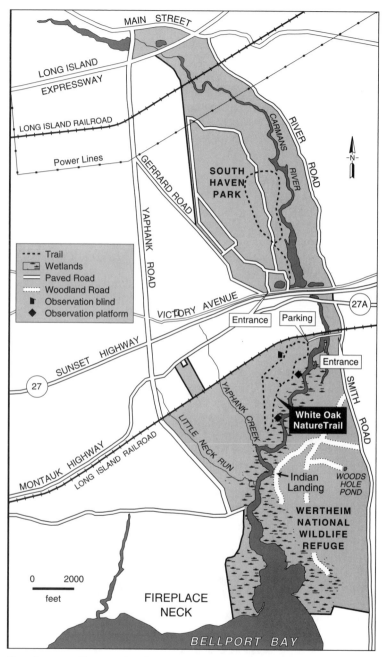

Legend

- - - - Trail
📭 Wetlands
—— Paved Road
- - - - Woodland Road
🚩 Observation blind
♦ Observation platform

MAIN STREET

LONG ISLAND EXPRESSWAY

LONG ISLAND RAILROAD

Power Lines

GERRARD ROAD

YAPHANK ROAD

CARMANS RIVER

RIVER ROAD

SOUTH HAVEN PARK

-N-

VICTORY AVENUE

27A

Entrance Parking

Entrance

SUNSET HIGHWAY

27

YAPHANK CREEK

White Oak NatureTrail

SMITH ROAD

MONTAUK HIGHWAY

LONG ISLAND RAILROAD

LITTLE NECK RUN

Indian Landing

WOODS HOLE POND

WERTHEIM NATIONAL WILDLIFE REFUGE

0   2000

feet

FIREPLACE NECK

BELLPORT BAY

Southaven County Park, Wertheim N. W. R., Brookhaven, NY

Weeks Pond. I have seen muskrats swimming around here. Look for the distinctive fuzzy buds of pussy willow in late winter along this stretch of the river. Hawks abound in this area as well. The upland portions of the trail are typical Pine Barrens terrain, but it is the river that makes this area appealing.

During the duck hunting season certain sections of the river should be avoided as riverside blinds are used by sportsmen. Signs are usually posted in their vicinity. Despite the lack of marked trails in the park, there is not a serious threat of becoming lost as the river bounds the east and fenced park boundary marks the west.

There is one interpretive nature trail that leaves the main parking area and heads north on a sandy woods road. A brochure available from a park office or through the Suffolk County Parks Department describes the eight numbered stations on the walk; it's a good introductory walk to the Pine Barrens. Blazed in white, it can be completed in less than an hour and is suitable for small children. It returns along the river where you may catch a glimpse of a fly fisherman.

Access

Car

Take LIE exit 68 for William Floyd Parkway south about 2.8 miles to Sunrise Highway. (27) and make a right (west). Stay on the service road (called Victory Avenue) for about 1 mile to the first park entrance on the right (north) just past the water. Parking and access to the trail is on the right a short way in.

The beautiful Carmans River can be seen along the paths of Southaven County Park

William Floyd Estate

Length: 2.2 mile loop. Blaze: blue

USGS topographic map: Moriches

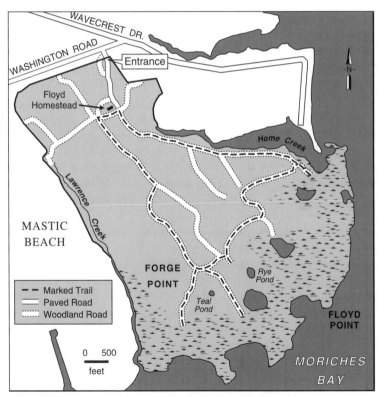

William Floyd was one of only two signers
of the Declaration of Independence from Long Island (the other was Francis
Lewis of Whitestone). These public patriots were all men of means who risked
death if the cause of liberty was lost or if they were caught. For that reason,
we honor their memories and the places they lived. The estate where William
Floyd resided once totaled 4,000 acres and went six miles north from the
grounds of the park named for him.

Built by Nicoll Floyd in 1724, the self-sustaining estate was inherited by son

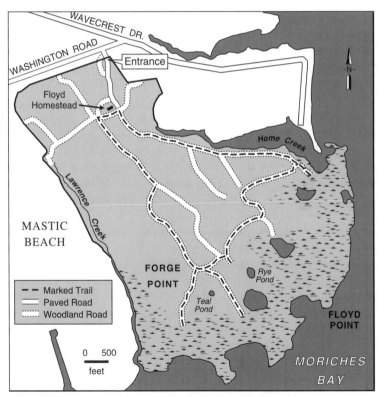

The William Floyd Estate, Mastic Beach, NY

William at age 18 when his parents died. Known for his hospitality, Floyd rose to the rank of major-general in the Continental Army. Like most patriots from Long Island, Floyd and his family fled to the safety of Connecticut when the British captured the island in August 1776. The British used the estate as well as the nearby Manor of St. George as bases of operation to protect the South Shore. The occupying forces ruined the place but Floyd returned after the war and rebuilt his estate to its former charm. It stayed in his family's hands as a summer home and hunting preserve into the 1970s. Today the 613-acre grounds on Forge Point contain a beautiful main house, a museum, a dozen-odd out buildings, and a family cemetery. The National Park Service runs the facility; it is open most of the year but has limited hours in winter. Call (631) 399-2030 for information.

To the walker this represents an opportunity to stroll unpaved roads through fields, woods, and salt marsh fronting Moriches Bay. There are 8.5 miles of trails that crisscross the property, including three marked trails. A crude map can be obtained near the parking area but a USGS topographic map or DOT map lists most of the main trails and will help locate some of the ponds in the southern section. The longest marked trail is **blue-blazed** and heads away from the southeast corner of the large open field in front of the main house. It goes along **Home Creek** on the eastern border of the property and reach-es a viewpoint near where the creek empties into Moriches Bay. It will loop around the southern section of the grounds and reach a merger with the short-er **Red and Yellow Trails**. All trails are on wide woods roads but they pass by fine open fields that contain many birds such as Carolina wren, northern cardinal, gray catbird, brown thrasher and bobwhite quail. Deer and fox can be spotted as well. The clearings help maintain a wider variety of wildlife than if the land was allowed to go entirely to woods. The forested areas are oak-hickory dominated by tupelo and a profusion of shadbush that blooms in late April and early May in the wetter sections. Try to explore some of the trails that take you down to the great view of the Fire Island barrier beach across Moriches Bay. Another goal is to locate little **Rye Pond**, which is not far from the bay. Although some of these overgrown paths can be quite wet at times, they will reward you with surprises like the great blue herons and egrets I spotted in the pond. The other larger ponds you will see on the map are sur-rounded by high phragmites and are somewhat inaccessible. You might want to find tiny **Teal Pond**, the farthest west of the five ponds. It was kept seclud-ed by the family so they would have a quiet place to observe wildlife. Wild ducks such as teal and wood ducks have been spotted here.

The William Floyd Estate is best walked (or cross-country skied) in the cooler season between October and June since there are many mosquitoes in summer.

Access

Car

Take LIE exit 68 for William Floyd Parkway south about 6.2 miles and make a left (east) onto Neighborhood Road. Proceed 1.9 miles and make a left (north) onto Whittier Drive which will run into Mastic Beach Road. Go 0.6 mile and turn right (east) onto Washington Avenue. The entrance to the estate is on the right (south) side in about 0.8 mile. The William Floyd Estate is only open from April through October at this time. Call (631) 399-2030 for more information.

The historic Floyd House is open to the public part of the year

Brookhaven State Park and The Brookhaven Trail

Length: 5.25 miles one way: Blaze: yellow

USGS topographic maps: Middle Island, Wading River

This undeveloped 2,500-acre state park is not well known to the general population and is used only by the hiking community familiar with it. Located between routes 25 on the south and 25A on the north with the William Floyd Parkway as its western border, this park brings many of the finer features of the Pine Barrens together in one place. It is currently under the jurisdiction of the New York State Office of Parks, Recreation and Historic Preservation (OPRHP), which is headquartered at Belmont Lake State Park. A free user permit for access is required so call the office at (631) 669-1000 to request one. There are plans to improve part of the park for horse and mountain bike use. From the hiker's perspective this could be a positive or a negative. Development would bring people into the park, which would undoubtedly spoil its solitude. However, along with this would come the enforcement so sorely needed to prevent increasing illegal dumping and motorbike/ATV destruction.

The property was once the northern part of the Camp Upton complex, which was a large army training base in both world wars. An interesting museum paying tribute to the camp is located in the Brookhaven National Labs where the camp was centered, south of Route 25. Irving Berlin was writing about old Camp Upton when he wrote his famous song, "Oh How I Hate to Get Up in the Morning." During the depression years of the 1930s the Civilian Conservation Corps (CCC) established camps at Upton that gave young men jobs preserving public land and planting trees.

Besides typical pine barrens terrain of ponds, open burn areas, and classic pitch pine and oak woods, Brookhaven State Park contains a section near its western boundary of oak-hickory forest with flowering dogwood in the understory and Christmas fern and wildflowers such as wood anemone and wild geranium on the forest floor. Ruffed grouse, great horned owls and the hermit thrush can be found breeding here. Wild turkeys now roam the forest floor. White-tail deer and red fox abound, along with the striped skunk. The eastern box turtle finds sanctuary within the park as does the beautiful northern ringed-neck snake. At night, bats fly through the clearings chasing insects, and whip-poor-wills sing from the thickets. In the burn areas the beautiful and increasingly rare bird's foot violet still holds on.

The Brookhaven Trail is the only marked trail currently in the park. It was originally intended to run all the way south to Great South Bay, but that idea was abandoned when problems crossing Brookhaven National Laboratory land

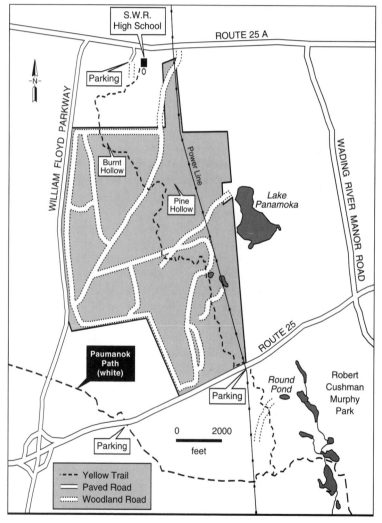

Brookhaven State Park, Brookhaven, NY

could not be resolved. This bright yellow-blazed trail winds roughly north to south to Route 25 and then goes 0.2 mile east and turns south onto county land where it eventually ends at the Paumanok Path. The total length to hike from Shoreham-Wading River High School to the Paumanok Path is **5.25 miles**. There are plans to extend the trail north to the Long Island Sound across land owned by the Long Island Power Authority, but these are being held up by concerns about crossing land adjacent to the Shoreham Power Plant.

Leaving the parking lot of Shoreham-Wading River High School off Route 25A, there is a nature trail just west (right) of the high school running track. Follow the small paved trail overlooking the track heading south and follow the crude white blazes on trees put there by the high school cross-country team. There are also yellow blazes that can be found here as the trail heads west away from the school. You will pass wooden benches for resting and cross a woods road at **0.5 mile**. Shortly after (**about 0.65 mile**) you will see a sign on the right explaining that this trail is for foot use only and requesting bikes and horses to stay off, a request that sometimes goes unheeded. This is where the yellow-blazed Brookhaven Trail leaves the white blazes which continue straight. The trail winds out through classic Pine Barrens rolling terrain. This section is actually on Brookhaven Town land that was once slated for development as a golf course but thankfully was preserved for walkers and runners to find some solitude. At **0.9 mile** from the school the trail crosses a woods road into Brookhaven State Park. In a little while it climbs gently up a slope and suddenly emerges at a viewpoint overlooking **Burnt Hollow**. Although the knoll is only 30 feet up hill, you get a panorama of a hollow that was opened up by fire a few years before. This is a special place with fox dens and signs of a resident great horned owl. Deer can often be seen here skulking up the opposite side of the hollow. The hollow is one of the cooler areas of the Island, and on clear nights the colder air tends to settle into it, causing a micro-climate. In mid- to late June while the surrounding woods are a vivid green the bottom of the hollow is a pinkish brown from the still-opening oak leaves. The trail follows along the top of Burnt Hollow and passes through shady pine woodlands and rolling terrain. Note that this area is loaded with bayberry on both sides of the trail. From the aromatic hard waxy berries of this plant the early settlers made candles that have come to be associated with the Christmas season. On a spring walk in this area I found the feathers of a ruffed grouse killed by an owl or fox. I have disturbed a great horned owl from its roost several times in these dense stands of pitch pines. When flushed, the ruffed grouse, an uncommon bird in most of Long Island, bursts out in a flurry of beating wings that can startle the unsuspecting hiker.

At **1.7 miles** the trail passes another woods road and winds along the west side of **Pine Hollow**. This pretty hollow filled with pitch pines contrasts sharply with Burnt Hollow since it has escaped fire for some time and is heavily wooded. Listen for the hermit thrush in June or July near here. Fox dens have also been found on the slopes of this secluded hollow in the most remote section of the park. Here the only sounds are bird's songs and the wind racing through the trees. The trail passes through open oak dominated woods and crosses another woods road at **2.4 miles** (this is an extension of Whiskey Road). Just before reaching it, a small scrub oak clearing is on the left (east). I have seen many large deer run across it in my travels. Notice the large burn to the west (right). It runs all the way south to Route 25 and the trail will skirt it again farther on. The trail winds for a while before eventually coming to a recent burn-site where there is extensive damage. The damage is not as much from the fire, since everything will grow back, as from the brush trucks of the local fire department that have obliterated sections of the trail. A future reroute of this section is not out of the question, but we will wait to see what healing the land does on its own. After passing a small vernal kettlehole (also freshly burned) the trail climbs up and crosses a dirt road called the Tarkill Road on old maps at the **3 mile** mark. Another recent burn here required repair work by the trail-maintenance crew of the Long Island Greenbelt Conference. A circular **pond** will appear on the left (east) side of the trail through the trees. There are a series of small ponds in this area. Some of their surrounding banks are in good condition and some have been seriously trashed by off-terrain vehicles and motor bikes. A little farther on the trail

A woods road in the southern part of the Park

crosses one more woods road at **3.25 miles**, this one created by the fire department a few years back to gain access to a fire in the park interior. The trail passes through an oak dominated forest with an open understory reminiscent of upstate woods. I have heard the elusive hermit thrush near here. This little bird's ethereal song is heard only in the deep woods. Naturalist John Burroughs thought it had the most beautiful song of all and poet Walt Whitman also waxed eloquently about it. In his poem "Starting From Paumanok," he wrote "And heard at dawn the unrivall'd one, the hermit thrush from the cedar swamps." A little farther on some of my colleagues once saw a rare albino deer while scouting the future route of the trail during a winter outing. Eventually the trail passes along the edge of the burn and through open scrub-land. There are "islands" of pitch pines that somehow escaped a fire that occurred in the early 1980s. These groves provide relief from the hot sun and cover for various birds and are reminiscent of the oak brush plains that once dominated western Suffolk County.

At about **4.0 miles** the trail comes out on Route 25. It goes **0.2 mile** east, crosses the road and heads south onto county land, passing through many burn areas. Birds that prefer these open areas, such as the prairie warbler, abound. Once recognized, the song of these bright yellow birds makes them easily identifiable. A scenic coastal plain pond called Round Pond can be seen through the trees on the left (east) when the leaves are down. Crossing a woods road shortly after (**4.7 miles**), the trail passes through a recent burn with a wide panorama, surprising considering the gentle sloping grade of the land. The trail reaches the white-blazed Paumanok Path at **5.25 miles** from its start. You can go east (left) and continue another 1.75 miles to Schultz Road where a shuttle car can be parked, or west (right) 1.55 miles to the Pine Trail Nature Preserve parking lot on Route 25.

Access
Car

To get to the north end of the trail, take LIE exit 68 for William Floyd Parkway north about 8 miles to its end on Route 25A and go east (right) only about 0.2 mile to the entrance to Shoreham-Wading River High School on the right (south). Proceed in to the main parking lot and park as far to the southwest corner as possible; the trail goes off in that direction along side the track. Another car can be left under the high power lines on the north side of Route 25 about 1.7 miles east of William Floyd Parkway. The yellow blazes of the Brookhaven Trail pass through here and go north into the park just to the west.

Robert Cushman Murphy County Park and the Coastal Plain Ponds

USGS topographic map: Wading River

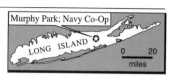
Murphy Park; Navy Co-Op
LONG ISLAND
0   20
miles

Dr. Robert Cushman Murphy was a well-known scientist and the Lamont Curator of Birds at the Department of Ornithology of the American Museum of Natural History. His book *Fish Shaped Paumanok*, published in 1964, describes the natural habitats of Long Island and the changes that proceeded from its settlement. He was one of the first, and certainly the most prominent, to speak out against the destruction of the vast tracts of Pine Barrens forests in central-eastern Long Island. He lead an initiative for Suffolk County to protect some of this land as parkland so the citizens of Long Island would be able to see its natural features close up. To honor this pioneer of Long Island's wild lands, the county named a large L-shaped parcel of land in the upper watershed of the Peconic River after him. It is fitting that the land set aside for this purpose contains the highest concentration of rare and endangered plants in New York State. In discussing this parkland, I have divided it into western and eastern sections, which are connected by a narrow corridor of parkland utilized by the Paumanok Path.

Robert Cushman Murphy Park, Western Section: the Coastal Plains Ponds

Length: 3.5 Miles

Blaze: none

Located south of Route 25 and west of Schultz Road, the western section of Robert Cushman Murphy Park contains a chain of coastal plain ponds in the watershed of the Peconic River. As noted earlier, this area contains the greatest concentration of rare and endangered plants in New York State. Coastal plain ponds are a rare global habitat. They are found on the coastal outwash plains of runoff from the last ice age and are highly dependent on rainwater for their water levels. The only other remaining coastal plain ponds in the world are found in parts of Siberia. The water levels shrink and rise from year to year and this has allowed some very adaptable plants to evolve. Some of these species of flowers have seeds that lie dormant under the ground

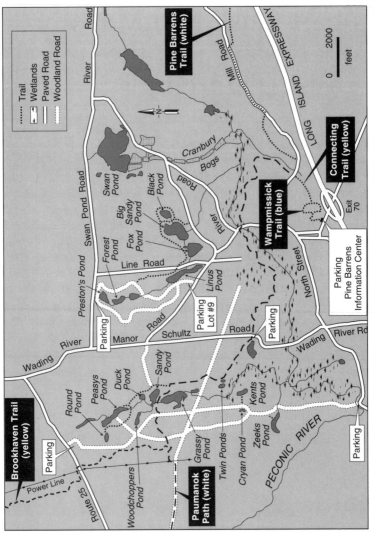

Robert Cushman Murphy Park; Navy CO-OP Area, Manorville, NY

beneath high water for years only to bloom prolifically along the shoreline when the water recedes to lower levels. In this park several rare wildflowers thrive, including slender blue flag, white-fringed orchis, pink tickseed coreopsis and small-flowered gerardia, and there are patches of wild cranberries. More numerous colorful flowers such as meadow beauty and golden hedge-hyssop make the shorelines very enjoyable scenes during August when these ponds are at their showiest. Probably the most fascinating plants of all are plants that trap insects to supplement the lack of nitrogen in the sterile acidic soil of these boglike ponds. These plants are the carnivores of the plant world, making them quite unique. Yellow and purple bladderworts as well as three species of sundews, round-leafed, spatulate-leafed and thread-leafed, all grow along the shores of the ponds.

Walking conditions in this area of linked coastal plain ponds vary depending upon the water levels and the season. Be careful not to tread on plants growing along the shorelines. The type of vegetation changes

The rare white fringed orchid grows along the shore of some of the ponds in early summer

abruptly from wetland species near the ponds to pine barrens pitch pine and scrub oak in the surrounding dry terrain. The Paumanok Path goes through this area, entering from the power lines on the west and passing over a wooden bridge at the **Sandy Pond** outlet. It then passes within sight of **Grassy Pond** before heading off towards Schultz Road. The Brookhaven Trail also comes into the parklands south of Route 25 through dry partially burnt woodlands before linking up with the Paumanok Path. These through trails can be used to gain access to this park. Some of the fire roads are also good walking trails. One such is a north-south trek through a 530 acre area of Brookhaven Laboratory managed by the U.S. Fish & Wildlife Service called **The Upton Ecological and Research Reserve**. The walk begins in Manorville on North Street about a mile west of the intersection with Wading River Road (Exit 69 on the LIE). There is room for a car or two on the side of the road. My car was once broken into on this secluded section of road – the only time this has happened to me while hiking – so be sure not to leave any valuables showing. A gate bars access to vehicles most of the year, the exception being during hunting season. The wide access road almost immediately crosses over the upper Peconic River that flows over a dam and water station here. There always seems to be some sort of wildlife in the river, especially in spring and summer. I have seen muskrats swimming near here, and large snapping turtles creeping along the dry center of the watercourse during a drought. Birds abound, and red-bellied woodpeckers creep along the trunks of tall trees overhanging the river. Once in the shrubs along the riverbank I saw a bright yellow prothonotary warbler, a bird quite rare on Long Island and found mainly in the wooded swamps and bayous of the South.

Beyond the river the road heads northward, passing close to **Zeeks Pond** on the left (west) in just under a mile. You will see signs warning of a firing range off to the left along the way. There is actually no range in close proximity but the yellow signs do let you know the land on the west side of the road is under the jurisdiction of the Department of Energy; no trespassing is allowed because the Brookhaven National Laboratory lies to the west beyond the river and a wide firebreak. A short walk on a wide sandy path will take you to the shore of Zeeks Pond, a sausage-shaped coastal plain pond that usually has wild ducks on it when filled. Don't stray beyond this short road to the pond; return directly to the main access road. The area around Zeeks Pond has been used by hikers for years but we have been told it is now off-limits and is patrolled. We hope that this won't be the case for much longer. A few minutes past the pond you will cross by a small wetland and reach a fork in the road. Go to the **right** past quaint little **Cryan Pond** on the left and continue left (north) once past the pond. Here the trail passes through a fine section of woodlands. A dim path off to the right will lead to secluded **Kents Pond**. Watch for ticks in the thick growth around this wetland.

Sandy Pond reflections

Continuing northward you will come to an intersection with another woods road a little less than 2 miles from North Street. The wetlands feeding the Peconic River are a short walk down to the right (east) and not passable most of the time. Nevertheless they make an interesting side trip to see the blue spikes of pickerel-weed rising out of the water in summer. I once flushed a large owl out of the trees along the waterway early one morning. Returning to the main road, continue northward and the vegetation will become more open and scrubby as you enter sections that have burnt more recently than the shady woods you just left. You may pick up the Paumanok Path as it crosses the woods road (look for the white blazes) at about **2.5 miles** and go in either direction. One car can be left at the Pine Trail Nature Preserve in Ridge to the west or on Schultz Road in Manorville to the east. A third option is to continue northward to a sandy intersection where a left turn will take you past pretty **Round Pond** on the right and eventually to Route 25 in about **3.5 miles** (that doesn't include any side-trips).

There are a few interesting areas the walker may want to investigate. There is a crossing at the south end of **Peasys Pond** where its outlet runs southward into **Duck Pond**. This was once known to local travelers as "the going over place" that connected Ridge to Manorville in the old days. It is easy to imagine this short crossing being bridged by branches and logs, much as it is today. In dry times it can be walked without getting your feet wet. To the east of here, take the north route of the path to come to a view of Peasys Pond (photo p. 38) from its south shore. A loop trail is planned going eastward and northward in the woods on the east side of the pond. It will cross back westward north of Peasys Pond and head between Round and Peasys ponds along a faint overgrown path southward along the west side of Peasys. Round Pond is a place to look for interesting migrating birds that seem to stop here each spring. I have seen hooded mergansers as well as least sandpipers running about its shallows.

Just southwest of here is **Woodchoppers Pond**. There are no trails going to its shores, but it's worth the short bushwhack. Though it's not far from a main woods road through the region, it nevertheless has a remote feel to it. Another set of ponds hidden away in the woods is **Twin Ponds**. These two small very pretty secluded ponds just off-trail probably look the same as they did hundreds of years ago.

Robert Cushman Murphy Park, Eastern Section: The Cranberry Bogs

Length: 1 1/2 miles.

Blaze: none

USGS topographic map: Wading river

East of Wading River-Manor Road is the eastern section of Robert Cushman Murphy Park. Dense thickets surrounding the Peconic River limit exploration of the river itself, but walks can be taken around the old cranberry bogs that run south of River Road in Manorville. This is just opposite Swan Lake Golf Club. Parking for one car is next to an entrance adjacent to the bog. A sandy road leads along the east side of the bog. On a map you will see it is a half-mile-long banana-shaped wetland segmented into five sections, each separated by a dike. This is the former Davis Bog, the last commercial cranberry bog on Long Island (it ceased operation in 1974). Many people don't realize that Long Island was once one of the leading producers of cranberries in the country (see Cranberry Bog County Park).

Although walking in the bog area itself is somewhat limited, you can follow the sandy road with the open bog on your right. Of main interest are the rare beautiful wild orchids that bloom here the third week of June through early July. The bright pink flowers of the grass pink (also called calopogon) can be found along the wet eastern shore of the bog along with the less-numerous rose pogonias. Please be careful not to tread on these rare gems of nature (or any plants for that matter) when you are seeking them out. Other unique bog plants, such as bladderworts, blue flag iris, ferns and sundews also grow in this acidic sterile environment. Many grasses and sedges are now taking hold in the bog and they add a texture of color and motion, feathery fronds swaying in the breeze in the center of the watercourse. As you get farther in, you will see cattails in great profusion in winter and you'll likely scare up some black ducks hiding among the rushes. Muskrats also are often seen near their large houses constructed from plant material. These houses can be up to eight feet long and three to five feet high. They are more likely to be seen in rainy seasons when water levels are high.

The top of the bog is reached in about half a mile; here, you can continue along the perimeter by following the trail to the right. The wetlands of the Peconic River are on your left and the length of the bog lies spread out to your right. You will see a concrete structure that goes over the outlet feeding into the Peconic wetlands. Continuing to the corner of the bog, you may wish to explore to the left (south) where more structures to channel and control water-flow for the former bog can be seen. Water-flow was a key element in the harvesting of cranberries and many signs of this type of manipulation are still in evidence. A narrow trail takes you out into the heart of the wide Peconic wetlands on an earthen, raised strip of land. There is much activity in the wetlands in late spring and summer; uncommon birds such as the blue-gray gnatcatcher and ruby-throated hummingbird have been spotted moving ever-so-quickly to and fro. Returning to the southeast corner of the bog you may want to explore some of the trails that penetrate the pine-oak woodlands just west of the bog. Close to the bog you may come across some dilapidated structures that were likely berrypickers' cabins.

The area east of the main bog is a dense forest with a smaller bog close to River Road. Access to this bog is about 0.2 mile east on River Road where a path takes you to the shore of an oval-shaped wetland overgrown with cattails, swamp loosestrife, pickerelweed. Orchids also grow here, and, of course, cranberries. A little farther down the road you will find another place to pull over that gives access to a large grassy clearing with a few tall trees in groves here and there. An old barn stood here until it was destroyed by a fire in the

An abandoned berry picker's cabin to be found by exploring the woods around the cranberry bog

early '90s. Nesting boxes have been put up to attract bluebirds and swallows to these clearings. This is a nice place to wander around amid tall grasses and thistle. These interesting areas can be tied together into one hike for those wishing to bushwhack the property. Swan Pond is on the opposite side of the road and is part of the county parkland. Swan Pond is available to anglers as boat access is directly off River Road, but the pond is surrounded by a golf course and is not open to hikers.

Access

Car

For access to the western section and coastal plains ponds take LIE exit 68 for William Floyd Parkway north about 4 miles to Route 25 east for 0.4 mile to Pine Trail Nature Preserve parking area on the right. For access to the ponds from the east, parking for one or two cars is available on Schultz Road in Manorville 1.6 miles north of LIE exit 69 just past a sharp turn on the left (west) side of the road.

For access to the eastern section and cranberry bogs take LIE exit 70 north to its end and make a right, go over the railroad tracks and make a right onto North Street. In about 0.2 mile bear right onto Wading River-Manor Road and in about 0.4 mile make a right onto River Road. Look for a place to pull your car off the road in about 1.1 miles opposite the entrance to the Swan Lake golf course entrance. There are other parking places farther along the road for those wishing to explore off trail in other parts of the park.

Cattails thrive in part of the cranberry bog

Navy Co-op Pond Walk

Length: 2.5 mile loop past Linus pond. Blaze: none

East of Line Road Nature Conservancy walk: 1 hour.

Blaze: yellow, white

USGS topographic map: Wading River

Wedged between Grumman Boulevard on the north, Wading River-Manor Road on the west and south, and Line Road on the east is a group of ponds forming part of the Peconic watershed. Many hikers ignore the ponds, some because there are no marked trails connecting them to the more popular Robert Cushman Murphy Park to the west, and others because they are surrounded by roads. But these roads actually allow more access and varying combinations of walks since they have many numbered parking lots used by hunters. A permit is required to park in these lots and to use the area; it's the same three-year permit used to access the Rocky Point Resource Management Area. Call the DEC at (631) 444-0273 for an application or send a request with a stamped self addressed envelope to NYSDEC, Division of Land and Forests, Building 40, SUNY at Stony Brook, Stony Brook, NY 11790-2353.

The land is part of a large swath previously owned by the United States Navy running from the huge Calverton Airfield southward into Manorville Hills. This sprawling area is still known as the Navy Co-op to veteran hikers and hunters who have used it for years. It is open to hunters in season as well as hikers or those wishing to fish the ponds. The land is patrolled by DEC forest rangers and the state is scheduled to take full possession when the Town of Riverhead acquires the Calverton Airport just to the north. Once intended to build and test Navy jets, the large hangars were used to reconstruct the wreckage of TWA Flight 800. The remaining federal lands outside the airport will revert to the state for recreational uses.

A good place to start is from parking lot #9 on the east side of Wading River-Manor Road about 0.25 mile north of Line Road. Head away from the road to a clearing where it's a good bet you'll see eastern bluebirds in spring, particularly in mid- to late March. Nest boxes are set up in this meadow to attract them. The narrow pond beyond is **Linus Pond**; it will likely have some wintering ducks on it at this same time of year. Look for ringed-neck ducks in small flocks in the more quiet northern section of the pond. They prefer the sterile acidic Pine Barrens ponds. Once I found a drake tufted duck in a flock of ringed-necks in early spring. The tufted duck looks like the ringed-neck but is rare on the Island since it is native to Eurasia. The pond is full of activity starting in April with the arrival of tree swallows constantly swooping over the water to catch flying insects. Although the pond is rather bare in early spring, it will be lush by August. Look then for the small bright-yellow flowerheads of the insectivorous bladderworts in the shallow water.

Continue beyond Linus Pond in a northward direction with the wetlands on your right. The short side-trails invite exploration of the wetlands lined with blueberry bushes and leatherleaf. Go straight past some feedlots and at the third intersection bear to the right, where, in a short distance, pretty **Middle Pond** will appear on your left (north). In mid-summer you will find the rare, dainty-looking pink tickseed growing in profusion along the moist shoreline. Looking like a forlorn daisy, this light-pink flower is rather inconspicuous and therefore your best look at it is in large patches like this.

Continue on past the pond until you reach another intersection of woods roads. Make a left and continue northward. Keep an eye out for deer; they're plentiful all around these ponds. You will pass **Forest Pond** on the left, where you can take a short path to get a closer look. If you do, you will notice that a narrow band of wet ground separates it from Middle Pond. Continuing along the main woods road, you will come into a large grassy clearing that has more nesting boxes set up along its edges. You will see **Preston Pond** on your left before circling around the north end of the pond just south of Swan Pond Road. The former Calverton Airport is beyond the chain link fence on the opposite side of the road.

The road will circle around to the west side of Preston Pond and head south. After passing a small pond, you can take a variety of ways back to your car. Make a left at the first woods road you cross to continue southward, keeping to the woods roads that stay away from the ponds so as not to overlap your walk on the return trip. You will pass through classic pitch pine-and-oak woods with the option to revisit the ponds at your discretion by making a left at one of the junctions. There is an old house foundation and well along here not far from Wading River-Manor Road. The Wading River quadrangle USGS topographic map or DOT map will assist you in this. The LIGTC Pine Barrens Trail map (western section) is also helpful in locating the various woods roads in the area. Even without these maps this is an easy pleasant walk that should not be overlooked by veteran hikers. It can easily be linked up to Robert Cushman Murphy Park just to the west.

On the east side, across Line Road, is the Calverton Ponds system featuring **Fox, Big Sandy** and **Block** ponds. The Nature Conservancy must be contacted for access to them. They can be accessed from my described walk on an unmarked woods road that becomes a narrow trail on the east side of Linus Pond. This trail comes out onto Line Road and if you turn right (south) for a few hundred feet and cross this lightly traveled rural road you can enter the Calverton Ponds Preserve. Please tread lightly here as the area is filled with rare and endangered plants and animals. These ponds are probably the best preserved examples of coastal plain ponds found anywhere. A well-marked trail system will take you to observation points on all three ponds. The blazes are plastic squares with The Nature Conservancy logo and are either yellow or white. If you choose to walk here, please stay on the trails. You should be able to cover both the yellow and white trails in about an hour or so.

Access

Car

Take LIE exit 69 north about 2.7 miles and make a right onto Wading River-Manor Road. Parking is available in about 0.8 mile on the left side in hunting co-op parking area number 9. Avoid the area during big game hunting season in January. A permit is required so call the DEC headquarters in Stony Brook for further info at (631) 444-0273.

Linus Pond seen from its western shore

Wildwood State Park

Length: 2.9. Blaze: blue

USGS topographic map: Wading River

Located on the North Shore of eastern Long
Island is Wildwood State Park. Since it is
known primarily for its campsites, most people don't realize that Wildwood is
a nice place to walk and explore the bluffs and rock-strewn shoreline. From
a rough trail along bluffs 160-feet high you have good views of the Long
Island Sound and Connecticut, especially when the leaves are down. There is
a haunting stunted American beech forest growing along its crest. In late summer look for a parasitic brown-stemmed flowering plant called beechdrops
that feeds off the roots of beech trees along the trail. They have an almost
magical look when viewed with a magnifying glass, revealing an orchid-like
appearance. Farther inland keep an eye out for the deer that live in the rolling
terrain of a rich beech-oak woods filled with hollows and strewn with glacial
erratics. Some of the hollows are even filled with eastern hemlocks, generally
considered a more northerly tree. I have seen great horned owls nesting in
pine trees among the campsites during February. In early November when
most color is fading, the forest is brightened with the yellow flowers of the
witch hazel tree. A freak of nature, witch hazel is the only tree to flower in the
fall. In springtime keep an eye out for trailing arbutus, jack-in-the-pulpit and
woodland violets off the side of the trail.

There are four marked trails set up by the park; they're blazed with painted
squares and they all revolve around the large circular path through the woods
of the park. There are many side paths to explore. The trails are easy to follow and blazed at intersections. A map can be picked up at the park office and
there are several stations along the way to let you know where you are. The
shortest trail is the **red trail** at **1.8 miles** long. It forms an elongated loop
through the rolling woods of the center of the park, passing along the edge of
the campground on its return to the main parking area. The next longest is
the **2.3-mile orange trail** that forms a wider loop in the park interior. Next
is the **blue trail** at **2.9 miles** in length that follows the main circuit around
the park, followed by the **yellow trail** at **3.8 miles** long. The latter differs
from the former by taking an excursion into some second-growth area on the
eastern edge of the parklands. Of course, the park lends itself to exploring on
other trails and woods roads. In the eastern section I have found a few very
intriguing old paths that go down to the beach through steep clefts in the
bluffs with large erratics guarding the way.

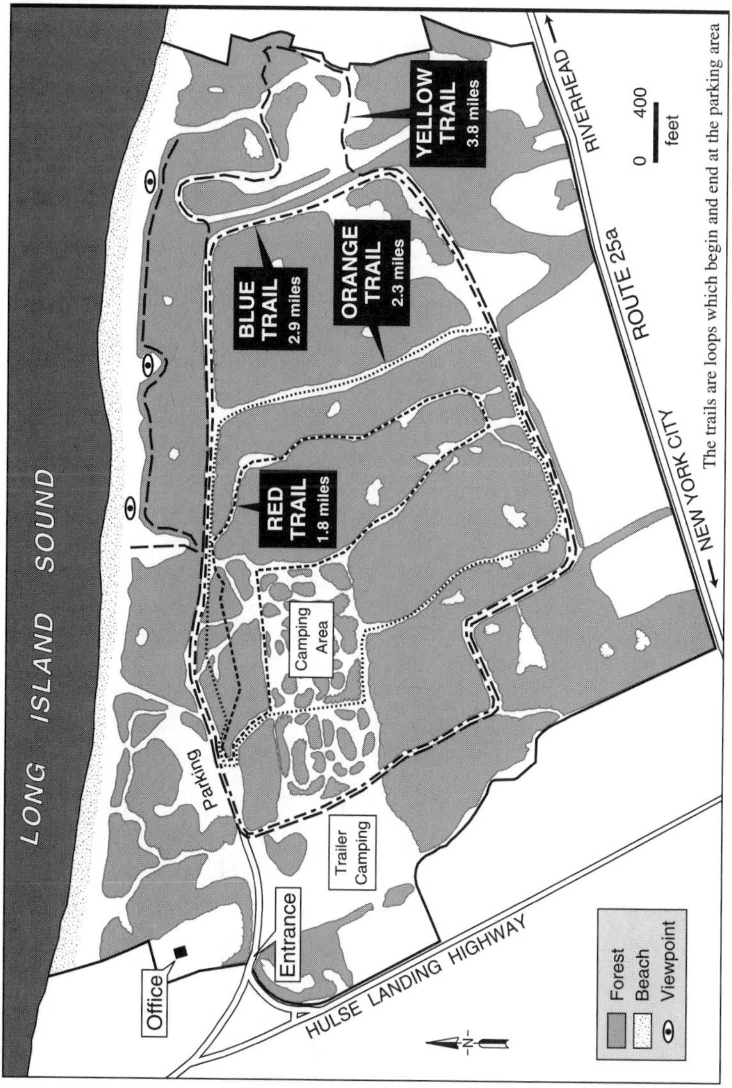

Wildwood State Park, Wading River, NY

YELLOW TRAIL 3.8 miles

BLUE TRAIL 2.9 miles

ORANGE TRAIL 2.3 miles

RED TRAIL 1.8 miles

The trails are loops which begin and end at the parking area

0 400 feet

RIVERHEAD

ROUTE 25a

NEW YORK CITY

LONG ISLAND SOUND

Camping Area

Parking

Trailer Camping

Entrance

Office

HULSE LANDING HIGHWAY

Forest
Beach
Viewpoint

N

In winter the gently rolling woods roads in the park are kept free of debris for cross-country skiing. Of course the beach is beautiful any time of year. I once saw some harbor seals swimming offshore. I especially like the winter when the desolation makes it all the more enjoyable. At points east there are large rocks on the beach for challenging scrambling and fine clefts in the bluffs to explore. The state-owned Baiting Hollow tidal marsh is separated from the eastern edge of the park by a small creek flowing into the Sound. It's fun to remove your shoes to ford it. A permit must be obtained from the DEC office by phone (631) 444-0275 for access to this tidal wetland.

Access

Car

Take LIE exit 69 north about 5.7 miles to Route 25A and make a right (east). Proceed about 1.2 miles and make left at the light onto Sound Avenue to continue east another mile or so and make a left (north) onto Hulse Landing Road. The park entrance will be on the right side in about 0.75 mile. There is the usual $5.00 parking fee for state parks in season between Memorial Day and Columbus Day.

Bus

SCT62

A view from the bluffs over Long Island Sound toward Connecticut

Terrell County Park

Length: 3 hours. Blaze: none

USGS topographic map: Moriches

This little-known park is a rare mixture of undeveloped fields and woods meeting Moriches Bay. Local people use the land for walking, horseback riding, and birding. Traffic is relatively light and most stick to the main woods road that loops through the property. Listed at 260 acres, the park seems much larger. I spent three hours exploring it with many stops to enjoy the views, the wildlife and to explore some side trails. The county threatens to develop the land into a golf course, but I hope to walk here again and again with friends and family.

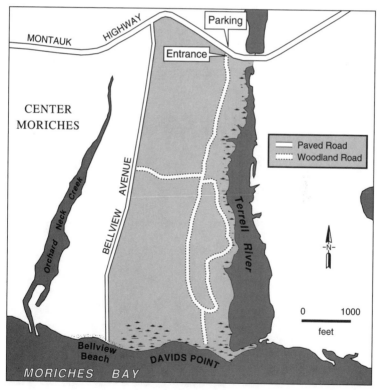

Terrel County Park, Center Moriches, NY

A USGS topographic map for Moriches will help you in getting oriented to the area. The park is not listed on most maps, but is shown as the undeveloped piece of property south of Montauk Highway bounded by Belleview Avenue on the west and the Terrell River on the east. The entrance to the park is simply a woods road with a gate across it to keep vehicles out. Look for a white sign with green lettering designating this as county-owned land. Park on the north side of the Montauk Highway directly across from the entrance. The Haven House on the north side of the road was once part of the park but is now maintained by the Center Moriches Historical Society. The local Audubon Society has a stake in the land also, as indicated by a sign on one of the buildings. The Haven family once farmed the land of the park, and the area is filled with second-growth trees. However, several non-native trees are very old, including the London plane tree, an uncommon ornamental with maple-like leaves that do not turn colorful in the fall, and the Norway maple and black locust. Old overgrown trellises adorned with grapevines and surrounded by large American holly trees reveal where sitting gardens once stood. All around the native woods is taking back the land. The western section of the park is in a more transitional state since many fields that were farmed up until the 1980s are reverting back to forest. The land along the river is classic Long Island woods and includes oaks, hickories, tupelos and pitch pines.

The showy pink flowers of sheep laurel grow at the edge of bogs of Terrell County Park

The main woods road takes you south with the **Terrell River** on your left (east) through the trees. Exploring side trails and deep paths throughout the park is one of the most interesting aspects of walking here. Some are dead ends with a view over the river (really a deep tidal creek); others may lead to a secluded pond with a great blue heron ready to spring skyward at your approach. On a head of land facing south on the river take a break on a fallen log, and you can see where the river empties into the bay, with the Fire Island National Seashore in the background and the Atlantic Ocean beyond it. Looking across to the east side of the Terrell River you can see the abandoned buildings of some of the many duck farms that once dominated this area. Long Island was a major duck producer for years and its ducks had a reputation in the finest restaurants along the eastern seaboard.

Continuing south on the woods road to the end of an old field you hear the waves on the beach at Great South Bay. On my visit there the wind buffeted us as we walked to the end of the sand spit where the river empties into the bay. Many odd water birds can be found here in the swirling water and shore. I saw American oystercatchers and marbled godwits among others. The godwit, with its long up-curved bill, is rare indeed since the nearest they breed is in the northern grasslands of Minnesota. They are a rare visitor during migration. The nearby beach is full of all sorts of flotsam and jetsam from Great South Bay. My children especially enjoyed walking here since the change in habitats always meant something new along the hike.

Access

Car

Take Sunrise Highway exit 59 south until it runs into Railroad Avenue. Follow Railroad Avenue. to Main Street (Montauk Highway) and make a left (east). The preserve entrance will be on the right (south) side in about 0.75 mile but parking will be on the opposite side of the road.

Bus

SCT90

Otis Pike Preserve

Length: 2 mile loop. Blaze: none

Longer walks possible

DEC topographic map: Wading River
quadrangle

Part of the land formerly known as the Navy Co-op Lands has been turned
over to New York State and made into a natural preserve named after former
Suffolk County legislator Otis Pike. The parcels were owned by the federal
government as buffer crash zones adjacent to the old Grumman airport in
Calverton where military jets were tested, and are somewhat disconnected
and jumbled in location. They are open to hunters in season as well as hikers
and others who have a state permit to be there.

The Peconic River as seen from the trail in Otis Pike Preserve

The area most hikeable is a parcel of land between River Road (Grumman Boulevard) on the north and the Long Island Expressway on the south. Long familiar to local hunters, this area is not much used by hikers mainly because there are no signs or obviously visible access points. The area appears in the north portion of the LIGTC map for the central section of the Long Island Pine Barrens Trail. The DOT topographic map is useful since it shows near-by development and wetlands among other interesting features. Canoeists may be familiar with the state boat launch on the east side of Connecticut Avenue. An easy access point is from the state designated hunter's parking area on River Road about 0.5 mile east of Connecticut Avenue. Small game season runs from October through the end of February, and there is a deer season for three weeks on weekdays only in January. It is best to avoid the area during hunting seasons. Hunters are required to make a large permit vis-ible on their dashboard. It is always a good idea to check with the DEC on the length and dates of the hunting season.

From River Road, there is a pretty view of the Peconic River just to the south of the parking site. It is a photogenic spot worth a stop to see the river make its way towards the bay that bears its name. A short loop of more than 2 miles can be made that is bordered by the river and surrounding wetlands on the north and east, Connecticut Avenue on the west and the LIRR Ronkonkoma branch on the south. This lightly used section of the railroad heads out to Greenport on the North Fork. There are some interesting wetlands to explore

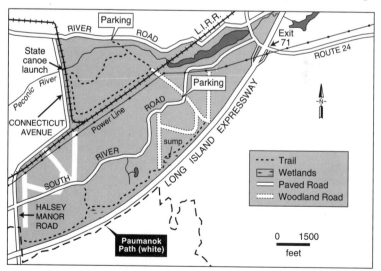

Otis Pike Preserve, Suffolk County, NY

in the center of the property; look for the section of overgrown railroad tracks in the southwest corner of the loop just beyond the unmarked path you will follow. This spur branched off the main railroad to supply the former Grumman facility located to the north. It is strange to see perfectly good tracks with vegetation growing out amongst them. In the southeast corner of this property the adventurous can continue on the woods road south across the tracks and under the power lines to where the land starts to rise away from the lowlands of the river. This is actually the beginning (or foothills) of the Manorville Hills located just to the south. You can cross South River Road and continue on public land as far south as the LIE. If desired, an unmarked trail can be picked up going westward about 2 miles to Halsey Manor Road thus linking up to the Paumanok Path.

Access

Car

Take LIE exit 71 (Edwards Avenue) north to River Road (second left just past the river) and turn left (west). Proceed for 1.2 miles to a state designated parking site #17 on the left (south side of the road).

Manorville Hills

Length: 2.8 mile loop. Blaze: slate gray, some unmarked.

Bushwhacks and woods roads can make for outings of varying lengths

USGS topographic maps: Wading River, Moriches, Riverhead, Eastport

The area south of exits 70 and 71 and Route 24 and north of County Route 51 is known as the Manorville Hills. In this tract as the Ronkonkoma Moraine starts to tilt towards the South Fork of Long Island, it rises to heights of 300 feet above sea level in a confusing landscape of hills and dips with no apparent pattern.

It has no paved roads for more than 8 miles between Halsey Manor Road on the west and the County Center on the east. This is the longest stretch of unpaved land left on Long Island; at its widest point it is nearly 4 miles wide. Much of the land is federally owned and has been called the Navy Co-op Lands, but is now part of the Otis Pike Preserve. The Manorville Hills comprise the "core" of a vast reservoir of pure drinking water in underground aquifers protected by the Pine Barrens Protection Act. Here hikers can experience real solitude with no signs of modern society, and feel what it was like to travel the island in colonial times. Bushwhackers can still come across a

This glacial erratic was named Gilbraltar for its shape like the famous mountian

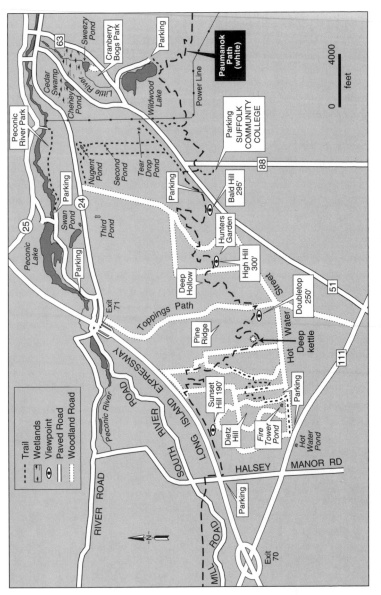

Manorville Hills, Peconic River Park, Suffolk County, NY

secluded hollow, a large glacial erratic in the middle of the forest or view-points from isolated hilltops. This is Long Island's "last wilderness." It offers hikers the best bushwhacking on the island.

It was in Manorville Hills that a Pine Barrens nomenclature was developed to help name some of the memorable features and have reference points to work off in this disorienting landscape of forest, paths, hills, and hollows. The greatest concentration of glacial erratics in the Pine Barrens is found here. Most wetlands are found in the eastern section of the land. At present, the Paumanok Path enters the area from Halsey Manor Road just south of the LIE overpass and follows within sight of the expressway for 1.6 miles before diving southward into the hills. It is hoped that the trail can be moved away from the LIE when some land acquisitions are made. The area is beset by destructive and illegal motor bike use. There is a debate between hikers who want more trails and those who fear new trails without better supervision and management will attract increased motorbike activity. Until that conflict is resolved, places like **God's Knuckles, Pine Ridge, Deer Run Hollow, Ridge Rock, The Western Edge, Deep Hollow, Twin Kettles, Table Rock, Erratic Hill,** and **Gibraltar** will remain known mostly to the few experienced hikers who found and named them. The public can learn about them on group hikes led by Pine Barrens veterans affiliated with the LIGTC.

Surprises abound. For example, the nameless hills about 0.75 mile north of Hunters Garden are traversed by a narrow trail with some of the most dramatic views on Long Island. Although only 210 feet high they nonetheless mark the point where the northern edge of the Ronkonkoma Moraine rapidly drops off, allowing you to see all the way to the North Shore bluffs and nearby ridges to the west. These hills definitely need names!

Navigating Manorville Hills off-trail is not always easy. Even experienced hikers may have trouble finding their features on the LIGTC map since it has no contour lines. It is best to explore gradually until you become familiar with the area. A USGS topographic map or DOT map is more helpful in this somewhat confusing landscape. But exploring has its rewards. On a crystal clear December afternoon near Toppings Path as the setting sun hit the tops of the taller hills I found a wonderful serene pine-clad knoll I call Roundtop. Manorville Hills offers the adventurous hiker the freedom to find unique features and special places relatively unknown to casual walkers.

A side trail called **The Loop Trail** partially blazed with slate-blue-and-gray paint follows existing woods roads and deer paths, and is virtually trailless at points. Although the entire loop is not yet blazed a full circuit can be done by using existing paths or by bushwhacking. The partially completed trail is marked on the LIGTC Pine Barrens Trail (central section) map. Much is left to the imagination of the walker to find his own way to complete this hike. The trailhead can be picked up off unpaved Hot Water Street about a half-mile east of County Route 111. An old blacktop paved road going off to the left (north) has room for a couple of cars to park. In wet weather you are safer parking closer to Route 111 and walking the short distance in to prevent getting stuck in muddy terrain. A gate across the entrance with signs will help in locating the road where the trail begins. Look for a blaze on one of the posts here. The paved road was constructed by the Sperry Corporation in the early 1960s for access to an experimental communications station located atop a hill less than a mile to the north. The land was subsequently purchased by the Dietz family, who sold it to the state in 1995. Today this 250-foot hill is known as **Dietz Hill** and has a clearing atop it. Some have suggested it would make a good place for designated camping in the future, but that is just talk at this time. This road appears on the USGS topographic map, Moriches Quadrangle, as a strung-out question mark ending on the summit of the hill. The Loop Trail proceeds up this old road through clearings that have been planted with evergreen trees in what was once apparently a tree farm. A small water hole known as **Fire Tower Pond** lies hidden off to the left (west) in the tangled underbrush not far from the trail's beginning. My research failed to turn up any reason for the name of this small somewhat hidden pond since no fire tower ever existed in the immediate area. At about **0.4 mile**, the trail makes a right onto a fainter path and then rather quickly a left to continue north onto another worn old path. It follows this path slightly uphill a short ways; keep an eye out for some blazes that go **off trail** to the right through a hollow between hills. It eventually uses an old path to climb up an unnamed **220 foot hill** that has limited views through the trees. You must be alert as the blazes are quite faint. It is kind of like bushwhacking off-trail with blazes to follow (a contradictory yet interesting concept), but watch carefully for sharp turns or you can easily lose the trail. The trail crosses a main north-to-south fire road (**0.9 mile**) and drops southward before joining the same road for a short distance. Watch for blazes (**1.4 miles**) where it dives back into the woods on the left (east) and winds back northward, where it eventually joins a major woods road (the blazes end here at **1.8 miles**). The hiker can link up with the Paumanok Path by continuing northward on this woods road for about a half mile. However, to complete the loop, turn south (right) on this road until it ends at Hot Water Street (**2.3 miles**), where you turn right again for the final half-mile return to your car (**2.8 miles**).

An area of interest that makes a worthy destination for the hiker is **Hunters Garden**. Originally a spring fed clearing, it attracted the attention of early residents who used it as a meeting place to gather and share news. Farmers from the south shore would meet friends and relatives from the north shore and eat wild game while catching up on the local news. Eventually, corn and crops were planted to attract deer which in turn were shot to provide food for the feast. The meetings took place on a designated day each May and October. Today, the Hunters Garden Association still meets to eat game, now eel chowder. This has been going on each year since 1833 without missing a meeting. There is no glitz or anything unusual about the meetings; they are only for the enjoyment of companionship and the outdoors. A visit to Hunters Garden which is located west of Bald Hill and north of County 51 still rewards the walker. The fresh water spring is still there and it attracts many birds in springtime. A road actually goes into the clearing, which also has a designated hunters site. A small stone monument commemorating this special site stands in the northwest corner. Unfortunately it has been damaged by someone who has apparently taken a shot at it with a shotgun. Nevertheless, the spirit of the great outdoors and love of nature live on here for those open to it. The actions of one deranged individual can not take that away.

The far-eastern section of the Manorville Hills becomes less hilly, but it contains several small attractive ponds that contain plants very different from the

Exploring during a winter bushwack

surrounding dry Pine Barrens terrain. The trail map lists four ponds, **Nugent (1st pond), 2nd Pond** and **Tear Drop Pond,** with **3rd Pond** farther west. The Riverhead topographic map reveals they are part of a series of wetlands running northwest of Wildwood Lake. You will find plenty of bird activity around these ponds. On a warm May afternoon the air was heavy with the sweet fragrance of the flowering highbush blueberries that abound in 3rd Pond. The terrain here is anything but flat with some excellent dry kettles sprinkled throughout. The woods roads, some quite overgrown, make very good exploratory walks as paths link the larger ponds in this sandy pine-oak habitat. Many loops can be fashioned using either Route 24, Route 51, Toppings Path or Hot Water Street as starting points. A good destination is to bushwhack eastward beyond the high power lines to the county preserve that contains a unique cedar swamp area. **Cheney Pond**, a large pond nourishing an Atlantic white cedar grove, is just north of County Route 51. It makes a good destination for those daring to brave the boggy, dense tick- infested growth that surrounds it.

Access

Car

There are many access points to such a large area. On the west, take LIE exit 70 south about 1.2 miles and make a left onto Halsey Manor Road. Cars can be parked in about 0.8 mile alongside the road just before it crosses over the LIE. The trail goes into the woods at this point. Another way into the area is to take LIE exit 70 south and make a left in about 1.7 miles onto the unpaved section of Hot Water Street. Proceed in about 0.5 mile to the beginning of the Manorville Hills loop trail on the left. This is an unpaved bumpy road and should not be used in snowy weather unless you have a four wheel drive vehicle. On the western end of Manorville Hills you can gain access by the gated woods road on the north side of County Route 51. To get there, take LIE exit 70 south for about 3.5 miles and get off onto County Route 51. Make a left and the access is about 2.6 miles farther on the left. You must go past it and turn around to park on the other side of the road. There are also several unpaved roads along north side of State Route 24 east of exit 71 of the LIE.

Bus

SCT8A

The Summit and Hampton Hills

Length: 6.7 miles, blaze: none

USGS topographic maps: Riverhead, Eastport

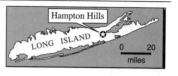

On its journey eastward, the Paumanok Path passes by the Riverhead campus of Suffolk Community College and into the hilly area to the east known as Hampton Hills. Located south of County Route 51 and east of Speonk-Riverhead Road, this was a major acquisition for the county made with the assistance of The Nature Conservancy. Most hikers stay on the trail as it heads towards Wildwood Lake but some excellent exploring can be had in the land to the south, including a 260-foot hill with superb views toward the ocean. Simply referred to as the Summit, this hill stands above the flat coastal plain to the south-southeast and affords startling views over this area. The white Federal Aviation Agency radar dome atop the Summit guides planes to Kennedy Airport. This reference point is visible from a hill or the nearby coastal plain. For a few months there were two of these dome towers, since they left the old one up while constructing the new one. The base of the old one is still visible.

A walk with many side trips and loops can be accomplished in this area. It has a wealth of diversity; you can pass through burnt-out areas from the fire of 1995, visit the dwarf pines, and reach viewpoints from windswept hilltops all in a few hours wandering. Use the LIGTC map for the eastern section of the Pine Barrens Trail to negotiate this area. Those wanting more detail can use the USGS topographic map or DOT map for Riverhead and Eastport. Linkups to the David Sarnoff Preserve to the north give hikers more options for extending their walk, especially if two cars are used.

I suggest a hike that takes in the best features of the region and can be done as a large loop in several hours, depending on the whims of the hiker. It will keep you mainly south of the Summit in county land. Although there are no marked trails, woods roads and unmarked trails are quite easy to follow, as seen on the map. As usual, a compass will help in staying on course in foggy or overcast weather. A glance at the map will show that you are staying north of Route 27 (Sunrise Highway), west of County Route 31 and south of County Route 51. Knowing this, you can head for one of these roads should you

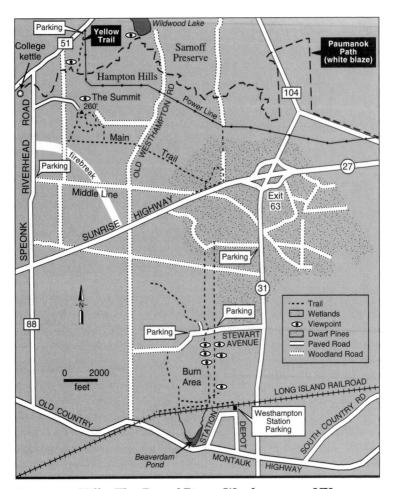

Hampton Hills; The Dwarf Pines, Westhampton, NY

become lost. Also, a power line on the north is a good reference point. Two old trails cross the area in a generally west-to-east direction. The more northerly of these is known as the **Main Trail**, while the **Middle Line** runs almost parallel and south of it. The Middle Line is most accessible from the road and you start there. Drive about 1.3 miles south of County Route 51 on Speonk-Riverhead Road and look for an old woods road that goes off to the east (left). There are actually two entrances at this point, the more northerly (left) created by brush trucks to fight the tremendous fire that burnt out of control here beginning on August 24, 1995. There is room for a few cars at this point. The **Middle Line**, a straight road created years ago, was part of a large purchase of land made by Captain Thomas Topping in 1662 from the Shinnecock tribe. Toppings Path, named for him, is a sandy path that has been around a long time and has been used as a fire road in recent times. The first thing you notice as you proceed eastward along this road is the dead snags that dominate the scene. The tree trunks were all blackened the first two years after the fire, but recently the bark on the oaks has dried up and peeled off, leaving bright gray almost silvery snags standing. The pitch pines seem to be retaining their tough scaly bark longer and still stand out blackened against the landscape. These snags will serve as nesting places for cavity-dwelling birds such as woodpeckers, black-capped chickadees, tufted titmice, nuthatches, great crested flycatchers, screech owls, and eastern bluebirds. The practice of letting these trees stand as long as nature allows has greatly helped these species find suitable nesting sites. Of course, nothing stays the same in nature for long and it will be interesting to watch as the weakened trees start to fall. A few minutes in, look to your left (north) and you may catch a glimpse of the white radar dome on top of the Summit, the eventual destination of this hike. You will pass some small paths on the right that go south into county land. If you choose to explore in this direction I recommend that you do not go off-trail, since the understory is rapidly growing back after the fires. It is a humbling experience as you ramble around in this area to imagine how immensely hot that conflagration must have been. After years without a major fire, large amounts of leaf litter had accumulated on the forest floor. Coming during a drought and swept by strong dry northwesterly winds, the 1995 fire burned more than 3,000 acres in this area alone. The other fire that occurred a few days earlier in the Rocky Point Natural Resources Management Area was a little smaller yet just as dangerous. More about the natural consequences of fire in the Pine Barrens is discussed in the Pine Barrens introduction. In any case, this is a great opportunity to see nature regenerating after a natural catastrophe. You will see stands of bracken fern, wild sedges and grasses sprouting up along with oak and pine seedlings.

At about **0.4 mile** from the road down the Middle Line you reach a major woods road which heads southward (right) and another shortly thereafter that goes north (left). The latter road heads north through a wide ugly firebreak that was obviously bulldozed but is growing back. Crossing the firebreak, find the continuation of your north-south trail. In a hundred yards or so the Main Trail comes from the right (look for an old downed log pole on the right here). This can be taken eastward for 100 yards or so where a faint path on the left heads northward up to the Summit. This route can be used if you want to do a short day-hike up to the Summit and back.

Continuing eastward on the Middle Line, almost **1.0 mile** from the road you cross the large firebreak that was bulldozed to contain the fire. If you are hiking very early or late in the day, you may spot a deer scampering for cover. Continuing a few more minutes you leave the burn area and enter thicker woods. At about **1.2 miles** you reach the intersection with a sandy woods road. This is the **Old Westhampton Road**, one of the oldest roads in the area dating back to colonial times. It shows up on old maps as a fairly direct route between Riverhead and Westhampton. Today it can be taken northward to DEC parking lot #1 at the southeast corner of Wildwood Lake some 2 miles away. I recall standing at this intersection and feeling like I was in a time capsule, since this is just what foot travel on roads was like in colonial Long Island. I noticed some sloppy blue paint blazes on a nearby tree, probably put there by a motorbiker. As you continue eastward, in winter you may pass a flock of chickadees; they fill the air with buzzes and chatter before fading away. Eventually you will notice that the trees become shorter and the sound of traffic from nearby Route 27 becomes more obvious. You are now entering the northwest corner of the **dwarf pines**, a unique and rare ecosystem. The sky really opens up and the trees seem to shrink towards earth as you approach. It is downright hot to hike in this sandy sun-baked section of the coastal plain during the summer; the best time to hike here is from October through April.

Once you reach the fence line on the north side of Route 27 (**about 2 miles**) continue eastward a short way until you are even with the exit sign on the opposite side of the eastbound automobile exit. Turn north here and you will pick up a sandy path that heads away from the road. You will see some of the hardier plants, like Pine Barrens heather (hudsonia) and reindeer lichen, that are able to withstand the harsh conditions in this ecosystem. Since you can see for great distances because of the low-growing trees, this is a good place to get oriented as to where you are and where you are heading. Looking to your left (west) you will see the radar dome atop the Summit, and straight ahead are the power lines that separate the dwarf pines from the Sarnoff Preserve. To the east (right) you can see the long green ridge of Flanders Hill a few miles off. Keeping your eyes on the trail, look for another unmarked trail going off to the left (west) about 200 yards north of Route 27. If you were to continue northward here you could stay on this trail beyond the power lines into the Sarnoff Preserve and eventually pick up the Paumanok Path. But we will make the turn left here to head back in the direction we approached the dwarf pines from. Although only a sandy break in the ground vegetation, this obscure path will take you back northeast and shortly turn southeast. It affords an opportunity to examine this queer forest of pygmy trees, some over a hundred years old and growing twisted, distorted, and horizontally along the ground like bonsai trees. Keep in mind that you are in the northwest corner of an area that once spread three miles across. Conditions may be desertlike at times but there is still plenty of life here. You may rouse a deer that has bedded down or spot an old wooden deer hunting stand off to the side of the trail. Fox tracks are not uncommon but actually viewing a fox is a matter of sheer luck. In October you may see the flight of the buck moth or catch sight of hawks overhead.

As you start to hear cars on Route 27 the trail heads northeast (right) again (**about 2.75 miles**). You will shortly leave the dwarf pine plains and move into a transition woods of short scroungy trees that are tall enough to muffle out the sound of any Route 27 traffic. It soon becomes quiet as the forest rises to engulf the walker. It is amazing how quickly the sounds of traffic can be absorbed by surrounding trees and woods. You are now on what is called the **Main Trail** on the LIGTC map. It was probably created as a firebreak some years ago, but is now becoming overgrown. You may not realize it, but you are slowly ascending as you amble away from the coastal plain towards the moraital hill ahead of you. You will see a faint side path off to the south (left) that is dimly marked on the map and a short time later you will reach the junction with the **Old Westhampton Road** again at about **3.6 miles**. An old downed tarred telephone pole is located here to help you define your exact position. As you continue westward, watch for another junction with a north-to-south trail crossing a few minutes later. There is a county survey marker put in the ground nearby and the southerly portion of this trail looks more newly cut, probably as part of a county acquisition as it is very straight. Just beyond this junction you will reach another trail leading north (right), but this trail doesn't go far before dead-ending; it's probably just an access trail for hunters.

The trees will become larger, especially the oaks, as you continue west on the Main Trail. You should notice the incline in the land. Your objective is to reach a **dim side trail** off to the north (right) at about **4.4 miles**. Although unmarked at this writing, plans are to eventually mark a trail here. This overgrown path is particularly hard to spot when the leaves are out. The only landmark I can find to identify this faint narrow path is one pitch pine tree that stands out at trailside where the path begins. This trail should be called the Summit Trail as it will take the hiker up the slopes of **the Summit**, the 260-foot hill that stands out above the flat coastal plains to the south. One sure way to know you have the right path is that the main trail ends and junctions with a wide woods road about 100 yards or so to the west of the Summit Trail junction. With this in mind you should have little trouble finding the Summit Trail.

Looking south from a viewpoint on The Summit

This closed-in path is one of the best surprises in the Pine Barrens as you steadily but gradually ascend until reaching a clearing with tall pitch pines overhead. Through the trees on your left (west) you will see the pine-clad ridge of 270-foot Rock Hill with the tall tower and blinking lights on it. Obviously, all of these views are better when the leaves are down. Looking back southward you can get an idea of how high you are in relation to the coastal plain, which seems far off in the distance. Nearby is a view through an opening in the trees. This is an impressive view of the ocean through the trees, although it is becoming obstructed by growth on the southern slopes of the hill. Hiking here a few months after the 1995 fires you could plainly see the black charred landscape, but as time goes by it is becoming harder to distinguish. What an astounding view this can be if the county decides to take out a few trees to open it up a bit!

From this little open area the paths split, one going off to the right (southeast) down to a spur of the Summit. It is best used as a return route as part of a loop exploring the Summit and its surroundings. For now, continue on the other path in a northerly direction to a small clearing where another junction is reached. Remember that none of these are well-traveled and are somewhat overgrown. Continuing northward here will shortly take you to the base of the radar dome where a fence marks the boundary of the FAA land on the top of the Summit. Back at the junction, the path that goes off to the right (east) takes you to another fine view through the trees. The small airport in Westhampton that houses the Air National Guard is visible beyond the dwarf pines you just left behind. A loop going around the base of the Summit can be explored by following this path eastward and southward until it links with the Summit Trail; a left here will take you back down to the Main Trail. The loop around the Summit is approximately a mile long. There is a large erratic that makes a good place to rest right alongside the path as it descends away from the hill on the east side. The area just north of here has excellent kettles that warrant exploration, and other views surely await the adventurous. Larry Paul, who first wrote about the walks in this area, said it best in describing a view from the slopes of the Summit: "To be here on a clear autumn day, with clouds massed overhead, with backlighting through the luminous wine-hued foliage of the oaks, to gaze far out upon that incredible flaring white mirror of the Atlantic, is to understand why the pinelands must be held forever wild."

Once back down on the Main Trail, make a right until a junction is reached in about 100 yards or so. Make a left (south) and you will shortly reach the large firebreak bulldozed during the fires of 1995. Cross this gash in the earth and pick up the woods road as it continues southward on the far side. You will see that the woods are regenerating from the fires here. In a few minutes you will reach the Middle Line at about **6.3 miles** where you make a right (west) and return to your car in 0.4 mile to complete a roughly **7 mile** loop.

Access

Car

Take LIE exit 70 south about 3.5 miles and get off onto County Route 51. Make a left and proceed for about 3.25 miles to Speonk-Riverhead Road. Make a right and a woods road giving access will be about 1.3 miles farther on the left. Turn around and park alongside the road here. Hampton Hills can be accessed directly from the yellow blazed trail on County Route 51. To get there follow the above directions to County Route 51 and go left (southeast) about 4.25 miles. Pull over on the right where the high tension lines cross over the road. The yellow blazes can be picked up there.

Bus

SCT8A

Dwarf Pines and Westhampton Burn Area

Length: various. Blaze: no marked trails

For trail map see p. 214

USGS topographic maps: Eastport, Quogue

The dwarf pine plains are an area around Exit 63 of Route 27 (Sunrise Highway). A few miles long, the plains are comprised of stunted trees that rarely reach 6 feet in height, despite being more than 80 years old and, in some cases, more than 100. The soil is very sandy; in fact it looks like nothing but sand, and it is a wonder that trees grow here at all. The area is one of only three like it in the world, the other two being in the New Jersey pinelands and atop the Shawangunk mountain plateau near New Paltz in upstate New York. Scrub oak and pitch pines are the two dominant trees that can tolerate the porous soil. Some trees have branches that grow out horizontally for several feet in a strange fashion. Not too many other plants grow readily here. Pine Barrens heather and a few scraggly blueberries can be found in the open sites. Hiking here should be done in cooler weather, since this is a very hot and uncomfortable place with no respite from the sun. Here you can see to the horizon most of the time since the pygmy trees do nothing to hinder the view. Landmarks such as the FAA radar dome on the Summit to the northwest, the water tower at the airport to the southeast or the exit signs at Route 27 can all guide the hiker.

You might expect this barren region to be devoid of wildlife but that is not the case. White-tail deer abound as well as several bird and snake species. Two endangered species, the buck moth and the northern harrier live here. The buck moth can be seen in flight for a two-week period in October. The northern harrier (once called the marsh hawk) is a large hawk that prowls over the open areas 10 feet off the ground looking for prey. This attractive hawk can hover over one loca-

A sandy path in the land of stunted trees

tion for a period of time before making its move. It probably never was all that common since it requires open marsh or grassland in which to hunt.

The dwarf pine plains have been cut into four quadrants by Exit 63; the larger two parts are on the south side of the road. The northwest quadrant is accessible from the woods roads that run east of Speonk-Riverhead Road and can be included in hikes up the Summit in Hampton Hills. Other access to the area can be from sandy roads on either side of County Route 31 (Riverhead Road, Exit 63). Suffolk County Airport is in the southeast quadrant but hiking is possible north of it. The burn areas left from the 1995 fires are located in the southeast quadrant a mile or so west of Route 31. This is a fascinating area to explore. The dwarf pines have serotinous cones that require fire to open and germinate. Unfortunately, it had been nearly 70 years since the last large fire in the plains, and initial studies show that only a small percentage of pine seeds are germinating. Only time will tell if this spells the end of the dwarf pines and begins a new dominance of scrub oaks, which are vigorously re-sprouting.

The burn areas as well as the dwarf pines can also be hiked from the south. To gain access from the south start from the Westhampton train station, walk west along the tracks past the thin yellow sign with the WH on it and cross over the tracks (no third rail here) and go over a dirt berm about 150 feet west of the station. This line of the railroad (Montauk Branch) is lightly used with only a few trains a passing each day, but exercise common sense safety when crossing it. Just on the other side of the berm, you will pick up a woods road that runs parallel to the tracks. Continue walking westward and you will soon come to a sandy trail on your right that will go off to the north. Walkers in this area should be armed with the LIGTC map for the eastern section of the Pine Barrens and a USGS or DOT topographic map for Eastport. The northward path will take you into the Westhampton burn area that was roasted in the hot fires of August 1995. Remembering that development and the village of Westhampton lie just south of the railroad tracks makes one realize how close we came to disaster and how hard the firefighters must have worked to stem the tide of the blaze. The area you will enter is very sandy; it might be described as desolate, though not in a negative sense of dread or disdain. Like a hiker in the arid deserts of the Southwest of our country, a feeling of isolation in awesome nature came over me. I explored in winter when the only true colors were the dark green hillsides of surviving pitch pine islands, the blue of the sky and the rusty burnt orange hillsides covered with the false heather known as hudsonia. In early June the hiker would see its small yellow blooms which gild the slopes for a short time. Because of the rolling terrain and the lack of high vegetation, vistas open up for long distances in all directions. You will actually be following a river valley which must have been quite a strong watercourse 10,000 years ago after the retreat of the glaciers. A check of the topographic map shows there were actually two forks. If you take the first trail on the left (west) about 0.4 mile north of the tracks you can explore the eastern branch, which is an interesting wetland as it flows south into Beaverdam Pond. The shores of this small creek are lined with wetland plants such as inkberry, red maples and even a few American hollies. While exploring along here, I flushed a common snipe. This small wading bird with an unusually long bill is anything but common on Long Island, and only passes through in migration or occasionally winters in our area. These wetlands were the only place on this walk where I saw small flocks of birds chattering in the trees. The surrounding dry hills had signs of fox and deer but no living animals, including birds, were seen on my visit. One may choose to continue westward and explore the other fork of the river valley which has long been dry. Farther off-trail exploring to the northwest is possible, as there are many tracts of public land here.

Continuing north on the center trail you will see a housing development on the left, the only sign of civilization. This development was spared from the fires by the efforts of firefighters, and you have to wonder why it was built in such a vulnerable isolated location. You may continue north and cross Stewart Avenue, the access road to the development. You can continue farther north into the dwarf pines and get a look at the regeneration of this unique ecosystem firsthand. As previously mentioned, the land for a few miles to the west makes for longer outings for the adventurous.

Access
Car
A good place to explore the dwarf pines is south of Sunrise Highway (County Route 31) exit 63. There is a sandy path into the area on the right (west) side about 0.6 mile south of that exit.

Train
From the Westhampton Train Station on the Montauk Branch walk west along the tracks only about 150 feet, cross over (no third rail here) to the north side and go over the earth berm to a woods road that will take you westward to other trails that go north. See the Dwarf Pines hike description for more details.

Bus
SCT90

David A. Sarnoff
Pine Barrens Preserve

Length: 6.5 miles. Blaze: red

USGS topographic map: Riverhead

This state-owned 2,749 acre preserve has
an interesting history and contains more

surprises than one would expect from a dry, sandy-soiled pine-oak forest habitat. The Ronkonkoma Moraine cuts through the property making for some
hilly terrain, including some wide views. Freshwater ponds, small swampy
wetlands, rolling terrain dotted with kettleholes, and windswept hills all come
together within the borders of the Sarnoff property to make this a great place
to explore. The Paumanok Path traverses the southern, and most hilly portion
of the land. Descriptions of that trail can be found in the section labeled
Paumanok Path. If you combine the Sarnoff Preserve with the adjacent
Hampton Hills property (on the west), the dwarf pines on the south, and
county holdings to the east, it's possible to plan longer hikes. A permit to hike
the property is required. The same permit that allows access to the Rocky
Point Preserve is good here. Write to NYSDEC, Division of Lands and
Forests, Building 40, SUNY-Stony Brook, Stony Brook, NY 11790-2356 for a
permit or pick up an application at the Pine Barrens Trail Information Center
just north of exit 70 on the LIE. You can also call the DEC directly at (631)
444-0276. Hunting is permitted on portions of the property. If you wish to
hike here during the three-week deer season in January be sure to wear bright
colors and stay on the trail. The chances of seeing a hunter are slim but it's
best to take precautions anyway.

Located south of Riverhead and north of Sunrise Highway (Route 27), The
Sarnoff Preserve straddles both sides of County Route 104, the larger piece
being on the west. There are six main access points to the property; five of
those are on blazed trails. The preserve has one red-blazed six-mile loop on
the west side to which four shorter yellow side trails give access. There is also
a 3.75 mile blue-blazed loop accessed by a yellow trail on the east side of
County Route 104. The landmark starting point is the five-road traffic circle
at Route 24 in Riverhead. The main access point where the red-blazed trail
can be reached is about 0.2 mile down county Route 63. Look for a wooden
state trail marker sign on the left (south) side of the road where you can pull
down a short road to a parking lot. If you continue another 0.7 mile (0.9 mile

from the traffic circle) on that same road you will reach one of the yellow-blazed side trails on the same side of the road. It is inconspicuous; there's just a place to pull a car over on the shoulder of the road. Beyond this Lakeview Road branches off to the left. If you follow this to the left it becomes Old Westhampton Road. Follow it along the scenic east side of Wildwood Lake to the end of the road, where a parking area has another yellow trail leaving it. The other yellow side trails are located on the east side of the property, starting from the parking lot on the west side of County Route 104, about 2.1 miles south of the traffic circle. Another access point is located 0.7 mile south of the

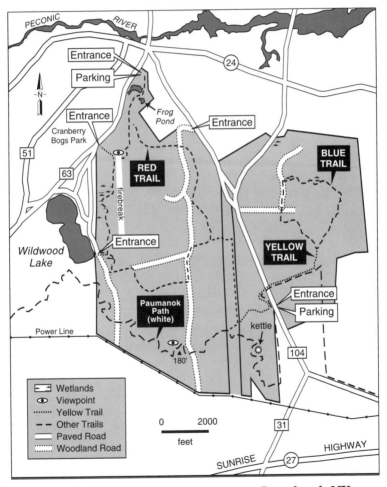

David A. Sarnoff Pine Barrens Preserve, Riverhead, NY

traffic circle where a small paved pull-off is designated by another trail marker sign. Although unmarked, this was once the main access road to the property when it was an active communications center. It will lead to the red loop trail in a few minutes' walk. The last yellow side trail is a direct north-to-south linkup between the red loop and the Paumanok Path. If this all seems kind of confusing, consult the LIGTC map for the east section of the Pine Barrens Trail and it will make sense. Think of the side trails as widely spaced spokes coming off the red loop trail at scattered intervals. The trail mileage information provided by the state is sparse so I have had to estimate the locations of some features. Overall, the total mileage is fairly accurate.

As mentioned in the Paumanok Path section on the Rocky Point Natural Resources Management Area, the Sarnoff property was instrumental in the development of wireless communication across the Atlantic in the earlier part of the twentieth century. It is here that some of the pioneers in short-wave radio developed methods of receiving radio messages from Europe in the 1920s. Some of the greatest minds of the time worked in this now largely forgotten location. David A. Sarnoff was one of these giants of his time. Today, remnants of tower fields are still scattered about the property but many of the disturbed sites are returning to their natural state. At the height of the property's use, there were 34 rectangular and 18 rhomboidal antenna fields spread over the area. Tall towers connected by wires dominated the landscape from a distance. The advent of satellite technology made the antenna fields outmoded, and operations ceased in 1975. The property was eventually acquired along with the Rocky Point property by the state from the RCA Corporation in 1978 for a token sum of $1, a gift that is much appreciated by hikers and hunters.

Starting out from the parking lot off County Route 63 you'll see a trail sign for the **red-blazed trail**. Follow the sandy path for a few short minutes until you reach **Frog Pond (0.25 mile)** on your left. A surprisingly busy little pond, there always seems to be some sort of wildlife activity going on here. In spring and summer you may see a deer drinking early or late in the day as well as lots of song bird activity, since the pond has many insects that fly above the surface of the water. In fall through early spring you may see wild ducks such as mallards and black ducks feeding quietly. Fragrant pond lilies dot the water with their bright white multi-pointed stars in summer, and there are even a few rare Atlantic white cedars growing along the bank in places. There is another larger pond on the opposite side of the trail but it is hidden away most of the year by thick plant growth.

Just past Frog Pond, watch for blazes that make a right at a junction. A left will take you past one of the old buildings on the grounds that was destroyed in a recent fire. The trail then loops around to the left through old pitch pine woods. Looking closely you can see the blackened evidence of a past fire on the trunks of these pines. An abandoned hulk of an old (1940s) pickup truck can be seen off to the right sitting like a ghost of past times in the now overgrown woods. You will also pass a healthy looking mountain laurel on the right side of the trail near here. This showy shrub is more common on the North Shore in western Long Island or the hilly sections of the South Fork than it is here. Beyond this spot the trail meets the merger point where the red trail branches off in two directions at the base of a 5-mile loop. This is about **0.5 mile** from the main parking lot. A trail marker sign gives mileage of some of the other junctions and features along this loop. I have always gone to the right when doing this loop, in a counterclockwise direction, and that is how I will describe it.

From the junction, the trail passes through a predominantly oak forest. Scarlet oak is especially prevalent here and in autumn the color red dominates the scene in various shades and hues. Shortly thereafter the trail joins an old overgrown woods road and continues its roughly southerly course before reaching an open sandy area. This is part of the original firebreak created to protect the main building in the center of the property. A look at any of the trail maps, whether the LIGTC map, the US topographic map for Riverhead or the crude map given out by the DEC will show a rectangular box-shaped area that was created when radio research and experimentation was going on. The topographic map in particular, although it dates to 1956, shows some strangely shaped cleared areas where transmission fields were set up over large areas to develop this "new" way of communicating overseas. Once in the old firebreak the trail makes a left and heads slightly uphill to a viewpoint back northward towards the village of Riverhead. The county complex buildings can be seen in the distance and seem farther off than the mile or so they actually are. You will notice that pitch pines have been the main tree to try to re-establish themselves in the very sandy open environment of the firebreak. There is also a lot of bearberry growing along the ground that seems to creep out into sunny locations wherever possible. Another member of the heath family, this ground cover has small paddle-shaped evergreen leaves that turn a pale maroon-like color in fall but do not fall off. It grows in creeping mats in exposed rocky or sandy sites that most other plants couldn't tolerate. Common in the far northern tundra, it nonetheless thrives in equally inhospitable locations in the Pine Barrens of the Northeast where its deep roots allow it to obtain moisture in extreme conditions. You will see it throughout the Sarnoff Preserve as it claims open ground cleared years before. The name apparently comes from the fact that bears feed off the red berries when they ripen each fall. They are edible for humans, too, but only for survival's sake, since they are mealy and tasteless. Small inconspicuous urn-shaped flowers bloom in late spring. Their dried leaves were smoked by Indians as a tobacco substitute.

Just as the trail starts to drop down, watch for blazes signifying a turn to the right where the trail heads back into the woods. At about **1.1 miles** the trail reaches another junction with a **yellow-blazed access trail** that heads in a few minutes time (approximately 0.2 mile) to County Route 63. Along the way it passes along the slopes of a vernal kettle before reaching the road. Back at the trail junction, you can make a left turn and continue to follow the red trail on a pleasant path. Looking off to the sides of the trail you will see more kettle-like depressions demonstrating that this terrain is far more variable than one might imagine. A glance at the topographic map shows that this is one of many dips in the area. This was one of the most surprising things about my first trip to Sarnoff. The other was the small swampy wet kettles you will skirt as you continue along this westerly portion of the trail. In early spring the high-pitched sound of spring peepers can be heard piping above the evening air. Tall bush blueberries, leatherleaf and sheep laurel all thrive in the wet area. The different vegetation is very colorful in October but peaks in early November when the surrounding oak dominated forest is in its full fall colors. In springtime, the differences in when these plants flower and leaf out are also evident. Thus, the wetlands lend a contrast and much-appreciated change to perceptive walkers through most of the year. The trail passes up and away from the first wetland before quickly coming to another at about **2.3 miles**.

Beyond the wetlands the trail snakes back and forth for a while, passing more wetlands along the way. You are now in an upland section of the preserve and when the leaves are down you will pass some places where Wildwood Lake can be seen through the trees on the right (west). One nice viewpoint is of the surrounding hills beyond the lake (the lake remains hidden by the nearby terrain here).

At about **2.9 miles** the trail drops down to another swamp where a

Hiking the Paumanok Path deep inside the preserve

yellow-blazed side trail comes in on the right. The trail sign says that it is 0.06 mile out to parking area #1 located at the end of Lakeview Road (also known as Old Westhampton Road), and indeed it is a short walk. The red trail circumvents the wetland on a very narrow path just along the border of the wet ground. You will then start an uphill climb through some bald areas under tall pines. The trail then reaches a hollow that shows signs of a more recent burn with scarred trees and some new growth in the understory. After passing up the open slopes of the hollow you will reach a wide woods road; turn left and follow it for a few minutes. The trail was not marked very well at this turn on my last visit.

The trail reaches an old clearing that has some concrete footing and cables lying about, telltale reminders of the tall towers that once stood here. There are four paths at this junction, and the trail follows the right one on an open narrow woods road. In a few minutes you will see a long tarred wooden pole, another reminder of this property's past. A kettlehole behind it is a nice place to poke around off trail for a little while. Many dense but small pitch pines now grow on either side of the trail as you continue along this quiet path. Follow it as it curves eastward, passes a deep kettle on the left and reaches a junction at about **3.9 miles**. Here, another **yellow-blazed trail** gives direct access to the Paumanok Path in about **0.6 mile** to the south. This wide old tote road is very straight and is probably one of the very old roads used long ago to cut across the pines between Riverhead and the South Shore towns. The Paumanok Path can then be taken to the right (west) uphill for a few minutes to an excellent vantage point northward from an open scrub-oak- covered 180-foot hill where a lot of sky and serenity heightens the scene. This is a worthwhile side trip to take, adding perhaps 1.75 miles to the walk. This hilly southern section is a good place for experienced bushwhackers to explore a pristine area of the Ronkonkoma Moraine. The woods road can be taken another 0.4 mile south past the Paumanok Path until it reaches power lines. On the other side of the power-line clearing, one can pick up a trail that will lead you into the dwarf pine plains making for many interesting possibilities for imaginative hikers.

From the junction, the red trail heads to the left (north) through the characteristic rolling terrain of this region. It reaches the old central firebreak at about **4.2 miles** where it makes a right and heads eastward a few minutes. At about **4.4 miles** it reaches the fourth **yellow-blazed access trail**, which continues straight at a point where the red trail heads to the left. This yellow trail leads through open scrub-oak-dominated land to a point where it turns right parallel to County Route 104. Silver survey monuments have recently been driven into the ground by Suffolk County around here; they can be seen in a few places. This trail will eventually make a sharp left (east) and bring you to the Route 104 parking area. Here, it meets with the Paumanok Path as well as allowing access to the blue loop trail on the opposite side of Route 104.

Back on the red trail, you now enter the woods on a much narrower trail and pass into another old antenna field that's now open second-growth pines. Concrete bases are visible in areas just now recovering from being disturbed years ago. Watch for blazes letting you know that the trail veers off to the right across the grassy field and into the woods again. It crosses another path before emerging into the central clearing of the property at about **5.2 miles**. This was the locus of activity for the communication research that once went on here. At one time it was thought that a ranger station could be set up in the building in the center of the clearing, but it was demolished because it posed a hazard to the curious.

The trail now follows the edge of the clearing in an area known as an ecotone, where two types of different habitats meet. They are good places for wildlife because they offer a combination of food and cover. The state has made brush piles that will help increase the local rabbit population. The trail crosses the old paved road and continues along the northern edge of the clearing until it takes a right (northwest) to head into the woods, joining an abandoned woods road before coming to the trail merger at about **5.9 miles**. With the loop completed, you follow the same route back out to the parking area, for a total hike of about **6.5 miles**.

Many options are open to the hiker who links the David A. Sarnoff Preserve trails to adjacent public lands: There are unlimited combinations of hikes in almost any direction. But Sarnoff itself has plenty to offer the walker in the way of its history, terrain, and wildlife.

Access

Car

Take LIE exit 71 and make a right (east) onto County Route 24. Proceed about 4.8 miles to a traffic circle and take County Route 63 0.2 mile to the parking area on the left. Other access to the Sarnoff Preserve can be found in this section.

Buses

SCT8A, 90

David A. Sarnoff Blue Loop Trail
(East of Route 104)

Length: 3.75 mile loop

Blaze: yellow, then blue

USGS topographic map: Riverhead

The blue-blazed loop on the east side of County Route 104 south of Riverhead makes for a fine introductory hike to the Pine Barrens or a walk to take the kids on. The total hike from the parking lot on the east side of Route 24 is about 3.75 miles round trip. There once was a small restaurant on this site and remnants of it can be seen. Pick up the **yellow trail** and head north (right) towards the woods. There is a lot of heather (or hudsonia) growing in the clearing before entering the woods. It is the upland Pine Barrens variety that blooms in pretty yellow flowers in late spring. The trail will turn to the east (right) and shortly cross Route 104. Be careful, as cars move very fast on this open highway. You may notice the white paint blazes of the Paumanok Path that follow this route for the time being.

The trail follows an old boundary road for about **0.4 mile** east of Route 104. It is straight and unexciting at this point and was used out of convenience. About **0.6 mile** out of the parking lot, look for the yellow trail to leave the Paumanok Path and head off to the north (right). The yellow trail ends and the 2 mile blue-blazed loop begins here. I chose to go to the left here. The trail passes through beautiful open Pine Barrens woodlands where the pitch pines stand out above the surrounding scrub oaks. The pines have the advantage of scaly resistant bark that allows them to survive fires whereas the oaks must sprout anew and therefore never seem to catch up to the pines. Red-tailed hawks often nest in these tall trees. The trail continues through nice rolling terrain, and there seem to be an unusually high number of wintergreen plants along it. On a winter hike in this area we ate wintergreen berries on a cold clear day. The small red berries give off the familiar fragrance we have become accustomed to in gums, candies, and toothpaste. Of course, the fragrance is now synthesized in laboratories at a much cheaper cost, but nothing beats the real thing. Be sure to properly identify any berries or plants with a field guide before eating them.

The trail passes three wetlands just off to the right side. Each is interesting in its own way. They make for an excellent opportunity to see some of the common plants that have adapted to the wetland habitat. Plants such as leather-leaf and swamp loosestrife are examples of those that can survive in acidic boglike conditions and fluctuating water levels. Wetland trees such as tupelo and red maple turn brilliant colors weeks before the surrounding upland flora does. Just past the last of these wetlands the trail crosses a woods road and turns south again. It skims the side of a low hill that poses a welcome relief to this flat section of trail. A little farther on the trail rejoins the yellow trail and can be followed the way you came in back to the parking lot on Route 104. The entire loop, including stops, can be done in 3 hours or so.

Access

Car

From Riverhead drive south to a parking lot on the east side of Route 24 about 2 miles from the traffic circle near the Suffolk County administrative complex. Or drive north to the Route 24 traffic circle from either exit 63 or 64 on Route 27 and the parking area will be on the left (west) side of the road about 0.6 mile north of the junction with route 31.

A wetland seen from the blue loop trail east of Route 104

Peconic River County Park

Length: under 1.3 miles one way.

Blaze: none

For trail map see Manorville Hills section
page 208

USGS topographic map: Riverhead

This area of county-owned land along the south side of the Peconic River west of downtown Riverhead is undeveloped parkland. It's a fine example of riverfront woods and contains some bogs that appear to be very much in their natural state. The tract is the northern part of a large piece of county land that extends from Route 51 on the south through Manorville Hills and north to the Peconic River. Wedged between state Route 24 and the river is the Peconic River County Park. The area suffers from some illegal dumping but this shouldn't deter walking here. Access on the east side is from a state boat launch just south of Route 25 and on the west side from a quieter setting at the end of South River Road just past where Forge Road goes over the Peconic River. From here a woods road goes eastward reaching a feeder brook that runs into the Peconic on the left. Skunk cabbages poke their hooded heads up in midwinter in this area. They are considered the first wildflowers of the year; as strange as they may appear, they are still flowers. Power lines are reached farther on. You can walk out to the left (north) to the riverbank to get a firsthand view of the Peconic, which is in very good shape considering how close to downtown Riverhead you are.

Back on the unmarked trail, continue past the power lines eastward and some interesting wooded bogs appear on the left in slight depressions. There are a couple of these wetlands along this stretch. Exploration around them will take some serious off-trail bushwhacking and is not recommended unless some type of natural history research makes it necessary. Continuing on from here, you'll come to the state boat launch site. A small LIPA substation is nearby. A southern night-calling bird called the chuck-will's-widow is known to be heard here on late spring to late summer evenings. Similar to the whip-poor-will, it is slowly extending its range northward. The song is mysterious; the bird seems to be repeating its name over and over again from the dark forest floor. A different return route can be taken along the power lines just south of the route you took in. A much dryer route through pines and oaks can be expected here. A USGS topographic map for Riverhead is useful in negotiating this area.

Access

Car

Take LIE exit 71 and make a right onto County Route 24. Make a left in 1.2 miles onto Pinehurst Boulevard. At the end of the road, make a right onto South River Road. Park at the end of the road.

A small creek in the park flows into the Peconic River in spring

Cranberry Bog County Nature Preserve

Length: more than 1 mile loop. Blaze: self-guide signs

For trail map see Manorville Hills section

USGS topographic map: Riverhead

Located between State Route 24 and County Route 63, just to the west and south of the Suffolk County Complex in Riverhead, are freshwater wetlands that drain into the nearby Peconic River. They contain bogs, swamps, and ponds with some of the most unusual and rare plants on Long Island. Because the tract has long been a favorite haunt for botanists and naturalists, Suffolk County has made this natural treasure a county nature preserve. Within these boundaries is possibly the best kept secret in the county park system, Cranberry Bog County Preserve. If you are traveling west away from the Route 24 traffic circle in Riverhead, the entrance is located on the right (north) side of County Route 63 (Old Riverhead-Moriches Rd) just past where Lakeside Drive forks off to the left almost one mile west of the traffic circle. A large sign designating the park is on the right. There is room to park off the road here.

The Cranberry Bog Preserve is a short walk that can be covered in less than an hour. It is an excellent introductory walk for children, but don't be fooled by the short distance: This unique area contains some uncommon plants in a scarce habitat. It also includes a bit of Long Island history since it was one of the last working cranberry bogs until it closed in 1965. Cranberries grow on creeping vines in wet acidic soils such as those found in bogs. The berries, which are rich in vitamin C and pectin, are North American natives found only in north-central and eastern states; they're common in large numbers only along the coast in the wet, sandy and well-drained soil of Pine Barrens wetlands from New Jersey through Cape Cod.

Used by Native Americans, cranberries were a part of the Pilgrims' first thanksgiving at Plymouth. They were first grown for sale in Massachusetts around 1817, and in the 1870s began to be grown commercially in some of the eastern Long Island bogs. By the early 1900s Long Island was the third-largest producer of cranberries in the world behind Cape Cod and the New Jersey Pine Barrens. However, the business of cranberry farming never reached its full potential due to a series of setbacks, including lack of local processing plants, pest problems, and finally a pesticide scare that made the industry unprofitable. The last local bog was used until in 1974. This cranberry operation was owned by S.H. Woodhull and was known as the Woodhull Bog. Commercial production requires open sunny bogs that are dammed so they can be flooded each fall to aid in gathering the fruit and to protect the plants in winter. The bog is covered with a layer of sand each year to stimulate new growth. Some folks still harvest the native berries each October from favorite spots in the Pine Barrens, but don't expect them to reveal the location willingly. Good berries should be firm and bouncy. If they are soft, they are not the best for eating. I have found the local berries to be a tart treat if eaten right off the vine.

Once you travel down the woods road that takes you into the preserve, you will shortly see a medium-size lake in front of you. This is **Sweezy Pond**, the centerpiece of the walk. Look for a path on your right which will take you counterclockwise around the pond. Notice how quickly the dry Pine Barrens flora gives way to wetland tolerant species such as sweet pepperbush, leatherleaf and sphagnum moss. As you follow the pond in this direction you'll soon see the first of several interpretive signs put up by the county. They explain

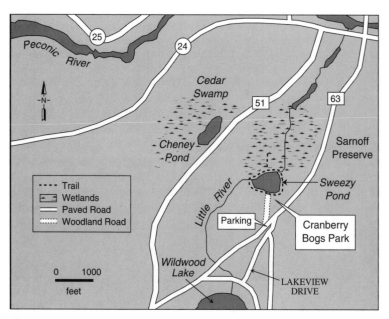

Cranberry Bog County Park, Riverside, NY

the workings of the bog and how cranberries were farmed here. The over-grown excavation pits where sand was removed are pointed out. Following the pond past the old pumphouse, you will make a left and proceed around to the other side. The thick wooded area between you and the pond at this point is a grove of Atlantic white cedars. They were cut for their rot-and-insect resistant properties. White cedars only grew in freshwater wetlands and since they were never very numerous they soon became a rarity. This small grove is still relatively young and appears healthy. Certain species of insects such as the rare Hessel's hairstreak butterfly thrive in these trees.

Along the back side of the pond you will come to a path that goes off to the right. It is a dead end but I have explored back this way and have found pitch-er plants growing along the borders of the overgrown wetlands on the left. This is another unique plant. It is insectivorous, meaning that it gets much of its nutrients by devouring insects lured into the tall pitcher-like leaf. Once inside, insects are trapped by downward-pointing hairs that give off a numb-ing secretion. Escape is impossible as the insect slips farther down past a slip-pery chamber to a water-filled base that contains enzymes to help break down the victim. The plant uses the insects for energy and to obtain nitrogen, which is not readily available in this sterile sandy soil. Other insectivorous plants such as bladderwort and sundews can be found in the preserve as well, but

Sweezy Pond seen from a bridge along the trail

pitcher plants are particularly rare on Long Island and this area is one of the few places they are found.

Back on the trail that skirts around the pond, continue past wet areas that seep into Sweezy Pond. Colorful flowers such as swamp milkweed can be found in the damp meadows here. In midsummer look for the small flowers of cranberries in bloom. These reminded the early settlers of the beak of a crane, a tall wading bird. Over the years craneberries became cranberries. The trail will go over a fine sturdy **wooden bridge** on the left and head back to the starting point.

To the north of Cranberry Bog County Park, and north of County Route 51, is **Cedar Swamp**, another part of the county nature preserve system. Basically trail-less, it is a wonderful place for serious naturalists and bush-whackers to explore. **Cheney Pond** is the large pond seen from Route 51 and is the centerpiece of the area. There are Atlantic white cedars here, along with gray birch and mountain laurel. Despite being so close to the road, the place has a wild look, and there are many rare and unusual plants here. The extensive wooded swampy area behind the pond will require proper attire to prevent getting too wet, and precautions against ticks must also be taken. Best left to more experienced hikers, Cedar Swamp will reveal surprises to those who research its more inaccessible spots.

Access

Car

Take LIE exit 71 and make a right (east) onto County Route 24. In about 4.8 miles you will reach a traffic circle. Take the second right onto County Route 63 and proceed to the entrance on the right in just under 1 mile.

Bus

SCT8A

Sears-Bellows County Park

Length: 4.4 miles. Blaze: white, then yellow

For trail map see Hubbard Creek Section on page 241

USGS topographic map: Mattituck

This park run by Suffolk County is best known for its public campground and adjacent horse stables. Yet it contains some beautiful ponds, the largest of which are **Bellows Pond** near the park entrance and campground area, and **Sears Pond** in the interior of the parkland. Other ponds in the park include **House, Division** and **Grass** ponds as well as many smaller unnamed but very pretty ponds scattered about. Some have small islands in them with stands of rare Atlantic white cedar. These scattered wetlands are a great attraction to the hiker not only for their aesthetic beauty but for the opportunities to see a variety of wildlife, especially birds. Ospreys, herons, egrets, wood ducks, warblers and many others are attracted to these ponds.

Like so many of the prime wildlife habitats on the Island, the park was once owned by a sportsmen's club called the Flanders Club, which hunted local waterfowl. At only 693 acres the park is not very large, but all the surrounding lands are either undeveloped or publicly owned so hiking opportunities are many and varied. The park entrance is off Bellows Road south of Route 24 in Hampton Bays about 1.5 miles north of Route 27 (Sunrise Highway). The Paumanok Path passes through the park as it traverses the south shore of Sears Pond, eventually crossing Route 24 before entering neighboring Hubbard County Park. The campsite has showers and is useful to hikers backpacking the Paumanok Path, since a short trail connects the camping area to it. The campsite is much-used in summer but it is deserted in the off-season. Some sections of woods road are chewed up from horseback riding, but there are enough paths and old woods roads to explore and loop around the park. One short day hike utilizing two cars begins by leaving one car at Spinney Road just off Route 24 and then driving to the parking area in Sears-Bellows County Park to start the hike. With the aid of the Pine Barrens trail map you can follow the access trail out on the main woods road, linking up with the Paumanok Path in a little while. Following the trail westward you will pass by Sears Pond and eventually lovely Owl Pond, reaching the yellow-blazed Birch Creek Trail that will take you back out to Route 24 and Spinney Road. This is about 4.4 miles and a nice introduction to the area. To extend this another 2 miles or so you can continue on past the Birch Creek Trail to Maple Swamp, eventually ending at Pleasure Drive.

Access

Car

Take Sunrise Highway (State Route 27) to exit 65 north for 1.5 miles. Make a left onto Bellows Road to the entrance of the park on the right in less than a mile.

Bus

SCT92

Sears Pond is one of the most beautiful bodies of water on Long Island

Hubbard County Park

Length: 3 miles out and back. Blaze: white, then unmarked road

USGS topographic map: Mattituck

The South Fork begins in Flanders, south of Riverhead. A series of creeks empties into the bay in this area. Here an expanse of magnificent salt marshes, beaches and red cedar savannahs extends out of the Pine Barrens woodlands. Suffolk County wisely acquired a large portion of the land, which today is known as Hubbard County Park. A few woods roads traverse the property north of Route 24. The area once was owned by private clubs and was prized for access to wetlands and upland close together. I have seen few hikers in this little-known gem of the county park system. Goose, Birch, Mill and Hubbard creeks all empty into Flanders Bay, creating salt flats (marshes with low growing grasses and plants) that are fascinating places for the naturalist to explore year round. In spring and fall many migratory birds can be seen in the large inlets where the creeks widen before they empty into the bay. Look for tall wading birds along the shorelines, and in winter large flocks of sea ducks in the bay. Ospreys can be seen in summer. Close observation of the unique plants that colonize the salt marshes will reveal their hardiness, despite appearing so fragile. These plants have had to adapt to strong salinity, poorly nourished soil, tide changes and constant exposure to the elements. The sea lavender that adds its splash of color to the marsh in late summer is a perfect example of this.

You can start a hike on Red Creek Road as it goes off to the northeast off Route 24 about 2 miles north of Route 27 (Sunrise Highway). There is a sign for the park at this point. A very short distance down Red Creek Road is a gravel road on the left. Park near here and walk the road heading north. You'll notice you are following the white blazes of the Paumanok Path. The road seems to be surrounded by classic Pine Barrens flora, but a closer look off to the side of the trail reveals tall evergreen mountain laurel widely scattered in the understory. Its showy pink and white blossoms bloom in mid to late June. Although fairly common on Long Island, the mountain laurel is quite rare in the Pine Barrens. This is the first patch of mountain laurel as you approach the South Fork, where it once again can be seen more regularly.

In a short distance the Paumanok Path leaves the road to the right to continue east. Continuing on the road, you will come to a clearing containing the

Black Duck Lodge and other buildings under the care of the parks department. The Hubbard family built part of the lodge after they purchased the tract in 1815. It was later bought by E.F. Hutton in 1937, who used it as a hunting lodge and extended the building on both sides. We saw red-bellied woodpeckers in the trees around the lodge. These are large handsome birds that have expanded their range northward in recent years. Farther on the road is

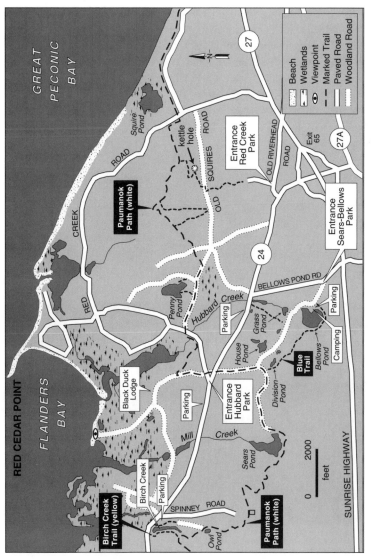

Hubbard Park; Red Creek Trails; Sears-Bellows Park; Suffolk County, NY

lined with tall pines with a grassy understory. There is a small freshwater swamp on the left where some Atlantic white cedars grow. A little farther along you'll come out in the sun amid a salt marsh. Notice the osprey platform on your left. This area is closed off during the warmer months so as not to disturb the birds as they breed and raise their young. Ospreys are sensitive to development, and constant approaches by people would force them to abandon this nest. Assuming you are hiking between October and April, continue along the road and you will see a grove of hardy eastern red cedars between you and the beach. This is a great place to explore. Notice the remains of a stone chimney, all that is left of a past habitation. Prickly pear cactus grows nearby. North across Flanders Bay you can see South Jamesport. The beach has a wealth of scallop and whelk shells, among others. There is even a tidal pond on the south side of the road. I hiked this area in winter shortly after a strong nor'easter and damage to the trees along the beach was evident, just another reminder Long Island is constantly being shaped and changed by nature.

A short detour takes you to Flanders Bay's tidal ponds and salt marshes

Returning the way you came, look for a trail on the right (west) side before you get back to Black Duck Lodge. This will take you past stands of mountain laurel and through open woods to a wooden walkway over an outlet of **Mill Creek** lined with shadbush that bloom in white profusion each spring. The property beyond here is a part of Hubbard County Park, which opened to the public in 1996 after an agreement with a local hunting club took effect. The county took title to the land five years after the last surviving member passed on. Brinkley Smithers was that last member, and this section of the tract was named the Smithers property after him.

The trail meets a park access road and follows it right (north) to the cabins of the hunting property. It is hoped that eventually the cabins will be made into overnight accommodations for hikers or campers. Currently a caretaker and his family live in a small home on the property. The spot is exceptional. South Jamesport lies directly across Flanders Bay. Red Cedar Point juts out into Great Peconic Bay to the east and Robins Island can be seen beyond. The salt meadows are undisturbed and wading birds and waterfowl can be viewed at various times of the year.

Another section of this sprawling park located west of **Birch Creek** is also worth exploring. An artesian well lies within the area and walking north toward **Goose Creek Point** is rewarding. The entire area would also be a fine place to cross-country ski. In order to explore parts of Hubbard County Park, experienced hikers will have to do some bushwhacking since no developed trail system runs east-to-west. However, the park does have some woods roads for walking in the woodlands along the bay. The USGS topographic map or DOT map of the Mattituck Quadrangle is a useful aid here.

Access

Car

Take Sunrise Highway (State Route 27) exit 65 north for about 2.4 miles to Red Creek Road. In about 0.1 mile you can park a car where the trail crosses the road at this point. If coming from the LIE, take exit 71 (County Route 24) east a little over 10 miles to Red Creek Road on the left.

Bus

SCT92

Red Creek Trails

Length: three hours. Blaze: yellow

For trail map see the Hubbard County Park section, page 241

USGS topographic map: Mattituck

Red Creek Park, located in Hampton Bays and run by the Township of Southampton, is a tract of Pine Barrens woodlands, ponds, and kettleholes just south of Great Peconic Bay near the beginning of the South Fork. The Paumanok Path passes through here on its way to the nearby Shinnecock Canal, where it ends. The park trail system is maintained by the Southampton Trails Preservation Society, a non-profit organization very involved in the extension of the Paumanok Path as well as the preservation of open space within the town. A map of Red Creek Trails is available from the society. It details some of the more interesting features in the park as well as adjacent Hubbard and Sears-Bellows county parks. These three parks combined yield an extensive trail system with plenty of loops and circuits to give hikers a full day of trekking. Blueberries are plentiful in the understory and fun to pick and eat when they ripen in mid-to-late July. The usual wildflowers found in woodlands are also here. One that is fairly localized on Long Island is germander, also known as wood sage. This tall mint can grow to 3 feet high with pink tubular flower clusters that bloom in July or August. It is found in woods, thickets and shores, and is a northern plant common in Quebec and western New England; it appears only as far south as Long Island.

Access the trails by taking Old Riverhead Road east from Route 24 to about a third of a mile north of the Route 27 cloverleaf at exit 65. If you are heading south on Route 24, look for a turnoff to the left less than a mile past Bellows Pond Road. Once on Old Riverhead Road look for the second left to Red Creek Park past Jackson Avenue Park on the northern end of the parking area. Proceed past the well-tended Little League baseball field to a break in the woods on the far side. There you will pick up the **yellow diamond blazes** of the **yellow loop trail** taking you into the shade of a mixed hardwood and pitch pine forest. In a few minutes time you'll reach the unpaved Old Squires Road onto which you'll make a right and go a short distance before heading back into the woods to the left. In a little while the trail will drop down to the nearest of two kettlehole ponds located here. The drop is quite sudden and this kettle is filled with water all year. You are likely to hear the meow-like call of a catbird in the thick undergrowth surrounding the kettle. Flycatchers swoop above the water in summer; there always seems to be some kind of bird activity in the warmer weather. The trail leaves the slopes and continues until it meets the Paumanok Path. The yellow trail makes a left here but you may want to go a little north to another small pond with a bench, perfect for quiet contemplation.

As the yellow trail continues westward it will pass the **white center trail**, which will go off to the left at the junction and take you back to Old Squires Road onto which you can make a left to shorten your walk. The yellow trail can be picked up again and taken to the right and back to your car making a total of about an hour's walk. The yellow loop trail continues past the white center trail a little farther, then heads left to make a similar but wider loop that will add about a half hour to the walk. At this left turn you will see the **yellow-white trail** which continues past Penny Pond and Hubbard Creek (see Paumanok Path). It will eventually cross Route 24 into Sears-Bellows Park and follow some park roads before heading back to cross Route 24 again. It then skims a wetland before linking up with itself. This hike can take about three hours to complete; the other sections are described in more detail in their appropriate park descriptions. Obviously, a map will help alleviate any confusion negotiating these trails.

Access

Car

Take Sunrise Highway (State Route 27) exit 65 north about 0.4 mile to Old Riverhead Road. Make a right and the park entrance is on the left in about 0.1 mile.

Bus

SCT10E

Fragrant water lily on Penny Pond

Quogue Wildlife Refuge

Length: 1.2 miles one way. Blaze: none

USGS topographic map: Quogue

This 200-acre refuge is owned by the Southampton Township Wildfowl Association and run and maintained by the New York State Department of Environmental Conservation (DEC). It is located on the north side of South Old Country Road about three quarters of a mile west of County Route 104 in Quogue. The entrance is just before the overpass over the railroad tracks. The **Charles Bank Belt Nature Center** is located on Old Ice Pond. It has a nature display and picture window overlooking the pond for quiet observing of waterfowl. There is also a wildlife complex at the beginning of the refuge where injured birds and mammals are cared for and then released if possible. Children especially enjoy the chance to see a hawk, owl, or fox up close. An enclosed pen with white-tail deer is behind this area.

The walk here heads away from the wildlife complex northward. The path is wide and flat with **Old Ice Pond** on your left. You will see nest boxes in clearings alongside the trail. The birds most likely to be using the boxes during breeding season are tree swallows. These birds are shiny blue-green above and white below and seem to be in constant motion as they swoop and dart above water in pursuit of flies and mosquitoes. The flora is typical of the Pine Barrens. Not many people use the refuge, so it is relatively peaceful. In winter there is a particular calm on this trail, except by the pond near the entrance where you may be mobbed by ducks and geese grubbing for handouts. The main trail can be taken more than a mile northward, crossing over parts of the Old Ice Pond (to the left) and going through a wetland near **North**

A freshwater pond and bog in Quogue Wildlife Refuge

Pond a little farther on. Both of these ponds drain southward into Quantuck Creek. Insectivorous pitcher plants can be found growing in the wetlands. I once startled a large snapping turtle in the water beside the wooden boardwalk. The Westhampton Airport borders this long, narrow preserve on the west, and undeveloped land is on the east, making the refuge seem much larger than it is. A walk to the northern limits of the land takes you into the fringe of the dwarf pines. This rare habitat is a fascinating place to explore but offers no cover from the hot sun in summer. One can spend several hours walking the refuge and the adjacent area to the north. Bring water if you choose to go into the dwarf pines. Binoculars will help in identifying some of the ducks on the ponds.

Access

Car

Take Sunrise Highway (State Route 27) exit 64 south about 2.3 miles to Old Country Road. Make a right and the preserve entrance will be on the right (north) side in about 0.7 mile.

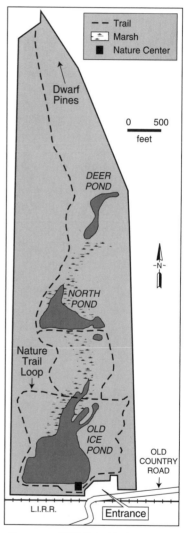

Quogue Wildlife Refuge, Quogue, NY

The Twin Forks

The Paumanok Path in Southampton

Big Woods to North Sea Road: 2 miles.
Blaze: white, some parts not blazed.

Majors Path to Great Hill Road: 2.5 miles
Blaze: white,

USGS topographic map: Southampton quadrangle

Big Woods to North Sea Road

The Paumanok Path currently runs nearly 50 miles from Rocky Point to the Shinnecock Canal. About 50 miles of trail is also completed from south of Sag Harbor to Montauk Point, mostly in East Hampton Township. That leaves the middle section in Southampton Township to be completed. The goal of completing this one hundred forty-five mile long trail is yet to be realized because the 1990s development boom has made it difficult to gain access across private land. Despite this, members of the Group for the South Fork are working on patching together sections where the trail will eventually run. The result is that some sections are walkable, but not all public land is blazed with the white rectangles that designate the Paumanok Path. Experienced hikers who can use a DOT topographic map and are accustomed to some bushwhacking here and there may try longer hikes in the area. For beginners or families with children there are several shorter walks in the area. The best times are winter and spring when several good views through trees are open.

After following a narrow corridor along the Shinnecock Hills, the South Fork widens north of the village of Southampton. East of the world-famous Shinnecock Hills Golf Club lies Tuckahoe Hill, which at nearly 130 feet affords views north towards Peconic Bay, west towards the interior of Long Island and south to the Atlantic Ocean. Parts of the hill are owned by the town and village of Southampton, but some development may occur on its west side. Unfortunately, I cannot recommend hiking on Tuckahoe Hill at this time even though the Paumanok Path is blazed over it. The Southampton police department has a small shooting range on the summit which could pose a hazard to hikers. The town and interested citizens are discussing ways to help the police find another location. There is also a problem on the north side of the hill where private land blocks access to the roads that will allow the trail to continue.

An interesting walk can be done from Big Woods on Millstone Brook Road to North Sea Road just east of Big Fresh Pond. This takes in land owned by The Nature Conservancy, the Peconic Land Trust, Southampton Town and Suffolk County. You can park at The Nature Conservancy Big Woods Preserve or at another parking area on North Sea Road near its junction with

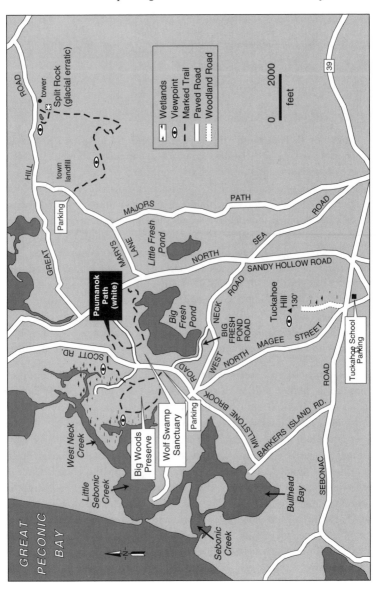

Paumanok Path, Southampton, NY

Millstone Brook Road. A street atlas is useful in finding these locations. You will also need a USGS topographic map, or even better the updated DOT Southampton quadrangle map which shows where homes and buildings are located.

Big Woods Preserve is maintained by The Nature Conservancy. Users of the preserve should consider supporting this organization, although it is not mandatory. You can hike a circuit trail within the preserve that will take you through beech-dominated woods and past **Little Sebonac Creek**. The mix of large American beech trees and eastern white pines is more reminiscent of upstate New York than Long Island. Land owned by the Peconic Land Trust is directly to the north. On the DOT map you will see one road that penetrates the area; it ends at a single building overlooking the open salt meadows of **West Neck Creek**. The Paumanok Path extension can be picked up inside the preserve going north and then east as it leaves the preserve traversing a rise of land overlooking the salt meadows toward the barn and silo on Cow Neck. This is not a common scene on Long Island and is more like the St. Lawrence Valley hundreds of miles to the north. The views are particularly good when the leaves are down. At one memorable turn the trail comes right down to the shore with an open view of the salt marshes. In spring look for ospreys nesting on a nearby platform and scan the marshes for egrets, herons and other shorebirds in season. In May the shores are lined with lacey looking sections of shadbush in bloom. Soon the trail crosses Scott Road (**0.8 mile**) and traverses uneven land, passing some large trees that went down in a recent storm. You shortly reach Millstone Brook Road (**1.2 miles**) onto which you can turn right (west) and back to your car if you parked near the entrance of Big Woods or near North Magee Street.

The Paumanok Path continues for another 0.8 miles to North Sea Road, where you will want to park a second car to avoid returning the way you came. The trail crosses Millstone Brook Road onto a sandy road that provides access for boats to put into **Big Fresh Pond**, which you will see straight ahead. To the right is land owned by The Nature Conservancy called **Wolf Swamp Sanctuary**. There is no access to it from here, but a small loop trail that gives a better look at Big Fresh Pond is accessible from Millstone Brook Road. Shortly before reaching the pond the Paumanok Path makes a left (east) onto a distinct but at this time unblazed trail (**1.5 miles**) that follows above the north shore of Big Fresh Pond coming into a clearing for Emma Rose Elliston Park with a small beach nearby. Only residents of Southampton Township are permitted to park in the lot off Millstone Brook Road. Although not blazed white at the time of this writing, the Paumanok Path follows the Rose

Elliston Nature Trail which has small yellow diamonds nailed to trees. Take it to the right as it passes above the south shore of Big Fresh Pond. On this delightful stretch the large pitch pines frame the pond and provide great photo opportunities. A little farther on you cross a brook flowing into the pond. At this point I flushed several great blue herons and black crowned night herons who voiced their annoyance with loud "quok" calls. I also saw an osprey flying over the pond searching for fish. Shortly after the trail turns away from the pond, the Paumanok Path leaves the nature trail going right (east) to cross the south and east perimeters of a farm field before reaching North Sea Road (**2 miles**). The trail is not complete east of here. You may return to your second car a few hundred yards up the road.

Majors Path to Great Hill Road

length: 2.5 miles. Blaze: white

Another section of the Paumanok Path is blazed and in place east of the Big Woods Preserve trail described above. To hike this section of trail you must park on Majors Path just south of the Town Landfill. Here you will see the Paumanok Path sign and white blazes going east. I estimate this section of trail to be about 2.5 miles from Majors Path to Great Hill Road. The first part of the trail circumvents the landfill on the south and east sides. The present path is seeing a lot of abuse from ATV (all terrain vehicles) use and is not the better for it. Once up on the heights behind the landfill there is a **wide view** north and northwest. It is a surreal view that includes both beauty and the beast. In the foreground is the landfill with its manmade hill and disturbed area that resembles a war zone. I have been told that the area in front of the landfill (in the foreground) is slated to be made into ball fields and a park. That should help the scene somewhat. Despite all of this, the view in the distance is excellent. It reminds me of the viewpoint overlooking the landfill in Montauk known as Panorama. Little Peconic Bay and the North Fork are easily visible with Robins Island prominent to the left. On clear days like the one I had, one can easily see Connecticut along the horizon beyond the North Fork. A tall tower rises above the trees at two o'clock, and it represents the ending place of this hike description.

Once the trail leaves sight of the landfill it becomes a pleasant walk in rolling oak-pine woods passing some nice kettles before reaching a historic old woods road known as Split Rock Road. The trail makes a sharp left (north) and follows this road for about 0.7 mile until it reaches a large erratic named what else but **Split Rock**. This is a historic landmark and a great place to rest for a little while. The trail leaves the road at this point and goes off to the left of the rock heading northwest and skimming a hillside with nice views through the trees toward the Peconic Bay in the winter. Shortly after you will reach Great Hill Road just west of the transmission tower where there is room for parking. At the time of this writing the trail ends at this point but there are already plans to extend it northward towards Turtle Pond and the old Bridgehampton Race Track.

Access

Car

Big Woods to North Sea Road: Take Sunrise Highway (State Route 27) east onto the south fork and make a left onto North Magee Street a little over 5 miles past Shinnecock Canal. To get to The Nature Conservancy's Big Woods Preserve just continue north on North Magee Street about 1.6 miles to a junction called five corners since five streets merge here. Take the second right (northeast) onto Millstone Brook Road and continue left at the fork to Scott Road to the preserve entrance on the left, a total of about 0.6 mile from five

corners. To get to North Sea Road, just continue at the last fork to the right, staying on Millstone Brook Road until the road ends on North Sea Road.

Majors Path to Great Hill Road: Take State Route 27 into Southampton and make a left (north) onto North Sea Road and then quickly take a fork to the right onto Majors Path. Follow this about 2.7 miles to the spot just south of the town landfill where the trail goes in on the right. To leave a second car on Great Hill Road, continue past the landfill and make a right onto Great Hill Road. Proceed about 0.5 mile to just before the tall tower and the trail will be seen on the right. There is room to park nearby.

View over wetlands from the trail

Laurel Valley County Park

Length: 2.8 mile loop. Blaze: white rectangle, white disk

USGS topographic map: Sag Harbor

This undeveloped county property located
in Noyack has been used by deer hunters for generations. After acquisition of
several smaller parcels by Suffolk County and the Town of Southampton, 183
acres now comprise a large L-shaped piece of property that appears on the
New York State DOT map as Noyack Hills County Park. It was recently
renamed Laurel Valley County Park for the dense stands of mountain laurel
that proliferate here. It is part of the Paumanok Path as it winds eastward
toward the Long Pond Greenbelt south of Sag Harbor. A map is available
from the Southhampton Trails Preservation Society (631-537-5202).

Access is off Deerfield Road, about 0.8 mile south of Noyack Road. There is
a small parking area with a kiosk at the trailhead. One landmark to look for
is a deep kettle that drops off on the east side of the road.

A new hiking trail called the **Laurel Woods Trail** has been marked with
white disks. The white rectangular blazes of the **Paumanok Path** also traverse the area here. The terrain is hilly with many rises to hilltops (the highest point being 210 feet) and drop-offs (lowest less than 50 feet) into laurel-
filled hollows and kettles that can be quite confusing and difficult to negotiate.
On my exploration of the area I spent most of my time bushwhacking and a
few times found myself crawling out of one of these "laurel hells." The experience was not all that bad and I look forward to returning to the area again.

Oak-dominated woodlands with some beech mixed in appear to have been
undisturbed for many years. The northwestern part of the property just north
of the kettle by the road has an abandoned field that's becoming overgrown
with black locust and eastern red cedars. East of this there are some very large
hickories and other uncommon species. The rest of the property is heavily
wooded, with one good view from a 180-foot hill in the northeastern corner.
This view is on the boundary of the Noyack Golf Course and overlooks a
pond on the course with visibility over Little Peconic Bay toward Nassau Point
on the North Fork. This rewarding vantage point will likely be included in the
loop trail being planned. It is best seen in winter or when the trees are bare.
The Laurel Woods Trail is discernible especially when the leaves are down,
but some of the turns in heavily grown stands of mountain laurel are obscure.

The Paumanok Path can be followed southward from the trailhead to unpaved Middle Line Road. A nearby vernal kettle pond has been identified as having a breeding population of spotted salamanders in springtime. Although some development is encroaching on the park boundaries, the homes are scattered on large wooded parcels and don't ruin the secluded nature of the park.

I saw hawks, migrating song birds and a garter snake in a few hours wanderings. This area is full of wildlife and worth a half day of exploration both on-trail and off trail.

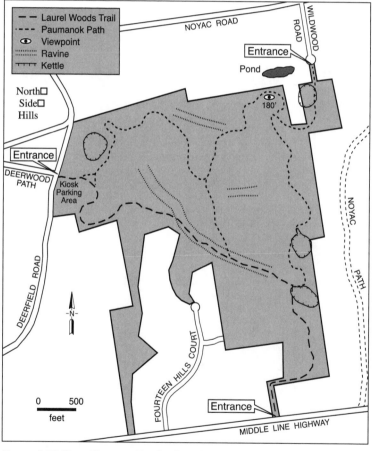

Laurel Valley County Park, Southampton, NY

Access

Car

Take Sunrise Highway (State Route 27) east onto the south fork. A little over 5 miles past the Shinnecock Canal make a left onto North Magee Street. Proceed north for 1.8 miles to the junction of five corners (stop sign); take the second right onto Millstone Brook Road and bear right at the first junction to stay on that same road. The road will end at North Sea Road in 0.8 mile. Make a left and then a right in about 0.2 mile onto Noyack Road. Go about 5 miles and make a right (south) onto Deerfield Road. A small parking area will be 0.8 mile on the left (east) side of the road.

Looking northwest across Peconic Bay to the North Fork

Laurel Valley County Park to Long Pond Greenbelt

Length: 5 miles

Blaze: white, side trail yellow on white

USGS or NYS DOT topographic map: Sag Harbor

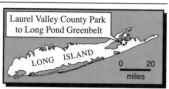

Laurel Valley County Park to Long Pond Greenbelt

LONG ISLAND

0   20
miles

The Paumanok Path leaves Laurel Valley County Park on Middle Line Highway about 0.7 mile east of Deerfield Road and 0.5 mile west of Millstone Road. It comes out near a small perched wetland resembling a vernal kettle-pond. For this hike you can leave your car here, but it is also possible to leave a car on Deerfield Road at the entrance to Laurel Valley County Park so you can include that hilly 1.3 mile section of trail in your exploration of this area. It takes about 30 minutes to walk that trail at a quick pace and is worth the while. See the Laurel Valley County Park section for a description of that trail.

The description of this hike begins at the exit from Laurel Valley County Park. If you include Laurel Valley County Park in your walk, you will need to add 1.3 miles and 30 minutes walking time to the distances given here. Development in the past few years has caused this section of Middle Line Highway to be paved, but the homes are spread out on 6 acre lots. Blazes are far apart on trees or poles on the south side of the road. Your walk will show how hilly this high section of the moraine is, as the trail along the road always seems to be going up or down. The trail goes east, crossing Noyak Path in 0.1 mile and passing a tall radio tower on the left (north) before reaching Millstone Road at 0.5 mile. Crossing the road it continues easterly into a large disturbed area of a sand mining operation which has been in existence for many years. Persevere past the noise and unsightly man-made canyon, continuing straight on the extension of Middle Line Highway. The pit will be on your left (north) and on the far side a blaze can be found on a telephone pole in the southeastern corner of the area at the start of the woods. This is 0.4 mile east of Millstone Road at 0.9 mile from the start at the Laurel Valley County Park boundary.

Before leaving this area behind, I suggest a slight detour to the left along the tree line. The view from the top of the canyon is surprisingly interesting. I worked my way to high points beyond the rim along the edge of woods with a view back west over a portion of Peconic Bay. Part of Robins Island and the bay front houses in Mattituck are in the foreground. The real surprise was how many familiar landmarks I could pick out with pair of binoculars. Following the water to the far shore, one can make out the concrete bridge where County Route 105 passes over The Peconic River as it empties into the bay. In the Manorville Hills above this one can pick out the FAA radar dome on the Summit and the squat water tank and the tall slim tower near Bald Hill. The Northville oil drums in the Mattituck Hills are visible to the right of these. The most startling thing was the sight of the tall stack from the reactor in Brookhaven National Laboratory jutting up above the horizon about 35 or more miles away. A glance at the topo map shows you are nearly 280 feet high. This elevation and the large clearing of the sand mine produce this unusual view.

Back on the trail, you continue eastward on the straight unpaved Middle Line Highway extension. The sounds of the mining operation slowly fade away as you pass into the buffer of forest. This is obviously an old established road. On my walk there was flagging tape on shrubs and branches, signs of the development that is due to occur here. I have been informed that the trail is scheduled to be moved off this straight path onto a more interesting route to the north of the sandmining operation in the future (probably the Racetrack Trail) but at this writing the Middle Line Highway extension is the still the only blazed route. Look along here for profuse stands of trailing arbutus blooming in April or mountain laurel blooming in June. Near this spot is the highest portion of the moraine on the entire south fork, reaching almost 300 feet in elevation. It would be nice if the trail could access some of these high sections, but much of that land is in private hands. After about 10 minutes of walking from the sand quarry I reached a junction where five trails meet. It reminded me of a similar trail junction in Harriman State Park aptly named Times Square; however, not all of these trails are marked. This junction is about 1.4 miles from the start.

The **yellow blazed Racetrack Trail** goes off to the left (north) from here. This trail may very well become the route of the Paumanok Path when the housing development takes place and necessary re-routes are complete. The yellow trail traverses rolling terrain, dipping into several shallow hollows before reaching the southern boundary of the old Bridgehampton Racetrack, now converted into a golf course. It continues around the northern side of the old racetrack property, staying out of sight of it most of the time. After ascending some high ground it drops into a fairly long steep hollow before reaching the unpaved Ruggs Path in about 2.3 to 2.5 miles. At this writing the yellow trail does extend south of Ruggs Path, but in a short distance it returns to this

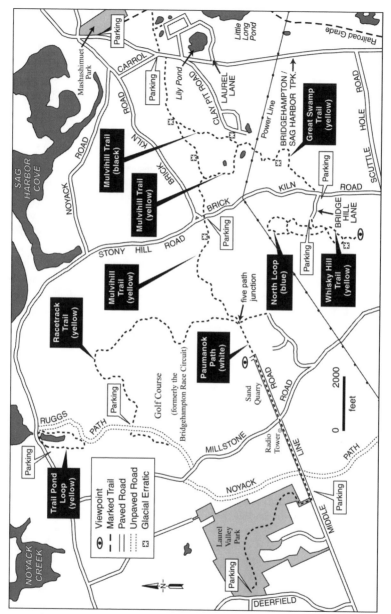

unpaved road a little farther west of this crossing. Plans are being made to extend it in the future. An interesting route can be made by walking 0.3 miles to the right (north) on Ruggs Path, which becomes paved in a short distance.

This is a backwoods type of road with a rural feel to it. One can pick up the Southampton Trails Preservation Society's **Trout Pond Looptrail** on the left (north) side of the road. The Town of Southampton's **Trout Pond Park** can be reached by car from Noyak Road with parking just west of the pond itself. Ruggs Path goes south from Noyak Road on the east side of the pond. A small loop trail circles the pond, and the south end of the loop comes very close to Ruggs Path.

Back at the five path junction, the Paumanok Path blazes became weak here as I was walking; they were just old silver paint on trees. They will likely be re-painted by the time of your reading this. I followed the silver blazes into a newly cut section that wound back and forth along somewhat uneven terrain. In just a few minutes a fork was reached with both branches weakly blazed in silver. I took the one on the right since it, too, was newly cut. The other one continued straight and was obviously an old established route. The right fork turned out to be the correct choice, reaching the fence line of a property with an H-shaped tower resembling an old fashioned football goalpost on the right in about 10 minutes walking time. Beyond this the trail came out onto the unpaved Middle Line Highway extension. A sign that said Wildlife Preserve is visible here and you will make a left (east) and walk past a very large glacial erratic on the left before reaching Brick Kiln Road in a couple of hundred yards. This is close to **1.7 miles** from the start.

Just across from Middle Line Highway you will see a white blaze and a Paumanok Path emblem on a tree. You will now enter some pleasant moist woods with tall hickories towering overhead and spicebush in the understory. Eastern red cedar trees and a few mature white oaks are signs this property was pasture land not long ago. Boundary ditches where borders were once established can be seen along here as well. In a few minutes (**1.8 miles**) at a place where the trail makes a sharp left you will see three **white diamond plastic markers** with yellow writing and an owl on them on the right. This is the beginning of the recently blazed **Mulvihill Preserve Trail** that was also cut by the Southampton Trails Preservation Society.

The Mulvihill Preserve is land donated by the Mulvihill family. This interesting side trail passes through a white pine forest and by a small pond on your right (south). Now blazed with black on white discs, the Mulvihill Preserve Trail continues eastward past the pond near several small wetlands and wooded swamps with a good concentration of glacial erratics sprinkled in. The Mulvihill Preserve Trail eventually links back with the Paumanok Path further east in about 30 minutes walking time.

The **yellow blazed Great Swamp Trail** is another side trail worth adding to your plans to walk in this area. It leaves the Mulvihill Preserve Trail just past the pond, turns right (south) and passes a farm where ducks are raised for a nearby hunting preserve. It's unlikely you've ever heard this many ducks quacking at one time, and the sound is quite amusing. In a short distance it crosses the high power lines and passes the border of wetlands known as **The Great Swamp,** where vivid foliage can be viewed in October. There are really several small ponds in this knob and kettle topography as well as some interesting erratics. One that I'll call **Table Rock** lies on a rise overlooking Great Swamp just alongside the trail. The trail curls through this beautiful property before reaching Brick Kiln Road in about a mile or so. You will come out just south of Bridge Hill Lane. Cross Brick Kiln Road and proceed up Bridge Hill Lane. This is a quiet court with stately well-kept homes. In about 0.3 mile at the end of the cul-de-sac you will see a split rail fence between two homes. Cars can be parked here if you choose to do so. The **Yellow blazed Whiskey Hill Road** trail continues through a right of way here and turns left (south) in about 100 yards to proceed into the woods. The trail will switchback as it goes uphill through big oak dominated woods and past some glacial erratics scattered on the slopes. You will be following white paint blazes as well as the yellow lettered Southampton Trail Preservation Society disks. Signs direct you to the **excellent viewpoint** from the open 220 foot portion of Whiskey Hill in about 10 minutes time. The NYS DOT or USGS maps show the Hildreth marker placed at that spot in 1938. Look for it on the ground on the top of the hill. At one time this hill was called Windmill Hill, as a state historic marker on Scuttle Hole Road explains. The windmill was well placed on this hill in 1700, more than 300 years ago. The panorama takes in all the open country to the south as well as the Atlantic Ocean. The north side of Long Island's south fork is still heavily wooded as opposed to the south side which was historically used for farming and pasture land. The hilltop represents the border between woods and fields. Return the way you came but follow the turn blazes left and pass a **tremendous erratic** on the left. Lying just below the 240 foot high point of this hill complex, this dramatic glacial erratic should have a name to establish its importance as a great natural feature. It is undoubtedly the largest rock in the area, perhaps in the entire south fork, although Split Rock on the Paumanok Path just south of Great Hill Road may be larger. Another erratic near it would have been considered a fine specimen if it was not dwarfed by the big rock nearby. Although there is a home on the top of the hill above this erratic, it does not reduce the impact of such a large monolith at such relatively a high elevation. From here the trail drops back down to the right of way clearing. If you wish to return the way you came, make a right and you'll reach Bridge Hill Lane in a few hundred yards. If you want to extend your walk another 25-30 minutes, continue across the right of way to another side trail loop **blazed with blue lettering.** This trail travels through hilly upland woods, thick mountain laurel and a couple of steep kettles before returning to the right of way. A left turn will return you to the top of Bridge Hill Lane in about 30 minutes total walking time. Obviously, there are a lot of alternatives for the walker to choose from in planning hikes in this area.

Back on the Paumanok Path from the start of the Mulvihill Preserve Trail (**1.9 miles**), you head downhill, cross an unpaved road and pass a small wetland on the left with a beautiful large erratic alongside the trail. Beyond that, you reach flat open woods containing a few erratics (with one particularly large one that needs a name!) before closing in amidst mountain laurel again. Eventually the trail comes out to a long driveway that brings you to the Bridgehampton-Sag Harbor Turnpike just south of Carrol Street at approximately **3.2 miles**. If you cross the road you can follow it eastward into a woodlot between a house and a commercial building. In a few minutes you reach the old railroad grade in Long Pond Greenbelt. If you chose to leave a car at Mashashimuet Park you can turn left (north) and walk this wide path out to it in 10 minutes making a walk of about **3.7 miles**. A nice alternative would be to leave a car on the other side of Long Pond Greenbelt at Widow Gavitts Road or Sagg Road, thereby continuing on the Paumanok Path eastward. This makes a 4 hour hike covering about 4.7 miles or so.

Access

See the Laurel Valley County Park section for directions if you choose to include that section of trail in this walk. To reach the trail where it meets Middle Line Highway, continue past the entrance to Laurel Valley County Park on Deerfield Road, make a left onto Middle Line Highway and proceed about 0.9 mile. Look for the white blazes coming in from the left (north). There is room to park on this quiet stretch of road.

Bus

Nearest is SCTB 10A dropping off on Noyak Road near Deerfield Road with a 1 mile walk to the trailhead.

Morton National Wildlife Refuge

Length: 5 miles out and back. Blaze: none

USGS topographic maps: Sag Harbor, Greenport

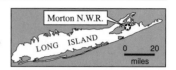

The north side of the South Fork has a 187-acre wildlife refuge run by the federal government. On a map the distinguishing feature of this refuge is a finger-like peninsula called Jessup Neck that juts almost 2 miles into Peconic Bay. It makes for a great walk for kids, especially in winter when they can hand-feed black-capped chickadees and pick up shells on the beach. Experienced hikers will find plenty to explore here as well. It is wise to choose a relatively mild and wind-free winter day to walk out on Jessup Neck. The total trip is about 5 miles and takes at least 3 hours if you want to enjoy the sights. The peninsula is closed from April through August to allow undisturbed breeding for two endangered species, the piping plover and the least tern. Waterfront development and beach vehicles along the Eastern Seaboard have dangerously diminished these birds' numbers. The Nature Conservancy is working hard to protect some beachfront locations so the birds can become numerous once again. A walk in Morton during the breeding season is limited to a short loop trail and a walk down to the beach and back.

The refuge is located off Noyack Road, about 5 miles east of its junction with North Sea Road. The original name of the landmark peninsula was Farrington Point after Southampton founder John Farrington. In 1679, John Jessup obtained possession of the land and renamed it Jessup Neck. I have read that Jessup's daughter Abigail was buried on a wooded bluff in the preserve. There is supposedly a distinctive headstone to mark the site, but I was unable to locate it. The land passed through two other families until Elizabeth Morton donated the property to the U. S. Fish and Wildlife Service in 1954.

Just beyond the unpaved parking area on the north side of Noyack Road you will notice a caretakers building and a wooden platform with information about the location of the over 500 wildlife refuges that the Fish and Wildlife Service maintains. You can also pick up a brochure describing the local refuges with checklists for the many birds that can be spotted at each one throughout the year. If it is winter you will notice bird feeders nearby and a

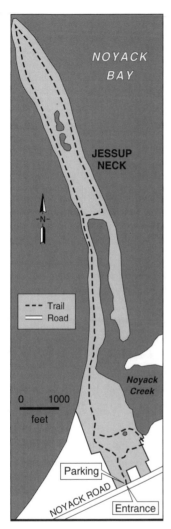

**Morton National
Wildlife Refuge,
Southampton, NY**

lot of bird activity, as food and cover is available here. Be sure to bring some sunflower seeds and you may be able to feed the local chickadees. Be patient and you will be rewarded by having one of these cheerful little birds alight on your hand, pick a seed and bolt to a tree branch to open and eat it. There is something special in making physical contact with a wild creature; the fact that it is only a tiny chickadee doesn't matter at all. Rather tame and curious by nature, chickadees are very adaptable creatures. They are gregarious, the noisy come-and-go companions of winter woods walkers. They also have a very high metabolism, which requires that they constantly seek food in the colder months. On frigid nights they roost together in tree cavities and their metabolism slows in a kind of temporary sleep; their heartbeat slows dramatically so they use very little energy. This adaptation enables them to stay in northern climates rather than migrating south. They can be seen on the loop trail in the southern part of the refuge as they prefer the cover of thickets along the trail.

The trail makes a right through thick second-growth shrubs and trees. Red cedars attest to this stage of forest development. This area was cultivated to grow mulberries, apples, and pears among other crops. Raising silkworms was also attempted here. Some grazing of sheep and cattle has also taken place, so it is no wonder the area is still a second-growth habitat. The trail loops to the left to small wooden bridges over several creeks and swamps. In colder months you will notice Noyack Creek with **Noyack Bay** in the distance through the trees. In a short while you will see a hidden pond with a bench to overlook the scene. Shortly beyond the pond the trail goes along the edge of an open field with bluebird boxes and an osprey platform in it, then joins the main trail again. This loop takes about twenty minutes or so to complete and you may then take a left to head back to your car if you wish. A right will take you along a wide path through red cedars to the beach in a few minutes.

There always seems to be some kind of wind or breeze blowing on the beach so dress accordingly; a nylon shell is most useful here. The view from here looks west (left) toward Little Hog Neck with Nassau Point jutting southward into Little Peconic Bay. To the left of Nassau Point is Robins Island in the distance. Looking straight ahead, you can see Jessup Neck with its wooded bluffs and long stretch of beach extending out into the water. Starting your walk along the western side of the peninsula you will notice changes in the texture of the beach. It starts as fine sand and later becomes gravelly, and eventually rocky. This is probably related to the constant wind erosion of the westerly facing bluffs. Various types of shells, particularly jingle shells, scallops, and whelks litter the beach, along with some very colorful and unusual rocks. There is the chance of spotting harbor seals in winter, and many attractive sea ducks winter on the water, usually off the eastern side. These include the old-squaw, a brilliantly contrasting black-and-white duck with a long pointed tail. On a hike to the point with my family we saw white-winged scoters and red-breasted mergansers. Buffleheads, common goldeneye and horned grebes are also seen here in winter.

The first stretch of beach is not very wide, as a lagoon connected to the bay has formed on the east side. Passing an osprey nesting platform you will then come to the wooded section in the center of the peninsula. There is a path that goes up into the woods past the foundation of an old house. On the right is a hidden protected pond that probably supplied the inhabitants with fresh water. The USGS topographic map has not been updated since 1956, and this house is on the map. What a secluded location to live! The sunsets must have been unimpeded and magnificent over the waters of the bay. There is also a herd of deer living out on Jessup Neck; I startled them from the spot where they were bedded down. The maritime forest drops down in the middle of the neck to open sands with an enclosed pond where you may see swans or ducks. The

The author on Jessup Neck

land rises up again to bluffs that reach 60 feet high. The beach here becomes more rocky allowing a close up look of the steeply eroded bluffs. Do not try and climb this fragile area as signs on the beach deny access; and besides, the catbriar is so thick on top you couldn't penetrate it anyway.

Out at the point you will realize that you are closer to the North Fork than you might have thought. Great Hog Neck is the piece of land that juts out toward you. Notice how the sand eroding from the bluffs you just passed is slowly extending the neck farther out. If not altered Jessup Neck will probably reach completely across and enclose Peconic Bay in a few thousand years or so. The walk back on the east side of the neck will probably reveal more sea birds in Noyack Bay because it is sheltered from the prevailing winds. This side only gets pounded in the severe nor'easters that occasionally strike the coast. An established red cedar grove is found beyond the bluff on the east side. It is strange to explore here; little grows on the forest floor because of a lack of sunlight filtering through. We found channeled whelk shells in excellent condition at least thirty yards back from the beach and twenty feet up. I wonder if they arrived there by way of the wind and wave action of a nor'easter. Or could gulls have dropped the shells? In the interior, in sheltered hollows, are some very old oak trees with long horizontal branches coming off their thick, ancient-looking trunks. This forest has obviously not been disturbed for a long time. Returning along the east side, be sure to cut back across to the west side after the second section of woods or you will walk out to a dead end where the lagoon cuts into the land. The path then leads you straight back to your car.

Access

Car

Take Sunrise Highway (State Route 27) east onto the south fork. A little over 5 miles past Shinnecock Canal make a left onto North Magee Street. Proceed north for about 1.8 miles to the junction of five corners (stop sign), take the second right onto Millstone Brook Road and bear right at the first junction to stay on that same road. The road will end at North Sea Road in about 0.8 mile. Make a left and than a right in about 0.2 mile onto Noyack Road. Go about 6.5 miles to the refuge entrance on the left.

Bus

SCT10A

Long Pond Greenbelt

Length: more than 3 miles. Blaze: white, some unblazed. Paumanok Path about 2.5 miles. Blaze: white

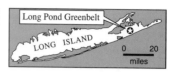

USGS topographic map: Sag Harbor

South of the village of Sag Harbor a series of wetlands and ponds forms a watershed stretching from Peconic Bay on the north across the entire South Fork and linking up with the Atlantic Ocean. The water depth in the ponds varies from year to year depending largely on rainfall. They are remnants from the last ice age and exhibit habitats that have elsewhere been greatly diminished as development progresses. The Nature Conservancy has identified over 30 globally rare plant species within the area, a concentration larger than anywhere else in New York State. The tract is home to specialized plants that have adapted to the freshwater environment. With this in mind, a partnership between Suffolk County, the Town of Southampton and The Nature Conservancy has raised money to preserve much of this beautiful area. Those wishing to explore here are asked to tread lightly and be cautious going off-trail, especially along the shores of the ponds where the rare plants are concentrated. The Southhampton Trails Preservation Society has put out a good map of the area listing some of the rare plants and animals found here. The Paumanok Path also passes through here and its white paint blazes can be found along this walk. Walkers with two cars may fasten together a longer hike into Sagaponack Woods to the east.

The largest pond in the chain is Long Pond; it is the centerpiece that gives this area its name. This greenbelt of land lies between the Sag Harbor-Bridgehampton Turnpike on the west and Sagg Road on the east. A good walk starts from Mashashimuet Park on the north end. Here you will pick up a straight woods road; it is actually an old railroad grade. Follow this in a southerly direction for a few minutes and you will soon enter a more wooded and quiet area. Look for evidence of the old railroad in the form of cinders along the outside of the wide path. The railroad grade runs roughly north-to-south through the entire area and forms a good central point to help you stay oriented while you wander on either side of it. The railroad was a fairly short line from the Bridgehampton Station to the Long Wharf in Sag Harbor. There was also a 1400 foot spur to Round Pond where ice was cut and shipped to New York City. The path will be shaded by trees at first but after passing a wide sandy road it opens up. Just past this junction take a smaller trail that

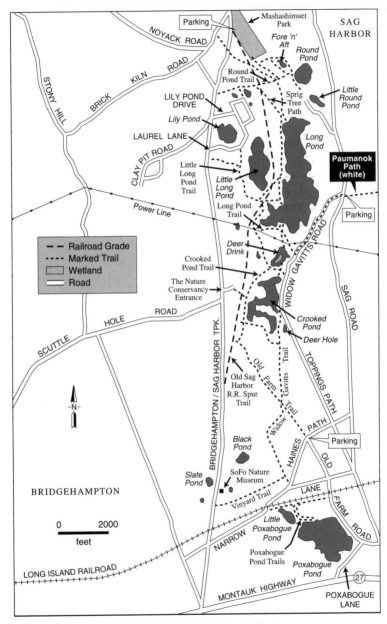

Long Pond Greenbelt, Southampton, NY

goes off to the left (east) marked by a sign designating it the **Sprig Tree Path**. This path winds through typical oak-dominated woods. There are no blazes to follow throughout this system of trails and woods roads, but the railroad grade is always there and serves as a focus for any walk. In a little while you may notice a change in the vegetation on the left as you near the wetlands of Long Pond. A gurgling noise on the left reveals a small outlet flowing out of the northern portion of the pond. This may not flow fast in dry seasons, but when it is moving rapidly it is more reminiscent of small streams upstate. Babbling brooks are a bit of a rarity on Long Island. **Long Pond** will soon come into sight on the left. Keep an eye out for wading birds and waterfowl. River otters are said to be making a comeback in these waterways. A pair of binoculars is a big help here as the pond is fairly large and one rarely gets very close to the shore itself. Wetlands trees like tupelo and red maple abound along the shore and bring early color in late September. The best colors can usually be seen in early-to-mid October.

Following this path along the west shore of Long Pond will eventually lead you back to the railroad grade. Sprig Tree Path continues across the railroad grade skimming the shores of **Little Long Pond**. The short **Little Long Pond Trail** around the south and west sides of the pond ends on Laurel Lane. If you are returning to your car in Mashashimuet Park, I suggest staying on the east side of the railroad grade on the way out and exploring the west side on the way back. This will minimize overlapping of your walk. From this point one can follow the railroad grade south and pick up another side trail on the left and once again catch glimpses of Long Pond. In a little while you will reach the power lines that bisect the area east-to-west. They can serve as a second guide to orient yourself on a topographic map. There is a short side trip to the left (east) along the power lines that is worthwhile. Go east a short distance and pick up a path left past a small overlook of the lower portion of Long Pond, then at the first junction follow it to a left to a boat launch where there's a sweeping view northward of the entire length of the pond. From here you can spot two bald cypress trees growing just to the left at the water's edge. They are a truly strange sight since the nearest this southerly tree is found in the wild is southern Delaware, hundreds of miles to our south. It is a cone-bearing member of the redwood family and a familiar sight in the large bayou swamps of the Gulf Coast. It has fine small needles that turn brown and fall off in autumn. Were these trees planted here or are they unexplained freaks of nature?

The Paumanok Path will diverge eastward just south of the power lines as it goes south of Long Pond and makes a left onto little used Widow Gavitts

Road for about 0.5 mile to Sagg Road where it crosses into Sagaponack Woods Road. The total mileage is estimated to be about 2.5 miles of Paumanok Path from Mashashimuet Park to Sagg Road. Let's return to the spot the spot where you diverged from the power lines. This whole area would be a great place to cross-country ski in winter. The paths are not steep and lend themselves to exploration of many side paths. If you want to continue hiking south from the spot where you diverged from the power lines, your next destination should be **Crooked Pond**. Sprig Tree Path leads south and goes into the woods just east of the junction of the power lines and the railroad grade. Here I spotted an abundance of an odd reddish-colored plant called pinesap. Somewhat uncommon on Long Island, this plant is saprophytic; it gets its energy from sources beneath the ground and not from sunlight through photosynthesis. The path bears to the right (west) onto Crooked Pond Path just before reaching the small pond called **Deer Drink.** This path will continue southward. You will notice the railroad grade is up on your right at this point. On the left **Crooked Pond** winds around the surrounding hilly landscape making it impossible to see all of it at once. Crooked Pond is enhanced by the low hills around it. There is some limited development near part of the eastern shore; nonetheless, it gives a feeling of seclusion and remoteness that make it worth exploring. I spotted wood ducks among the waterfowl in this setting.

Many flowers, including purple bladderwort, cover the pond's surface in summertime. The paths around it have late-summer flowers such as purple stiff asters in abundance. It should be noted that one can hike the entire area end

Crooked Pond

In September the light purple stiff aster grows in profusion around the ponds

to end by leaving a car at the northern end of Old Farm Road where it ends on Haines Path. Here directly opposite the end of the road a Southampton Town sign designates an old path to Crooked Pond, which from here is more than a mile to the north. I estimate an end to end hike to be more than 3 miles. If you choose to go this route, bear left at an X shaped intersection of trails that will bring you to Haines Path. If you have one car, make your way back to Mashashimuet Park by following the railroad grade back and exploring some of the side paths on the west side. Another worthy area to explore is the land around **Black Pond**, which is near a winery that was purchased to add to the public land here.

You may wish to visit the old whaling village of Sag Harbor after working up an appetite on this hike. It is a bustling attraction in summertime, with fine restaurants. In the first part of the 19th century it was the major coastal port in New York.

Through foresight and hard work by a number of groups working together the Long Pond Greenbelt will serve as a model for future land preservation.

Access

Car

From Sag Harbor drive south on Main Street, which becomes Sag Harbor-Bridgehampton Turnpike, until a junction with County Road 38 (Brick Kiln Road) where there is a small pull-off parking area in Mashashimuet Park on the right (east) side.

Paumanok Path: Sagaponack Woods and Miller's Ground

Length: 2.5 miles. Blaze: white; side trails unblazed

USGS topographic map: Sag Harbor

The Paumanok Path now continues east-ward from the Long Pond Greenbelt into East Hampton Township, where it links up with the Northwest Path on the other side of State Route 114. It traverses heavily wooded Sagaponack Woods in Southampton Town before entering East Hampton Town in another wooded area north of the East Hampton Airport known locally as Miller's Ground. The trail is very easy to follow but attention must be paid for turn blazes or at junctions since the area has many bike paths throughout. The remainder of the area, mainly south of the power lines, must be bushwhacked by those familiar with the use of map and compass. In seasons when mountain bikes are not in use, for example when there is substantial snow on the ground, those bike trails can give the walker easier access to some less trodden sections. It is very rewarding to explore this upland region in the middle of the terminal moraine that makes up the South Fork.

The DOT Sag Harbor map of the region is well updated and shows all the new homes that have sprung up around here in recent years. The mountain biking map for Miller's Ground showing the hiking trail east of Town Line Road is useful to hikers as well. It can be purchased at local bike shops in the area. Sagaponack Woods currently comprises 188 acres of county and town lands with more scheduled to be purchased. It certainly seems like a much larger parcel of woods, although some development is infringing on it from the southeast and the north. Miller's Ground has seen development since the building boom of the late 1990's but the trail is in place. This section is about 2.5 miles long.

The trail can be picked up heading east off Sagg Road just south of Widow Gavitts Road. This is just south of a house on Sagg Road, and there is enough room for a few cars to pull over in this sparsely populated area, but be careful of the birdfoot violets that bloom here along the road. White blazes indicate the new trail here. The DOT map shows the area is crisscrossed by two old unpaved roads that form a somewhat crooked X and by power lines that run almost east-to-west through the heart of the region. These serve as good reference points and don't spoil the natural beauty of the walk. I explored this area on a sunny day in mid-April and found the elusive trailing arbutus blooming throughout the entire walk. The area is best explored when the leaves are down: views open up, tick activity is at a minimum, and off trail navigation is less difficult.

The first thing you'll notice is that the terrain is undulating; there are many dips into kettleholes and rises to small hilltops. For the most part the forest is oak-dominated with few pine trees scattered about. The understory has healthy stands of mountain laurel with blueberry covering the forest floor. A

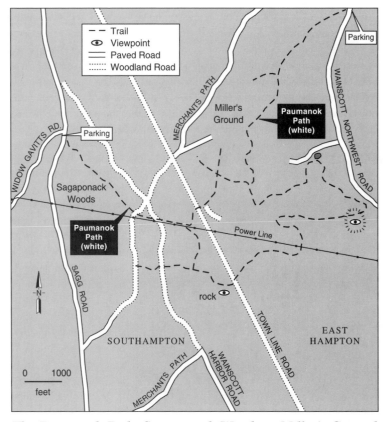

The Paumanok Path: Sagaponack Woods to Miller's Ground

few minutes into the walk you will pass a long depression on the left filled with water in wet seasons and bordered by mountain laurel. I noticed a large stick nest on the opposite side of the trail near here. This is undoubtedly the nest of a large bird, either a red-tailed hawk, a great horned owl or possibly even a crow. The trail will then climb gently to higher ground and eventually reach power lines near the place where the unpaved Merchant's Path crosses them in a roughly north-to-south direction. The white blazes of the Paumanok Path go left here (east) and follow the power lines for about 0.2 mile before taking a left (north) back into the woods. A **large glacial erratic** is on the south side of the power lines at this turn. In a short distance you will cross unpaved Town Line Road and continue through the fine rolling terrain of oak-dominated woods. There are several junctions with bike trails here but the trail is well blazed at these points. This is Miller's Ground; it is a nice mix of kettles, hills and mountain laurel which is in full bloom in mid-June. There is one hill where you can see the land in the distance off to the east when the leaves are down. A few minutes farther on the trail makes a left and quick right around a small vernal wetland shaded by tall pitch pines. Within 15 minutes the trail reaches Wainscott-Northwest Road in a new development. This is about 0.6 mile south of State Route 114 and there is room to park a few cars nearby. The trail makes a left and goes back into the woods following between homes until it reaches State Route 114 about 0.6 mile farther on. Parking is across the street by Edwards Hole Road where the trail continues onto the Northwest Path.

Open woods, hills and small erratics are characteristic of this area

From the first junction I choose to continue on Merchant's Path southward a short ways and explore quaint little kettles off either side of the trail before farther exploring in a generally easterly direction. Other than the occasional hunter's tree stand and a narrow bike path, the land is in good shape. The trees are not particularly large, probably since they are second growth and growing in sandy soil. The spring I hiked here was a particularly wet one; I was surprised to find a swamp with a small stream running out of it. It was probably spring-fed and there was much bird activity around it. Spring wildflowers such as the Canada mayflower bloomed in the cooler moist woods where the water drained out. This pleasant little wetland was located south of the power lines between Merchant's Path and Town Line Road (both unpaved). Navigation in this area is uncertain and will keep even the most experienced hikers constantly consulting the map to pinpoint their location. If one continues exploring in an easterly direction, a rewarding goal is an unnamed **130 foot hill** just west of Town Line Road. This knoll has stunted oaks on it and a **large erratic** on which you can stand to get a **view westward** toward the high pine-clad hills south of Noyack. Looking southward, one can see the ocean in a few places where the land dips. A well-used unmarked trail leads off this hill to the south and then branches off in several directions. Just to the east of this hill you will cross unpaved Town Line Road and pass into East Hampton Township. Farther east I found another hill with an active fox den and views towards the Atlantic. You are now in Miller's Ground and hills reaching 160 feet can be explored here amid the dry, uneven land. One can also explore the rolling terrain in the area north of the power lines. In the eastern section of this walk there is much high ground to explore, with pitch pines and many small erratics scattered along hillsides and ridges. A return toward your car north of the power lines should reward the walker with some of these interesting features, but remember that this is almost completely trailless land and you will be checking your map often.

Access

Car

Take State Route 27 eastward onto the South Fork. About 1.25 miles east of the village of Bridgehampton make a left (north) onto Sagg Road. Proceed about 2.8 miles to where the trail goes into the woods on the right. This is just before the junction with Widow Gavitts Road. There is room to pull a few cars over here. For parking at the other end, take State Route 27 east to Wainscott and make a left (north) onto Stephen Hands Path. Proceed for 1.3 miles to State Route 114 and make a left and proceed for 1.8 miles to parking where Edwards Hole Road goes off to the right.

Barcelona Neck

Length: 4.25 miles. Blaze: blue disk

USGS topographic maps: Sag Harbor, Greenport

East of Sag Harbor is a little-known penin-
sula surrounded by pristine salt marshes called Barcelona Neck. Although the
state sign says Barcelona Neck is only 341 acres, it seems much larger since
there is more public land just to the west. New York State has built a small
nine-hole golf course in the center of the lower part of the peninsula but hilly
mature upland forest dominates the center and northern sections. There are
high bluffs with excellent views on the north side. Wetlands woods are common in the southern section and there is even a mature white pine forest to
hike through, and a fine stretch of beach. There is surprising diversity all within a few hours' walk, making this is a great hike for all ages. My wife, three
daughters and I did the entire walk in three hours. Though no official
mileages were available, I estimate the entire hike to be about **4.25 miles**.
Our moderate pace included stops at viewpoints and for an occasional break.
The state has put in a blue-blazed trail that traverses the entire exterior of the
peninsula. As you will see there are places where one can bail out and cut the
hike short if needed. The USGS topographic maps for Greenport and Sag
Harbor give more details on the terrain. The DEC also has a trail map that is
useful for this walk.

From the entrance to this state-managed land located off Route 114 (south of
Sag Harbor), drive east on the paved road and park near the golf course clubhouse. Watch for flying golf balls since the road crosses some tee-off areas and
fairways! Take the dirt road behind the clubhouse heading in a northeasterly
direction away from the golf course. In a short distance make a right onto the
first woods road you come to. This will curve to the left and straighten out. At
the first fork go left onto a lightly used woods road and you will cross the
blue-blazed disks of the state-maintained trail you will follow around
Barcelona Neck back to this spot. Go left (north) and follow the trail along the
east side of the peninsula. The first thing to notice is the distinct difference
between the plants on either side of the trail. On the left is typical second-
growth dry woods, and on the right are wetland species such as cinnamon
fern, tupelo and red maple. Northwest Creek is visible through the trees on
your right. This is one of the most pristine saltwater estuaries on Long Island,
a place where many species of fish breed and spend part of their lives before

setting out for open waters. A variety of fish and shellfish, including oysters, depend on these waters for their continuance. The salt marshes also provide an important habitat for waterfowl during winter and migration stopovers. The first human inhabitants of the area gathered shellfish here. Early European settlers also set up dwellings along the shores of Northwest Creek. In fact, it was a bustling profitable port in the early 1700s. A little farther along

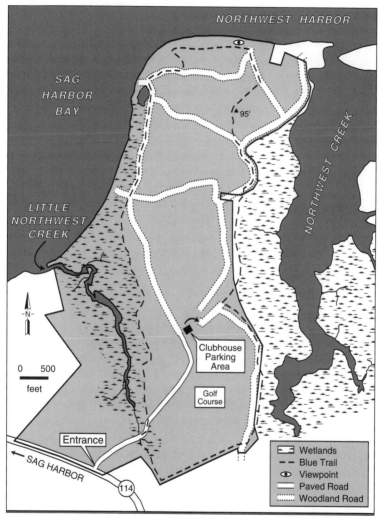

Barcelona Neck Natural Resources Management Area, Sag Harbor, NY

the trail you pass an abandoned house on the left. It is easy to pick out the older trees by their size; they dwarf the younger ones. What a beautiful homestead this must have been with the view east over **Northwest Creek** cleared so the sun would rise each morning over its blue waters. There are other outbuildings nearby. Because they are all dilapidated, it's hazardous to get too close to them.

Leaving the old homestead behind you, the trail shortly comes to a woods road and continues north. There is an even closer view of Northwest Creek on the right. We saw an active osprey nest on a manmade pole in the salt marsh. After a little while, the trail turns left onto a less-used woods road. The road you are on then continues through the only private land left on Barcelona Neck. Once you are on the less-used road keep an eye out for trailing arbutus, the low-growing wildflower that is plentiful here. It blooms in springtime and is one of the first wildflowers of the season. In a little while look out for a spot where the trail goes off to the right on a newly cut path through the woods. No turn blazes were at this spot on my last walk. In warmer weather take precautions against deer ticks as the brush here is not cut back well. This section of rolling hilly terrain is a mature upland woods and has many older trees. We found lots of low-growing wintergreen in this section, identified by that familiar wintergreen smell when you crush its leaves. The red shiny berries are edible as well but make positively sure that they are wintergreen. They have the same pleasant fragrance as the rest of the plant.

As the trail crests the hill nearly 100 feet above sea level, a view through the trees in winter opens up toward Northwest Creek. After winding up and down through the woods, the trail goes down to meet another old woods road and makes a left. The bluffs at the head of the peninsula are on your right. You will notice sand spilling over into the woods at several places along this section of trail. By all means climb up and be treated to a wonderful view overlooking Northwest Harbor. The view is all the more wonderful because most of what you are looking at is land that has been preserved so it will never be developed. It is nice to know that the view looks the same as it did in the past and will look the same for years to come. Directly across the harbor is the stone houselike structure of the Cedar Point Lighthouse at the tip of Cedar Point which is all a part of Cedar Point County Park. To the left of the lighthouse is Mashomack Point on Shelter Island, part of a preserve that encompasses the entire southeast portion of Shelter Island. To the right is the land of the Grace Estate, owned by the Town of East Hampton (See the Northwest Path section for details on this area). Orient Point, Plum Island and even Connecticut are visible beyond the lighthouse on clear days. There are several viewpoints to explore along these bluffs for the more adventurous. A walk along the beach to the east (right) will take you to the head of Northwest Creek, adding a little extra time to the estimated three hours for the walk.

Returning to the trail proceed west with the bluffs on your right (north). Shortly after reaching the last viewpoint, the trail turns away from the bluffs and heads southwest. In a short time it turns right onto a woods road that eventually leads to the beach at Barcelona Point at the northwest point of the peninsula. Walk out to the beach past a groundsel tree; its showy, white silky tufts are on display in October. On the left is a pond that attracts many wad-

Shelter Island seen from the tall bluffs at Barcelona Neck

ing birds. From the beach you can see Sag Harbor village identified by the many masts of sailboats in the marina. The beach goes to the right along the north end of Barcelona Neck. Back on the trail you will head south on a wide well-used dirt road along the west side of Barcelona Neck; the salt marshes along Sag Harbor Bay will be on the right and woods will be on the left. Wildflowers, including several species of violets, grow along here in springtime. A couple of woods roads on the left offer explorations of the interior of the Barcelona Neck Peninsula. The entire area is suitable for cross-country skiing since wide roads as well as narrow trails abound throughout. The hilly interior is not so challenging that inexperienced skiers cannot traverse it.

Continuing along the wide dirt road the golf course will eventually become visible on the left through the trees. This is important because the trail leaves the road off to the right with no turn blazes. You have the option here to bail out to the parking lot where your car is located. Beware of flying golf balls if you choose to head across to your car. If you stay on the rest of the hike you will be rewarded with some fine walking, but be aware that the trail is sparsely blazed in sections. Look for a faint trail with the first blue disk blaze about twenty yards into the woods. This section of trail goes into the wet woods bordering Little Northwest Creek and is strikingly pretty in autumn as swamp (red) maple, tupelo and cinnamon fern have attractive colors. Although faint the path can be followed and the change in flora is obvious. I found the red spikes of pinesap popping out of the ground on this stretch of trail. They are saprophytic fleshy plants that lack chlorophyll and hence do not have the green color of most plants. Since they do not produce energy through photosynthesis they have evolved a way to obtain nourishment from fungi in the roots of pines or, in this case, oaks. These relatives of the more common white Indian pipe are not very plentiful on Long Island.

The trail soon skirts very close to the golf course and you may get strange looks from nearby golfers as they approach one of the greens. It then heads into the swampy woods close to **Little Northwest Creek** and crosses wet areas on wooden planks. The red maples are especially brilliant here in October. The trail is very overgrown as it passes through stands of sweet pepperbush and other wetland species. Amid this setting are some very large pitch pines growing on drier sections of soil.

A road is reached shortly thereafter, the same one you took to get into the area, and offers the opportunity to cut the hike short by walking left to the parking lot, which is just a few minutes away. The trail turns right and crosses over where Little Northwest Creek flows under it. It then makes a left and proceeds in a southeasterly direction through another wet wooded area. There are many wildflowers here in spring despite the fact that this area was once used as a dump. Scattered pieces of old glass bottles and other debris still can't take away from the beauty. Wetlands are on your left and mixed woods are on your right. So much of this hike goes through the edge of differing habitats, providing a chance to see many types of plant and animal life. The trail turns left (northeast) and cuts across the wet woods at the head of Little Northwest Creek. Crossing wooden planks it comes into an elegant mature **White Pine forest** with wintergreen underfoot. It crosses another old woods road and reaches the border of the saltwater marshes of Northwest Creek as it turns north, once again traversing the edge of different habitats. The marsh on the right is very colorful in autumn.

The golf course is now on your left and you have almost completed a circuit of this entire area. You will come out onto a woods road that can be followed back to the parking area, or follow the trail as it leaves this road to the right. It eventually reaches the point where you originally picked up the blue trail. Turn left here and retrace your steps back to the car.

Access

Car

Take State Route 27 (Sunrise Highway) eastward to the south fork. About 1.25 miles east of the village of Bridgehampton make a left (north) onto Sagg Road. Proceed a little over 3 miles into the village of Sag Harbor until the road becomes Main Street. In the village, turn right (southeast) onto State Route 114 (East Hampton-Sag Harbor Turnpike) and look for the entrance to Barcelona Neck in 2 miles on the left.

Bus

SCT92

Northwest Path

Length: 6.5 miles one way. Blaze: yellow triangle

USGS topographic maps: East Hampton, Gardiners Island West

The area northwest of East Hampton village is heavily wooded and undeveloped. This entire area is known as the Northwest Woods and there is much public land here with some private landholdings in between. Walkers in East Hampton Town have put together an excellent trail that passes through some of the finest features in the area. They have even managed to get private landowners to let the trail pass through their land, quite an accomplishment on Long Island in this day and age. You can see several glacial kettleholes and freshwater ponds (known as holes in these parts), mature native white pine forests (rare on Long Island), glacial erratics, secluded hollows, moraine hills, tidal ponds, salt marshes, and a pebbly beachfront. The perceptive hiker will also see signs of prior human uses of the land. A map of the area can be obtained from the East Hampton town clerks office, phone (631) 324-4143 for information.

The Northwest Path is estimated to be **about 6.5 miles long** and is blazed with yellow triangles. The trail can be walked in four to five hours, but an extra hour should be left for side trips to features off the main trail. The starting point is at a small dirt parking area where Edward's Hole Road (a dirt road) forks off of Route 114. You can easily find the yellow triangles going east from here. The white blazes of the Paumanok Path can be seen here also.

The trail dives right into the woods and winds away from the road; the traffic noise quickly fades. It soon climbs across the north side of **Winter Harbor Hill**, so named because Northwest Harbor and Cedar Point Lighthouse can be seen from here in winter. We heard a hermit thrush singing near here and got a good look at a white-tail buck off the side of the trail. It gently descends to cross Two Holes of Water Road and in a short distance one can see Chatfield's Hole through the trees down to the left (north). The trail then takes a left and crosses a dirt road heading around the east side of the pond. There was a lot of bird activity when I visited this area. **Chatfield's Hole** appears to be a coastal plain pond very reliant on rainwater to maintain a high water level. It was quite low when I was there and motorbike damage was evident in the drier areas. A unique mixture of eastern white pine and pitch pine grows along the pond. The trail follows just above the shore; there is a nice view of the length of the pond before moving away from the north shore. All typical wetland flora can be found here. An old woods road is soon reached. It is called Lone Grave Road since it leads north to a grave of one of the Hubbards, who died of smallpox long ago. The grave is on the north side of Swamp Road, one of the main roads in the area. We explored a little north on

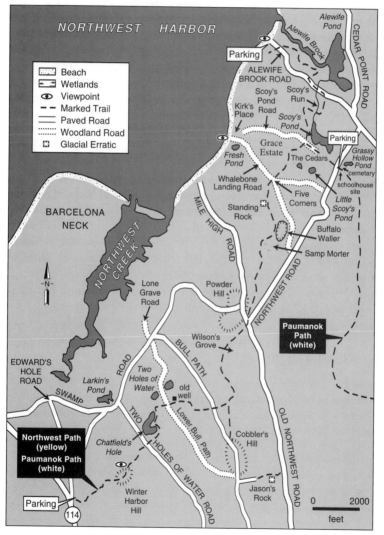

Northwest Path, East Hampton Township

the road to see the **Two Holes of Water**. They are two ponds on either side of Lone Grave Road. The larger and more easily seen pond is on the east side. It has a large home on the far shore. The other pond located to the west is set off-trail and has a wildness about it. Bushwhacking down to it you get the feeling of what it was like for early settlers to explore this land. The hole is nearly inaccessible, surrounded by swampy growth and sphagnum moss. There are many mature native white pines scattered about; they are the most distinguishing feature of the Northwest Woods. Returning to the trail you may wish to explore Lone Grave Road south of the Northwest Path. It becomes Lower Bull Path and skirts Cobbler's Hill near Bull Path, a paved road. You may also wish to go east to **Jason's Rock**. This large glacial erratic is named after an Algonquin named Jason who used this rock as a stopping place between Sag Harbor and Freetown near East Hampton in the 1800s. It is said that a depression in the top of the rock always contains water and this is where Jason would refresh himself on his daily trip. Back on the Northwest Path you will find the remains of an old well a little east of Lone Grave Road and just on the north side of the trail. A ring of stones marks the place where the well was located. Past this point the trail turns southerly and skirts the north side of a private driveway. A home comes into view as the trail crosses Bull Path. The homes here are few and far between and blend nicely into the landscape. That is, they do not ruin the rural feel of the area. After crossing along the border of another home, the trail turns northerly and passes a grove of mountain laurel. In a little while the trail drops down into a hollow and passes into **Wilson's Grove**, a magnificent grove of mature white pines named after the landowner, who, thankfully, allows hikers to pass through. You may note that signs direct mountain bikers away from the area. Not many plants grow under the pines because so little light gets in and the pine needles make the soil extra acidic. I noted some scattered lowbush blueberries and trailing arbutus but not much else in the shady open forest floor.

The trail comes out of Wilson's Grove and passes through a damper area with a profusion of highbush blueberries (ripe in July!) and tupelo trees. In a little while the trail comes out into an intersection of the Old Northwest Road and Mile Hill Road and crosses both.

The trail now enters land known as the **Grace Estate** after industrialist W.R. Grace, who acquired the land in 1910. There were plans in the early 1980s to put in a large condominium complex complete with a golf course and polo grounds with stables. Fortunately, local opposition turned the project away, with critical assistance from The Nature Conservancy. The Town of East Hampton acquired the land in 1985. The tract connects Cedar Point County Park to the east with the public lands of Northwest Harbor and Barcelona

Neck to the west. Three distinct Algonquin settlements have been found within the property. The trail is narrow and unused as it heads through quiet woods, passing several deep hollows along the way. The most prominent kettle along the trail is **Samp Morter**, a deep wetland teeming with bird and animal life. Farther along another less-conspicuous depression called the **Buffalo Waller** is passed. The trail winds through woods where the wood thrush can be heard before eventually reaching a large glacial erratic called **Standing Rock**. It is an ideal resting spot perched on the slope of a small hollow that lends itself to quiet contemplation. I was told that this rock was once an Algonquin

Walking under the huge white pines in Wilson's Grove

meeting place, and the rock is hence called "meeting rock" in some literature. Continuing on from Standing Rock you will reach an intersection of trails known as **Five Corners**.

This is a great place to launch another side trip off the Northwest Path. Make a left (west-northwest) here and proceed down an old road called Whalebone Landing Road. Years ago a 600-acre farm was located here. The woods are all second-growth forest. Stay straight on this path and in a few minutes you will emerge out of the woods and onto the shore of Northwest Harbor. Take time to scout the beach and walk it in either direction. You may choose to walk west (left) as far as Northwest Creek, a pristine tidal creek and estuary rich in its diversity of life. This area was the most bustling port in East Hampton Town, and Northwest Harbor was a thriving farming community back in the early 1700s. Sag Harbor took over as the main port in the area late in the 1700s and the important port of Northwest Harbor has all but been forgotten. Most of the land seen from the beach is protected from development. To the west (left), the bluffs of Barcelona Neck are prominent. Straight out lies Mashomack Preserve on Shelter Island. The Cedar Point Lighthouse is visible, looking like a tall house off in the distance. Be sure to explore the area of woods and thicket just south and east from where you came out. This is known as **Kirk's Place** after Josiah Kirk, who owned the farm after the civil war. Kirk was an "outsider" and never hit it off with the locals. He spent much time and money trying to prevent them from gathering eel grass from the beach in front of his house. This practice of gathering eel grass as a source of fertilizer had been going on for generations and the local folk were not about to stop because someone new to the area told them to. Go back about 30 or 40 yards down the trail you took and bushwhack east from there, and you will find the old stone foundation of the root cellar Kirk owned. Traces of his barn can be found farther east across an old woods road. Overlooking the beach near here are two large linden trees and a huge old horse chestnut tree that someone disfigured with an ax. This was the front of Kirk's large home. What a great view Kirk must have had as tall-masted ships came and went from Sag Harbor. There are several old overgrown foundations to explore here as well.

Alewife Creek and Shelter Island as seen from the eastern section of the trail

After taking the trail back to the Northwest Path, proceed east (left) and pass through an area known as **The Cedars,** named for the eastern red cedar trees clinging to life here. The trees are being gradually shaded out by the taller oaks and hardwoods. They are evidence that this was once an open field, since red cedars are pioneer trees that take hold in clearings and abandoned fields. A little farther on you will come to an intersection with Scoy's Pond Road, another abandoned woods road. To the left (northwest) the road goes back to Kirk's Place. The white blazed Paumanok Path goes off to the right reaching Northwest Road in less than a half mile. Cars can be parked at that point.

You may opt for a sidetrip to the south (right) on Scoy's Pond Road and in a few minutes make a left to take a look at **Scoy's Pond**. This is the largest of the many ponds and kettles found in the Grace Estate property. In summer the pond will be covered with fragrant water lilies and abuzz with dragonflies. Swallows swoop over the surface chasing insects and you may also spot a heron wading about. But be warned: this is prime habitat for deer flies, which inflict their stinging bite in hot weather (late June through July). Returning to the Northwest Path, continue east and the trail will make a right turn and pass around the north side of Scoy's Pond, although it cannot be seen well from here. The trail crosses **Scoy's Run**, the outlet of the pond, at a place called **the Sluice**. Erosion from mountain bikes is evident here. A pink flower caught my eye on the slope of the waterway. It turned out to be a wild pink, a flower associated with the Appalachians that is surely rare on Long Island. A little farther on the trail comes out onto a dirt road and makes a left (north) to Alewife Brook Road. The entire section of trail that goes over the Sluice to this point may be eliminated in the future to avoid further damage to this sensitive area.

The trail follows Alewife Brook Road to the left (northwest) for a few minutes of quiet walking. It passes over Scoy's Run again along the way and makes a right to enter Cedar Point County Park through an unlocked gate. The trail comes out on the eastern side of **Alewife Pond**. This tidal pond is accessible from Cedar Point County Park farther up on the other side, where small rowboats can be rented. Alewives are small members of the herring family related to shad. They grow to about 15 inches long when mature and are migratory: They are born in freshwater ponds and creeks during late spring and swim out to the ocean when three or four inches long in the autumn. The following spring, they congregate at the mouth of the tributary they came from, an amazing feat considering the vastness of the ocean and the small size of the fish. There is much debate as to how alewives find their way back to their place of birth. Large runs of the fish occur every spring as they return upstream to spawn. Although once quite common, there are only a half-dozen or so remaining places where the fish migrate upstream on Long Island. **Alewife Brook**, as its name implies, is one of these places.

The final section of trail follows along the bank of the brook, which empties into Northwest Harbor. There is a fine resting spot above this tidal creek where a bench has been placed. Belted kingfishers, fish-eating birds with large crests on their heads and long bills, frequent this area. Their distinctive loud rattling call emitted while on the wing gives them away. The trail finishes up by exiting another gate back onto Alewife Brook Road and turning right for a short walk to the shore of Northwest Harbor. The Cedar Point Lighthouse is directly across the harbor from this point.

Access

Car

This trail crosses a few paved roads but access is best from the west near State Route 114. Take State Route 27 (Sunrise Highway) to the south fork and out to Wainscott (the village just before East Hampton); make a left (north) onto Stephen Hands Path. In 1.5 miles, make a left onto State Route 114. Proceed 2.5 miles and look for a fork onto unpaved Edwards Hole Road. Pull off onto the small parking area between Route 114 and Edwards Hole Road. The trail crosses the road at this point and continues eastward from here. Another place to leave a car or start a hike is where the Paumanok Path crosses Old Northwest Road 0.7 mile south of Alewife Brook Road.

Bus

SCT92

Cedar Point County Park

Length: 4 mile circuit. Blaze: none

USGS topographic map: Gardiners Island West

Cedar Point County Park on the north side of the South Fork offers the opportunity to see several different types of habitat in one hike. This park offers three-season overnight camping. As with many Suffolk County parks a brochure with descriptions of numbered stations along the trail can be obtained at the park office. One gets a truly woodsy feeling just approaching the park by car as winding roads pass nearby Northwest Woods and Barcelona Neck.

The trail starts near the park office and takes off into rolling woods dotted with occasional glacial erratics. One noticeable feature of the forest is that the dominant tree is the chestnut oak, which is not particularly common on Long

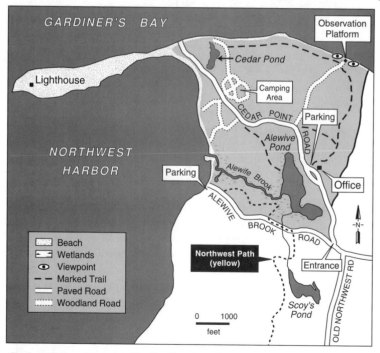

Cedar Point County Park, Sag Harbor, NY

Hikers can reach the Cedar Point Lighthouse which once stood on an island

Island. The understory consists of dogwood, shadbush and even an occasional chestnut. The trail suddenly breaks out of the woods and comes to a **magnificent view north overlooking Gardiners Bay**. From this observation platform on a bluff only 60-feet high I counted five lighthouses with the aid of binoculars. Nowhere else offers a better panorama of the end of the North Fork, including views of Orient Point, Plum Island and the Gull Islands, with the shore of Connecticut 15 miles in the distance. Gardiners Island, with its rich history of early settlement and the legendary buried treasure of Captain Kidd, is just off to the right. A large white windmill can be seen on its western shore. To the west (left) is Shelter Island. The platform is about 1.5 miles from the park office. Follow the trail westerly along the top of the bluff and you will pass several small lookouts before finally coming to a junction with a dirt road that will take you back to your car at the park office to complete a 4-mile circuit. This hike takes you through the public campsites and past

Alewife Pond along the way.

The hiker can choose to walk the beach another 1.5 miles to the point and visit the **Cedar Point Lighthouse**. This lighthouse was originally located on a small island dominated by cedar trees that were destroyed by a hurricane. Shifting sands have extended the point beyond the lighthouse, which was reachable by foot only at low tide at one time. The beach is a wonderful place to pick up shells, especially colorful scallop shells that seem particularly common here. The entire walk from the park office to the observation platform and out to the point and back is approximately 7 miles. Either section makes an excellent hike for families with children.

Access

Car

Take State Route 27 (Sunrise Highway) out the south fork to the village of Wainscott. Make a left (north) onto Stephen Hands Path. In just under 2.5 miles make a left onto Old Northwest Road. In 2.2 miles the road forks right. Proceed about 2 miles from the fork and make a left onto to Alewife Brook Road. Follow the signs to the park entrance on the right.

Paumanok Path: the Grace Estate to Stony Hill

Length: 8.2 miles, Blaze: white

USGS topographic maps: Gardiners Island West, East Hampton

This link in the Paumanok Path leaves the Northwest Path in the Grace Estate Preserve and heads southeast through historic woodlands, between housing developments, across open farm fields, and finishing in the magnificent wooded hills of Stony Hill. I estimate this hike to be more than 8 miles from the Northwest Path to Red Dirt Road. It is a much-needed link in the Paumanok Path to Montauk Point and is surprisingly varied. Although the path often travels close to houses, the character of the woods is not lost. The South Fork in East Hampton Township has extensive development, and credit should be given to the East Hampton Trails Preservation Society and the Group for the South Fork for making it possible for the walker to hike from Sag Harbor to Montauk with very little road walking. This hike includes some of the more interesting natural features of the landscape, along with past historic sites. The Town of East Hampton trails maps for the Northwest Area are useful in negotiating the first few miles of this hike. They can be purchased at the Town Hall located on Route 27 just east of the village of East Hampton. It would probably take the average hiker about five hours with breaks to cover the 9-odd miles from Northwest Road where parking is available to Springs-Amagansett Road near Red Dirt Road north of Amagansett. Of course you may choose to make your own hike by leaving a car at any of a number of crossroads and shorten or lengthen your route.

The first 0.5 mile of this section of the Paumanok Path lies north of the closest available parking on Northwest Road with the balance of the hike going south of the road. This section of trail begins in the **Grace Estate** where it leaves the Northwest Path on an old woods road called Scoy's Pond Road on the local hiking map. It heads southerly past **Scoy's Pond** which is off to the left (east). There are several small wetlands as well as **Little Scoy's Pond** on the west side of the trail. The wide old woods road is also marked with orange blazes alongside the white of the Paumanok Path. This orange-blazed trail will eventually be a continuous route but is not yet complete. Take note that turn blazes are in the shape of an inverted L to designate when and which way the trail turns. This is important since there are many turns off woods roads and some diagonal road crossings, so you have to be alert throughout this hike.

The best place to begin this hike is from Northwest Road, where there is parking for a few cars. The trail now leaves the Grace Estate property and enters an old area that was first settled by the Van Scoy family in the late 1700s. The

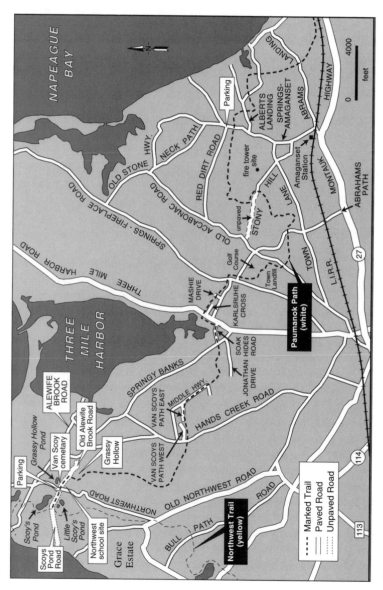

The Paumanok Path: Grace Estate to Stony Hill

area was once known as **Grassy Hollow** and the swampy pond on the east side of the trail bears the name **Grassy Hollow Pond**. The **Van Scoy Cemetery** is also here, with headstones dating back to the eighteenth century. Just opposite this is the site of the **Northwest Schoolhouse,** the main school in these parts in colonial times. You may notice that there are orange blazes with the white of the Paumanok Path at this point. These mark a more recent trail called **Foster's Path** that is open to mountain bikes. Hikers can use this 5 mile long trail which stays south of Northwest and Old Northwest Roads and links up to the Northwest Path near Chatfield's Hole. Continuing along the trail you may notice some old red cedar trees mixed in with the flowering dogwoods in the understory. This is a telltale sign that the area was once pasture land since these trees are pioneer species which need the open light of clearings to grow. The woods here are oak-dominated with some pitch pines and stands of white pine. White pine seems to be a signature tree for the nearby Northwest Woods, and, although not common on most of Long Island, it has done nicely in this corner of the South Fork. The trail turns off the old woods road, known locally as the Old Alewife Brook Road, and continues through slightly rolling uplands. A few more turns off old woods roads occur as you continue in a southwest direction. Keep an eye out for a classic boundary tree that was bent sideways many years ago and continued to grow; branches sent upwards from the main trunk give it a weird shape. At about 45 minutes steady walking time (**about 2 miles**) the orange-blazed Foster's Path leaves off to the right. The Paumanok Path continues straight ahead on an old overgrown woods road that must date back to colonial times. The fact that the trail is worn down and moss-covered along its borders alerts the hiker to the fact that its use was heavy some time long in the past.

At about **2.75 miles** you reach Hands Creek Road which you cross and then continue into the woods on an old woods road just south of Van Scoy's Path West. Here you travel between homes that are separated by woods according to the zoning laws. You continue past more houses and cross Van Scoy's Path East diagonally at this point. From here the trail will pass by the end of new streets or follow an old sandy woods road as it continues generally south and east. Just watch for turns and you should be all right. The dry oak-dominated terrain is very rolling, and the trail makes a sharp left at one point just before a large kettlehole. Your inclination is to continue on over the small ridge into the kettle, but if you do you will miss the turn (as I did). If you recognize that the blazes have suddenly stopped, you can easily retrace your steps and find your way again. At most of these road crossings there are Paumanok Path logos to guide you to where the trail continues. Be particularly aware of diagonal road crossings on these quiet residential streets.

The trail comes out onto Springy Banks Road (**about 4 miles**) and crosses it to the corner of Soak Hides Road, which is a small connector to Three Mile Harbor Road. Watch for the blazes designating a left turn onto an unpaved road that enters the **Soak Hides Preserve** run by the Town of East Hampton. At the end of the road you will see the sheltered waters at the cove on the southernmost

Hiking among the huge beech trees in Stony Hill

portion of **Three Mile Harbor**. Three Mile Harbor is a large sheltered harbor that empties into Gardiners Bay. The trail takes a sharp right near the end of the preserve road and heads back towards the creek. You may notice two patches of creeping low growing evergreens, the larger one on your left just alongside the trail and a smaller group off to the right in the open woods. This variety of low growing juniper, uncommon for this area, is much more prominent in winter. A little further on (**4.3 miles**) on the left you will come to a long wooden bridge over Tanbark Creek where it drains into the base of Three Mile Harbor. The names **Tanbark Creek** and Soak Hides Creek come from the practice of soaking animal skins in the tannin-laden water to turn tough hides into soft leather. This area is rich in archeological finds, as it was used by the original inhabitants before the arrival of Europeans. The bridge is a welcome change from the old route that traversed Soak Hides Road. On a winter visit I was amazed by how many kinds of birds I observed here. There were white throated sparrows foraging in the leaf litter along the shore, white breasted nuthatches and golden crowned kinglets flitting in the branches overhead as well as downy woodpeckers pecking away at tree trunks. This was not to mention the more common resident birds that were present as well. At this writing the view towards the harbor to the north (left) is somewhat obscured but I have been informed that the town is going to remove the tall invasive phragmites that have closed in on both sides of the creek. That should open up a nice lookout over the area at the base of Three Mile Harbor.

On the other side of the bridge the trail takes you through a patch of woods dominated by red maples with a few tupelo trees mixed in. These species are typical of wetlands on Long Island. The trail then turns left through very wet soil that will soon need wooden walks to protect the soil and the hiker's feet. Keep an eye out for a short path on the left to a view over the water. At **4.4 miles** the trail reaches the end of Gardiner Cove Road, where a car can be left if you are planning a shorter day hike. Turning right, you will come out to busy Three Mile Harbor Road at **4.5 miles**. There is a small deli a few hundred yards up the road to the right should you need to pick up something to eat or drink.

The trail crosses Three Mile Harbor Road and proceeds onto Karlsruhe Cross Highway, a quiet dead end road. At the end of this road, where I saw chickens roaming around freely, the trail continues on the straight path off to the left side of the road (about **4.7 miles**). Evidence of motorbike, horse and mountain bike damage illustrates the multi-use problems that are present on the south fork as well as the rest of the island. Along this section of trail, on a clear cold winters day, I observed a flock of eastern bluebirds feasting on the blue berries of large red cedar trees near the trail. Usually thought of as birds that arrive early from their winter migration, many bluebirds tough it out through our unpredictable Long Island winters. After crossing Mashie Drive, the trail continues in the woods adjacent to and just northeast of Abraham's Path before approaching Springs-Fireplace Road at **5.2 miles**. The trail used to cross the road at this point, but a re-route now has it turning left and following the road about 0.1 mile until it meets Shadom Lane. Cross the road and follow the blazes another 0.2 mile where you turn right and once again enter the woods (**5.5 miles**).

You now enter **Accabonac Preserve** managed by the Peconic Land Trust. The woods here near the road are almost exclusively made up of oak trees. I noticed an old worn boundary ditch a few yards off to the right of the trail a short distance in. These ditches marked off properties in colonial times before fencing became popular. The old forest was cut for cordwood to heat nearby cities. In a few minutes time you will see a sign put up by the Peconic Land Trust and cross an unmarked path. Soon thereafter you may notice beech trees start to mix in and eventually become the dominant tree in the surrounding woods. The trail climbs gently up a rise and then passes an area that looks like it was mined for sand at one time. Some pitch pines seem to flourish in the sandy soil at this spot. Reaching an old woods road, the trail turns left, follows it a short distance, and then turns right back onto a narrow path.

In a short distance the trail drops into a dry kettlehole where you pass a fairly large American holly tree. This is a forerunner of the holly trees that will become more numerous the further east you travel in the hardwood forests of the east end. You will reach Old Accabonac Road (**6.5 miles**) directly opposite Stony Hill Road. The trail crosses the road and proceeds down unpaved Stony Hill Road for 0.6 mile before it makes a left into the woods of Stony Hill at **7.1 miles**.

An interesting historical note is the fact that the only state run fire tower on the south fork once stood on a 150-foot hill just south of here. The tall steel structure was erected in 1930 and closed in 1946. It was torn down in 1961 because of the hazard it posed to the curious.

The next section of trail traverses private land, where it is important to respect property rights and stay on the trail even though the temptation to wander maybe strong. This section of the forest is a real treasure. These are big woods, and old woods; some of the ancient American beech trees have a girth of five or more feet. Copper beech is the nickname for this tree in some parts of the country because its buds are a shiny copper color and its leaves turn yellow and copper in fall; I have distinct memories of this copper hue set against a bright blue sky on a winter's day hike.

The old trail through Stony Hill woods showcases old growth trees and rolling hills; deep kettles pock mark the land in this isolated stretch of woods. It is

Bridge over Soak Hides Creek

surely one of the best walks on Long Island. Woodland flowers can be found in the spring. In the late summer and fall you will see saprophytic plants such as beechdrops, Indian pipe and pinesap adding color to the forest floor.

The trail reaches a property border and makes a sharp right turn. It skirts the top of a great kettlehole shaped like a big round crater. A glacial erratic sits near the rim, an ideal place to rest and take in some very dramatic topography. Continuing up and around this crater, you will reach a fence line marking the boundary of a secluded residence. The height of the fence is necessary to keep deer from eating the ornamental shrubs around the house. In a few more minutes walking you will reach Springs-Amagansett Road, just south of Red Dirt Road (**8.2 miles**). There is room to park a couple of cars near here or on Red Dirt Road. The trail continues on as the George Sid Miller Trail into Amagansett Woods before reaching Napeague.

Access

Car

Take State Route 27 (Sunrise Highway) out the south fork to the village of Wainscott. Make a left (north) onto Stephen Hands Path. In just under 2.5 miles make a left onto Old Northwest Road. In 2.2 miles the road forks right. Proceed about 1.5 miles and look for the place where the trail crosses. There is a woods road (Scoy's Pond Road) on the left at this point. You can pull a car over on the right (south) side of the road here. A second car can be left where the trail crosses Springs-Amagansett Road just south of Red Dirt Road. See the next section for this parking spot.

Train

Access to this section of the Paumanok Path from the Amagansett Train Station: Cross the tracks going east on Abrams Landing Road and immediately make a left (north) onto Old Stone Highway. At 0.5 mile, make a left onto Side Hill Lane, cross Town Lane at 0.8 mile and proceed up Stony Hill Road until the Paumanok Path comes out from the left to join the road just before it becomes unpaved at 1.25 miles. The trail is blazed in white. If you continue on the unpaved road for another 0.25 mile, look for the turn blaze where the trail leaves on the right and enters the hilly woods of Stony Hill.

Bus

SCT10B

Paumanok Path: Amagansett Woods and Napeague State Park

Length: 8.5 miles. Blaze: white

USGS topographic maps: Gardiners Island West, East Hampton, Napeague Beach

The South Fork of Long Island reaches its narrowest point just beyond the village of Amagansett in East Hampton Township. This isthmus was created by the action of wave-deposited sand over a period of thousands of years. Before this, Montauk was an island isolated from the rest of Long Island by a channel that probably had a strong tidal flow. This would explain the Montauk Indian words niep and eague, which mean "water" and "land." With the Atlantic pounding it on the south side and Napeague Bay with its deeply cut Napeague Harbor on the north, one is never far from the shore. In modern times the narrowest section of Napeague was overrun by the high tidal surges of some hurricanes, the most recent being in 1957. The land was originally used for wood cutting, salt-hay harvesting and grazing, but no permanent settlements were established here until 1935 when a small development was built on the north side, but salt in the ground water discouraged further building.

Today Napeague is very much in its natural state, a land of pitch pines and dunelands, of tidal marshes and ponds, cranberry bogs and thickets. It seems an inhospitable place where wildlife must find a way to survive with what the land will give it. Yet it is one of the most intriguing places to explore on Long Island. Subtle beauty in an almost surrealistic sense awaits the hiker here. Although the Napeague area has a variety of habitats, great diversity can be added to this walk by hiking the section of the Paumanok Path directly to the west in the wider section of the South Fork north of Amagansett, which is the hike I describe here. Although no exact measured mileage is available, I estimate the end to end walk to be about 8 to 8.5 miles long. By leaving a car at each end of the trail you can spend four or five hours traversing this area, and certainly an entire day if you choose to do a bit of exploring off the beaten path. Only small groups should stray from the main path, being careful not to trample fragile plants and dunes that have taken decades to reach their present state and can easily be damaged.

To start this hike on the west it is best to leave one car on Napeague Harbor Road just north of the railroad tracks. A Suffolk County Hagstrom map is useful in finding your way in this area. Drive back to Amagansett Springs Road and park the other car on the west side of the road just south of Red Dirt Road. You should see signs on the trees across the road indicating that the land is owned by The Nature Conservancy. White blazes along with the Paumanok Path logo can be picked up going east on the opposite side of the

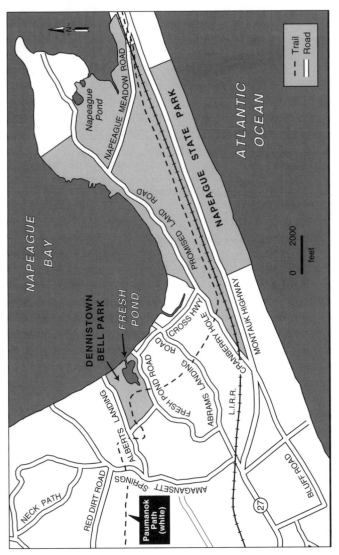

Napeague State Park, East Hampton, NY

road. A few older triangular plastic blazes marking the **George Sid Miller Jr. Trail** are still in evidence. They honor one of the early trail planners in this area. Miller was an avid horseman and hence the horse-head logo on the blazes. The trail beginning may be a little tougher to find in summer since it does not receive a lot of use. Although blazes do go west from here, they do not go very far. The East Hampton Trails Preservation Society

A holly tree and wetland are distinguishing marks of this area

and Group for the South Fork have linked this section to the Northwest Path in Cedar Point Park to the northwest. There is now a continuous trail from Sag Harbor to Montauk through some wonderful and varied terrain, undoubtedly some of the best on the Island.

Upon entering the woods you will notice it is hilly terrain with many dips and rises. Vernal depressions abound in this moraineal land. Vernal depressions are areas that retain water only in spring. They are important places for amphibians like frogs and salamanders to lay eggs and breed before dispersing into the surrounding woods for the rest of the year. The trail dips up and down in very pleasant surroundings through this uneven terrain. It crosses what looks like a private driveway before going back into the woods. The edge of a steep crater-like depression is skimmed by the trail. Its unnaturally steep sides suggest it was manmade many years ago.

The trail crosses Alberts Landing Road and goes back into the woods to avoid the steepness. This excavation is one of several clay pits where clay was removed for brick-making. Farther on watch for L-shaped turn blazes pointing to the right (west) of where the trail comes out on the road. Relatively new large upscale homes can be seen through the trees from higher points along the trail when the leaves are down. The area is covered with oak-beech woods with an understory of American holly, some reaching 30-to-40 feet high. The hollies are easy to spot in winter since they are evergreen. The contrast between the smooth silver-barked stately American Beech, a tree associated with the northern hardwoods forest of upstate, and the dark evergreen American Holly, normally associated with southern woods, is a great example of the overlapping of north-south flora zones found on Long Island. The evergreen ground pine can also be seen in places along the trailside.

The trail makes a left onto what appears to be an old overgrown woods road, passing close to one home in particular up on a hill. Keep an eye out for old overgrown boundary ditches that long ago were used to mark property. You will make a left and descend slowly to another road, Cross Highway, a quiet back road. Crossing the road the trail enters **Fresh Pond Park**, which is run by the Town of East Hampton. In a few minutes the trail goes up and over a small hill and gives an impressive view of **Fresh Pond** off to the left (east) when the leaves are down. The pond is not completely fresh water as there is a creek that connects it to Napeague Bay on the east side. The trail quickly turns to the right away from the pond and enters an old clearing that was probably an excavation from our colonial past. There is an old fox den on the slopes of this dig site. Watch for blazes as the trail makes a sharp left from the clearing and heads towards Fresh Pond Road. Before crossing the road take a short detour to the right (west) and read the historic plaque marking the site of the easternmost brick kiln in the area. Some old brick remains are visible nearby.

Back on the trail, just before it goes south of the road you'll pass a small wetland on the right surrounded by some American hollies. Keep an eye out for inkberry along here. It is an evergreen member of the holly family that usually grows in wet areas. This section of trail south of Fresh Pond Road was newly cut when I hiked it. You pass a small **wooden-fenced gravesite** for early resident Isaac Conkling who died in 1744. Farther on the trail passes through a preserve in the middle of a subdivision, crosses an access road, and then climbs gently through the rolling terrain. It appears that the homes are spread out and only seen through the trees at points.

Reaching unpaved Cross Highway to Devon the trail heads south (left) for a quarter mile or so before crossing Abrams Landing Road and passing behind a small home on a public right-of-way. I have been told that the "No Trespassing" sign here does not apply to this small section of trail. This short cutoff takes the trail back to Cross Highway (which is paved at this point) where some road walking southward is necessary. After following the road for almost a half-mile, you will come to a small triangular intersection where Cranberry Hole Road meets Cross Highway. Cross this and look for a small path leading up to a high point (70 feet) under power lines with a **view of the Atlantic Ocean**. From here you will be heading east into Napeague State Park. The change in vegetation is dramatic as pitch pines dominate, and there's much catbriar and scrub oak in the understory. Heather blooms in late spring as well as sickle-leafed Aster in summer. Both are yellow flowering plants that can tolerate the dry sandy soil found here. After dropping down off the hill make your way just to the left (north) a short distance and pick up an overgrown road that follows old telephone poles. This is the Old Montauk Highway path, abandoned about 1912 when the current Montauk Highway was paved. I have found this a more quaint path to follow than the power-lines trail. It can be followed straight easterly if you so choose; however, be warned that in wet weather this path becomes flooded in spots and reroutes may be necessary.

To keep your bearings in **Napeague State Park** remember that the Montauk branch of the Long Island Rail Road will be to your south (right) and Cranberry Hole Road will be to your north (left). Of course a USGS topographic map for Napeague Beach will help you stay oriented in this area, which has few landmarks to go by. For some really interesting exploration you should head into the land north of the Old Montauk Highway and roam dune-lands where pitch pines have branches growing horizontally (similar to the dwarf pines). Bearberry carpets large areas, and fox dens can be found dug into the wind- carved side of dunes. Various sedges, grasses and heather have grabbed a foothold in this land where surface water is scarce most of the time. Be careful not to trample any of these hardy plants that help to stabilize the dunes.

Only deer and fox tracks break up the isolated surrealistic feeling you encounter in this unique place. As one goes farther east there is a nearly impenetrable thicket of scrub oak, bayberry, and cranberry that grows in a swale to the

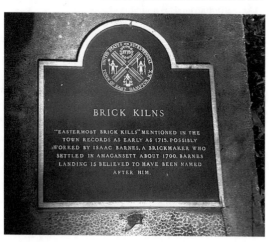

Plaque marking the site of the old brick kiln

south. In wet weather it is filled with water, making it more of a barrier to cross. Staying north of this you can wander the duneland until the abandoned railroad tracks are reached. They run southwest-to-northeast and once went to the old Smith Fish Factory in Promised Land on Napeague Bay to the northeast. The buildings can still be seen from some of the higher points in the dunes; they are being used for aquaculture study.

Hiking the dunelands is a unique experience

Continuing eastward at this point you will run into Napeague Meadow Road and can continue exploring on a sandy road on the north side of salt meadows towards Napeague Pond. A car left on Napeague Meadow Road near here is suggested if you choose this route. A longer and more interesting alternative is to take the old rail bed back to the southwest and head east again just north of the active LIRR tracks. The area here is on the edge of a swampland bordered by a mixture of dead snags and thickets to the north and the tracks to the south. Exploring east from here you enter a pitch pine forest crossed by deer "herd paths," and the forest floor is covered with pine needles and blowdowns. This is what a true old forest looks like, and except for the occasional hunters' stand or piece of flagging tape this place has been undisturbed for a long time. The Paumanok Path follows this course, staying out of the wetlands. I found this pure pine forest fascinating for its contrast to the open dunes I'd just left. In late spring pink lady's slipper can be found growing alongside wintergreen. The trees provide shade and make a pretty good wind-break.

Eventually the LIPA substation or the access road to it are reached. You can continue east along the power lines to Napeague Meadow Road and your car. The Paumanok Path continues eastward at this narrow point crossing two channels on short walkways. It eventually comes out at Napeague Harbor Road where it will continue into Hither Hills to the east.

At present only limited access is permitted to the oceanfront section of Napeague State Park south of Montauk Highway. It is a good area for natural-history study since rare orchids grow in cranberry bogs there. For that reason only very small groups should carefully explore this area of undisturbed woods, dunes, and beach.

Access

Car

For Amagansett Woods: Take State Route 27 out to the village of Amagansett. Just east of the village make a left onto Abrams Landing Road and then another left immediately after crossing the railroad tracks onto Springs-Amagansett Road (named Stone Highway here). Proceed about 1.4 miles to the place where the trail (white blazes) crosses the road. This is just before the junction with Red Dirt Road. There are places to pull a car over on the north side of the road here. To perform the walk described, leave one car on Napeague Road just north of the railroad tracks, and position another car at this hike's east terminus. See the Hither Hills access description for the directions.

Train

From the Amagansett train station walk north on Amagansett-Springs Road about 1.4 miles to the place where the trail crosses the road.

Hither Hills State Park and Hither Woods Preserve

Length: 11.3 miles, or a loop of varying length from 12 to 16 miles. Blaze: white

USGS topographic maps: Gardiners Island East, Montauk Point

Hither Hills State Park is known primarily for the state campground and ocean beach on the south side of Montauk Highway. Many people are not aware that the bulk of this 1,800 acre park lies north of the road, an area of wild, shifting dunes and hilly forests with a large body of fresh water within. Some of the finest hiking on Long Island is to be found here. Unusual plants common farther north thrive undisturbed because the ocean acts to cool the general temperature of the area. This is a wild place where ocean, bay, and wind shape the character of the land, and solitude for the walker is the rule. Combine it with the larger contiguous Hither Woods and Lee Koppleman County Preserve to the east, and the area becomes one that simply cannot be fully appreciated in one day, or two for that matter. Maps are available at the East Hampton town clerk's office; call 631-324-4143 for information.

The main trail that traverses the area roughly west to east is called the **Stephen Talkhouse Path**; it is also the Paumanok Path, blazed white. The remainder is quite easy to follow for an experienced hiker versed in the use of a map. Mileage is difficult to estimate but a full round trip of the area is close to 16 miles. The turn blazes are marked by an inverted L leaning in the direction of the turn. The trail heads uphill through a low pine-oak forest on the southern fringe of an area called the **Walking Dunes**. The forest seems to show some stability here. Just to the north the land is shaped by the shifting sands that give the Walking Dunes their name. To fully appreciate this unique area one must get off the trail. Tread lightly if you choose to bushwhack here. I discovered an active fox den in this land of dunes and pines fighting to stay above the moving sands. This is prime habitat for the puff adder, also known as the eastern hognose snake. There are dramatic views north over Gardiners Bay, east toward Napeague Harbor, south towards the Atlantic Ocean, and west over Fresh Pond. Goff Point to the northwest makes a good destination in cooler weather. A short trail through the Walking Dunes is explained at the end of this section.

The trail shows signs of erosion from mountain bike use in the steeper sections where the sandy soil is particularly susceptible. After a short climb into the hills, there is a short side trail off to the right (south) leading to the **Nominicks Overlook** (**0.3 mile**) with a fine view westward over Napeague Bay. A second viewpoint a little farther past the first opens up to the vast Atlantic to the southwest. Back on the trail on a late spring hike, I was delighted to find the beautiful starflower covering the forest floor. It was joined by

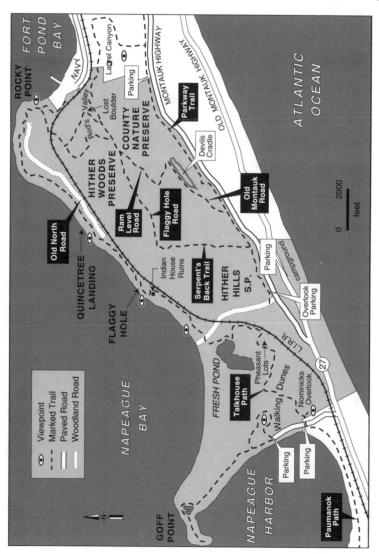

Hither Hills State Park, East Hampton, NY

the leafy but less conspicuous flower of wild sarsaparilla growing among the fine grasses of the woodland floor. The trail dips down behind the wooded dunes into a secluded protected hollow and the vegetation abruptly changes. Red maple, hickory, and beech mix in with the oaks with an understory of flowering dogwood and witch hazel, resembling a typical North Shore forest. Wildflowers such as the petite pink wild geranium and the more discreet whorled loosestrife are dominant. I even saw the beautiful orange lantern-like flowers of the wild columbine growing along the trail here. This is possibly the rarest wildflower in the park and certainly one of the rarest on Long Island. Listen for the flutelike song of the wood thrush in this section. To me the change of habitat is the biggest surprise of the area. Finding plants with a southerly and a northerly disposition growing together makes Long Island different from so many areas. Nowhere is this more pronounced than in Hither Hills. After a while the trail turns to the north (left) and enters an area called the **Pheasant Lots** (**1.75 miles**), due to the fact that in the 1930s and '40s the state kept it mowed so the open grasslands could hold pheasants released for sport shooting. Today you can still see much high grass in the open woods. I saw a turkey hen with a clutch of chicks in this area; the hen feigned injury and stayed within 10 yards of me so as to take my attention from her chicks, enabling them to find a safe place to hide. I saw another turkey hen and a chick which I nearly stepped on later that day in the Hither Woods section of the park; that mother abandoned her young in fright!

View westward across Napeague Bay from the Nominicks Overlook

The trail then turns and stays in the woods just on the northwest side of the Long Island Rail Road tracks. After leaving the tracks you head down toward **Fresh Pond (2.6 miles)**. When you come to the dirt road that gives fisherman access to the pond, turn left and walk down to the wild and untouched shore. Return to the trail heading almost due north above the east shore of the pond, where attractive views are limited by leaves but open in winter.

As the trail pulls away from the pond it climbs up and crosses a dirt road known as Fresh Pond Road that gives four wheel vehicles access to the beach on Napeague Bay. Cross the road and walk to the right a short distance where the blazes can be picked up again heading northeast (left). This hilly area follows parallel to the bluffs on the north side of the South Fork. In a short distance take the path to the left to **Waterfence Overlook** at **3.1 miles** for a view of Napeague Bay toward Gardiners Island, with its old whaler's lookout tower on Whale Hill. To the left (west) is Goff Point with Shelter Island beyond. In the opposite direction is Block Island, and on clear days Connecticut visible in the distance

Back on the trail you now walk with the bluffs on your left and the railroad tracks on the right. Views through the trees on your right give you a glimpse of the water now and then. The area is full of songbirds, especially the brightly colored American redstart. In a few minutes you reach the site of the **Indian House Ruins (4.0 miles)** where Stephen Talkhouse lived the last years of his life. One of the Pharaohs, a well-known Montauk tribe family, Talkhouse led the legal battle to keep his ancestral homelands at this very spot. He lived an interesting and varied life, and was renowned for his ability to walk great distances in unbelievably short times. He claimed to have walked from Montauk to Brooklyn and back in a single day! P.T. Barnum signed him up as "The Last King of the Montauks" although he was neither the last one or the king of anything. He was respected in his time and even more so after his death in 1879. Fittingly, he was found dead on a trail at the age of 60. A famous photograph taken of this dignified man in 1867 accents the nobility of his character. He may have been the first Long Island native American photographed, and the image invokes strong emotions to this day. Round stones around a depression just off the trail mark the site of his homestead, The Indian House Ruins.

A short distance farther on the trail takes you out of the woods into a wide-open area along the bluffs where they descend to near beach level. A striking contrast to the heavily wooded section you just left, the trail turns east again and follows the contours of the land down towards **Flaggy Hole (4.2 miles)**. Flaggy Hole is a large break in the tall bluffs that run along this stretch of shoreline. The LIRR Montauk branch runs behind a wetland here. As the trail descends with Napeague Bay on the left (north), the bluffs to the east provide a dramatic contrast between water and land. In late spring there are small white wildflowers here called grove sandwort, a flower related to the sandwort seen above the tree-line in the mountains of northern New England and the Adirondacks. The purple five-petaled flower called blue-eyed grass, a member of the iris family, also grows here. White beach roses are here mixed in with the more common pink ones. Another rarity found here in June is yellow thistle, which grows along the East Coast from Maine south. It is the only native yellow thistle found in the East.

It is believed that a house for cattle herding was once located here, but it has fallen into obscurity, probably due to its out of the way location. Three other houses are all marked in one way or another in guides explaining local Montauk history. If you refer to the USGS topographic map for Gardiners Island East, which covers this area, you will notice that Flaggy Hole is incorrectly called Quincetree Landing. Sources familiar with the area explained to me that Quincetree Landing was an old loading place located farther east along the shore. The East Hampton Town Trails map has the correct location listed on it. The trail starts to ascend the bluffs again, climbing gradually among beach plums and a couple of large glacial erratics. The view here back to the west is almost as dramatic as the easterly view from the other side of Flaggy Hole. After passing back into the forest in higher ground the white blazes become more spread out but easy enough to follow. You will pass into the Hither Woods Preserve. This entire area has long been known as Hither Hills, but recent public purchases have divided the area into two separate sections. The trail merges with a woods road called the **Old North Road** (**5.3 miles**) that continues eastward. It will eventually be blazed to the north of the Old North Road. At this point, you meet three successive side paths to the left (north), the first two of which dead end at the beach. The trail leaves Old North Road as the white blazes turn left onto the third path at about **6.1 miles**. It passes a **fine overlook** in a cleft in the bluffs, reaches another path onto which a right turn will take you to a trail that continues easterly (right) again. The trail will eventually come out alongside the low bluffs and then down to the beach. Make a right and then a left into the woods to follow the trail as it rounds the corner of land and reaches a clearing facing **Fort Pond Bay** on the east. I noticed a lot of fragrant lavender clusters of wisteria in full bloom here in early June. The head of land to the left (north) is known as **Rocky Point** due to the numerous rocks along this section of shore. The long pier to the right (southeast) is the long abandoned Navy pier. It is said that submarines once docked here, since the water is nearly 60 feet deep in Long Pond Bay. I would estimate that you have covered about **7.5 miles** at this point, a good 4 hours of hiking.

The Paumanok Path heads right (west) as a small path into the woods in a notch in the land. The first thing noticeable is the mountain laurel that grows along the trail. It is worthwhile to plan a trip in mid-late June when the showy clusters of flowers are in full bloom. The trail then crosses the railroad tracks and the Power Line Road just on the other side of them. In a few minutes you will come to an intersection (**8.0 miles**) where you may wish to continue straight, eventually reaching Flaggy Hole Road which runs through the middle of the area. The Paumanok Path turns left here and is fairly wide. This section of trail, known as the **Riah's Ridge Trail**, gradually climbs up and drops down into **Rod's Valley**. Rod and Riah were two elderly African-Americans who lived on the shore of nearby Fort Pond Bay. Rod was a woodcutter who logged this area in the post-Civil War period. The trail makes a sharp right (west) and ascends a ridge. In winter when the leaves are down a sharp-eyed hiker can see the Montauk Lighthouse from along the trail, probably the only place in the park this can be accomplished. The ridge has several scattered small glacial erratics along the crest, and mountain laurel proliferates here. After a quick descent to the **Flaggy Hole Road** at **8.8 miles**, the Paumanok Path goes to the left (east) and then makes a right in about 0.2 mile to start up another ridge. Called the **Lost Boulder Trail**, this relatively new section of trail is a gem as it passes some large old beech trees and reaches the **Lost**

Coming out of the woods onto the open bluffs overlooking Gardiners Bay.

Boulder on the ridge top at about **9.1 miles**. This large erratic is one of the most interesting I have ever seen. The steep wall facing the trail is embedded with white quartz, pink granite and shiny mica, parts of which are green with moss. Past this point the trail goes through a thick growth of mountain laurel on an ancient looking path. Mountain Laurel are very slow growing and these are obviously old plants from their size.

Eventually the trail reaches an old woods road and takes a right (south) heading within view of the town landfill, which looks like a large grassy hill looming up in front of you. The trail cuts to the left just before the landfill and traverses along the side of a slope overlooking Fort Pond Bay on the left (north). This is a great section of trail and will show its view best on a clear winter day when the blue waters of the bay stand out beyond the large trees in the foreground. The trail switches back into a sheltered cleft in the land called **Laurel Canyon** at **about 10.2 miles**. There are medium sized glacial erratics scattered on the slopes of either side of the hollow that is covered with stands of mountain laurel. As mentioned earlier, these showy native bushes are in full bloom in mid-late June.

After reaching Upland Road, an old woods road, the trail takes a right (northwest) and heads towards the landfill. The trail is scheduled to be taken directly across into the woods but at this writing it climbs along an open edge of the southeastern border of the capped landfill. At the top, probably about 180 feet in elevation, is an expansive view called **Panorama** (**11.0 miles**). Despite the bizarre grassy mass of landfill in front of you, an amazing view of Plum Island, Great Gull Island and the waters of Long Island Sound dominates the scene. Binoculars will help reveal such landmarks as the tall lighthouse on Little Gull Island and the battle monument at New London, Connecticut, some 23 miles distant.

Beyond here the trail climbs up into the woods and over the hill, reaching near Montauk Highway in a few minutes walking (**11.3 miles**). The Paumanok Path continues left (east) following alongside the road to reach the village of Montauk in a little over a mile. A right will take you back a couple of hundred yards or so to the landfill entrance where you may have left a car. The total mileage is probably about **11.4 miles**, and it takes a good 6 to 7 hours to complete with stops for lunch and observing. If you choose to do the entire circuit hike back to Napeague Harbor Road in one day it can easily extend to 15 to 16 miles depending on the chosen route. I have done it by taking Flaggy Hole Road back through Ram Level and estimate it to be about 12 miles long. A car left at the overlook on Montauk Highway can cut about 1.5 miles off that distance.

The Hither Hills and Hither Woods areas offer opportunities for exploration, with many combinations of routes possible for the adventurous. For instance, one may choose to take the Flaggy Hole Road back through the center of the park, passing into an area showing new growth from a major fire that swept through these parts in 1986 when 2,000 acres burned. Farther on there is much mountain laurel, especially on the west side of the Power Line Road that pretty much bisects the area from north to south. The Old North Road can then be picked up and taken towards Montauk Highway with a number of opportunities to get back across the railroad tracks and hence to the Stephen Talkhouse Path, which is the main route on the west side of the tracks. There is also the **Serpents Back Trail** which runs parallel and just west of the power lines. This hilly trail is a strenuous but fairly direct route back towards the parking overlook on Montauk Highway. Another nearby trail a little north of Montauk Highway can be picked up from the Serpents Back Trail heading westerly over a hill with a view of the ocean; it eventually ends at the Old North Road. It is called the **Ocean View Trail**. Another alternative is to take the Ram Level Road through **Ram Level**, a large maritime grassland. Although they were once common, these native grasslands are fast becoming rare as fire suppression permits trees to invade. A serious effort is being undertaken by The Nature Conservancy to set prescribed fires to preserve these grasslands. Controlled burns will prevent terrible conflagrations like the 1986 fire. They prevent a buildup of fuel on the ground, and they return nutrients to the soil.

One worthwhile goal to reach as you head back west is the Old Montauk Road that runs just north of an elongated depression known as **The Devils Cradle**. I know of at least one reason the area earned its name: I bushwhacked it and paid dearly with cut and torn legs and arms from the tremendous growth of catbriar on the slopes. Not to mention the ticks I picked off myself! But the giant erratic called **Split Rock** affords the hiker a fine resting place on the Old Montauk Road. Farther west the trail opens up into glades of hay-scented fern before merging with the **Parkway Trail** from which you hear traffic on nearby Montauk Highway. Another name for this trail is the **Indian Jumps Trail**, which hints at another bit of interesting folklore. There are three depressions called the Indian Jumps. According to legend, a brave was engaged to be married to a maiden. A second jealous suitor hid in the bushes and mortally wounded the first with an arrow. In his agony he took three final leaps; hence, the Indian Jumps. One should not bypass the fine overlook on Montauk Highway if taking the Parkway Trail. Expansive views as well as interpretive signs make it a worthy place to stop, and it's nice to see the Atlantic Ocean after spending a day under the trees of Hither Hills.

Between the Old North Road and the Serpents Back Trail, the **Ocean View Trail**, although not long, affords clear views of the ocean.

To the west of the overlook on Montauk Highway is **Elisha's Valley**, named after a Montauk who lived there in the 1870s. The entire area has hidden surprises at any time of the year. It features hilly terrain and many roads and makes for a myriad of options for hikers of all abilities. Combine this with the colorful history of the area and this is undoubtedly one of the premier hiking places on the Island.

Access

Car

Take State Route 27 (Sunrise Highway) out to the south fork past the village of Amagansett. After the long desolate stretch of Napeague, make a left (north) onto the first road, Napeague Harbor Road. In a short distance you will cross the railroad tracks and look for white blazes on a telephone pole where the trail goes in on the right (east). Places to pull over a car are along the road here. Cars can be left at the overlook a little farther east on Route 27. For an end to end hike of the area, make a left (north) off Route 27 about 3.2 miles farther east of Napeague Harbor Road into the Town recycling center. Park just off to the left outside the gates of the recycling center.

Bus

SCT10C

Walking Dunes

Length: 1 hour. Blaze: interpretive signs

USGS topographic map: Gardiners Island
East

On the northwest border of Hither Hills lies
a unique land of shifting dunes containing plants that have adapted to a harsh
environment. Access is from the end of Napeague Harbor Road where there
is parking for a few vehicles. An interpretive sign explains the plight of the
endangered piping plover that breeds in protected areas in a few scattered
locations on Long Island beaches. You will see numbered signs on posts
throughout this short walk, which can be completed in a little under an hour
with stops to observe and take pictures. Please stay on the trail and avoid stepping on plants since they have a hard enough time surviving the elements and
lack of water.

Those who have studied this unusual area believe that early industries such as
fish factories cleared the land of trees just to the north, causing a loss of
ground cover. The result shows what the forces of wind at work through the
centuries can do. The prevailing northwesterly winds that sweep off the water
have pushed sand inland, where it covers trees, shrubs, rocks, and just about
anything in its path. You will see several examples of this during this relatively short yet engrossing walk.

The trailhead goes off to the right from the end of the road on a narrow sandy
path. You will see many of the plants you'd associate with this type of sandy
porous soil. Bearberry creeps in large mats along the trail. This low-growing
plant with paddle-shaped leaves has inconspicuous flowers in late spring that
become red berries . They are edible and sustaining, but mealy and tasteless;
not something you would go out of your way to pick and eat. Bearberry is
found throughout the Pine Barrens and sandy coastal areas on Long Island,
but interestingly it is also common in the far northern tundra where harsh
conditions of a different type exist. Beach plum, black cherry, Virginia creeper and poison ivy also close in on the trail.

In a short distance you will see a tall dune in front of you with a trail sign letting you know that you should make a right turn at its base. First you may
choose to scamper up to the open top where a **fine view** back toward
Napeague Harbor with Lazy Point on its western shore gives you a good perspective of the area. Return to the trail and continue southward with the big

dune on your left. The dry sandy slope is covered with gray-green mats of beach heather, a hardy plant sometimes known as "false heather" since it is not really an old-world heather like those found in the British Isles, but a member of the Rockrose family. The plant is covered with small bright yellow flowers in late spring that add a nice touch to the drab dunes for a few short weeks each year. Looking to your right you will see plants associated with a wetland since this is the fringe of a freshwater swamp. Tall shrubs such as highbush blueberry, sweet pepperbush, swamp azalea, bayberry and winterberry can be seen here. Beyond this the scrubby maritime forest of Hither Hills rises.

Follow the trail as it curves up to the left along the contours of the rounded sandy dune. At the crest look off to the right (south) and you can actually see the huge smooth-sided dune in its advance on the nearby wetland. The tops of trees that are partially covered can be seen in places! Now turn and walk out a little in the opposite direction and you come to a superb view of Napeague Bay with Gardiners Island prominently situated in its midst. You can also follow the adjacent beach all the way out to Goff Point. In the foreground you will see a large swale (which is a depression behind a dune). This one is a large horseshoe-shaped bowl sculpted by the strong northwesterly winds that come in unimpeded over the waters of the bay.

The view north toward Gardiners Island from atop a high dune

Dropping down into the swale in summer I found the temperature can be much higher; there's little or no breeze to cool you off. At the base of the bowl there is a sign explaining the **Phantom Forest** that once stood there. The shifting sands covered the trees in this forest and have moved on, leaving only the bare trunks as evidence of their existence. Continue on keeping the wetland to your left. This is a cranberry bog that has developed in this somewhat sheltered location. Other wetland plants like yellow-eyed grass, wood mint and some beautiful wild orchids such as grass pink and rose pogonia are in bloom at different times of the summer. Of course, the cranberries are edible and best picked in October when they ripen to a deep red color. In some of the drier locations you may see a small yellow daisy-like flower during the hottest days of mid-summer. This is the sickle-leafed golden aster which is the earliest of the asters to bloom and thrives in sandy sunny locations many other plants can't tolerate. The trail will come out to the beach on **Napeague Harbor**. Turning left, you may return to your car a few hundred feet down the beach.

Turning right, one can combine this walk with an excursion out to **Goff Point** which loops around into the mouth of the harbor. Excellent tidal mud flats allow some of the best shorebird watching anywhere on Long Island. Sandpipers, plovers, egrets and large wading birds can be seen here, especially during low tide. The endangered piping plover makes visits here from nearby nests; be sure to watch out for signs identifying which areas to avoid so as not to disturb them. The sights and sounds of the seashore are everywhere. Shells can be found all along the beach walk. Clammers, both commercial and locals, are usually out raking the shallow water for steamers. Terns and gulls are always on the move looking for fish in the shallows. As you reach the curve in the beach to the left, you can pick up a sandy road on the right which will take you out to the bay side where the colder waters of the open bay await. Continuing to the left you can go all the way to Goff Point, or as far as you like, eventually returning on the harbor side. You should give yourself at least two hours to do this round trip and be sure to bring water and snacks. A note of caution: the beach is littered with sharp shells at many points and some type of footwear is necessary or the going can be slow and painful!

Hikes in the Walking Dunes or out along the beach on Napeague Harbor can be extended to include Hither Hills. By using two cars or fashioning together a loop using the Stephen Talkhouse Path, you can make this an all-day excursion including Fresh Pond to the west and much of the heavily wooded surrounding hills.

Theodore Roosevelt County Park
(formerly Montauk County Park)

Length: two to three hours

Blaze: unmarked nature trail

USGS topographic map: Montauk Point

Roosevelt Park/Point Woods

LONG ISLAND

0   20
miles

East of the salt water inlet called Lake Montauk is a large piece of public land owned by Suffolk County that has a long and varied history. Easily overlooked by those heading out to see the majesty of Montauk Point, Theodore Roosevelt County Park is a surprising gem that contains freshwater ponds and swamps, pristine dunes and beachfront, woodlands, grasslands, and panoramic views. This diverse 1,073 acre park abuts Montauk Point State Park to the east, so virtually all the land to the Montauk Point is public. Long day-hikes can be put together by utilizing both parks. By itself the county park offers a day's worth of opportunities for exploring.

The main park office is located just north of Montauk Highway, east of Montauk village. It is the site of the old Deep Hollow Dude Ranch and today the county runs the stables on the property and offers horseback riding. This was the first cattle and sheep ranch in the nation, the grass and heathlands of Montauk providing ideal places for livestock to spend the winter. The surrounding shorelines made natural barriers to keep the animals contained. The park office is located in the historic **Third House**, one of the three houses put up for the men who tended the flocks. The other two were built earlier and of those two only the Second House stands today; it's located to the west of Montauk village. Third House was built in 1797 and is inexorably linked to Theodore Roosevelt, who stayed here in 1898 with his famous Rough Riders upon their return from the Spanish American War. They were actually quarantined as they recovered from the various tropical diseases they had contracted. Here President McKinley persuaded Teddy to run for governor of New York. Photographs of Roosevelt and his men are located inside the house. The park was renamed after our 26th president on the 100th anniversary of his stay here.

The hiking (nature) trail is not located near the Third House. At the park office you can pick up a map to show its whereabouts. A USGS or DOT

topographic map for Montauk Point, or the Town of East Hampton trails map
are helpful in negotiating the area. The town map can be purchased from East
Hampton Town Hall just off Montauk Highway east of East Hampton village.
From the starting point off East Lake Drive, a map board at the trailhead has
the layout of the trail system. Several short loops and boardwalks in the nature
trail system traverse the many wetlands to the east. The nature trail system
can be done in a round trip of one-to-two hours of easy walking and observing. It makes a great walk for families with young children. It is blazed with
colored arrows on trees. There are kiosks with maps at key trail interesec-
tions, and some benches for resting. Following the numbered nature stations
in order will lead you back to your car. The nature trail is a good place to link
up with some of the wider woods roads or bridle paths in the area to make a
day-long hike out of it. An even more extensive walk can be fashioned by
extending the hike around Oyster Pond into the adjacent state park and either
looping back or continuing on to Montauk Point, where you can leave a second car. Don't forget to bring a pair of binoculars and camera to this scenic
area.

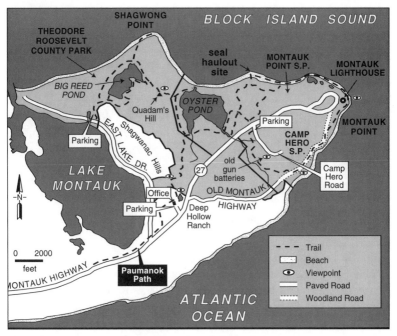

Roosevelt County Park Point Woods Loop, Suffolk County, NY

Starting out from the parking area you immediately head into a second-growth area of briars and thick viney growth. In a short while you cross a woods road and enter a moist woodlands where you find many wildflowers on the forest floor in springtime. Of special note is the trout lily, a rare Long Island wildflower I first became familiar with in the cool rich woodlands of the Catskill Mountains. It is a small drooping yellow lily with brown mottled leaves said to resemble the patterns on brown and brook trout. It is one of the wildflowers known as the "spring ephemerals" that bloom for a short time on the forest floor just before the leaves open.

You soon arrive at a clearing with a bench and two wooden bridges. The forest here is dominated by tall hickories that turn bright yellow in fall. Red

Looking east to Block Island from Squaw (Quadam's) Hill

maples and tupelo also grow well in the damp soil. The understory contains southern arrowood, American holly and witch hazel. Take the trail to the left (northeast) and it will bring you across a wetland down toward **Big Reed Pond**. This beautiful body of fresh water was a big surprise when I first visited here. I expected to see a pond surrounded by tall invading reeds or phragmites but what I found was a photogenic lake in excellent condition lined with cattail marshes rich with wildlife. Wild ducks abound here and warblers fill the trees in spring and fall migration seasons. The colors of the tupelos, sumacs and red maples in autumn are memorable. And all this is only a tall layer of dunes away from the windswept shores of Block Island Sound!

Returning to the clearing, proceed to loop around and explore the trails with the notion of making your way south and eastward following the numbered stations. You will pass into an area where a feeder stream gurgles as it runs towards the pond. American beech and American hornbeam trees flourish here along the banks of this peaceful stream. Hornbeam is not a common tree on Long Island since it prefers rich soil along river bottoms—not the usual habitat found here. The smooth blue-gray bark is fluted, or muscular looking, and the wood is known for its unusual hardness. You soon come to a view of Big Reed Pond. In late summer you may see the large showy pink flowers of the swamp mallow adding some color to the marshy shoreline. In winter the orange-red berries of winterberry stand out amidst the drab browns.

Proceed along the narrow path that parallels the south shore of the pond. You occasionally see paths that lead down to the shoreline, and one leading to a duck blind; investigate them at your leisure. At one point you can see the tall dunes to the north beyond the pond. The trail will pass around the southeastern cove of the pond and reach a wooded clearing. Here you can return by way of the more southerly section of trail away from the pond, or extend your trip to include one of the best views in these parts. If you choose the latter, follow the trail a little bit farther eastward and pick up the main woods road (it is used as a bridle path). It is suggested you take this trail during the week in the off-season, after Labor Day or before Memorial Day, to avoid any conflicts with the horseback riders. Follow this road uphill past a building on the left and make a left shortly thereafter. You proceed uphill and come out onto an open grassy hilltop with a **spectacular view** eastward. This is **Quadam's Hill**, also known as **Squaw Hill**, and is a great place to have lunch and enjoy the scenery. At only 97.5 feet it demonstrates that you don't necessarily have to get very high to see great distances when the surrounding terrain is flat. The view includes Montauk Point Lighthouse and Block Island in greater detail than you will ever get from sea level. Coastal Rhode Island can be seen across the open waters on a clear day. Oyster Pond is sprawled out in the foreground, surrounded by a mix of woods and grasslands. To the southeast is hilly terrain with the tall abandoned radar facility in the Point Woods area. Directly south you see the hilly terrain of the Shagwanac Hills with Prospect Hill reaching to 142 feet. Third House lies hidden somewhere at the southern base of these hills. On a clear autumn day here, we sat and watched a northern harrier (marsh hawk) cruising above the grassy hills surveying the ground for prey. Many other hawks and falcons were seen as they migrated along the coast southward.

From here the walker has many options. You can wander the paths southward, crossing over streams that feed into Oyster Pond and working your way back northward along other paths. You may even check out the archeological site south of Big Reed Pond or stray into the Shagwanac Hills for another view of the surroundings. Another option is to head for the northern shore of **Oyster Pond** and observe shore birds foraging along the sandy shoreline. A short walk from here is the open beach, which can be walked up to **Shagwong Point**. In the dunes behind Shagwong Point I saw a young eastern milk snake that headed for cover after I almost stepped on it. The dunes here are in a natural state with a few narrow paths allowing access to them. The raw power of wind and open water is a sharp contrast to the peaceful woods along the shore of Big Reed Pond. A wide woods road leads back toward your car along the north side of Big Reed Pond, passing through a narrow wooded area full of tupelo trees that turn crimson in early fall. You can pick up the original trail on the right to take you back to the parking area in a few minutes.

Access

Car

Turn left (north) off State Route 27 (Montauk Highway) onto East Lake Drive for 1.8 miles. Then pull into an unpaved road that takes you to a grassy parking area.

Bus

SCT94 (summer only)

The Point Woods Loop

Length: 5 1/2 mile loop. Blaze: white for first half and then none

Roosevelt Park/Point Woods

LONG ISLAND

0   20
miles

For trail map see Theodore Roosevelt County Park, page 319

USGS topographic map: Montauk Point

This loop is a half-day affair that takes the walker around the easternmost point of Long Island through some pristine old growth woods to spectacular bluffs overlooking the boundless Atlantic Ocean. It continues past the historic Montauk Point Lighthouse and then along windswept beach, returning back to your car through a rare maritime forest, all without any backtracking. The trail is clearly cut and blazed in white up until the Montauk Point Lighthouse. The USGS Montauk Point topographic map, the DOT map and the East Hampton Town map for the area will serve you well in keeping track of your whereabouts on this circuit hike. The first section, which goes to the lighthouse, is the final leg of the 145 mile long Paumanok Path. The hike is entirely on public land, starting out in Camp Hero State Park and passing into Montauk Point State Park. The trail is clearly cut and heads into the woods right off the road. Parking for a single car is possible here but other cars can park along the short road.

Along this trail are evergreen American holly trees that are quite old (although not particularly large, due to the slow growth of these native trees) and evergreen mountain laurel. They are particularly noticeable with the leaves down on the deciduous trees since the contrast with the bare woods highlights the dark greens of the holly and mountain laurel. The trail almost immediately dives under the closed-in evergreens then drops down into a small valley where a brook runs through an open woods filled with red maple and tall American beech trees. The trail takes a sharp left down to the stream, which it crosses on a short wooden walkway. The section that continues straight here is the connector to the west where the Paumanok Path comes in after crossing Montauk Highway. You will be following white blazes all the way to the lighthouse. On one April visit here the large bright-green leaves of skunk cabbage were emerging from the wet ground around the small waterway. The trail continues through undulating terrain as it winds through an oak-beech forest with some dense stands of mountain laurel and plenty of holly. It is possible that these woods were never cut down, or at the very least they are very old second-growth. There are also some fine groupings of shad-bush, a small tree that bursts out with attractive white flowers in late April. Here and there lies a small vernal kettlehole filled with water; in fact you are never far from small brooks with associated wetlands in this entire section. In springtime birds are plentiful as they forage through the trees, and there are amphibians here since water is never far off. One of the few places that the blue spotted salamander is found on Long Island is in this area of Montauk, the other being near Greenport. It is 3-to-5 inches long with a dark gray or black body with bluish-white flecks on the sides and tail. The best chance of seeing one is at one of the small kettles or vernal wetlands that dot the area in March or April when they find their way to these sites to breed and lay eggs. Another critter, the gray fox, a catlike canine that can climb trees, is also found out at Montauk but is extremely rare in other parts of Long Island. There are also several plant species found only here.

Be careful to pick up one sharp left turn (south) after being on an old wide path for a short distance. You will know you have missed the turn if you come to a stream with an aged chain-link fence beyond it. Called **The Sanctuary** by locals, this large trailless area is open to hikers who are skilled in the use of a map and compass. Exploring this wetland-dominated terrain to the west makes for some great bushwhacking and nature study. This fence marks the old boundary of the U.S. Air Force Station that once guarded this section of our coastline from foreign invaders. As far-fetched as this seems today, during the first two world wars and during the cold war, our shores were vulnerable due to the limits of early technology for the location of submarines, fast-moving boats, or planes. The old USGS topographic map of Montauk Point for 1956 is still in print, and it clearly shows the boundaries of the Air Force Base and adjacent Camp Hero. Both are now included in the state park that bears the latter name.

You will notice that the mixed holly forest is left behind as you enter a recent second growth area of short trees and thickets. An old access road to the military installation is crossed. It heads northeast-to-southwest and is worth exploring. Beyond this you pass an area that slopes up to the left (north) with a few big oaks and even some sycamores. If the leaves are down you may see the tall building topped with radar towering over the surrounding land. I chose to leave the trail and explore uphill (north) for a little while and was rewarded with a view of the ocean about a half-mile away, atop an old concrete installation built into the side of a steep hill 110-feet high. This is a **gun battery** where big 16-inch guns were placed during World War II to ward off attacks from the sea. There were active fox dens on the hillside and the top was covered with dense vegetation. The area just to the east containing the tall relict tower is **Camp Hero State Park**. A paved road through the old Army base makes an interesting stroll in a part of our coastal defense system once disguised as a quaint fishing village. It was an active base from 1947 to 1982.

The trail heads southward crossing a couple of more streams and goes through an area with a wealth of bird life before reaching Old Montauk Highway. It took me and hour and a half to reach this point, including much exploration and stops; without side trips, the hike takes less than an hour.

The trail crosses a small wetlands tributary

Old Montauk Highway was the original route to Montauk Point until the present highway was built and this one abandoned more than 80 years ago. Just as in Napeague State Park it makes a good route for hikers since it is overgrown yet sufficiently open for walking. The trail makes a left (east) and shortly comes to a south entrance of the old Camp Hero facility. Continuing eastward it slopes downhill, giving views of the ocean straight ahead and at one point the top half of the Montauk Point Lighthouse. Dilapidated ruins of old buildings can be seen off the side of the trail but they really do not spoil the charm of the hike, especially if you know a bit about the history of the property. As the old road winds down near the water it presses close to steep eroded bluffs rising some 70 feet above the Atlantic Ocean. Robert Cushman Murphy referred to these sections as a "badlands" topography in his classic book *Fish Shaped Paumanok*, and indeed they are strange features. In winter and early spring you may see many sea birds just offshore; they migrate here from the far north and visit this stretch of coastline up to Montauk Point.

Farther on you will see the numbered parking spots for fisherman who come for the world-class surf-fishing here. Continue eastward toward the Montauk Point. If you stay with the white blazes they follow the road and veer away from the water, ending at the base of the Montauk Point Lighthouse in a 10 minute walk. To return to the beach keep to the right at junctions. Use extreme caution near the top of the bluffs as cornices or overhangs have formed at the top and can give away under the weight of the unsuspecting hiker who ventures too close to the edge.

The **Montauk Point Lighthouse** was commissioned in 1790 by George Washington. Built in 1795, it is 100-feet high and constructed from red lime-stone imported from Connecticut. Standing on Turtle Hill 69 feet above the sea, it has been a beacon to ships for more than two centuries. Yet nature is taking its toll on the land upon which it sits. When first built it stood 297 feet from the edge of the bluffs. Today it is about 50 feet from the edge. Much has been made of this situation in the media, and celebrities and musicians organized by local resident Paul Simon have held concerts to raise money to help the Army Corp of Engineers shore up the land and stabilize the incessant erosion. This is a battle against the natural order: the currents take sand from here and move it westward to lengthen the barrier beach we call Fire Island.

On my visit here I saw along the base of the bluffs huge gray rocks enclosed in metal wiring bluffs that are designed to stop the erosion. They made a great place to duck out of the wind, take my boots off and have lunch in the sun. Here at the tip of Long Island as I gazed at Block Island some 14 miles away, I could make out the lighthouse on the bluffs on the southwest part of that island. A flock of brightly patterned harlequin ducks went speeding by. I became tuned-in to the soft whistling of some black scoters swimming near-by. Other sea ducks from afar were spread out from the shoreline at my feet into Block Island Sound as far as the eye could see. Beautiful white common eiders, three different kinds of scoters, buffleheads with large white patches on their heads and red-breasted mergansers were also seen here. Most of these were species I had never seen before, since it takes a special effort to come out to Montauk Point in the winter with binoculars in hand to see them. This is one of the best places on the East Coast to observe wintering ducks.

To continue your hike you have two options. If the weather is nice (and wind calm), you can continue on the beach westward. On the beach route you will likely feel the wind in your face if it's a clear day, since fair weather winds often blow out of the north or northwest. You will need to protect your skin from the sun and wind. On this stretch of beach I noticed patterns made in the purple-tinged sand by the wind. A little bird scurrying ahead of me turned out to be an Ipswich sparrow, a rare subspecies of the savannah sparrow that breeds only on Sable Island, Nova Scotia. This one was likely stopping here on it's trip back home. There are ponds on your left as you approach a small point in the land where Shagwong Point becomes visible across the water.

To finish this circuit hike proceed westward along the beach and look for a duck blind that looks like a tiny house on a short bluff. This is a good 15 to 20 minute walk from the lighthouse. The group of rocks in the water near here is a well-known "haulout" site where wintering harbor seals sun themselves. Between December and April you may be lucky enough to see them at low tide, but keep your distance since seals can be aggressive if approached too closely.

Behind the blind you can pick up a woods road that goes by at this point. Take it to the left (southeast) and follow the yellow blazes for a short distance to a right turn into the woods and out of the incessant wind. The way is well marked. You will now pass through a maritime oak-beech-holly forest dotted with small wetlands. Some of the shad-bush trees here are the largest I've ever seen. The walk is about 15 minutes back to a wide unpaved road. Turning left (south) will take you back to Montauk Highway just west of Camp Hero Road and your nearby car.

The alternative to the beach trail is to follow the Money Pond Trail. Opened in the spring of 2002, this path is a good route on windy days. To find the trailhead, walk north on the road in front of the concession building (to the right coming out of the building) about 100 yards. Just before reaching the 15 mph speed limit sign, look for the green plastic blazes with the New York State Parks Department discs on the right. Immediately a fine view northward opens up from an elevated vantage point. Soon the trail crosses somewhat hilly terrain with views through the trees north to the water when the leaves are down. In 15 to 20 minutes walking time you reach **Money Pond**. This lovely little body of water surrounded by thick vegetation has an isolated feeling to it. Legend has it that the infamous pirate Captain Kidd buried treasure here in the late 1700's. Farther on, the trail passes through woods with taller trees, including many large shadbush trees. After about 35 to 40 minutes of walking, the trail junctions with the **yellow-blazed Seal Haulout Trail**. You can either take a right to the haulout site or a left which will take you back to Montauk Highway.

A good half day can be taken up on this walk if you explore off the trail. This is one hike where the walker will be rewarded by any venture off the trail, and will find interesting sights at all seasons. A longer 9 to 10 mile loop can be made if you start farther west at Third House in Theodore Roosevelt County Park, loop back to your start via the beach near Oyster Pond and take one of the trails heading south through the park grounds.

From Montauk Point

I stand as on some mighty eagle's beak,

Eastward the sea absorbing, viewing, (nothing but sea and sky)

The tossing waves, the foam, the ships in the distance,

The wild unrest, the snowy, curling caps–that inbound

urge and urge waves,

Seeking the shores forever.

Walt Whitman

Access

Car

To get to the beginning of this walk take Montauk Highway out past the village of Montauk. After passing the Oyster Pond lookout on a hill with a fine view northward, make the first right turn onto paved Camp Hero Road (no sign) and park close to Montauk Highway. Look for access to the white blazed trail on an unmarked path that goes off to the west (right) a few hundred feet down. The trail also can be picked up where it crosses Montauk Highway a little west of Camp Hero Road.

Bus

SCT94 (summer only)

Mashomack Preserve

Length: 11 miles. Blaze: Blue

USGS topographic map: Greenport

Sheltered by the North and South forks of eastern Long Island lies aptly named Shelter Island. A hundred miles east of New York City, it is surrounded by Peconic Bay on the west and Gardiners Bay on the east. The southeastern portion of the Island, fully one third of the land mass, is an undeveloped nature preserve owned and operated by The Nature Conservancy. This 2,039-acre sanctuary is one of the most pristine and spectacular natural places on the northeast coast. Known as the "Jewel of the Peconic," it is the largest preserve the Long Island East End and South Fork chapters of The Nature Conservancy maintain. Containing a mixture of tidal creeks and salt marshes, fresh water swamps and ponds, open meadows, upland mature forest and rocky beaches, this preserve has more diverse habitats open to hikers than anyplace else on the East Coast.

Naturally the area is a haven for all sorts of wildlife. It contains one of the densest populations of breeding ospreys in the east. Harbor seals sun themselves on offshore rocks in winter, and otters have been spotted in the preserve. Eighty-two species of birds have been found to breed there, including eastern bluebirds, ruby- throated hummingbirds, various owls and hawks, wading birds and waterfowl. In winter, another 56 species have been sighted. Deer, fox, and salamanders share the land with other creatures large and small. The variety of plant life is equally impressive.

"Mashomack" means "where they go by water" in the language of the Manhasset tribe. It was later called Sachems Neck, a name that persisted into this century. These early native inhabitants found the woods, sheltered creeks, and coves of the area to be ideal for shellfishing and hunting. Although the land was subdivided by English settlers, it was never completely cleared or exploited as much of mainland Long Island was. Its preservation was due chiefly to the Nicoll family, which had possession of Sachems Neck from the early 1700s until 1931. The land eventually became the property of a hunting club before The Nature Conservancy purchased it in 1980. Today, it looks much as it did when the Nicoll family sold it so many years ago.

A visitor center is located just beyond the parking lot. The preserve is open 9 a.m. to 5 p.m. daily; it is closed on Tuesdays. Nature programs and guided hikes for all ages are held throughout the year. Contact the preserve office at (631) 749-1001 for further information.

There are four hikes of varying lengths available to the walker, ranging from 1.5 miles to 11 miles. There is also a cross-country ski trail. Mashomack is a great place to hike any time of the year, as it showcases the seasons in so many different ways. One memorable day I hiked the full 11 miles in February after a foot of snow fell on the East End. The sky was the rich blue color only dry winter days can bring. I seemed to have the entire preserve to myself, but the animal tracks in the snow told me I wasn't really alone. Noisy mixed flocks of winter birds occasionally passed by to keep me company. Mashomack is also beautiful in late March or early April when the ospreys have just returned and

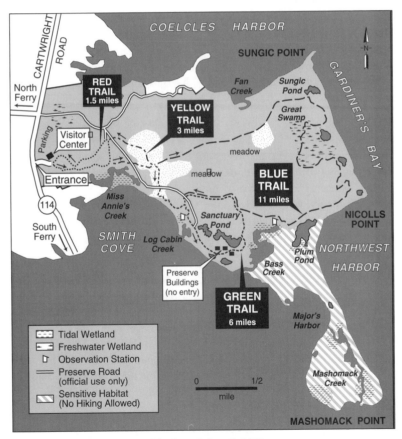

Mashomack Preserve, Shelter Island, NY

the spring peepers are giving evening concerts in the wetlands.

The shortest trail is the **Red Trail, 1.5 miles** long, and the next shortest is the **Yellow Trail, 3 miles long**. Either of these hikes is fine for young children. One note of caution: Shelter Island has a high density of deer ticks. The trails are wide enough to avoid picking up ticks in most places, but youngsters don't always stay in the middle of the trail, so take the usual precautions and check them frequently. You should be able to get a map at the nature center. A small donation will help defray costs of maintaining this huge preserve. From the map you may notice that the shorter trails are completely overlapped by the longer ones so a full description of them all separately is unnecessary. To avoid repetition I will describe the **11 mile Blue Trail** and the **6 mile Green Trail** sections which do not overlap.

Leaving the visitor center, all trails head east through the southern portion of a freshwater white pine swamp. This area and the one just to the north are known as the **Pine Swamp Complex** and are considered to be of unique local importance by the New York State DEC. A series of long depressions have become waterlogged because of the rising water table since the last glaciers receded. The result is a boglike environment in which locally rare plants such as eastern white pine and mountain holly thrive, isolated from their strongholds on the mainland. Continuing through rolling terrain you will notice that the woods are second growth, with species such as gray birch taking over what were once clearings. In a few minutes you reach a nice view over the waters of **Miss Annie's Creek** with **Smith Cove** beyond. A gazebo here makes a nice place to relax and take in the scene. On one trip here I observed an osprey dive into the water and come up with a fish, a sight not often seen. Shortly after this the Red Trail goes left and starts back to the visitor's center. The other trails continue through low-lying ground and then cross the main preserve road, reaching a trail junction in a large meadow shortly thereafter.

In warmer seasons wildlife is active in this meadow. Nesting boxes are busy with parent birds feeding their young. Swallows swoop and dive after flying insects in a quiet aerial battle, and red-tailed hawks drift on the air currents overhead. The smell of grass and wildflowers is in the air. The Nature Conservancy keeps this meadow free of invasive shrubs so native plants and wildlife flourish. The clearings are also important to deer and other animals who find prime nighttime feeding here.

From the intersection the Yellow Trail goes off to the left toward the visitor center while showcasing more of the open fields. You will also be going back on that same path if you choose either of the longer trails. The Green Trail goes right here but we'll continue eastward on the Blue Trail. About 60 yards farther along you may notice a short path off to the right. This takes you to the **Nicoll family cemetery**, a neat fenced-off clearing in the woods containing the graves of Nicoll family members dating back to the 1700s. It is obviously well-maintained and cared for, unlike some overgrown forgotten cemeteries I have come across in central and eastern Suffolk County.

Getting out early the day after a big snow

The trail soon passes into a fine oak-beech-hickory forest with small kettleholes here and there. After about an hour of peaceful walking through woods reverting to old growth forest you pass **Sungic Pond** on your left. Shortly thereafter the tree canopy opens and reveals a view of Gardiners Bay as the trail turns southward. You are only about 30 feet above the water but this is sufficient to allow a **fine overlook**. Gardiners Island is prominent several miles off.

The trail soon heads to the right (west) away from the bay. It is making a large half circle detour around **Great Swamp**. The swamp is a large wetland ringed with tall reeds called phragmites, which tend to dominate an area once they become established. Although they may be attractive when they take on a purplish color in flower or when they sway together in the wind, they offer little food or cover for wildlife. You will not see so many animals here as in a healthier more diverse wetland. Nevertheless, you are apt to spot an egret or heron wading through the shallower waters of Great Swamp.

Coming back toward the bay, the trail passes another small pond before following along the bluffs again. You can take one of the paths down to the rocky beach near **Nicolls Point** and, if it's not too windy, find a great place for lunch. Looking south (right) from the beach you can see Cedar Point with its lighthouse appearing to stand alone above water. The bluffs and hills of the South Fork rise along the horizon line behind it. Straight out is Gardiners Island and to the north (left) is Ram Head, another small peninsula of land on Shelter Island. The large erratic boulders at Nicolls Point may have harbor seals sunning themselves in wintertime. In colder months with binoculars you may spot hardy sea ducks riding the swells just offshore. In warmer seasons look for ospreys nesting in the trees behind the beach. Heading back down the trail you will pass more views to the south towards Mashomack Point, a narrow peninsula closed to hikers. Proceeding westward there is a fine overlook of **Plum Pond** on the south side as well as another of the **Bass Creek** tidal complex. Many ducks seek the refuge of this inlet, especially in wintertime. You will eventually reach the junction of the green trail.

The Green Trail rejoins the Blue Trail here from its loop along **Log Cabin Creek** and other small tidal coves. If you follow this Green Trail loop there are fine views of Shelter Island Sound and beyond, including North Haven, Jessup Neck (on the South Fork) and Nassau Point (on the North Fork). Be sure to check out the ospreys nesting on the platform in front of the observation blind just off the trail. The ospreys arrive in mid-March and stay until September or so. The Green Trail passes the regal Manor House on a rise overlooking the waters. Keep an eye out for the small but active least tern along the beachfront near here. This attractive little bird is listed as endangered since much of its habitat on the East Coast has been developed and its nests left open to predation. Behind the Manor House the green trail will start to loop back northward and pass between Bass Creek on the right (east) and **Sanctuary Pond** on the left (west) where much bird activity takes place. In season swallows pluck flying insects out of the air and white great egrets wade the water looking for a small fish dinner. A little farther on the Green Trail joins the Blue Trail for the return trip to the parking lot. The Green Trail is a scenic route and is recommended if you don't have the time (or energy) to do the longer Blue Trail.

The Blue Trail continues past the park access road and up to a section of bluffs overlooking Smith Cove. You may see the South Ferry shuttling between

North Haven and Shelter Island. Off to the right is **Miss Annie's Creek** and inland beyond is the visitor center where you are headed. After re-crossing the road you go through the meadow again, following the arrows on the Yellow and then Red Trails back to the visitor center. This long hike can be covered in four to five hours, but it is best to allow at least another hour to explore the beach and observe wildlife.

Access

Car

You'll need to take a ferry to reach Shelter Island. The preserve is just off the east side of Route 114. After landing on the island go three miles south from the Greenport/North Ferry or one mile north from the North Haven/South Ferry, where a sign will lead you to a small parking area on the east side of the road.

Hiking the wide paths of Mashomack on a spring day

Orient Beach State Park

Length: 2 miles one way. Blaze: none

USGS topographic maps: Orient,
Greenport

In contrast to the dramatic bluffs of
Montauk Point to the south, at Orient Point on the tip of the North Fork the
Harbor Hill Moraine has been worn down to sea level and Long Island sinks
subtly into Long Island Sound. Here at Plum Gut the strong currents between
Long Island Sound and Gardiners Bay tug at each other with each switch of
the tide. This area is not well traveled; a walk here is likely to be a solitary
one. The North Fork is like coastal New England. After all, many of the farmers who settled here came from New England, and some families have been
tilling the soil in the area for hundreds of years. Local people are more likely
to be Red Sox fans than Mets or Yankee fans. Here white church steeples rise
over a bucolic setting of vineyards, farmstands and village greens. History
seems undisturbed in the people and the land; Southold Town especially has
preserved the rural character and the natural beauty of the land.

At the end of Route 25 just before the ferry terminal is the entrance to Orient
Beach State Park on the right. Located on a 4 mile long spit of land going
back westward, this state park is usually not crowded. Recent storms have
wreaked havoc on this thin peninsula and forced closing of the park when
water rises over the roadway and floods park buildings.

Orient Beach State Park is unique; there simply is no place like it that I know
of anywhere on Long Island. Start your walk down the sandy road just to the
right (north) of the building that houses the restrooms (near the playground).
You will soon leave any noise or people behind you. It seems strange to be
walking back toward the southwest when you have driven this far east to walk
to the place, in this case Long Beach Point, where the land ends. On the left,
to the south, is the expanse of **Gardiners Bay**. Gardiners Island is prominent
in the foreground. On a clear day you can barely see land just above the
southern horizon; this is the high ground of Hither Hills on the South Fork.
Farther to the right (west) the South Fork is closer and the bare sandy bluffs
of Cedar Point County Park are visible. Looking farther west you can see the
old Cedar Point Lighthouse looking like a tall home rising out of the water.
Shelter Island is close by also with Ram Head a prominent feature. Notice
that sheltered **Long Beach Bay** is to the right (north). You'll likely see a

clammer working the shallows from a small boat. A little farther on I once found a group of weathered trees with the empty shells of channeled whelks stuck on their branches. I wondered if they had been put there by people or by sea gulls trying to eat the animal inside.

If you decide to walk the beach keep an eye out for the breeding areas of the endangered piping plover or least tern. These nests should be avoided during the breeding season of April through August when the birds lay their well-concealed eggs right on the beach. Disturbing these birds could have an

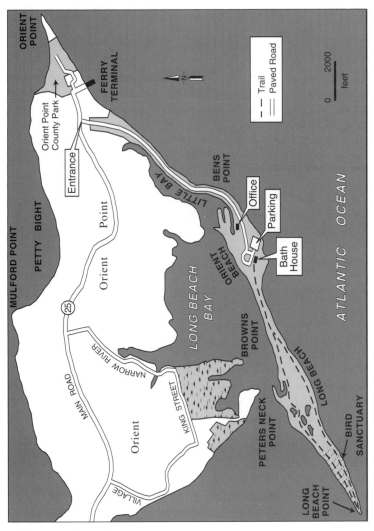

Orient Beach State Park, Orient, NY

adverse impact on their population. A tidal pond connected to the water by narrow channels on the north side is the first of several breeding locations. Look also for tall wading birds like the great egret whose white plumage stands out against the background of earth colors in the marsh.

A little farther on you reach a forest of red cedar trees that now extends down to the water on the south side when the tide is high. You may have to pick your way through some blowdowns here. Note the dead trees along the water line, destroyed by shifting sands and storms. On calm humid days you can smell the fragrance of the oil in the cedar trees. Look for the remains of an

Red Cedar growing in sandy soil near the tip of the point

old road that goes to the interior here. Note the reddish sand colored by erod-ed bricks from a fish factory located nearby years ago. There are ponds on each side. You may also see the prickly pear cactus, the only native cactus in the northeast. I have found it here and there on Long Island, but nowhere does it grow in such profusion as in this park. If you are here in early sum-mer you may be able to see the beautiful yellow flowers of this oddity. There are post oaks and Japanese black pines mixed in with the many cedars on this point. The oaks are native but the pines are not. Japanese black pines have been under attack from a pine borer insect that has devastated most of the Long Island population. Following the road you will come out on the north side of the peninsula with a lovely view across Orient Harbor towards the village of Orient with its tall white church steeple. The scene probably looks much as it did during the Revolutionary War when the village was called Oysterponds and was commanded by Benedict Arnold after he defected to the British side. Note the profusion of whelks, Atlantic scallops and jingle shells mostly unbroken on this untrodden section of beach.

On an early spring hike we saw and heard loons in the water here. Ospreys are all over the place on this walk. Do not linger too long near the nests of these big birds as they are skittish and will not return until you have passed by. Continue to the west along the shore and notice how the cedars become low growing and stunted near the point from exposure to salt and wind. At **Long Beach Point** there are usually many shore birds like oyster catchers, grebes, brants and cormorants to name a few. Bring a pair of binoculars. It is two miles to the point. At low tide you may be able to see the remains of the old lighthouse which used to be here. The new lighthouse known as the "Bug Lighthouse" was erected in 1991 and is visible just to the south of the point. It is interesting to realize that this point is being continually extended to the west and that the sand is being removed from the area you passed back to the east where the cedars came right down to the water. You may return by way of the beach on the south side if you choose.

Access

Car

Take State Route 25 to the end just before the Orient Point Ferry terminal. The entrance to the park is on the right.

Bus

SCT92

Other Parks and Preserves in Suffolk County

Other than the large parks that the longer Greenbelt Trails pass through, there are many smaller places for shorter walks if your time is limited or you are just getting started hiking. They are also great places to start with small children, since you are never far from the car and the hike is short enough to keep young minds occupied. There are too many to include them all, but some small better suited ones I have discovered are listed here.

In western Suffolk County there is **Twin Ponds Nature Center** in Centerport located just off Route 25A or the unheralded **Makamah County Preserve** accessed off Makamah Road in West Fort Salonga. With small brooks and hilly morainal uplands Makamah's 160 acres are a delight for walkers in springtime and a magnet for migrating warblers and other songbirds. The **South Shore Nature Center** is 206 acres of boardwalks and trails through salt marsh and maritime woods fronting Great South Bay. Farther east, **Indian Island County Park** offers some wandering within its 287 acres on Flanders Bay in Riverhead. Another small park to explore is **Goldsmith's Inlet Park** on the North Fork which offers a short trail and exploring of the rocky beach on Long Island Sound. Other shor woalks that show case the woods and wetlands of the North Fork are **Dam Pond Maritime Preserve**, **Arshamomaque Pond Preserve** and the **Down Farm Preserve**.

The Nature Conservancy has dozens of preserves sprinkled all over both Nassau and Suffolk Counties. One of the largest is the 93 acre **Uplands Farm Sanctuary** in Cold Spring Harbor that houses the Long Island Chapter's headquarters. The trails traverse grassy fields and hedgerows of a farm as well as typical north shore woodlands. There is a link to the Nassau-Suffolk Greenbelt in a wild looking hollow. The 124 acre **David Weld Sanctuary** in Nissequogue has a fine loop that provides some beach walking and offers a chance to see the largest tulip tree on the island. Not to be missed is the **Calverton Ponds Preserve** (mentioned in the Navy Co-op Pond Walk) where you can see some rare coastal plains ponds and wildlife in a pristine setting. Other Conservancy preserves which represent various habitats around the Island are the **Daniel R. Davis Preserve** in Coram, a fine example of pine barrens habitat. **Wading River Marsh Preserve** in Wading River and the **Merrill Lake Sanctuary** in Springs showcase the beauty of the salt marsh in an undisturbed state. They are good short introductory walks but since they are preserves no picking of plants or otherwise disturbing the habitat is allowed. For information you should join The Nature Conservancy and obtain a detailed list of all the preserves they maintain.

Suffolk County has public holdings throughout the entire county, and these are open to those wishing to explore them. Most have been described already, but some of the smaller ones can be linked up to larger public land-holdings for an interesting day's exploring. One example of this is the **Eastport Property** located just south of County Route 51 about 1.1 miles east of County Route 111. You will see a county parklands sign that has a symbol of a hiker designating that the land is open to hikers. As you hike the main dirt road southwest the pine-oak woods will be on your left, and a field on your right is a savannah with eastern red cedars and pitch pines growing inde-pendently in the grasslands. The profile of some of the taller southern ridges of the Manorville Hills appear on the horizon in that direction. There is an access road on the left about a half a mile in that allows exploration of the interior of the property. You can pick up paths eastward here and with some bushwhacking eventually traverse parts of the burn areas from the 1995 fire before reaching Speonk-Riverhead Road south of the Suffolk Community College. From here you can hike into the burn areas on the east side of the road and head for the dwarf pines or go for the views from the Summit. Link-ups such this are available in many parts of the county if you know how to use a DOT map to avoid buildings and the like.

Dusk at Peasys Pond in Robert Cushman Murphy Park, Western Section

Appendix

Mass Transportation

Some trails or public lands are accessible from train stations or bus stops. Consult them if you are interested in seeing if you can fashion a hike without a car.

Long Island Rail Road
New York City (718) 217-LIRR
Nassau and Suffolk Counties (516) 822-LIRR

Suburban Buses
Nassau County (516) 222-1000
Suffolk County (631) 447-8601
Huntington Township (HART) (631) 427-8822

Campsites

This is a list of campsites available to hikers within reasonable distance of trails or hikeable public lands. There are other campgrounds (such as **West Hills County Park** and **Cathedral Pines County Park**) that are in prime hiking areas but are only open to large organized youth groups or camping clubs. Most are seasonal but may be open late into the fall. You must call each individual campground for directions and reservation information.

Blydenburgh County Park in Smithtown has 30 general campsites for tents and trailers with full sanitary facilities (showers). Located just off the Long Island Greenbelt Trail within Blydenburgh Park, it can be used by hikers wishing to stop near the mid-point of the trail or as a base to day-hike from. Beautiful Stump Pond is a short walk away. Phone campground (631) 854-3712 or office at (631) 854-3713.

Heckscher State Park has 69 sites located along the south end of the Long Island Greenbelt Trail within the state park. For details call (631) 581-2100.

Southaven County Park is located in Brookhaven. There are trails and many woods roads to explore in this park. With 219 general sites for tents and trailers available, it is a good place for larger groups. Call (631) 854-1414 for information.

Fire Island National Seashore has primitive camping open to backpackers on the barrier beach adjacent to a federally designated wilderness area. Call

(631) 597-6633 at Watch Hill or (631) 289-3010 at Smith Point for further details since there are only 25 sites available.

Smith Point County Park has sites available on the oceanfront for trailers and campers only. The campground (631) 852-1316 or office should be called for information.

Wildwood State Park is located in Wading River on the North Shore. With 322 sites, it is the largest campground on Long Island. Full sanitary facilities with direct access to the bluffs, beach and wooded trails within the park. Call the park office at (631) 929-4314 for more information.

Indian Island County Park in Riverhead has 150 campsites for tents or trailers. Its central location allows you to travel either fork or access the central Pine Barrens by car. Call the park at (631) 852-3232.

Sears-Bellows County Park offers 70 sites on the scenic shores of Bellows Pond. A short side trail from the Paumanok Path in Hampton Bays, it makes a good backpacking destination or home base for day hikes in this beautiful park. Phone the park at (631) 852-8290 for details.

Cedar Point County Park in East Hampton has access to the great trails within the park as well as the nearby Northwest Path. 190 wooded sites with full facilities are a short walk from the beach on the bay side of the south fork. The park can be reached at (631) 852-7620.

Hither Hills State Park in Montauk has 165 open beachfront sites. Great access to the eastern section of The Paumanok Path and the wild lands of Hither Hills north of Montauk Highway. Try (631) 668-2544 for availability or information.

Theodore Roosevelt County Park allows outer-beach camping for trailers and campers near Shagwong Point. Call (631) 852-7878 for information and availability.

Eastern Long Island Campgrounds located in Greenport on the North Fork has 148 sites within a short drive of Orient Beach State Park at the tip of the fork. A private campground, it offers full sanitary facilities with partially wooded sites. For information, call (631) 477-0022.

Hiking and Outdoor Clubs

East Hampton Trails Preservation Society
P.O. Box 2144
Amagansett, NY 11930
(631) 329-4227

Group For The South Fork
P.O. Box 569
Bridgehampton, NY 11932
(631) 537-1400

Hiking Long Island
P.O Box 36
Mt. Sinai, NY 11766
www.hike-li.com
(631) 331-5938

Long Island Greenbelt Trail Conference
23 Deer Path Road
Central Islip, NY 11722-3404
(631) 360-0753

New York-New Jersey Trail Conference
156 Ramapo River Road
Mahwah, NJ 07430
(201) 512-9348
e-mail: info@nynjtc.org
www.nynjtc.org/

Nassau Hiking and Outdoor Club
139 Cambridge Drive E
Copiague, New York 11726
(631) 766-7950
www.nhoc.org/

The Nature Conservancy, Long Island Chapter
250 Lawrence Hill Road
Cold Spring Harbor, NY 111724
(631) 367-3225

The Nature Conservancy, Suffolk Fork–Shelter Island Chapter
P.O. Box 5125

East Hampton, NY 11937
(631) 329-7689

Southampton Trails Preservation Society
Box 1171
Bridgehampton, NY 11932
(631) 537-5202

Governmental Offices

US Fish and Wildlife Service
Wertheim National Wildlife Refuge
P.O. Box 21
Shirley, NY 11967
(631) 286-0485

New York State Department of Environmental Conservation (DEC)
SUNY Building 40
Stony Brook, NY 11790-2356
(631) 444-0354
permits (631) 444-0273

New York State Office of Recreation and Historic Preservation
Belmont Lake State Park
P.O. Box 247
Babylon, NY 11702
(631) 669-1000

NYS Office of Cyber Security & Critical Infrastructure Coordination
30 S. Pearl Street, 11th floor
Albany, NY 12207-3425
(518) 443-2042
www.nygis.state.ny.us
USGS & NYS DOT topographic maps available

Nassau County Department of Recreation and Parks
Eisenhower Park
East Meadow, NY 11554
(516) 572-0200

Suffolk County Department of Parks, Recreation and Conservation
P.O. Box 144
West Sayville, NY 11796

(631) 854-4949

United States Geologic Survey (USGS) for topographic maps
Box 25286
Denver, Co 80225
www.ask.usgs.gov
(888) ASK-USGS

Useful Publications

This is a list of books the walker will find useful in explaining and under-standing more about the outdoors.

Long Island Outdoors

Albright, Rodney, and Priscilla Albright. *SHORT NATURE WALKS ON LONG ISLAND.* Old Saybrook, Connecticut: Global Pequot Press, 1974, revised 1998. As the title suggests, short walks are highlighted on the Island in various settings.

BOCES, Third Supervisory District. *PADDLING THE NISSEQUOGUE.* Suffolk County, New York, 1985, rev. 1989. Short guide to exploring the Nissequogue by canoe with highlights of wildlife and human history.

Borg, Pamela, and Elizabeth Shreeve. *THE CARMANS RIVER STORY.* 1974. Guide to natural and human history of the Carmans watershed.

Falorp, Nelson P. *CAPE MAY TO MONTAUK.* New York: The Viking Press, 1973. Pictures and descriptions of coastal Long Island.

Giffen, Alice M., and Carole Berglie. *WALKS AND RAMBLES ON LONG ISLAND.* Woodstock, Vermont: Backcountry Publications, 1996. Short walks are described (a maximum of a mile or so), for those wishing to start walking in some of our natural areas.

Kulik, Stephen, Pete Salmansohn, Matthew Schmidt and Heidi Welch. *THE AUDUBON SOCIETY FIELD GUIDE TO THE NATURAL PLACES OF THE NORTHEAST: COASTAL.* New York: Pantheon Books, 1984. Several shorter hikes on Long Island preserves are included here.

Long, Robert P., William and Barbara Wilhelm. *CANOEING THE CARMANS RIVER.* Cutchogue, New York: Peconic Publishers, 1985. Short guide to exploring the Carmans River by canoe.

Long, Robert P., William and Barbara Wilhelm. *CANOEING THE PECONIC RIVER*. Cutchogue, New York: Peconic Publishers, 1983. Short guide to exploring the Peconic by canoe.

Mackay, Robert B., Geoffrey L. Rossano, and Carol A. Traynor, eds. *BETWEEN OCEAN AND EMPIRE, AN ILLUSTRATED HISTORY OF LONG ISLAND*. Northridge, California: Windsor Publications, 1985. Long Island history with illustrations giving insight into the uses of the land and the people who resided in it.

Murphy, Robert Cushman. *FISH SHAPED PAUMANOK: NATURE AND MAN ON LONG ISLAND*. Great Falls, Virginia: Waterline Books, 1964. Concise yet thorough descriptions of the different habitats and historic uses of the land by the Island's famous native naturalist.

New York-New Jersey Trail Conference. *NEW YORK WALK BOOK*. 7th edition. New York: New York-New Jersey Trail Conference, 2001 A general description of hiking opportunities on Long Island, New York City and upstate. Carries on the tradition started years ago by the largest hiking group in the New York metropolitan area.

Puleston, Dennis. *A NATURE JOURNAL*. New York: W.W. Norton & Company, Inc., 1992. Beautifully illustrated with color drawings, this easy-to-read guide by a respected veteran Long Island naturalist takes the reader through the seasons of natural Long Island.

The Nature Conservancy. *NATURAL HISTORY OF LONG ISLAND*. 1974. An out of print book one can still find at some libraries. Despite being somewhat out of date, this book nonetheless is well-written and clearly explains the habitats the hiker will encounter on the trail. An interesting description of the plants and animals still found on the Island.

Turner, John L. *EXPLORING THE OTHER ISLAND: A Seasonal Guide to Nature on Long Island*. Great Falls, Virginia: Waterline Books, 1994. Seasonal guide to best places and ways to observe wildlife around the Island. A must for the amateur naturalist to explore well known and lesser known wonders on the Island.

Villani, Robert. *LONG ISLAND: A NATURAL HISTORY*. New York: Harry N. Abrams, Inc., 1997. Beautiful, full-color photographic trip through natural Long Island with text to match. The best visual book on the Island.

Flora and Fauna

Identifying and understanding the wonders of nature enhances any outing. These books will help one in learning more about the plants and animals encountered in the wild.

Eastman, John. *BIRDS OF FOREST, YARD, & THICKET.* Mechanicsburg, Pennsylvania: Stackpole Books, 1997. Fine book with drawings and explanations of the behaviors and details of each bird's habits.

Eastman, John. *THE BOOK OF FOREST AND THICKET: Trees, Shrubs, and Wildflowers of Eastern North America.* Harrisburg, Pennsylvania: Stackpole Books, 1992. Easy-to-read descriptions of the plants that surround us in the woods, from the smallest flower to the tallest tree. Invaluable to the amateur naturalist.

Eastman, John. *THE BOOK OF SWAMP AND BOG: Trees, Shrubs, and Wildflowers of Eastern Freshwater Wetlands.* Mechanicsburg, Pennsylvania: Stackpole Books, 1995. Same as above except it centers on wetlands.

Hostek, Albert. *NATIVE AND NEAR NATIVE: An introduction to Long Island Plants.* Smithtown, New York: The Environmental Centers of Setauket-Smithtown, Inc., 1977. Descriptions of common plants found on the Island.

Museum of Long Island Natural Sciences. *A FIELD GUIDE TO LONG ISLANDíS WOODLANDS.* Stony Brook, New York: 1996. Nicely illustrated guide to some of the more common plants and animals found on Long Island.

National Audobon Society. *NATIONAL AUDUBON SOCIETY FIELD GUIDE SERIES.* New York: Alfred A. Knopf, Inc. This series does a good job of identifying wildlife; the distinguishing feature is the text, which give facts about each subject. There are guides on subjects from birds to wildflowers to weather and astronomy.

Newcomb, Lawrence. *NEWCOMB'S WILDFLOWER GUIDE.* Boston-Toronto: Little, Brown and Company, 1977. Considered by some to be the best field guide for wildflowers; a detailed guide to identification.

Peterson, Roger Tory, et al. *THE PETERSON FIELD GUIDE SERIES.* Boston: Houghton Mifflin Company. These excellent guides cover the wildlife one might see while hiking.

Stokes, Donald W. *A GUIDE TO NATURE IN WINTER: Northeast and North Central North America.* Boston-Toronto: Little, Brown and Company, 1976. Useful in making sense of the myriad of signs and traces of natural things that are surprisingly detectable in winter if one knows what to look for and where to look. Also, look for Stokes other nature guides in this invaluable series.

Other Outdoor Interests

Rey, H. A. *THE STARS: a new way to see them.* Boston: Houghton Mifflin Company, 1952. This book makes the sky more fun to observe as sensible arrangements are given to the constellations. It is for young and old alike since it gives a basic understanding to the movements we take for granted in the sky.

Van Diver, Bradford B. *ROADSIDE GEOLOGY OF NEW YORK.* Missoula, Montana: Mountain Press Publishing Company, 1985. Easily readable descriptions of geological features on Long Island and the rest of the state.

Index

NEW YORK-NEW JERSEY TRAIL CONFERENCE 1920

We invite you to join

the organization of hikers, environmentalists, and volunteers whose tireless efforts produced this edition of *Kittatinny Trails*.

Since our founding in 1920, the **New York-New Jersey Trail Conference's** mission has been to provide the public with the opportunity to directly experience nature and, by doing so, help preserve the region's environmental integrity. The Conference's three-pronged approach—protection, stewardship, and education—is achieved largely through the efforts of volunteers.

Join now and as a member:

■ You will receive the *Trail Walker*, a bi-monthly source of news, information, and events concerning area trails and hiking. The *Trail Walker* lists hikes throughout the New York-New Jersey region by many of our 88 member hiking clubs.

■ You are entitled to purchase our authoritative maps and books at *significant discounts*. Our highly accurate trail maps, printed on durable Tyvek, and our informative guidebooks enable you to hike with assurance in the New York-New Jersey metropolitan region.

■ In addition, you are also entitled to discounts of 10% (and sometimes more!) at most local outdoor stores and many mountain inns and lodges.

■ Most importantly, you will become part of a community of volunteer activists with similar passions and dreams.

Your membership helps give us the clout to protect and maintain more trails. As a member of the New York-New Jersey Trail Conference, you will be helping to ensure that public access to nature will continue to expand.

NEW YORK-NEW JERSEY TRAIL CONFERENCE
156 Ramapo Valley Road ❖ Mahwah, NJ 07430 ❖ (201) 512-9348
www.nynjtc.org info@nynjtc.org

Other Hiking Books Available From the Trail Conference!

Authoritative Hiking Maps and Books
by the Volunteers Who Maintain the Trails

CIRCUIT HIKES IN NORTHERN NEW JERSEY

Fifth Edition (2003), Bruce Scofield
Revised and expanded, the author describes 25 hikes in the NJ Highlands that can be walked without the need for a car shuttle or significant retracing of steps.
sc. 176 pgs, 4 3/4 x 6 3/4," B&W photos with maps for each hike

NEW JERSEY WALK BOOK

Second Edition, Edited by Daniel Chazin
Illustrations by Jack Fagan
Essential source book for the New Jersey hiker. Indispensable reference book, full trail descriptions, illustrations, color maps, ecology, geology, and history. Companion to the *New York Walk Book*.
sc. 442 pgs, 53/8 x 81/8, B&W illus.

DAY WALKER: 32 hikes in the New York Metro Area

Second Edition (2002)
A collection of 32 walks in the New York metropolitan
area for new and experienced hikers. The *Day Walker* presents a sample of walks within 60 miles of the George Washington Bridge, of varying levels of difficulty and most accessible by public transport.
sc. 301 pgs, 53/8 x 8 1/8, B&W photos and maps.